BARRELHOUSE

BARRELHOUSE WORDS

A BLUES DIALECT DICTIONARY

STEPHEN CALT

UNIVERSITY OF ILLINOIS   Urbana and Chicago

Library of Congress Cataloging-in-Publication Data
Calt, Stephen.
Barrelhouse words: a blues dialect dictionary /
Stephen Calt.
p.   cm.
Includes bibliographical references and index.
ISBN 978-0-252-03347-6 (cloth : alk. paper) —
ISBN 978-0-252-07660-2 (pbk. : alk. paper)
1. Blues (Music—Texts—Dictionaries.
2. Blues (Music)—History and criticism.
I. Title.
ML3521.C35   2009
781.64303—dc22   2009021912

To the memory of

Raymond and Nora Calt,

two lovers of language

CONTENTS

This work was begun in the late 1960s, a time when neither the vocabulary of blues songs nor the subject of bygone black language appeared to claim anyone's attention. It was initially fueled by simple curiosity, a love of language, and by what was then a startling discovery, for me at any rate: that the most striking expressions found in blues songs were not, as usually depicted, poetic or metaphorical turns of phrase, but rather were slang terms. Blues abounded in slang that seemed to belong to the ordinary vocabulary of the singers and their peers. Moreover, many unfamiliar terms occurring in blues songs were contained in dictionaries that did not classify these expressions as black or even American slang.

On the premise that every enigmatic expression found on an old blues recording had been an aspect of actual speech, I compiled a list of such terms and attempted to track them down as best I could. In catch-can fashion, I questioned various aging blacks (particularly blues singers) regarding their meanings.

Every discovery was fortuitous. The most unlikely one occurred at a Manhattan bus terminal eatery, where I was startled to hear a scruffy, middle-aged customer denounce the counterman as a "jambooger"—a vexing word on my want list I had never encountered outside of a 1930 recording titled *Jambooger Blues*. The belligerent customer (whom I anxiously followed outside) was willing to indulge my curiosity about the term, though he obviously regarded me as something of a lunatic.

Unable to interest a publisher in the manuscript I had crafted, I became disheartened and abandoned it in 1976 in the fashion of a love affair gone bad. But for Ted Gioia, a fellow author with whom I began corresponding in 2005, the present work would have remained a stillborn enterprise. His curiosity about the dictionary led me to exhume the remains of the manuscript from a closet. Unexpectedly, most of my original papers were still intact after thirty years.

It was on the basis of Ted's enthusiasm that I returned to this project and updated it. In a palpable sense, this work is his as much as mine; apart from encouraging me, Ted took it upon himself to bring my manuscript to the attention of the University of Illinois Press. I am certain that no writer has ever received greater assistance from another writer than I have received from my unusual benefactor, a man I have never even met in person. In a field where competitive egos run riot, he is a rare, magnanimous soul.

In addition to Ted Gioia, I owe substantial debts to various people who assisted me in assorted ways, particularly Renatha Saunders (who provided first-hand information on entries surviving in black speech), Tim Aurthur, Christopher Calt, Owen D'Amato, David Hinckley, Denis Lisica, John Miller, Maggie de Miramon, Xiomara Vogel, and Steven Wexler. I further wish to convey my gratitude to Richard Nevins of Yazoo Records, who graciously supplied me with his entire catalogue of CDs for this project, and to Chris Smith of *Blues & Rhythm* magazine, who (with equal generosity) provided me with copies of his informative column, "Words Words Words," devoted to the language of blues songs.

I also wish to thank Suzanne Ryan of Oxford University Press for her kind comments and beneficial criticisms concerning a version of this manuscript, and (posthumously) B. F. Skinner, for steering the original version to his own publisher on my behalf. Finally, I would be considerably remiss if I failed to thank my editor, Joan Catapano, and Rebecca Crist of the UIP Production Department for their helpful and judicious stewardship, along with associate editor Tad Ringo, with whom I enjoyed a productive working relationship.

INTRODUCTION

This idiosyncratic, discursive dictionary was assembled to unravel the most unusual, obscure, and curious words, expressions, and proper or place names found on race records, the music industry trade term for recordings intended for blacks. As a special category, such records were promoted between 1923 and 1949, when the term was replaced in *Billboard* by its own clumsy confection, "rhythm and blues," put forth in the interests of appearing less racist, and to retire a term that was associated with musical smut.

Most race recordings consisted of blues songs, which served as the popular music of black Americans from around the turn of the twentieth century until (roughly) the outset of the Second World War, a span I have designated as the blues era. These songs attracted virtually no attention beyond the record industry when they were current; to the extent they were even noticed, they aroused contempt or indignation: "[h]undreds of 'race' singers have flooded the market with what is generally regarded as the worst contribution to the cause of good music ever inflicted on the public. The lyrics of a great many of these 'blues' are worse than the lowest sort of doggerel . . ." (*Talking Machine Journal*, February 1924).

Blues songs did not operate along the lines of conventional song composition, as it existed from the 1890s through the 1950s in what has become known as the Tin Pan Alley era of popular music. As much as a method of music making, blues were a medium of language. Blues songs were not written compositions in the customary Tin Pan Alley manner, involving literary or poetic diction on at least a rudimentary level. As declaimed by the singer-guitarists and singer-pianists whose lyrics are the crux of this dictionary, the blues lyric was a snippet of vernacular speech set to song, ostensibly referring to events and sentiments of the moment or recent past. The casual, often crude, colloquial style of blues expression became an essential building block of rock and roll, which to this day is rooted in informal spoken English.

At the turn of the twentieth century, when guitar blues were becoming fashionable among black entertainers in the South, blues stanzas apparently consisted of thrice-repeated conversational statements:

I'm goin' where the Southern cross the Dog. (3)
I got arrested, no money to buy my fine. (3)

The real subject of such songs was the singer himself, who was always at the forefront of his lyrics. The peculiar scaffolding of blues (generally employing lengthy ten-beat vocal phrases) enabled blues songs to exist as a series of complete sentences set to a meager melody. As blues evolved into stanzas of rhymed lyrics, dispensed in couplet form with the first line repeated, they retained their initial relationship to unadorned speech. A blues song would typically involve disconnected, discursive statements in the form of verse held together by rhyme rather than by an express theme or topic.

Throughout the 1920s, when blues were at their peak popularity, the blues lyric that was its prime selling point was a form of rhymed speech, conveyed in the style of English that was otherwise employed by the performers. These largely male individuals were African American, usually Southern (or from a Southern background), and denizens of what could be termed "barrelhouse culture." Indeed, one Mississippian (Willie Moore) characterized the blues expressions he was asked to elucidate in the 1960s as "barrelhouse words"—the slangy speech one typically heard in bygone night spots known as barrelhouses, where revelers congregated to drink, dance, gamble, or consort with prostitutes. The patrons of such illegal establishments were not respectable figures in the eyes of society (black or white), and blues singers themselves had an almost Victorian sense of their own disreputable identities:

> I like low-down music, I like to barrelhouse and get drunk, too
> I'm just a low-down man, always feelin' low-down and blue.
> —Freddie Spruell, "Low Down Mississippi Bottom Man," 1928.

"In the beginning, *anybody* who sang blues was regarded as low-down," reported J. Mayo Williams, the first black person to gain employment as a recording executive. To W. C. Handy, who encountered blues in 1903 while working in a Mississippi Delta brass band and became the first person to exploit the music commercially, blues songs were the product and province of "small-town rounders and their running mates"—the kind of ne'er-do-wells or riffraff that patronized barrelhouses or loitered around nearby railroad depots. Blues reflected both their consuming interests and their style of language.

Partly because one did not pay money to listen to them, whether on the street, at a barrelhouse, or at a plantation house frolic, musicians who trafficked in early blues were not hailed as notable entertainers. Notwithstanding Handy's ambitious efforts to put blues on a pop music footing by offering them as Tin Pan Alley compositions, blues enjoyed only a brief early 1920s vogue as a pop commodity in the hands of white performers and black theater singers. The failure of blues songs to appeal to white record buyers caused record executives to begin promoting these works to blacks as "race" records.

Barrelhouse language and the jaded outlook of "small-town rounders" would permeate the genre in the mid- and late 1920s, when the recording industry began replacing female blues singers from the black theater circuit with relatively unvarnished self-accompanied Southern singers in an effort to duplicate the astounding sales of Blind Lemon Jefferson, an itinerant Texas street singer-guitarist with a flair for devising lyrics. Recorded blues of the period are so saturated in slang and assorted colloquialisms as to create a peculiar dialect that is only half-intelligible to present-day listeners. Apart from barrelhouse culture, the language of blues songs was rooted in everyday African American speech as it then existed, some six decades after slavery ended. Indeed, these songs constitute the earliest direct, authentic record of black English dialect on an appreciable scale.

In the 1930s, blues recordings became increasingly mannered, and tended to feature a particular theme, usually conveyed in unremarkable language. At the same time, the emphasis of blues remained fixed on the formulaic tribulations of the blues singer. Familiarity, and the vinegary quality of the blues sensibility, ultimately made it a fringe music, confined to small, insignificant pockets of the black community or to venues established and subsidized by white blues enthusiasts, whose patronage would eventually make blues the prestigious commodity it has since become. Songs from this declining post-blues period have been excluded from this volume, if only because they are unrepresentative of any group other than blues performers.

As the aim of this dictionary is to illuminate spoken language, the author has excluded seeming nonce words (unless they are of special interest), as well as metaphoric words and phrases that appear to have been the product of a blues songwriter's pen or poetic imagination (however feeble).[1] Most of these artificial blues terms were double entendres that rested on forced or nonvernacular comparisons between sex and some ordinary object, activity, product, and the like:

> Don't a man feel bad when he can't yo yo no more?
> Broke my yo yo strings, an' I can't go home no more.
> —Blind Lemon Jefferson, "Yo Yo Blues," 1929

> Bumble bee, bumble bee, please come back to me
> He made the best ol' honey, any bumble bee I ever seen.
> —Memphis Minnie, "Bumble Bee," 1930

These often ludicrous excursions were concocted with an eye toward generating hit records; some of them became so popular that their operative figures of speech ("yo yo," "bumble bee") became part of the clichéd blues vocabulary.

Generally, the records drawn upon for this dictionary were not the products of such commercial calculation, which resulted in full-blown themes; rather, they were produced by itinerant singers who did not anticipate their own discoveries and were given little or no direction by record executives.

The main influence that such record executives had on blues singers was to act as an inhibiting presence, causing the latter to soften or omit blunt sexual language. In live performances, the Delta blues singer Son House recalled, audiences relished raw sexual references: "You could sing anything at them Saturday night balls, I don't care how dirty you made it; they liked to hear it." In the recording studio, an indifference born of a racial double standard on the part of executives enabled blues singers to be sexually suggestive at a time when such material was considered pornography and was actually illegal to merchandise:

> You can play with my pussy, but please don't dog it around
> If you're going to mistreat it, no pussy will be found.
> —Jane Lucas, "Pussy Cat Blues," 1930

By contrast, the works of white performers were closely monitored for "off-color" material. When the white roustabout Harmonica Frank Floyd attempted to sing even slightly suggestive lyrics for Sam Phillips's Sun Records label in 1952, he was quickly rebuffed: "In *Swamp Root,* where it says: 'Let me see your underwear,' he made me say: 'Let me see your socks,' so I didn't get to make it just like I wanted to. . . . He [Phillips] said it's too 'rough' . . . gettin' too vulgary, and probably was, back then," Floyd recalled.

No such strictures were applied to black performers, whose avidity for sexual slang was evident as early as the Civil War, when Thomas Wentworth Higginson noted a seemingly inscrutable song called *Hangman Johnny* produced by mirthful black soldiers:

> O, dey call me Hangman Johnny!
> O, ho! O, ho!
> But I never hang nobody . . .[2]

Unknown to Higginson (who would have been mortified by the discovery), "hanging Johnny" was a contemporary slang term for penis.

According to Mayo Williams, blues singers of the early to mid-1920s did not know how to euphemize sexual expressions. He reported suggesting double entendre alternatives to various recording acts, thus helping to foster what became a burgeoning blues genre unto itself. Even at that, blues developed a reputation for being salacious or smutty; W. C. Handy claimed that "a flock of lowdown dirty blues" appeared on the recording horizon and undermined his own publishing career. A black sociologist of the late 1920s saw a virtual racial conspiracy in the contemporary race record:

> Worse than denying him [the Negro] the opportunities of developing a taste for the higher types of leisure time activities is the practice . . . of forcing upon the Negro a taste for degraded forms . . . [an] example is the quite general practice of larger talking machine companies of America, of almost forcing upon the Negro race records that are distinctly immoral in their title and content. Some of these records are so obscene that the companies have not the courage to advertise them in their regular catalogues, but issue special booklets for Negroes. Not content with issuing these booklets to Negroes these companies also flaunt the suggestive titles of these records, accompanied by obscene pictures, in the Negro newspapers.[3]

This diatribe found its way into the leading study of black American life, *The American Dilemma,* a work cited by the Supreme Court in issuing its desegregation decision of 1954: "Unfortunately, certain companies producing records have issued a special category for Negroes, 'race records,' many of which are vicious and obscene, and these were widely sold in the rural areas."[4] Race records became a virtual synonym for smut, so much so that the *American Thesaurus of Slang* would define "race songs" in 1942 as "pornographic blues written in a twelve-bar arrangement."

Such passé assessments indicate how distasteful race records were to whites and middle-class blacks, when considered from the standpoint of what was then regarded as morality. In retrospect, it is easy to forget that sex was actually a main selling point of many blues records and was a consuming interest of many blues singers. It is in fact questionable if the white listeners whose avidity for blues sparked a blues revival in the 1960s would have taken so readily to the music were it not distinguished for its strong sexual content.

A Note on Language

This dictionary makes no attempt to label each entry in terms of presumed racial origin or to exclude any idioms on racial grounds alone. Numerous terms contained herein were derived (directly or unwittingly) from facets of white speech. In some exotic instances (*hand, in good time, shave (one) dry, sling snot*), the vocabulary of blues singers appears to hark back to the seventeenth century, when slaves and white indentured servants toiled together on Virginia tobacco plantations. However, the means by which assorted idioms were transmitted to blacks, who sometimes used them long after they had lost currency among whites, remain speculative.

Apart from black English, the basic categories by which this dictionary classifies words are those employed by most dictionaries:

Standard English: written or formal English, as used by or associated with well-educated people. Although standard English is a seemingly snooty, restrictive designation, it constitutes the broadest category of words and encompasses many terms that might appear too casual at first glance to merit such labeling. The basic arbiter of this category (in terms of vocabulary) is the *Oxford English Dictionary,* whose pronouncements I have generally followed.

Colloquial English: spoken or informal English, once typecast as uneducated speech, and regarded as language that was unfit to publish outside of a dictionary, except as part of dialogue in fiction or a news story. With the erosion of class distinctions, the spread of radio and television, and the growing influence of realistic movies and lowbrow music, colloquial English (in post-1950s America, at any rate) has become increasingly blended into mainstream English, to the point of losing much of its original validity as an informative category.

Dialectal English (now often termed "regional English"): regionally, culturally, or ethnically isolated speech, historically connoting provincial, often obscure English, employed by rustics who had little contact with standard English. This category would include the speech of a majority of black Americans of the race recording era; in 1920, 85 percent of the nation's blacks lived in the South, and 75 percent of the latter lived in rural areas. Some 29 percent of the nation's blacks were then counted as illiterate. (It was not until the Second World War that the majority of blacks lived in urban areas.) Dialectal English is noted for retaining words that have fallen out of more general use, and such is the case with blues dialect.

A fourth category of English is slang, a novel addition to spoken language, usually fostered by a clannish social or occupational group that lies outside rank-and-file society (such as criminals, youths, or baseball players), reflecting its particular or unique interests, needs, or preoccupations. While the tenor of standard English is polite, slang is often brash, if not coarse. Once-fashionable slang invariably becomes exhausted with overuse or grows moldy as the group that uses it ages, to the point of finally passing out of existence. It is the latter situation that prevails with many significant blues or barrelhouse slang terms: they went the way of the singers who used them.

It is not always easy or even useful to distinguish slang, colloquial, dialectal, and standard English. The meanings of words are far more important than the niche they occupy, and this is particularly true of blues idioms. However, it is enlightening to note the place a given blues/black idiom occupies in the broad scheme of language, if only because of the long-held belief that blacks spoke a nonsensical brand of English. The latter view was commonly taken by recording officials who trafficked in blues material, one of whom said of blues lyrics: "You couldn't understand half of 'em. A lotta of it was a whole lotta moanin,' you know; didn't mean anything. You couldn't even <u>call</u> it a language."[5] Such a stereotype harks back to 1830s blackface minstrelsy, which was partly predicated on the seemingly ridiculous racial English embodied by such works as *Jump Jim Crow* (the original minstrel hit). Another widely held view was that black speech was notably grandiloquent; the first American dictionary devoted to colloquial English (by John Russell Bartlett in 1877) actually contained an entry, "Negro Nomenclature," that maintained: "A peculiarity of the colored race is their fondness for high-sounding words in their conversations, sermons, and speeches." This trait is not discernable in blues recording, and it will be seen from this dictionary that blues performers used standard English with a finely calibrated sense of meaning, despite being totally or virtually uneducated and being left largely to their own grammatical devices.

Rather than denigrated, the particular language of blacks has been more often ignored or treated carelessly by lexicographers. Although blacks have been in America since the seventeenth century, the first glossaries of black slang were not compiled until the 1920s, appearing in the form of appendices to two novels associated with the Harlem Renaissance. Black idioms scarcely figure in the *American Dialect Dictionary* (1944), a 15,000-word compilation that made extensive use of material gleaned by the American Dialect Society. The authoritative *Oxford English Dictionary* took almost no note of black idioms before 1972.[6] Its determined efforts to remedy this defect have been somewhat impeded by its reliance on printed sources, and the current edition actually contains a nonexistent black idiom, *policy blues,* which was culled from the work of a blues commentator who applied it to blues songs dealing with policy.

Too often, writers on the subject of black music or black language have produced misleading or ill-considered material, some of which is enshrined in dictionaries. The present attempt represents the best the author could do, within his powers and limitations; it cannot be free from error. The meaning of some terms is moot; had any significant research been done on the subject of black language when blues music was current, their meanings would be more intelligible.

■ Because words and expressions appearing in this volume are defined in terms of their use in various recorded couplets, the couplets themselves appear before the applicable definition. Songs are annotated by the year in which they were recorded, as listed in Dixon and Godrich's *Blues and Gospel Records, 1902–1942,* from which song titles (as given by the record manufacturers) were also taken. Phrases are alphabetized according to what appears (to me) to be their most significant word, which may not be the one that stands out for a reader. For example, *on a wander* is alphabetized in terms of *on,* rather than *wander.* Because such entries are not cross-referenced, locating them may require cross-checking.

Definitions are conveyed in the present tense for purposes of concision, although most of the indicated terms have long since passed out of black speech. If a term is construed as surviving in black speech, the author does not mean to thereby suggest that it does so on an appreciable scale or would be explicable to people under sixty. A slang expression labeled "contemporary" was current general slang at the time the cited blues couplet containing it was recorded. If a word or expression is described as dated, obsolete, archaic, or passé, the implication is that it was so at the time of its appearance in race recording, within the framework of standard English or general slang. These terms are used more liberally than is customary in the dictionaries I have drawn upon. It is impossible to date any of the black-originated expressions of pre-1930s lineage with anything resembling accuracy, let alone precision. Nor can various terms be rightfully assigned to any geographical area or location, given the footloose lifestyles of most blues performers and the skeletal nature of information regarding bygone black speech.

If a term is described as a "misnomer" for its standard English predecessor, the author means only to suggest that the term in question originated as such a misnomer, whatever its subsequent status. When the terms *penis* or *vagina* appear inadequate to make for an accurate definition, I have written *dick* or *pussy* to signify the blunt perception of these organs solely as vehicles for sexual pleasure. When a particular term has appeared in a given dictionary used as a resource, was invoked by an author listed in the bibliography, or defined by a black informant (usually a musician) of the blues era, I have usually indicated this fact by placing the pertinent reference in parentheses so that the basis of my information will be readily apparent. If an existing dictionary definition appears particularly apt, or better than any equivalent I could concoct, I have quoted it directly rather than filch or paraphrase it. A detailed definition of the somewhat murky term "blues" appears in the appendix.

NOTES

1. On this basis I have rejected *lemon,* a term that J. E. Lighter (cued by blues lyrics) puts forth as black English slang for genitals in his invaluable *Historical Dictionary of American Slang.* Yet it was apparently originated by Bo Carter, a recording artist who specialized in double entendres, many of them far-fetched, and who followed up his *Let Me Roll Your Lemon* (1935) with a similarly strained *Squeeze Your Orange.*

2. Higginson, *Army Life in a Black Regiment,* 172.

3. Forester B. Washington, "Recreational Facilities for Negroes," *Annals of the American Academy of Political Social Science,* 1928 issue. Such was one view. Of male race record customers, salesman J. B. Long said: "Ninety percent of 'em back in that day was a backdoor man." Another Southern salesman, Earl Montgomery, opined: "They used the records to fuck by."

4. Gunnar Myrdal, *The American Dilemma* (New York: Harper Publications, 1936), 1436.

5. This figure, Polk Brockman, supervised Okeh sessions of such artists as Blind Lemon Jefferson, the Mississippi Sheiks, and Hambone Willie Newbern.

6. Instead of acknowledging this omission, an Oxford University Press editor maintains that "there simply were not many prominent black idioms in general circulation" before 1972.

SELECT ANNOTATED BIBLIOGRAPHY
OF DICTIONARY SOURCES

Bartlett, John Russell. *A Dictionary of Americanisms.* Boston: Little, Brown, 1877. This was the first American dictionary devoted to colloquial terms: its retinue of black expressions amounts to *Bango!*, *buckra, cotch* (for caught; a "negro vulgarism"), *he's done come* ("negro vulgarism"), and *juba*.

Berrey, Lester V., and Melvin Van den Bark. *The American Thesaurus of Slang: A Complete Reference Book of Colloquial Speech.* New York: Thomas Y. Crowell, 1942.

Burley, Dan. *Dan Burley's Original Handbook of Harlem Jive.* New York: c. 1944. The author of this privately published work was a blues pianist on the Chicago rent party circuit in the 1920s who subsequently became a Harlem journalist. His *Handbook,* an elaboration on the dictionary of his associate Cab Calloway, follows the path of Rudolph Fisher in treating Harlem as a linguistic island, possessing a special vocabulary distinct from that of other black population centers.

Calloway, Cab. *Cab Calloway's Hepsters Dictionary: Language of Jive.* New York: 1939. This popular pamphlet by a leading swing-era musician, containing a hundred entries, was the first dictionary authored by a black person.

Cassidy, Frederic G., ed. *Dictionary of American Regional English,* Vol. 1, A–C. Cambridge: Belknap Press of Harvard University, 1985. Although it rejects the category *slang* as "too indefinite and too often used merely to condemn," numerous DARE entries that are pertinent to this dictionary (such as *dead cat on the line, doney, fanfoot, jellybean, jive,* and *meal ticket*) are clearly slang rather than "regional English."

———. *Dictionary of American Regional English,* Vol. 2, D–H. Cambridge: Belknap Press of Harvard University, 1991.

———. *Dictionary of American Regional English,* Vol. 3, I–O. Cambridge: Belknap Press of Harvard University, 1996.

Clapin, Sylva. *A New Dictionary of Americanisms: Being a Glossary of Words Supposed to Be Peculiar to the United States and the Dominion of Canada.* Detroit: Gale Research, Book Tower, 1968. Reprint, c. 1902. This interesting compilation, which seeks to exclude "linguistic abortions of merely ephemeral vogue," offers a meager assortment of black idioms: *biggity, buckra, hant, hoodoo, massa, misery, obeya-man, shank,* and *white folks.*

Chapman, Robert L., with Barbara Ann Kipfer. *Dictionary of American Slang,* 3rd ed. New York: Harper Collins, 1995. A revamped version of Wentworth and Flexner's *Dictionary of American Slang* that assigns unsupportable dates to various passé black terms.

Davies, T. Lewis O. *A Supplemental English Glossary.* London: George Bell and Sons, 1881. Most of its terms are taken from literature.

Dalzell, Tom. *The Slang of Sin.* Springfield, Mass.: Merriam-Webster, 1998.

DeSalvo, Debra. *The Language of the Blues: From Alcorub to Zuzu.* New York: Billboard Books, 2006. An ill-informed work containing chronically faulty definitions and etymologies.

Eliason, Norman E. *Tarheel Talk: An Historical Study of the English Language in North Carolina to 1860.* Chapel Hill: University of North Carolina Press, 1956.

Farmer, John S., and W. E. Henley. *Slang and Its Analogues.* New York: Arno Press/New York Times facsimile edition of the 1890–1904 work, 1970. This monumental seven-volume work was largely devoted to British slang and colloquialisms. It is evident from the number of its entries that crop up on race records that there was considerable undocumented linguistic traffic from England to America with regard to slang and colloquial English.

Fisher, Rudolph. *The Walls of Jericho.* New York: Arno Press/New York Times reprint of the 1928 original, 1969. This novel contains a 115-word "Introduction to Contemporary Harlemese," which ranks as the first glossary of black idioms produced by a black writer.

Folb, Edith A. *runnin' down some lines: the language and culture of black teenagers.* Cambridge, Mass.: Harvard University Press, 1980. This work contains a glossary of terms (referred to as a "black English vernacular vocabulary") used by black teenagers from south-central Los Angeles during the course of the author's research from 1967 to 1976.

Goldin, Hyman, Frank O'Leary, Morris Lipsuis. *A Dictionary of American Underworld Lingo.* London: Constable, 1950. The primary authors were themselves convicts and thus created a uniquely authentic slang dictionary.

Green, Jonathon. *The Dictionary of Contemporary Slang.* New York: Stein and Day, 1985.

Grose, Francis. *A Classical Dictionary of the Vulgar Tongue.* New York: Barnes and Noble, 1963. Reprint, 1796. A vivid reflection of its age, this is the only dictionary that is actually fascinating to read, rather than consult.

Hall, Joan Houston, ed., *Dictionary of American Regional English,* Volume 4, P–Sk. Cambridge: Belknap Press of Harvard University, 2000.

Hendrickson, Robert. *Whistlin' Dixie: A Dictionary of Southern Expressions.* New York: Facts on File, 1993.

Hotten, John Camden. *The Slang Dictionary: Or, the Vulgar Words, Street Phrases, and "Fast" Expressions of High and Low Society.* London: 1869.

Hurston, Zora Neale. *Mules and Men.* New York: Harper and Row, 1970. Reprint, 1935. A casual glossary is appended to this singular work.

———. "Glossary of Harlem Slang," word list affixed to "A Story In Harlem Slang," 1942, reprinted in *Spunk: The Selected Stories of Zora Neale Hurston.* Berkeley: Turtle Island, 1985.

Irwin, Godfrey. *American Tramp and Underworld Slang: Words and Phrases Used by Hoboes, Tramps, Migratory Workers, and Those on the Fringes of Society.* London: E. Partridge/Scholartis Press, 1931.

Lighter, J. E., ed. *Random House Historical Dictionary of American Slang,* Vol. 1, A–G. New York: Random House, 1994. This ongoing work, the most comprehensive slang dictionary since Farmer and Henley's *Slang and Its Analogues,* rests on published citations, as well as television and film references.

———, ed. *Random House Historical Dictionary of American Slang,* Vol. 2, H–O. New York: Random House, 1997.

Major, Clarence. *Dictionary of Afro-American Slang.* New York: International, 1970. This casual work was the first full-fledged dictionary devoted to black slang.

———. *Juba to Jive: A Dictionary of African-American Slang.* New York: Penguin Books, 1994. The author is impervious to the relationship between black speech and standard English. Nonetheless, this is the most comprehensive work of its kind.

Mathews, Mitford M. *The Beginnings of American English.* Chicago: University of Chicago Press, 1931. This valuable work reprints several early American glossaries.

———, ed. *A Dictionary of Americanisms on Historical Principles,* Vol. 1 and 2. Chicago: University of Chicago Press, 1951. The editor was the leading American language scholar of his era.

Oxford English Dictionary, www.oed.com. A gift of the gods. The online version contains its most recent updates, including draft additions.

Partridge, Eric. *A Dictionary of Clichés.* New York: Macmillan, 1940.

———. *A Dictionary of Slang and Unconventional English,* 4th ed. New York: Macmillan, 1953. The author was the foremost slang specialist of his age. This edition updates the 1937 edition that forms the bulk of the dictionary, which is largely comprised of Farmer and Henley's *Slang and Its Analogues* with respect to pre-twentieth-century terms and generally only recognizes American slang that permeated England.

———. *Shakespeare's Bawdy,* 3rd ed. London: Routledge and Kegan Paul, 1968.

———. *Slang To-Day and Yesterday,* 2nd ed. London: Routledge & Sons, 1935. This study contains a glossary.

Shipley, Joseph T. *Dictionary of Early English.* Totowa, N.J.: Littlefield Adams, 1968.

Smitherman, Geneva. *Black Talk: Words and Phrases from the Hood to the Amen Corner.* rev. ed. New York: Houghton Mifflin, 2000. Although the focus of this compilation is current black slang, some thirty terms it contains hark back to the blues era.

Spears, Richard A. *Slang and Euphemism: A Dictionary of Oaths, Curses, Insults, Ethnic Slurs, Sexual Slang and Metaphor, Drug talk, College Lingo, and Related Matters,* 3rd rev. ed. New York: Penguin Books, 2001. This work emphasizes sexual expressions.

———. *McGraw-Hill's Dictionary of American Slang and Colloquial Expressions,* 4th ed. New York: McGraw-Hill, 2006.

Taylor, Archer, and Bartlett Jere Whiting. *A Dictionary of American Proverbs and Proverbial Phrases, 1820–1880.* Cambridge, Mass.: Belknap Press of Harvard University, 1958.

Thornton, Richard H. *An American Glossary: Being an Attempt to Illustrate Certain Americanisms upon Historical Principles.* Philadelphia: J. B. Lippincott, 1912.

Townley, Eric. *Tell Your Story: A Dictionary of Jazz and Blues Recordings, 1917–1950.* Essex, England: Storyville, 1976. This volume, devoted to explaining the meaning of various jazz and blues recording titles, is marred by glibness (such as defining *shave 'em dry* as "[s]exual intercourse without preliminary love-making").

Tucker, Gilbert M. *American English.* New York: Alfred A. Knopf, 1921. This study contains a glossary.

Turner, Lorenzo Dow. *Africanisms in the Gullah Dialect.* Columbia: University of South Carolina Press, 2002. Reprint, Chicago: University of Chicago Press, 1949.

Urban Dictionary, www.urbandictionary.com. This Web site consists of voluntary reader contributions and affords some idea as to what expressions from the blues era are still around.

Van Vechten, Carl. *Nigger Heaven.* Champaign: University of Illinois Press, 2000. Reprint, 1926. This white-authored novel contains a fifty-word "Glossary of Negro Words and Phrases" that ranks as the first such published list.

Wentworth, Harold. *American Dialect Dictionary.* New York: Thomas Y. Crowell, 1944. This was the only dictionary of its kind before the advent of DARE.

———, and Stuart Berg Flexner. *Dictionary of American Slang,* New York: Thomas Y. Crowell, 1960. The first broad-based dictionary to include an appreciable number of black idioms, most of them associated (in the authors' minds) with jazz use. The definitions themselves are sometimes unreliable.

Wex, Michael. *Born to Kvetch: Yiddish Language and Culture in All Its Moods*. New York: Harper Collins, New York, 2007.

Wright, Joseph, ed. *The English Dialect Dictionary, Being the Complete Vocabulary of All Dialect Words Still in Use or Known to Have Been in Use during the Last Two Hundred Years*. London: Henry Frowde, 1898–1905. This classic dictionary documents British dialectal terms for the preceding two hundred years.

GENERAL BIBLIOGRAPHY

Anderson, Nels. *The Hobo: The Sociology of the Homeless Man*. Chicago: University of Chicago Press, 1961. Reprint, 1923.

Baker, Ray Stannard. *Following the Color Line*. New York: Harper Torchbooks, 1964. Reprint, 1908.

Blesh, Rudi, and Harriet Janis. *They All Played Ragtime: The True Story of an American Music*. New York: Alfred A. Knopf, 1950.

Born in Slavery: Slave Narratives from the Federal Writers' Project, 1936–1938. Washington, D.C.: Library of Congress. http://lcweb2.loc.gov/ammem/snhtml.

Botkin, B. A., ed. *A Treasury of American Folklore: Stories, Ballads, and Traditions of the People*. New York: Crown, 1944.

———, ed. *Lay My Burden Down: A Folk History of Slavery*. New York: Dell, 1989, Reprint, Chicago: University of Chicago Press, 1945.

———, and Alvin F. Harlow, eds. *A Treasury of Railroad Folklore: The Stories, Tall Tales, Traditions, Ballads, and Songs of the American Railroad Man*. New York: Crown, 1953.

Broonzy, Big Bill, as told to Yannick Bruynoghe. *Big Bill Blues*. New York: Oak Publications edition, 1964.

Brown, Henry Bates. *Cotton: War Department Education Manual*. New York: McGraw-Hill, 1938.

Bugliosi, Vincent, with Curt Gentry. *Helter Skelter: The True Story of the Manson Murders*. New York: Norton, 1974.

Calt, Stephen. *I'd Rather Be the Devil: Skip James and the Blues*. Chicago: Chicago Review Press, 2008.

Calt, Stephen, and Gayle Dean Wardlow. *King of the Delta Blues: The Life and Music of Charlie Patton*. Newton, N.J.: Rock Chapel Press, 1989.

Ginzburg, Ralph. *One Hundred Years of Lynching*. New York: Lancer Books, 1962.

Gwaltney, John Langston. *Dry Long So: A Self-Portrait of Black America*. New York: Random House, 1980.

Handy, W. C. *Father of the Blues: An Autobiography*. New York: Collier Books, 1970. Reprint, New York: Macmillan, 1941.

Higginson, Thomas Wentworth. *Army Life in a Black Regiment and Other Writings*. New York: Penguin Books, 1997. Reprint, 1870.

Hughes, Langston, and Arna Bontemps. *The Book of Negro Folklore*. New York: Dodd, Mead, 1958.

Johnson, Charles S. *Growing Up in the Black Belt*. New York: Shocken Books, 1965. Reprint, Washington, D.C.: American Council on Education, 1941.

Jordan, Don, and Michael Walsh. *White Cargo: The Forgotten History of Britain's White Slaves in America*. New York: New York University Press, 2008.

Krehbiel, Henry Edward. *Afro-American Folksongs*. New York: G. Schirmer, 1914.

Lepore, Jill. *The Name of War: King Philip's War and the Origins of American Identity*. New York: Alfred A. Knopf, 1998.

Lomax, Alan. *Mister Jelly Roll: The Fortunes of Jelly Roll Morton, New Orleans Creole, and "Inventor of Jazz."* New York: Grosset and Dunlap, 1950.

Martens, Frederick H. *The Book of Good Manners: A Guide to Polite Usage for All Social Functions*. New York: Social Culture Publications, 1923.

Mayer, Brantz, ed. *Captain Canot, an African Slaver*. New York: Arno Press, 1968. Reprint, 1852.

Mezzrow, Milton "Mezz," and Bernard Wolfe. *Really the Blues*. New York: Random House, 1946.

Morgan, Edmund S. *American Slavery, American Freedom: The Ordeal of Colonial Virginia*. New York: Norton, 1975.

Olmsted, Frederick Law. *The Cotton Kingdom: A Traveller's Observations on Cotton and Slavery in the American Slave States, 1853–1861*. New York: Modern Library, 1969. Reprint, 1859.

O'Neal, Jim, and Amy van Singel. *The Voice of the Blues: Classic Interviews from Living Blues Magazine*. London: Routledge, 2001.

Parrish, Lydia. *Slave Songs of the Georgia Sea Islands*. Hatboro, Pa.: Folklore Associates, 1965. Reprint, New York: Creative Age Press, 1942.

Puckett, Newbell Niles. *Folk Beliefs of the Southern Negro*. New York: Dover, 1969. Reprint, 1925.

Talley, Thomas. *Negro Folk Rhymes: Wise and Otherwise*. New York: Macmillan, 1922.

Randolph, Vance. *Ozark Folksongs: Religious Songs and Other Items*. Columbia: University of Missouri Press, 1980.

Stearns, Marshall and Jean Stearns. *Jazz Dance: The Story of American Vernacular Dance*. 1979. Reprint, New York: Macmillan, 1968.

Thompson, Thomas. *Blood and Money: A True Story of Murder, Passion, and Power*. Garden City, N.Y.: Doubleday, 1976.

Washington, Booker T. *Up from Slavery: An Autobiography*. Garden City, N.Y.: Doubleday, 1951. Reprint, New York: Doubleday, 1901.

Waters, Ethel, with Charles Samuels. *His Eye Is on the Sparrow: An Autobiography*. New York: Doubleday, 1951.

White, Newman Ivey. *American Negro Folk-Songs.* Hatboro, Pa.: Folklore
    Associates, 1965. Reprint, Cambridge, Mass.: Harvard University Press, 1928.
Wilson, Edmund, and Leon Edel, ed. *The Twenties: From Notebooks and Diaries
    of the Period.* New York: Farrar, Straus and Giroux, 1975.
Yetman, Norman R., ed. *Voices from Slavery: 100 Authentic Slave Narratives.*
    Mineola, N.Y.: Dover, 2000.

INFORMANTS CITED IN TEXT

The following people were consulted or interviewed between 1964 and 1971:

Ted Bogan (1910–90): A guitarist and string band musician who worked with such performers as Memphis Minnie in Chicago during the 1930s.

Vivian (Sam) Chatmon (1899–1983): The brother of Bo Carter and Lonnie Chatmon, he worked in a family string band near Bolton, Mississippi, and recorded in 1936 for RCA Victor.

Gary Davis (1896–1972): Davis worked as an itinerant street singer in Georgia and South Carolina from around 1912 to 1943, when he moved to New York. He recorded as "Blind Gary" in 1935, by which time he had become a gospel performer.

David Edwards: Born in 1915 in Shaw, Mississippi, Edwards became a nomadic Delta blues singer in 1932. As of this writing, he was still appearing in concerts.

Albert Evans: A native of St. Louis who worked as a sanctified preacher and morgue attendant in the 1960s, when he was consulted for his knowledge of church-related terms.

Frank Floyd (1908–84): A white singer-guitarist from Arkansas whose music reflected his keen appreciation of blues.

Pete Franklin (1927–75): An Indianapolis blues player and protégé of Scrapper Blackwell; his mother, Flossie Franklin, had been a girlfriend of Leroy Carr.

Sol Henderson: A part-time musician and contemporary of Robert Johnson, interviewed in his native Robinsonville, Mississippi, by Nick Perls in 1964.

Henry Hill: Born in 1902 in Virginia; an avid consumer of race records who worked as an Illinois Central railroad laborer and as a bartender in Kansas City before moving to St. Louis in the 1920s.

Son House (1902–86): A historic Delta blues performer who was rediscovered in 1964.

Skip James (1902–69): A historic Mississippi blues performer, also rediscovered in 1964, who variously functioned as a laborer, pimp, bootlegger, professional gambler, and entertainer.

Bessie Jones (1902–84): An a cappella singer who formed part of the Georgia Sea Island Singers, which she joined in 1933.

Willie Jones: An inveterate gambler born in 1915 at Moorhead, Mississippi; worked as a janitor in St. Louis when consulted for gambling terms in 1969.

Furry Lewis (1899–1981): A Memphis street singer who began recording in 1927 and was rediscovered in the late 1950s.

Eurreal (Little Brother) Montgomery (1906–85): A renowned blues pianist who originally hailed from Louisiana.

Willie Moore: A onetime associate of Charlie Patton and Robert Johnson, Moore was born in 1898 and raised in the Mississippi Delta, where he worked as a professional gambler, barrelhouse musician, and minstrel trouper between c. 1916–35. (Interviewed by Gayle Wardlow, with questions furnished by the author.)

Tom Shaw (1908–77): A native of Brenham, Texas, who became a professional musician around 1926 under the tutelage of Blind Lemon Jefferson and later (in the 1960s) worked as a faith healer/landlord in San Diego.

Johnny Shines (1915–92): A second-generation blues performer whose career began in Arkansas in 1932 and who emigrated to Chicago in 1941.

Walter Vinson (1901–75): In tandem with Lonnie Chatmon, Vinson recorded as the Mississippi Sheiks, one of the most popular race recording acts.

Bukka White (1906–77): A historic Mississippi blues performer rediscovered in 1963.

J. Mayo Williams (1894–1978): A pioneering figure in the race record industry who worked as a recording director for three companies (Paramount, Vocalion, and Decca) between 1923 and 1946, discovering such acts as Ma Rainey and Papa Charlie Jackson.

ABBREVIATIONS AND SYMBOLS USED IN TEXT

a. = adjective or adjectival phrase

ADD = Wentworth, *American Dialect Dictionary*

adv. = adverb

ATS = Berrey and Van den Bark, *American Thesaurus of Slang*

cf. = consult, see by way of comparison. When this abbreviation appears
before a cited glossary or dictionary, it indicates that the author is applying
its information selectively, rather than verbatim.

DAH = Mathews, *Dictionary of Americanisms on Historical Principles*

DAP = Taylor and Whiting, *Dictionary of American Proverbs and Proverbial
Phrases*

DARE = Cassidy, *Dictionary of American Regional English,* Vol. 1

DARE 2 = Cassidy, *Dictionary of American Regional English,* Vol. 2

DARE 3 = Cassidy, *Dictionary of American Regional English,* Vol. 3

DARE 4 = Hall, *Dictionary of American Regional English,* Vol. 4

DAS = Wentworth and Flexner, *Dictionary of American Slang*

DAS 3 = Chapman and Kipfer, *Dictionary of American Slang*

DAUL = Goldin, O'Leary, and Lipsuis, *Dictionary of American Underworld Lingo*

DC = Partridge, *Dictionary of Clichés*

DCS = Green, *Dictionary of Contemporary Slang*

EDD = Wright, *English Dialect Dictionary*

F&H = Farmer and Henley, *Slang and Its Analogues*

LC = Library of Congress (as opposed to commercial) recording

n. = noun

OED = *Oxford English Dictionary*

Partridge = Partridge, *Dictionary of Slang and Unconventional English*

q.v. = which see

SB = Partridge, *Shakespeare's Bawdy*

STY = Partridge, *Slang To-Day and Yesterday*

TT = Eliason, *Tarheel Talk*

UD = *Urban Dictionary*

v. = verb or verbal phrase

WD = Hendrickson, *Whistlin' Dixie*

? = problematic definition; undecipherable passage within lyric

Note: Parts of speech are indicated only insofar as they are helpful for clarification.
The use of quote marks within lyrics indicates either a spoken utterance, or the
singer's representation of someone else's (typically a girlfriend's) words.

act the fool

Now you take these young folks, that goes to high school
They sometimes really, do act the fool.
—Scrapper Blackwell, "Be-Da-Da-Bum," 1929

To behave foolishly or idiotically in a conspicuous manner; a still-current black colloquialism, synonymous with *to clown*.

actions

His ways an' actions is hard to beat
For he's the sheik, of Desplaines Street.
—Papa Charlie Jackson, "Sheik Of Desplaines Street," 1927

Conduct; a colloquialism embodied in the now-proverbial 19th-century American saying "Actions speak louder than words," and found in Stephen Crane's *Maggie: A Girl Of The Streets* (1893): "'Anybody what had eyes could see dat dere was somethin' wrong wid dat girl. I didn't like her actions.'"

after

When I'm gone, don't grieve after me
Don't you forget I went away.
—Sam Collins, "It Won't Be Long," 1927

? About; a Southern colloquialism found in Roark Bradford's 1931 black dialect novel *John Henry* ("'... all dat gal do is grieve after me when I'm gone.'") and Opie Read's 1897 Ozark dialect novel *Old Ebenezer* ("'There's a case in our neighborhood of a young feller goin' crazy after a woman he wanted.'") It also figures as an inexact preposition in:

Now go on girl don't flirt after me
Got good stuff an' it's all I need.
—Joe McCoy, "I'm Wild About My Stuff," 1930

afterwhile

My mama told me, when I were quite a child:
"Havin' a good time now but trouble afterwhile."
—Pink Anderson and Simmie Dooley, "Every Day In The Week Blues," 1928

Eventually; elliptical for *after a while*, and associated with Southern speech (cf. DARE).

Afro (a.)

> *And when she promenade in them Sunday clothes*
> *She tantalize those Afro gigolos.*
> —Lovin' Sam Theard, "That Rhythm Gal," 1934

Slang for African American.

aggravatin' papa

> *When I find that aggravatin' papa, that tried to two-time me*
> *I know I'll spend a great long sentence in the penitentiary.*
> —Barbecue Bob, "Ease It To Me Blues," 1928

A noted seducer of other men's girlfriends or wives, to the point of being a general aggravation to men. The Indianapolis blues singer Leroy Carr (1905–35) was locally known as "Aggravatin' Papa" because "he fucked everybody's wife" (Pete Franklin). This term arose by means of a popular 1923 Alberta Hunter recording, "Aggravating Papa," where it referred to an unfaithful lover. A pop version by Sophie Tucker resulted in its circulation as general American slang for "a refractory lover" (Martens, who listed it in *The Book of Good Manners* [1923] among "Slang and Colloquialisms Which Will Not Pass Muster").

airy

> *You can get yourself together*
> *You can go out with the weather*
> *We don't need no airy man.*
> —Papa Charlie Jackson, "Airy Man Blues," 1924

Conceited (Clapin, c. 1902); an apparent carryover of obsolete standard English signifying one who puts on airs (cf. OED) that is misconstrued by Major (1994) as a black term dating to the 1960s.

Alcorub

> *Every day of the week, I goes to Midtown Drug*
> *An' get me a bottle o' snuff, an' a bottle o' Alcorub.*
> —Son House, "Clarksdale Moan," 1930

A brand of rubbing alcohol manufactured by the United States Industrial Alcohol Company, which also produced *Sterno* (*Time Magazine*, 4/13/1931). Although toxic to drink, it was imbibed by some derelict alcoholics of the blues era.

Algiers

> *I was born in Algiers, twelve o'clock at night*
> *An' the moon wasn't shinin', and it wasn't a bit of light.*
> —Charlie Spand, "Evil Woman Spell," 1929

A New Orleans community on the west bank of the Mississippi, once fabled among blacks for its conjurers. The above lyric reflects an antebellum superstition: "They used to be a sayin' that chillun born at de dark of de moon ain't gwinter have no luck" (Aunt Pinkie Kelly, as quoted in *Born in Slavery*).

all-around man

> *Now I ain't no milkman, no milkman's son*
> *I can pull your titties 'till the milkman comes*
> *'Cause I'm an all-around man . . .*
> *I mean I'm all-around man I can do 'most anything that come to hand.*
> —Bo Carter, "All Around Man," 1936

A black term for a handyman. "Then I quit and went to working as an all-round man in the shop" (James Williams, as quoted in *Born in Slavery*).

all in all

> *I was lookin' out my window, Lord at how that rain did fall*
> *The onliest woman I loved has left me, and she was my all in all.*
> —Walter Davis, "Fallin' Rain," 1936

A romantic partner to whom one is completely devoted; one's soul mate; from the standard English use of the term as meaning "[a]ll things in all respects, all things altogether in one" (OED). In black sermonizing, Jesus is sometimes construed as the devout believer's *all in all*.

all, to have it

> *Starch my jumper, iron my overalls*
> *My brown done quit me God knows she had it all.*
> —Barbecue Bob, "Barbecue Blues," 1927

To have no shortcomings; a synonymous expression, *to have everything*, is used by the same performer:

> *It seems cloudy brown, I believe it's going to rain*
> *Goin' back to my regular, 'cause she got everything.*
> —"Cloudy Sky Blues," 1927

Another blues song scoffs at this notion:

> *Just as sure as the winter follows the fall*
> *There ain't no one woman got it all.*
> —Papa Charlie Jackson, "All I Want Is A Spoonful," 1925

all right with one, to be

> *"Boy, you know where I'm from?*
> *I'm from the Black Belt!*
> *If you be all right with me I'll carry you there too."*
> —Lucille Bogan, "Baking Powder Blues," 1933

To make a favorable impression; from the general slang superlative *all right* (cf. Lighter, 1994).

alley baby

> Papa got a watch, brother got a ring
> Sister got her arms full, of alley-boogin' that thing
> She's wild about her boogie, only thing she choose
> Now she's got to do the boogie, to buy her alley baby some shoes.
> —Lucille Bogan, "Alley Boogie," 1930

As used above, a child born as a result of alley debauchery or prostitution. See *boogie*.

alley rat

> I got a brownskin woman, she walks like a maltee cat
> Well she's a fine-lookin' mama, she ain't no alley rat.
> —Lee Green, "Maltese Cat Blues," 1930

A slang term for someone "who dwells in or frequents slum alleys; a guttersnipe" (Lighter, 1994).

alligator bait

> She said: "How I hate you, you alligator bait you
> You the ugliest thing I ever seen."
> —Sam Theard, "Ugly Child," 1930

A contemptuous term for a black person, dating in print to 1901 (Lighter, 1994) but of antebellum origin: "One of dem blue debils [Yankee soldiers] seed me an' come running. He say: 'What you doin', you black brat! You stinkin' little alligator bait!'" (Ida Adkins, as quoted in *Born in Slavery*).

along

> I was at home last night, I was all alone
> 'long about twelve o'clock, my baby come pullin' in home.
> —Bo Carter, "What Kind Of Scent Is This?," 1931

Sometime; a colloquialism of 19th-century vintage (cf. DARE).

ambeer

> I've got a head like a freight train, an' I walk just like a grizzly bear
> An' I use my skeetin' Garrett, and I skeet my ambeer everywhere.
> —Lucille Bogan, "Pig Iron Sally," 1934

Tobacco juice (cf. OED). In Southern usage, *ambeer* also signifies spittle mixed with tobacco juice (cf. WD). *Garrett* refers to a popular brand of chewing tobacco. See *skeet, skeetin' garrett*.

ambitious

> I started to kill my woman till she lay down 'cross the bed
> An' she looked so ambitious 'till I took back every word I said.
> —Willie Brown, "M&O Blues," 1930

Angry, ready to fight; a dated colloquialism associated with rural whites. Thornton (1912) traces its printed appearance to 1837, while Bartlett (1877) found its use restricted to Georgia and Western states. The above singer, however, hailed from the Mississippi Delta.

amen corner

> *There's a preacher in the pulpit, Bible in his hand*
> *And the sister's way back in the amen corner hollerin': "That's my man!"*
> —*Papa Charlie Jackson, "I'm Alabama Bound," 1925*

In black Fundamentalist usage, (1) a section of the church set aside for repentant sinners, equivalent to the mourner's bench of white churches; (2) a claque engaged by a minister to act as a cheering section in order to impress the congregation with his authority (Evans). As a black idiom, the term is found in Joel Chandler Harris's *Uncle Remus* (1880) in the form of a dialectal variant, *amen cornder*. In white Southern speech, *amen corner* connotes a vocally responsive group of churchgoers (WD) and dates in print to 1860 (DARE).

any old

> *My home ain't here, it's in 'most any old town (2)*
> —*Robert Wilkins, "Alabama Blues," 1929*

No particular; "a general term of vagueness" (DCS).

apron overalls

> *A woman is like a dresser, some man's always ramblin' through its*
>   *drawers*
> *It caused so many men, wearin' apron overalls.*
> —*Robert Johnson, "From Four Until Late," 1936*

A misnomer for overall aprons, once worn by rural females (cf. OED at "Mother Hubbard"). The performer is suggesting that women "wear the pants" of *monkey men*.

ash can

> *She sure shakes a mean ashcan*
> *I sure don't understand*
> *She can take any woman's man*
> *Lord she sure shakes a mean ashcan.*
> —*Pigmeat Pete and Catjuice Charlie, "She Shakes A Mean Ash Can," 1931*

A euphemism for "ass," perhaps originating in the above song.

ashes hauled, (to get) one's

> *When you catch my jumper, hangin' upside your wall*
> *Well you know by that baby I need my ashes hauled.*
> —*Sleepy John Estes, "The Girl I Love, She Got Long Curly Hair," 1929*

To fulfill one's sexual urges through intercourse; said primarily and probably originally of men. This inelegant expression arose from the presence of ash barrels in pre-gas and electric kitchen stoves; cf. *to burn one's coal and wood*. It anticipates the synonymous *empty one's trash*, associated with black speech of the 1980s (DCS). As a seeming term for sex drive, *ashes* appeared in the following:

> *Spied a spider, spied a spider, crawlin' on the wall*
> *Ruined his ashes but he's crazy 'bout his alcohol.*
> —Sam Butler, "Devil And My Brown," 1926

ash hauler

> *Well I went out last night, it was day when I came home*
> *Yes I was lookin' for my ash hauler, Lord Lord an' she was gone.*
> —Big Bill, "Ash Hauler," 1935

A female sex partner.

association

> *Elder Green told the deacon: "Let's go down in prayer,"*
> *There's a big 'ssociation in New Orleans, come an' let's go there."*
> —Charlie Patton, "Elder Greene Blues," 1929

An obsolete colloquialism for a convention of clergyman. The term was first noted in 1829, when it was attributed to New England speech (cf. Mathews, 1931).

awful fix

> *If you get one ol' woman, you better get you five or six*
> *So if that one happen to quit you, it won't leave you in no awful fix.*
> —Buddy Boy Hawkins, "Awful Fix Blues," 1927

Dire straits; a common colloquialism in the 19th century (F&H, 1890).

baby child

> *Your mother treated me like I was her baby child*
> *That's why I tried so hard to come back home to die.*
> —Bukka White, "Fixin' To Die Blues," 1940

A black colloquialism for offspring; particularly, the youngest child in a family. The latter sense is conveyed in a slave reminiscence: "My pappy was a old man when I were born—I were de baby chil'" (Sam McAllum, as quoted in *Born in Slavery*). The term appears in Ralph Ellison's *Invisible Man* (1952): "'It sounds like a woman who was watchin' a team of wild horses run down her baby chile and she can't move.'" Although DARE defines it as simply "baby," it was also used as a term of endearment for adults:

Mama say I'm reckless, daddy say I'm young and wild
"Reason he's so reckless 'cause he's my baby child."
—Isaiah Nettles, "So Cold In China," 1935

backbite

I will sure backbite you, gnaw you to the bone
I don't mean maybe, I can't let women alone.
—Sylvester Weaver, "Can't Be Trusted Blues," 1927

To have sex with a friend's bedmate.

backbiter, backbiting

My mama told me when I was about twelve years old:
"Son you're nothin' but a backbiter, may God bless your soul."
" . . . I am a backbiter; I'll bite any man in the back."
—Ramblin' Thomas, "Back Gnawin' Blues," 1928

One who backbites; a corruption of biblical terminology that may have been fostered by *biter*, a slang term for deceiver (Partridge). See *bite*. The adjectival form appears in the following:

I'm goin' to Louisiana, get myself a mojo hand
'Cause these backbitin' women, are tryin' to take my man.
—Ida Cox, "Mojo Hand Blues," 1927

backbone

I don't want no hoghead, don't eat no chitlins
Don't want no spareribs, don't eat no backbone
Mama got a hambone, I wonder can I get it boiled?
Because these Chicago women now, 'bout to let my hambone spoil.
—Rube Lacy, "Ham Hound Crave," 1928

Pork taken from the backbone area (DARE).

back door

Sun gonna shine in my back door someday
An' the wind gonna change gonna blow my blues away.
—Tommy Johnson, "Maggie Campbell Blues," 1928

Ass. The above couplet may have arisen from the phrase *where the sun don't shine* (i.e., anus). The statement "Sun gonna shine in my back door someday" was a proverbial blues or black indication (perhaps wistful) of coming good fortune, surviving in a Sea Island phrase: "The sun shine on a dog's ass any day." See *front door*.

back door (v.)

> *Honey can't no woman back door me*
> *I'm your one in all, or else your used to be.*
> —Emery Glen, "Back Door Blues," 1927

To cuckold; see *back door man.*

back door man

> *Ashes to ashes, sand to sand*
> *Every married woman has got a back door man.*
> —Seth Richards, "Skoodledum Doo," 1928

The secret lover of a married female, so named on the premise that he calls at the back door of her home. This figure was practically proverbial in black speech of the blues era. The association of a back door and illicit assignations is itself proverbial, reflected in the sayings "A nice wife and a back door, do often make a rich man poor" (John Ray, *A Collection of English Proverbs,* 1678) and "The postern door makes a thief and a whore" (Thomas Fuller, *Gnomolgia,* 1732). It appears in Ellison's *Invisible Man* (1952):

> *"BOY, WHO WAS BRER RABBIT?*
> *He was your mother's back-door man, I thought."*

bad, (badder, baddest)

> *Ain't nothin' in the jungle, that's any badder than me*
> *I'm the baddest man, ever came from Tennessee.*
> —Papa Charlie Jackson, "Jungle Man Blues," 1928

Tough; lawless; indomitable; black nuances attached to an old standard English sense of *bad,* as meaning morally depraved, wicked, or vicious (OED). In a general sense, *bad* = impressive: " ... Those music cats ... when you make some pretty good music note; kinda bad, out-of-sight chords, they look at one another, hunch one another" (Skip James, quoted in Calt, 2008). Although such was seemingly the primary connotation of *bad* as a dated black superlative, lexicographers see the word only as a jazz-originated inversion of *good* (cf., for example, OED). See *bad man, too bad.*

bad company

> *Bad company you must shun*
> *Or from the policeman you must run.*
> —Lottie Beaman, "Don't Speak To Me," 1930

The company of felons or social undesirables. This expression appeared in Benjamin Franklin's *Autobiography* of 1771 ("having no friend to advise him, he fell into bad company ... grew necessitous, pawned his clothes, and wanted bread.") and in the 1904 O. Henry story, *The Reformation of Calliope* ("' ... Keep away from bad company and work honest and sleep sweet.'"). The consequences of ignoring such advice are advertised in a 1963 Blind Gary Davis recording, "Bad Company Brought Me Here":

It is sad hurt to my heart

Bein' around about eleven o'clock

All of my veins are going to stop

An' they come into the cell

They gonna screw the death cap on my head

Well bad company brought me here.

bad, in

I wouldn't listen to my mother, wouldn't listen to my dad

And by my reckless way of livin' I done got myself in bad.

—Peg Leg Howell, "Low Down Rounders Blues," 1928

In bad repute, out of favor; an American slang term first recorded in 1911 (OED).

bad hair

Your sister was a teddy, your daddy was a bear

Put a muzzle on you mama 'cause you had bad hair.

—Charley Jordan, "Keep It Clean," 1930

Nappy or kinky hair, as opposed to *good hair*; a still-used black expression (*Smitherman, 2000*) that is also current among Hispanic Americans.

bad man

Police officer, how can it be?

You can 'rest everybody but cruel Stack O'Lee

That bad man, oh, cruel Stack O'Lee.

—Mississippi John Hurt, "Stack O'Lee Blues," 1928

A notorious gunfighter or outlaw. Farmer and Henley (F&H, 1890) offer a disquisition on the then-current term: "A BAD MAN, in the West, is a perfectly mixed character. The term is generally understood to mean a professional fighter or man-killer, but who, despite this drawback, is said . . . to be some-times . . . perfectly honest. These are the men who do most of the killing in frontier communities. . . ." In at least two instances, blues-era works invoke such figures by means of the modifier *bad*:

'Kinney says to Marget: "Come to me I said

If you don't come in a hurry, I'll put a .38 through your head."

Wasn't he bad? Just wasn't he bad?

—Henry Thomas, "Bob McKinney," 1927

Do you want your friend to be bad like Jesse James?

Get two six-shooters, highway some passenger train.

—Blind Lemon Jefferson, "One Dime Blues," 1927

baking powder man

> *Dice jumped to hustlin', I swear my money won't lose*
> *I got to win tonight and buy this baking powder man some shoes.*
> —Lucille Bogan, "Baking Powder Blues," 1933

Black slang for a "big bluffer," "blowhard," or "know-it-all" (Hill). It was once fashionable to squelch such persons with the question, "What blowed you up?," the inference being baking powder.

balk

> *Now, I changed walk, I changed talk*
> *I changed babies just keep from being balked.*
> —Sleepy John Estes, "Everybody Oughta Make A Change," 1938

Dated standard English meaning "[t]o check, hinder, thwart (a person or his action)" (OED, which offers 1821 and 1855 as its most recent citations for the term).

ball (n.)

> *I'm gonna get my pistol, forty rounds of ball*
> *I'm gonna shoot my woman, just to see her fall.*
> —Furry Lewis, "Furry's Blues," 1928

Units of ammunition; superseded by *bullet* with the early-20th-century advent of cylindrical shell casings. "When my marster went to de war him got a ball through his leg" (Charlie Robinson, as quoted in *Born in Slavery*).

ball (v.)

> *Ball on baby, you can have your way*
> *Each an' every dog, sure must have his day.*
> —Charlie Patton, "Hammer Blues," 1929

To carouse; probably derived from the use of *ball* as a term for a dance. Although treated as a "jive term" of the 1930s by DAS, it is of older, more rustic derivation (as per the above).

Ball the Jack (v.)

> *I can line the track, an' I can Ball the Jack*
> *I can beat anybody gettin' a good girl back.*
> —Sam Collins, "Hesitation Blues," 1927

To do the dance of that name. Nationally, this dance enjoyed a brief vogue created by a 1913 Tin Pan Alley composition, "Ballin' The Jack," written by a black songwriter, Chris Smith. Unaccountably, it figured in Chuck Berry's "Oh Baby Doll" (1958), in reference to high school antics: "We had a portable radio, we was Ballin' the Jack." To *ball the jack* was originally a railroad expression meaning to attain speed (ATS). "Ballin' the Jack was before my time, but it wasn't gone plumb out . . . you know what Ball the Jack is? People put their knees together an' then hit two knees together.... They tell me a woman was Ballin' the Jack one Sunday mornin' an' she couldn't stop. She just Balled an' Jacked until she died. I heard that." (Bukka White).

ballyhoo

> *She got a kitchenette, an apartment, too*
> *She don't do nothin' but ballyhoo*
> *Oh sister Jane, right across the hall*
> *Oh she drinks her liquor and she sure God has a ball.*
> —Kokomo Arnold, "Sister Jane Cross The Hall," 1937

To brag; an uncommon slang term dating to 1930 (DAS).

'bama, the

> *I'll sing this verse, ain't gonna sing no more*
> *Got a gal in the 'bama an' can't tell you all I know.*
> —Sam Butler, "Jefferson County Blues," 1926

Alabama; also rendered as *'bama:*

> *Mister engineer, please turn your train around*
> *I believe to my soul, my man is 'bama bound.*
> —Ida Cox, "Bama Bound Blues," 1923

Bamma is a current northern black pejorative for an unsophisticated arrival from the South (cf. Smitherman, 2000).

bamalong

> *Ain't gonna be in the second bamalong (2)*
> —Andrew and Jim Baxter, "Bamalong Blues," 1927

A brawl or police raid, particularly one that disrupts a party (Hill). This term may have been derived from the English dialect term *bammel,* to knock or beat (EDD).

banana

> *An' I'm tellin' you baby, I sure ain't gonna deny it*
> *Let me put my banana in your fruit basket, then I'll be satisfied.*
> —Bo Carter, "Banana In Your Fruit Basket," 1931

A conventional slang term for penis (DAS).

banty

> *I'm gonna buy me a banty, put him in my back door*
> *'Cause see a stranger comin', he'll flap his wings and crow.*
> —Charlie Patton, "Banty Rooster Blues," 1929

Bantam rooster; a widespread colloquialism (cf. DARE). In the above couplet it is deployed as a sentinel against the threat of a *back door man,* reflecting a rural black superstition: "When de rooster crows in the house it is a sign of a stranger coming" (Marshal Butler, as quoted in *Born in Slavery*).

barbecue

Talkin' 'bout barbecue, only thing I sell

An' if you wanna get it you got to come to my house at twelve.

—Lucille Bogan, "Barbecue Bess," 1935

Pussy, barbecue having been a black slang term for a sexually attractive woman (DAS).

barefooted

I'm gonna tell you why I got Lemon's low-down worried blues

I left my meal-ticket rider barefooted, my partner's sister's bought a new
*   pair of shoes.*

—Blind Lemon Jefferson, "Lemon's Worried Blues," 1928

Bereft of resources, a sense communicated by the current genteel catchphrase *barefoot and pregnant* (applied to impoverished lower-class wives). In the above depiction, the narrator has cleaned out a woman who supported him, and lavished money on her sister. See *meal-ticket rider.* "We was turned loose barefooted and had no schools den and when dey had schools I had to work" (Louis Hall, as quoted in *Born in Slavery*).

barrelhouse (n.)

An' I tol' my woman, 'fore I left the town:

"Don't you let nobody tear the barrelhouse down."

—Hambone Willie Newbern, "Roll And Tumble Blues," 1929

As used by Southern blacks, an illicit commercial establishment serving as an all-purpose tavern, gambling den, dance hall, and often brothel, located (if not in a city) near the railroad depot of a small town or in a sawmill or levee camp. These white-owned enterprises probably arose in the late 1800s; because their main attraction was bonded liquor, they were decimated by Prohibition. There is no truth to the frequent dictionary supposition, perpetuated by jazz writers, that the term *barrelhouse* arose from the presence of whiskey barrels on the walls of such places. Rather, the term stems from the outmoded use of *barrel* to mean liquor, which survived into the 19th century and produced the term *barrel fever* (Partridge).

Barrelhouse appeared in American colloquial speech by 1883, when it signified a low-class tavern (DAH); another source (Anderson, 1923) describes it as "a rooming-house, tavern, saloon, and house of prostitution, all in one," which approximates the black understanding of the word while omitting gambling. The latter held that barrelhouses (described as "a thing of the past" in 1923) catered to tramps; that was not true of black barrelhouses, which sometimes enforced dress codes and were more decorous than juke joints. Skip James said of them: "You used to pay to go in those places, maybe a dollar and a half, or two dollars for a couple. You would be served perhaps a small drink, and sandwiches. Then you had a chance to gamble, and anything else that you wanna do in there" (Calt, 2008).

barrelhouse (a.)

I don't want no barrelhouse woman, messin' around with me
If you 'bout to get drunk baby, mama please just let me be.
—Leroy Carr, "Barrelhouse Woman," 1934

Alcoholic; given to late hours and disreputable conduct in the manner of barrelhouse patrons, as in the following description: "You just one of them ol' barrelhouse gals, runnin' around up an' down ol' alleys, drinkin' this ol' bad alcohol an' stayin' out all night." (Bill Gaither, "Georgia Barrel House," 1940).

barrelhouse (v.)

And my poor mother's old now you know, head is turnin' gray
I know it would break her heart if she found I was barrelhousin' this way.
—Kid Bailey, "Mississippi Bottom Blues," 1929

To patronize barrelhouses or emulate the behavior of barrelhouse habitués, marked by intemperate drinking, gambling, and womanizing.

barrelhouse habit

Whiskey is my habit, good men is my crave
This old barrelhouse habit goin' to drive me to my grave.
—Lucille Bogan, "Cravin' Whiskey Blues," 1927

Immoderate whiskey drinking. In the blues era, commercially manufactured whiskey was dispensed to black Southerners only at barrelhouses; the product offered at plantation juke joints was corn liquor. See also *habits, to have one's on.*

barrelhouse people

My mama told me when I was a lad:
"Barrelhouse people gonna be your ruin at last."
—Charlie Spand, "Soon This Morning Blues," 1929

Barrelhouse habitués, also called (in Mississippi) *Saturday night people*, expressions used with the implication that their subjects had no interests other than carousing. Cf. *Saturday night.*

barrelhouse ways

I believe I believe, I will stop my barrelhouse ways
For I feel myself sinkin' every day.
—Teddy Darby, "Built Right On The Ground," 1931

Habitual carousing in a manner associated with barrelhouse patrons.

battle-ham

> *She got a great big nose, she got crooked toes*
> *I love my Tillie Lee*
> *She got big thick lips, she got battle-ham hips*
> *Nice as she can be*
> —William Moore, "Tillie Lee," 1928

A variant of *battle-hammed*, a black term signifying thick or unsightly hips. The earliest recorded use of this idiom, dating to 1742, was a description of a runaway slave (cf. DARE). Its first element perhaps derives from a 17th-century adjective, *battled*, applied to fatted animals (OED).

b.d. (1)

> *B.d. women, you know they work an' make their dough*
> *And when they get ready to spend it, they know just where to go.*
> —Lucille Bogan, "B.D. Woman's Blues," 1935

Bull dyker.

b.d. (2)

> *So woman you leavin', I reckon I have to let you be*
> *Babe you done got tired, Lord of this here old b.d.*
> —Walter Roland, "O.B.D. Blues," 1935

? Big dick or black dick. The two performers who used the expression *b.d.* were associates and may have contrived one or both terms as recording euphemisms.

be easy

> *Be easy mama 'cause trouble's bearin' down*
> *Be easy mama my trouble's bearin' down.*
> —William Harris, "I'm Leavin' Town," 1927

An admonition meaning "do not hurry, don't be so eager" that is "[n]ow considered an 'Irishism'" (OED).

beau (bo) dollar

> *You need not think because you're yeller*
> *I'm gonna give you my last beau dollar.*
> —Son House, "Am I Right Or Wrong," 1941 (LC)

Silver dollar; a Southern colloquialism associated with blacks (DARE, WD).

begone

> *I'm gonna get me a mama, I mean with lots of bucks*
> *I want you to begone mama, so I can change my luck.*
> —Blind Lemon Jefferson, "Change My Luck Blues," 1928

An old scolding expression, meaning "be off, get out of here," that is still heard in the South (WD).

bear down

Be easy mama 'cause trouble's bearin' down

Be easy mama my trouble's bearin' down.

—William Harris, "I'm Leavin' Town," 1927

To pull to the ground; overwhelm. Although construed as standard English by the OED, this expression appears to have been passé and associated with blacks in American speech. It occurs in the Roark Bradford dialect novel *John Henry* (1931): "'Well,' said John Henry, 'my troubles bearin' down mighty hard, but hit ain't got me down on my knees yit.'" In blues usage it is similarly coupled with trouble:

Trouble done bore me down

But here I sit a-moanin',

Trouble done bore me down.

—Barbecue Bob, "Trouble Done Bore Me Down," 1929

beat it

Now all you women love to fuss an' fight

Come on around an' let's us, beat it up tight

Now I can beat it; I can beat it tonight

I can beat it baby, got somethin' to beat it right.

—Kansas Joe McCoy and Memphis Minnie, "Beat It Right," 1931

To fornicate. In recent black slang, *Can I beat it?* is a male request for sex. See *boot it* and *kick it*.

bed-shaker

Don't you feel lonesome, when your bed-shaker's gone?

And you ain't got nobody, to carry your bed-shakin' on.

—Bill Gaither, "Pains In My Heart," 1936

A bedmate.

bedspring(s) poker

Says you may be brownskin, woman, great God your hair's long as my
*   arm*

Can't do a bedspring poker, you sure done lost your home.

—Will Batts, "Country Woman," 1933

An act of sexual intercourse; apparently, an embellishment of *poke*, a term of like meaning (F&H, 1890). It appears as a vocal aside in the Mississippi Sheiks' "Bedspring Poker" (1931): "Oh look at that old bed shaking. That's what we call 'bedsprings poker.'"

beedle um bum

Oh, my beedle um bum

Come and see me if you ain't had none

It'll make a dumb man speak, make a lame man run
You'll miss something if you don't get none
—The Hokum Boys, "Beedle Um Bum," 1928

A slang term for *pussy* current among female partygoers in Chicago during the 1920s (Tom Dorsey). It seems to have arisen from "Beedle Um Bo," a 1908 ragtime piano composition by Charles L. Johnson that probably bore no sexual connotation.

been here and gone

Aw listen fair brown it's something going on wrong
It's the woman I love she done been here and gone.
—Blind Lemon Jefferson, "Shuckin' Sugar," 1926

Vanished, apparently not to return; a blues or barrelhouse catchphrase.

believe to one's soul, to

I can't drink coffee and the woman won't make no tea
I believe to my soul sweet mama's gonna hoodoo me.
—Blind Lemon Jefferson, "Dry Southern Blues," 1926

To feel strongly convinced; a Southern colloquialism used in the first person. "'I remember well that Joe Whitaker frequently drank like a fish,' says Mama. 'I believed to my soul he drank chemicals.'" (Eudora Welty, *Why I Live at the P.O.*, 1936).

Belly Roll

Crawlin' lizard's got a crawl they call the "Belly Roll"
He can crawl, all in my door.
—Lucille Bogan, "Crawlin' Lizard Blues," 1930

A reference to *Roll the Belly*, a barrelhouse dance of the 1920s (Skip James).

between the devil and the deep blue sea

I'll never let another man fool me
I'm just as worried as a girl can be
I've been between the devil an' the deep blue sea.
—Virginia Liston, "I Don't Love Nobody," 1924

Mired in difficulty to which there are only grim alternatives; a clichéd figure of speech of mid-18th-century origin as *between the devil and the deep sea* (DC). The latter-day form (involving "blue") served as the title of a 1932 Ted Koehler–Harold Arlen Tin Pan Alley tune, popularized by Cab Calloway.

biddy (1)

Rooster chew tobacco and the hen dip snuff
Biddy can't do it but he struts his stuff.
—Blind Willie McTell, "Kind Mama," 1931

A chicken; a standard English term construed by the OED as obsolete except in dialectal speech.

biddy (2)

"You ain't nothin' but a no-good biddy, nohow."

—Sonny Scott, "No Good Biddie," 1933

A slang term, often pejorative, for a female (cf. F&H, 1890; OED).

big as a barrel

I'm five feet standin', six feet layin' down

I'm big as a barrel, but I'm round, round, round.

—Lucille Bogan, "Struttin' My Stuff," 1930

A colloquial simile found in Twain's *Tom Sawyer* (1876) and in Stephen Crane's dialect story *The Knife* (1899), where it is applied to melons by a black speaker: "'Seems like I nev' <u>did</u> see sech mellums, big as er bar'l, lain' dere.'"

big boy

Put both hands on her hips, and these is the words she said:

"Big boy I wouldn't miss you if the good Lord told me you was dead."

—Hambone Willie Newbern, "Hambone Willie's Dreamy-Eyed Woman's
* Blues," 1929*

A black pejorative that "in the South . . . means fool and is a prime insult" (Zora Neale Hurston's *American Mercury* note on Harlem speech (1942) quoted in DARE). This term has a similarly pejorative connotation in the Pine Top Smith recording, "Big Boy, They Can't Do That" (1929).

big chief

Baby when I marry, gonna marry an Indian squaw

So the big chief Lord, be my daddy-in-law.

—Furry Lewis, "Big Chief Blues," 1927

The perceived ruler or decision maker of a Native American tribe containing lesser chiefs; a colloquialism of the 19th century, racially unknown origin. ". . . he was one of the best known Creeks in the whole nation, and one of his younger brothers, Legus Perryman, was made the big chief of the Creeks . . ." (Phoebe Banks, as quoted in *Born in Slavery*).

big house

Now I'm on my way to the big house, an' I don't even care

I might get lifetime, then again I might get the 'lectric chair.

—Aaron Sparks, "Workhouse Blues," 1935

A state prison; construed as a Western term in DAUL.

big mama

Big mama owns, everything in her neighborhood

But when she's makin' money, is when she moves to the piney woods.

—Blind Lemon Jefferson, "Piney Woods Money Mama," 1928

A black term for grandmother; cf. Smitherman (2000) (which renders it "big moma") and DARE ("big mamma"). This idiom may be of antebellum vintage:

"Aunt Judy—some called her 'Big Mama'—lived down under the hill. She was old and saw after the children" (Mahalia Shores, as quoted in *Born in Slavery*). "All my grand-chillun calls me 'Big Mama,' but I's so lil' now dey ought to call me 'Li'l Mama'" (Sallie Wroe, as quoted in *Born in Slavery*).

big road

Lord I ain't goin' down the big road by myself
If I don't carry you gon' carry somebody else.
—Tommy Johnson, "Big Road Blues," 1928

A 19th-century plantation idiom applied to all but the most insignificant back roads. It frequently occurs in *Uncle Remus* (1880).

big-time (adv.)

All last winter I was sleepin' by myself
You're gone big-time and lovin' someone else.
—Bumble Bee Slim, "Cold Blooded Murder No. Two," 1935

An intensifier used to underscore the significance of a situation, perhaps of black origin; now common in colloquial speech.

big-timing (v.)

I remember the nights, sleepin' all by myself
While you was out big-timin', lovin' someone else.
—Bill Gaither, "You Done Ranked Yourself With Me," 1941

Carousing; from the Southern expression *big time* for an enjoyable party, celebration, and the like (WD), as in "First Saturday night they had a big time" (Delta black quoted in Calt and Wardlow).

biggest, the

There won't be enough Japs to shoot a little game of craps
Because the biggest of them all will be dead.
—Son House, "American Defense," 1942 (LC)

Most, the greatest amount; a black colloquialism of probable 19th-century vintage. A former slave related: "The biggest what they would give the field hands to eat would be ... what us had on the place, like greens ..." (Botkin, 1945).

billed

My babe took a ship, she says: "Daddy I'm bound for Mexico"
She says: "I'm billed out sweet papa, your sweet mama bound to go."
—Lee Green, "Down On The Border," 1930

Entered in a railway book as a passenger; American slang of 19th-century vintage applied here to boat travel (cf. OED).

bird liver

I wanna give you folks a warnin', I mean this mornin',
An' I want you all to strictly understand:

Now you can call me what you choose, but I'm a bird liver-cravin' man.
—*Sylvester Kimbrough, "Bird Liver Blues," 1929*

An elderly woman; black slang synonymous with *hogmeat* (Hill). The statement "you can call me what you choose" is put forth with the assumption that the singer will be regarded as a gigolo.

bird's nest on the ground, a

Come on mama, go to the edge of town
I know where there's a bird's nest, built down on the ground.
—*Charlie Patton, "Bird Nest Bound," 1930*

Contemporary slang (associated with white Southern criminals) meaning something that is there for the taking, equivalent to "a piece of cake." It occurs three times in Edward Anderson's *Thieves Like Us* (1937), a depiction of Texas bank robbers:

> "I cased that bank in Zelton four times," T-Dub said. "It was a bird's nest on the ground, but every time something came up."
> "Who goes in first?"
> "Nigger. The porter. Around six o'clock. It's a bird's-nest on the ground to go in with him."
> "This bank here is a bird's-nest on the ground," T-Dub said. "And it will go for fifty thousand or not a dime."

Though largely obsolete, it figured in a 2005 broadcast of the *Judge Judy* television show, as spoken by a black court officer (5/2/2005):

> *Judge Judy: "Do you see how easy that was?"*
> *Officer Byrd: "Like a bird's nest on the ground."*

biscuit

Every evenin', half-past eight
Hobblin' around, rich man's gate
Workin' and studyin', seekin' out the plan,
How to get that biscuit out that, rich man's hand.
—*Blind Lemon Jefferson, "Beggin' Back," 1926*

Slang for a young female, or "[a] flapper who pets" (quoted in Lighter, 1994). In the above context it is applied to a female who is laboring as a white man's cook and used with the implication that she is sexually available for the latter. Elsewhere in the song, *biscuit* is used to mean *pussy:* "You got to use a new biscuit, the way you been actin' the last thirty days."

biscuit roller

Now don't your house feel lonesome when your biscuit roller gone?
You stand in your back door and cry by yourself alone.
—*Robert Wilkins, "Rolling Stone, Part Two," 1928*

A live-in female companion, apprehended as a food and sex provider; an extension of the same term (associated with ranch slang) as meaning a cook, without gender or sexual implications (ATS). See the synonymous *dough roller*.

bite

> *She's a married woman but she says she likes me*
> *Hate to bite my friend but somebody been bitin' me.*
> —Charley Lincoln, "Hard Luck Blues," 1927

To *backbite*. The above reference to being "bitten" is probably a pun based on the word as meaning bothered or "bugged" by something. (Cf. Crane's *Maggie, A Girl Of The Streets* (1893): "'Ah, w'at's bitin' yeh?'")

bite one's tongue

> *Now don't you hear me talkin' to you,*
> *I don't bite my tongue*
> *You want to be my man you got to fetch it with you when you come.*
> —Ma Rainey, "Hear Me Talking To You," 1928

To remain silent or fail to speak one's mind, a now-common colloquialism perhaps occasioned by *to bite one's lips*, a 19th-century slang phrase meaning to regret one's words (F&H, 1890). "He didn't bite his tongue about tellin' you how much he was gettin' paid; if he didn't like the money, he would just leave." (Walter Vinson on duet partner Lonnie Chatmon)

black (a. 1)

> *Black man is evil, yellow man so low-down.*
> *I walk into these houses, just to see these black men frown.*
> —Barbecue Bob, "Chocolate To The Bone," 1928

Black-complexioned, as opposed to (for example) brown-skinned; the customary sense of the word as used on race recording. The above couplet was likely based on a catchphrase, recounted in Gwaltney (1980): "My Uncle Matt used to say this little saying: 'Black is evil, yallah so lowdown, look here honey, ain't you glad you brown?'"

black (a. 2)

> *I'll tell you what all the boys on Beale Street know*
> *It is the black man in the tree, and 4–11–44.*
> —Jim Jackson, "Policy Blues," 1928

African American, a sense that rarely occurs in blues recording. The above reference to lynching so riled Memphis whites that its performer was said to have been run out of the city in consequence.

black (a. 3)

It's a mean black moan, an' a, black moan my God
An' the strike in Chicago, Lord it just won't stop.
—*Charlie Patton, "Mean Black Moan," 1929*

"Clouded with sorrow or melancholy; dismal, gloomy, sad" (OED, which offers three citations, from 1659, 1715, and 1809).

black (a. 4)

Now when I had my black money, I used to spend
in almost any bar, without a doubt
But there is one thing funny, no one knows you
when you are down an' out.
—*Leroy Henderson, "Good Scufflin' Blues," 1935*

? Used as an intensifier, or (in the above) signifying money belonging to an African American.

black and tan

There's one thing about my woman I can't understand
Every night she go to bed she wanna, do that ol' black an' tan.
—*Blind Boy Fuller, "Black And Tan," 1936*

? An obscure slang term that almost certainly connotes oral sex, an activity some male blues singers found objectionable (see *come down on*). *Black and tan country* stood for the South (F&H, 1890), while *going South* was a conventional term for performing oral sex.

Black Belt, the

"Boy, you know where I'm from?
I'm from the Black Belt!"
—*Lucille Bogan, "Baking Powder Blues," 1933*

The prairie region extending from the south central part of Alabama to northeastern Mississippi. Booker T. Washington wrote of it: "So far as I can learn, the term was first used to designate a part of the country which was distinguished by the colour of the soil. . . . Later and especially since the [Civil] war, the term seems to be used . . . to designate the counties where the black people outnumber the white" (*Up from Slavery*, 1901).

Black Bottom (1)

She said: "When you go in Black Bottom, be sure an' put your money in
your shoe.
If you don't, Black Bottom women'll take it away from you."
—*Charlie "Dad" Nelson, "Michigan Shoe Blues," 1927*

A term first applied to a *bottom* (lowland) region with dark topsoil; so used in 1908 by Baker. As with *Black Belt*, it evolved into a nickname for a black neighborhood, particularly one with a rough character. Although the above song refers to the Detroit Black Bottom, the most storied one was located in Nashville, of which Ethel Waters remarked: "The Negroes who lived in the Black Bottom neighborhood in Nashville were so bad, aggressive, and hurly-burly that the bravest white coppers didn't dare invade their streets" (Waters).

Black Bottom (2)

> Me and my feets is skippy, how
> You oughta see me doin' the Black Bottom now.
> —Blind Lemon Jefferson, "Hot Dogs," 1927

A barrelhouse dance that enjoyed a brief national vogue by virtue of being featured in George White's *Scandals* (a famous Broadway production) in 1926. The latter utilized the following composition describing the dance:

> Now you hop in front, doodle back
> Mooch to the left, Mooch to the right
> Do the Mess Around
> Break a leg until you're near the ground.
> —Sadie Jackson, "Original Black Bottom Dance," 1926

A black-produced *Black Bottom* musical and dance revue appeared in Chicago's *Monogram Theatre* as early as 1923 (noted in the *Chicago Defender*, 11/3/1923).

black cat bone

> I believe my good gal have found my black cat bone
> I can leave Sunday mornin' Monday mornin' I'm tippin' 'round home.
> —Blind Lemon Jefferson, "Broke And Hungry," 1926

A hoodoo charm held to confer magical powers upon its possessor, including invisibility and the ability to triumph over sexual rivals. In the above song, the performer is suggesting that his girlfriend has been able to prevent abandonment by virtue of using his own *black cat bone*. As dispensed by some conjurers, the charm was represented as a bone boiled from a live black cat that made no reflection in a mirror (Puckett, 1925). An ex-slave noted: "First, the cat is killed and boiled, after which the meat is scraped from the bones. The bones are then taken to the creek and thrown in. The bone that goes up stream is the lucky one and should be kept" (Minnie R. Ross, as quoted in *Born in Slavery*). At the same time, the phrase was loosely applied to mean "just a bone they put in that hoodoo bag ... [with] a piece of lodestone, some kind of red cloth; they got it mixed up together" (Willie Moore).

black is evil

They say black is evil, and they don't mean you no good
But I would not quit my black woman, baby if I could.
—Leroy Carr, "Good Woman Blues," 1934

A black catchphrase of the blues era, used to denigrate black-hued African Americans, and applied in blues song exclusively to females. See *evil*.

black snake

My woman signified, my black snake was dead
But she never knowed it, till I went to bed.
—Sam Collins, "Signifying Blues," 1931

The penis of a black person.

Black Snake Wiggle

Do the Black Snake Wiggle an' the Boston Trot
Scratchin' Gravel in a vacant lot.
—Jane Lucas and Georgia Tom, "Come On Mama," 1930

In all likelihood, a reference to sex, disguised as a dance; in another recording (produced three months after the above), the term refers to the motions of a penis during intercourse:

Black snake wiggle, he wiggle both night an' day
When he wiggle his tail, you almost pass away.
—Peggy Waller, "Blacksnake Wiggle," 1930

black 'spatch

You can go if you choose, but the world is certainly gonna read bad news
'Cause when I tell you my troubles, you say I've got the black 'spatch blues.
—Ethel Waters, "Black Spatch Blues," 1924

Black dispatch, a black term for any widely publicized news about blacks, applied to either an informal grapevine or black-oriented publications like the *Chicago Defender*. It was defined by Zora Neale Hurston as "Negro gossip" (glossary affixed to the 1934 novel *Jonah's Gourd Vine*, where it was used synonymously with *Black Herald*). A black-owned Oklahoma City, Oklahoma, paper extant from 1914–82 bore the name *Black Dispatch*, supposedly in response to the use of "black dispatch" by whites as a term for unreliable gossip or falsehoods.

blacker the berry, the sweeter the juice, the

Blacker the berry, sweeter is the juice
I got a good black woman, and I ain't going to turn her loose.
—Leroy Carr, "Good Woman Blues," 1934

A still-invoked black proverb, used in blues song to extol the sexual properties of black-complexioned females.

blazes

> I got the blue, blue blazes blues
> . . . they burns all night long.
> —Emery Glen, "Blue Blazes Blues," 1927

Hellfire. Farmer and Henley noted in 1890: "This, an allusion to the flames of hell, was the original meaning; constant use, however, has lessened the force of the expression. . . . In most cases the word is now a meaningless intensive. . . ."

blind (v.)

> I just wanna blind it, far as (?) town
> When she blows 'fore to cross it, I'm gonna ease it down.
> —Ed Bell, "Mean Conductor Blues," 1927

To ride the blind; see *blind, the; blind(s), ride the.*

blind, the

> Lost John settin' on the railroad track
> Waitin' for the freight train to come back
> Lost John thought he'd have to ride the top
> 'Long come a Dixie Fly *then just behind*
> He missed the cowcatcher when he caught the blind.
> —Papa Charlie Jackson, "Long Gone Lost John," 1928

In passenger trains, the blind baggage car, described in 1901 as "a car that ain't got no door in the end that's next to the engine" (OED). This popular refuge for hoboes had a small platform on which to support a rider (Irwin, 1931).

blind(s), ride the

> I'm leavin' here tonight if I have to ride the blinds
> Take a freight train special, tell the engineer lose no time.
> —Papa Charlie Jackson, "Salt Lake City Blues," 1924

To cadge a train ride by standing on the platform attached to the blind baggage car. This term (of unknown vintage) superseded the synonymous *jump the blinds* (recorded in 1895) and *beating the blinds* (1893), becoming almost a metaphor for hoboing in the 1930s.

blind pig

> Blind pig, blind pig, sure glad you can't see
> 'Cause if you could it would be too tight for me.
> —Barbecue Bob, "Blind Pig Blues," 1928

A conventional slang term for a speakeasy dating in print to 1887 (DAH).

blood in one's eye, to have

> He packed his grip and went away with blood in both his eyes
> Her friends asked Sally where he went, and boldly she replied.
> —Trixie Smith, "I Don't Know And I Don't Care Blues," 1924

To be furiously angry or disposed to homicidal violence; a black idiom occurring in a 1971 prison memoir by George L. Jackson (*Blood in My Eye)* that subsequently influenced rap expression.

blow (1)

> *Believe me brownie, please don't throw me down*
> *I'm gonna pack my suitcase, I'm gonna blow this town.*
> —*Peg Leg Howell, "Fo' Day Blues," 1926*

A conventional slang term (dating in print to 1902) meaning to leave, usually hastily (DAS; Partridge).

blow (2)

> *There once was a girl she bought a hornright whistle*
> *Come blowin' it right down the street*
> *Every time she blow she blow "Toodlee-oo"*
> *An' she blow for everybody she meet.*
> —*Hambone Willie Newbern, "She Could Toodle-oo," 1929*

To fellate, a now-standard term that perhaps arose from double entendre imagery such as appears above, fostered less by the act of "blowing" a penny whistle or some such instrument than its phallic shape. As sexual slang, *blow* may have been novel at the time of the above recording (cf. OED, which traces it to 1933). See *toodle-oo.*

blow-in

> *I'm a stranger here I just blowed-in your town*
> *If I ask for a favor, don't turn me, don't turn me down.*
> —*Willie Baker, "No No Blues," 1928*

To arrive; an American colloquialism dating in print to 1895 (DAH).

blow one down

> *I met this joker one mornin', he was out on the edge of town*
> *I had to talk and plead for to keep him from blowin' me down.*
> —*Blind Lemon Jefferson, "Mean Jumper Blues," 1928*

To kill with a firearm.

blue notes

> *Blue notes, true notes*
> *Weird chords, Lord Lord.*
> —*Sara Martin, "Cushion Foot Stomp," 1926*

Musical jargon for departures from the major diatonic scale held to characterize blues, differentiating it from pop music. It variously connotes the minor thirds and minor sevenths that abound in blues song, and thirds sung as quarter tones, between minor and major intervals. In any event, this term is a misleading misnomer, as such intervals also abound in spirituals, and were simply characteristic of black singing during the blues era. They had small bearing on the tenor of blues: Henry Spaulding's "Cairo Blues" (1929) attains an authentic blues sound without utilizing so-called blue notes. See Appendix.

blues, to have the

I don't see why white folks don't have no blues
They got our cash money, an' brownskin women too.
—*T. C. Johnson, "JC Johnson's Blues," 1928*

Apart from the customary meanings of feeling dejected or depressed, this phrase is used in blues songs to express a general sense of disquietude. *To have the blues* variously means to feel out of sorts, to feel agitated, or to be disgruntled. When coupled with a noun or adverb, it connotes a feeling of wretchedness attributable to some external circumstance (specified in the modifier):

I'm gonna put some, wings on my shoes
An' I ain't gonna stop rollin' till I kill 'em homeless blues.
—*Seth Richards, "Lonely Seth Blues," 1928*

Some people say the Green River blues ain't bad
Than it must not a-been them Green River blues I had.
—*Charlie Patton, "Green River Blues," 1929*

See *sing (one's) blues, to.*

bo' hog

Pigmeat's all right, but pigmeat soon gives out
I'd much rather have my big bo' hog, he knows what it's all about.
—*Irene Wiley, "Rootin' Bo Hog Blues," 1931*

Boar hog; literally, an adult male swine. In the above song, *bo' hog* connotes a middle-aged or sexually experienced boyfriend, as contrasted with *pigmeat*, and may represent a nonce term. See *pigmeat* and *hogmeat.*

bo' hog shuffle

Where you get your shoes and your dress so fine?
Doin' the bo' hog shuffle an' the Georgia Grind.
—*Kansas City Kitty and Georgia Tom, "Close Made Papa," 1931*

A slang term for sexual intercourse, based on the connotations of *bo' hog* or *bo' hog's eye:*

She's got a little bitty foot, Lordie got them great big thighs
Well she's got something under yonder, winks like a bo' hog's eye.
—*Jack Kelly, "Men Fooler Blues," 1939*

Of itself, *hog-eye* is a slang expression for the vagina (ATS; Lighter, 1997).

bobo

> *Your face all wrinkled, your back's all bare*
> *If you ain't doin' a bobo, what's your head doin' there?*
> —Tampa Red, "The Dirty Dozen No. 2," 1930

An act of oral sex, probably used in reference to male activity. This term may have been suggested by "Georgia Bo-Bo," a 1926 Louis Armstrong recording that the latter related to "a dance that originated in Georgia."

boggy

> *I will cut your kindlin', I will build your fire*
> *I will tote your water, from the boggy bayou.*
> —Charlie Patton, "Heart Like Railroad Steel," 1929

Swampy, a standard English locution (OED). The above lyric is an arch way of suggesting that the performer will do little or nothing for his mate, fetching water having been children's plantation work.

bold

> *She's got a man on her man, got a kid on her kid . . .*
> *She done got so bold, Lord she won't keep it hid.*
> —Charlie Patton, "It Won't Be Long," 1929

"Audacious, presumptuous, too forward; the opposite of 'modest'" (OED), the invariable implication of the term in pre-1960s usage when the subject was a female. It is invoked to suggest promiscuity in Little Richard's "Slippin' And Slidin'" (1956): "I been told baby, you been bold . . ."

bone

> *Some men like lunch meat, and some they likes old tongue*
> *Some men don't care for biscuits, they like the doggone big fat bone.*
> —Bo Carter, "Your Biscuits Are Big Enough For Me," 1936

Erect penis. As a term for erection, *bone* dates to the mid-19th century, when it was associated with Cockney slang (Partridge). See *hambone*.

bone, to the

> *Aw they taken my woman, hurt me to the bone*
> *That's the reason why you hear me cry an' moan.*
> —Barbecue Bob, "Atlanta Moan," 1930

Thoroughly; to the core; a standard English figure of speech (OED).

bones

> *"Let's go, bones!"*
> —Blind Blake, "Dry Bone Shuffle," 1927

A makeshift percussion instrument of slave origin. "Some nigger women go back to de quarters and git de gourd fiddles and de clapping bones made out'n beef ribs, and bring dem back so we could have some music." (Charley Williams, as quoted in *Born in Slavery*)

bone orchard wagon

> *Oh when that bone orchard wagon, rolls up in front of my door*
> *I won't have to be cryin', and pleading with the blues no more.*
> —Ida Cox, "Bone Orchard Blues," 1928

An obscure term for a hearse, from a conventional slang term for cemetery (cf. Lighter, 1994). See *death wagon*.

booger, pitch a

> *I can tell when the blues is comin', I can't help but feel so low-down*
> *An' I want to get drunk and pitch a booger all over town.*
> —"Funny Paper" Smith, "Corn Liquor Blues," 1931

To carouse. The term also appears as *pitch a boogie*:

> "Give me half a bottle of moonshine, two-three bottles of beer;
> We gonna pitch a boogie right here."
> —Will Ezell, "Pitchin' Boogie," 1929

In the latter instance, *pitch a boogie* means to throw a party.

booger rooger

> "Now listen, my feets done failed on me but once,
> That was last Saturday night, down at that booger-rooger."
> —Blind Lemon Jefferson, "Hot Dogs," 1927

An obscure term for a dance party that may have been the parent term of *boogie woogie*.

boogie (n. 1)

> *Papa got a watch, brother got a ring*
> *Sister got her arms full, of alley-boogyin' that thing*
> *She's wild about her boogie, only thing she choose*
> *Now she's got to do the boogie, to buy her alley baby some shoes.*
> —Lucille Bogan, "Alley Boogie," 1930

Sexual intercourse. This term apparently fostered or was derived from *boogie house*, a black idiom for brothel at the turn of the 20th century (cf. Handy, 1941). Ultimately, *boogie* may be a black modification of an obsolete Scottish colloquialism for sex, to *dance the reel o'bogie*, which dates to the 18th century (Partridge).

boogie (n. 2)

> *Lonesome an' blue, here I stand*
> *Holdin' my boogie in my hand.*
> —Oscar's Chicago Swingers, "I Wonder Who's Boogiein' My Woogie Now,"
> 1936

Penis, used with an implied analogy to *woogie* (q.v.).

boogie (v.)

> *Mama it ain't no need, you keep raisin' sand*
> *I know you been boogyin' by the way you stand.*
> —Kokomo Arnold, "Feels So Good," 1935

To have sexual intercourse. *Boogie* was taken up by 1960s rock performers who employed it as a broad term for partying, in which sense it is currently familiar. The original sexual sense was retained by black teenagers of the 1960s and 1970s (cf. Folb).

boogie woogie (n. 1)

> *"I want everybody to dance 'em just like I tell you ...*
> *When I say, 'Get it!' I want you all to do a boogie woogie."*
> —Pine Top Smith, "Pine Top's Boogie Woogie," 1928

Taken at face value, a specific dance or dance step, a sense indicated by the above patter and the 1931 Tampa Red recording, "They Call It Boogie-Woogie":

> *Down in Georgia on Decatur Street*
> *They got a new dance an' it can't be beat*
> *Well they call it boogie woogie ...*
> *Everybody doin' that boogie woogie now.*

This dance, however, is of doubtful authenticity, and *boogie woogie* was more likely a veiled term for sexual intercourse with no vernacular application to dancing. The term and its cognates form the most flexible sexual slang invoked on race recording, variously connoting either sexual activities or male/female sex organs, often according to context.

Although *boogie woogie* had no discernable musical pedigree or connotations, jazz enthusiasts who were taken with "Pine Top's Boogie Woogie" misconstrued it as a musical term, associated with a stylized piano instrumental featuring a "walking bass" line, in which form it entered mainstream English after being promoted in a 1938 New York concert. In response to the popularity of such music, a dance of that name soon materialized, Calloway recording *boogie woogie* as "a new dance introduced at the Cotton Club in 1938." For other seemingly fictitious dances, see *boot that thing, doodle it back, get off, scronch,* and *shake that thing.*

boogie woogie (n. 2)

> *Now my gal's dressed in green*
> *Got good boogie woogie but she won't keep it clean.*
> —Lovin' Sam Theard, "Rubbin' On That Old Thing," 1934

Pussy.

boogie-woogie (v.)

> Keep talkin' about the woman next door
> I caught her boogie-woogyin' down on the floor.
> —Kokomo Arnold, "Busy Bootin'," 1935

To have sexual intercourse.

boogie-woogish, woogie (adv.)

> "Oh Mr. Cow Cow [Davenport], you're playin' it so boogie-woogish."
> —Tampa Red's Hokum Jug Band, "Saturday Night Scrontch," 1929

Evidently, a short-lived slang term (perhaps confined to Chicago) indicating horniness or randiness. It figured as part of vocal patter on Romeo Nelson's "Head Rag Hop," recorded two months after the above piece:

> "Daddy, that makes me feel so boogie-woogish!"

Woogie surfaced as part of vocal patter on Blind Blake's "Hastings Street" (recorded a month after "Saturday Night Scrontch"):

> "Goin' out on Hastings Street where they doin' the boogie. Doin' it very woogie."

See *woogie*.

booked

> I got three lanes to truck on, boy please don't block my road
> I be feelin' 'shamed 'bout my rider, baby I'm booked an' I got to go.
> —Robert Johnson, "Stones In My Passway," 1937

Engaged, bound; colloquial English dating in print to 1840 (OED). This term is coupled with imminent departure in blues poesy:

> I'm singin' this piece, I ain't gonna pick it no more
> Jim Strainer killed poor Lula, I'm booked an' bound to go.
> —Memphis Jug Band, "Jim Strainer Blues," 1930

boot (v.)

> Busy bootin' an' you can't come in
> Come back tomorrow night an' try it again.
> —Kokomo Arnold, "Busy Bootin'," 1935

To have sexual intercourse; applied to male sexual activity. A cognate expression, *boot it,* also occurs in blues:

> Says when I get to bootin', I boots it right
> Boot for these women both day and night
> You've got to boot it, you've got to boot it, sho'
> Lord you really got to boot it, every mornin' 'fore you go.
> —Bo Carter, "Boot It," 1931

This term was employed as a vocal aside, used to suggest a vigorous performance on guitar or piano:

> "Aw boot it, Mister strange man!"
> —Cow Cow Davenport, "State Street Jive," 1928

"I can't pick it, I'm just learnin' how, but I will

go head on an' boot it."

—Little Hat Jones, "Corpus Blues," 1929

boot that thing

"Boot that thing!"

—Blind Blake, "West Coast Blues," 1926

By itself, this phrase meant to fuck (Hill). As with *boot it*, it served as a catch-phrase on race records, ostensibly referring to one's performance on an instrument. It was also employed as the name of a bogus blues dance:

There's a little dance, just in town

It must be easy 'cause I got it down

They call it Boot That Thing, aw Boot That Thing

Aw you better stay home, learn how to boot that thing.

—Bessie Tucker, "Better Boot That Thing," 1929

bootie wah bootie

Big boys everywhere tryin' to bootie wah bootie

. . . Come put that bootie wah bootie on me.

—Lillie Mae, "Bootie Wah Bootie," 1931

A reference to sexual intercourse and (apparently) one's sex organ that is an obvious embellishment upon *booty*, formed by analogy to *diddy wah diddy* (q.v.). As a term for the female body or vagina, *booty* has been in circulation among blacks since the 1920s (cf. Lighter, 1994).

bosom friend

I stole my good gal, from my bosom friend

That fool got lucky, he stole her back again.

—Blind Willie McTell, "Stole Rider Blues," 1927

"A specially intimate or beloved friend" (OED).

boss card

I am the black ace, I'm the boss card in your hand

. . . I'll play for you mama, if you please let me be your man.

—Black Ace, "Black Ace," 1937

Chief card; winning card. The term appears in Roark Bradford's dialect novel *John Henry* (1931) as part of a gambling song: "He laid down de ace and he laid down de king/He laid de boss cyards down all around." This expression illustrates how various slang terms have been bandied between whites and blacks over the past two hundred years. In the sense of being primary or principal, "boss" was an Americanism of 1840s vintage, becoming a general superlative meaning "champion, excellent" before 1890 (Partridge). In these senses it was appropriated by blacks, and became associated with them to the degree that DAS would attribute *boss* to blacks and jazz musicians.

bottle in bond

> *Aw some folks say that it's bottle in bond*
> *You know it ain't nothin' but home-made corn.*
> —Mississippi Sheiks, *"Don't Wake It Up,"* 1932

Prohibition-era slang for any liquor produced before Prohibition, which began in 1920 (cf. ATS). The term was derived from *bottled in bond*, a distiller's label for hundred-proof whiskey aged four years under government supervision.

bottle up

> *I'm gonna tell my ma, listen to my pa*
> *I wouldn't say yes but I can't say no*
> *We got to bottle up and go, oh bottle it up and go*
> *See high-powered mama, your daddy got your water on.*
> —Memphis Jug Band, *"Bottle It Up And Go,"* 1934

To restrain or hold back; said of feelings. This expression entered colloquial language in the 17th century (F&H, 1890); the black variant *bottle it* was recorded by Van Vechten (1926) as "equivalent to the colloquial English *shut up.*"

bottom

> *Twenty years in the bottom, that ain't long to stay*
> *If I can stop my man, from makin' his getaway.*
> —Ma Rainey, *"Louisiana Hoo Doo Blues,"* 1925

A standard English term for an alluvial lowland region (OED), generally applied in blues to the Mississippi Delta.

bound

> *Bobby said to Ben Ferris: "I'm bound to take your life.*
> *You caused trouble, 'tween me an' my wife."*
> —Henry Thomas, *"Bob McKinney,"* 1927

Compelled, obliged; standard English (OED). In this sense it is used in the following:

> *Oh, I can't stay here no more*
> *Done did murder, now I'm bound to go.*
> —Bertha Henderson, *"Terrible Murder Blues,"* 1928

bound down

> *Now I wish I'd listened at what my mother said*
> *I wouldn't've been bound down in this trouble I'm in.*
> —Robert Wilkins, *"Jail House Blues,"* 1928

A black embellishment of *bound*, used in the standard English sense of confined or tied down (cf. OED). "Mr. President Davis wanted us to stay bound down" (Will Sheets, as quoted in *Born in Slavery*).

bow-legged

Tell all you men somethin', don't you raise no fuss
'Cause most of these here women won't do to trust
They are all bow-legged, from the ankle to the knee
Anything they got, they will give it away free.
—*Willie Baker, "Ain't It A Good Thing?," 1929*

Apparently, accustomed to spreading one's legs for sexual intercourse. To call a female *bow-legged* indicates "she can move that thing" (Hill). Similarly, *pleasure-bent* is a present-day jocular expression for a bow-legged female (cf. DARE 4).

box (n.)

Now my mother often taught me: "Son, quit playin' a box.
Go somewhere, settle down an' make a crop."
—*Sleepy John Estes, "Floating Bridge," 1937*

Among blues singers, a conventional term for guitar, carried over from its antebellum application to the banjo: "... I was at my best in de job of pickin' de banjo. I shorely did love to pick that box ..." (George Dillard, as quoted in *Born in Slavery*).

box-back

I say you need not think because you're little an' cute
I'm gonna buy you a box-back suit.
—*Elvie Thomas and Geeshie Wiley, "Over To My House," 1929*

A style of square-cut suit jacket considered old-fashioned by the 1920s. According to jazzman Rex Stewart, Louis Armstrong created a jazz musicians' vogue for them by wearing one when he played in New York in 1924. Their appearance in blues song dates to Clara Smith's "Uncle Sam Blues" (1923; set in World War I) and culminates in Memphis Minnie's "Memphis Minnie Bumble Bee" (1932).

box up (v.)

You can box me up and send me to my ma
If my ma don't want me, send me to my pa.
—*Henry Thomas, "Texas Worried Blues," 1928*

To enclose in a box or casings (OED); standard English that blacks applied to persons as well as objects: " ... they boxed us up in covered wagons and carried us to Texas ..." (Silus Dothrum, as quoted in *Born in Slavery*). The above reference may have suggested by the late-19th-century slang use of *box* for coffin (cf. Partridge).

boy

>*I'm a poor ol' boy, an' a long ways from home*
>*An' she causin' me to leave my plumb good home.*
>*—Charlie Patton, "Jim Lee Blues, Part Two," 1929*

A substitution for *man* noted by the OED with respect to Cornwall, Ireland, and American speech of the far West, but also characteristic of Southern speech (as in the phrase *good ol' boy*, q.v.).

boyfriend

>*You told me you loved me, an' told my boyfriend, too*
>*And I would not have been here, if it didn't be for you.*
>*—Clifford Gibson, "Hard-Headed Blues," 1929*

A male friend. In the blues lexicon, *boyfriend* does not exist as a term for a romantic or sexual partner.

boy in the boat, the

>*Ever since the year tootie two*
>*Lotta these dames had nothin' to do*
>*Uncle Sam thought he'd give 'em a fightin' chance*
>*Packed up all the men and sent 'em on to France*
>*Left the women at home to try out all their new stunts*
>*His face is all wrinkled an' his breath smells like soap*
>*I'm talkin' 'bout that boy in the boat.*
>*—George Hannah, "The Boy In The Boat," 1930*

A slang term for clitoris dating to the 19th century (Partridge). In the above couplet it appears in the context of lesbian sex.

bread

>*I smell your cabbage burnin' baby turn your good bread around*
>*'Cause in your kitchen baby is where that good stuff can be found.*
>*—Leroy Carr, "Bread Baker," 1934*

A black slang term for vagina (cf. DAS). A variant term, *sweetbread*, appears in Charlie Spand's "Got To Have My Sweetbread" (1929):

>*I love my sweetbread, baby, when it's good an' hot*
>*And the way you make it, it really takes the spot.*

Terms involving cooking or baking were a prime source of black sexual idioms, largely owing to the obvious association between heat and sexual excitement.

break and run

>*I stepped two feet forward, started to break and run*
>*(If) a man don't run, a cannon is same as a gatlin' gun.*
>*—Blind Lemon Jefferson, "Lemon's Cannon Ball Moan," 1928*

To make a sudden dash away from someone; a Southern colloquialism found in Faulkner's *Sanctuary* (1931): "'You can't stop me like this,' Benbow said. 'Suppose I break and run.'" This expression is an embellishment of *break* (to move suddenly; cf. DARE):

> Now Lucille has got ways like a fox-squirrel in a tree
> Every time she sees me comin', she'll break an' hide from me.
> —Bo Carter, "Lucille, Lucille," 1938

Breakaway

> I'm gonna upset your back, I'm gonna put your kidneys to sleep
> Do the Breakaway on your liver
> And dare your heart to beat.
> —Robert Johnson, "They're Red Hot," 1936

An improvised segment of the Lindy Hop, which came into vogue with the swing band craze of 1935; also called the Swing Out. The above couplet is an obvious barrelhouse catchphrase, in which a familiar dance is inserted. Another singer had it:

> If I ever catch you down on Hastings Street
> I'll do the Two Step on your liver and dare your heart to beat.
> —Calvin Frazier, "Lilly Mae," 1938 (LC)

break down

> . . . I had a gal like you once before
> She'd break down everywhere she go
> She'd drink moonshine, get high as a kite
> If someone speak she's ready to fight.
> —Papa Charlie Jackson, "Don't Break Down On Me," 1929

To behave boisterously. As a noun, the term *breakdown* first appeared in print in 1819 (DARE) and was associated with (if not originated by) blacks. It is recounted by Bartlett (1877) as "a dance in the peculiar style of the negro," but actually referred to a dance party put on by blacks. (David Edwards: "My father's and them days, they used to give them breakdowns . . . after I come along, the folks was still just givin' them country dances . . .") *Breakdown* probably derived its name from the real or imagined sight of floorboards breaking from the weight (or stomping) of the dancers. In any event, *to break down* became a general 19th-century expression meaning "to dance riotously, to be boisterous and 'spreeish'" (F&H, 1890). The expression was revived in a Robert Johnson blues:

> Every time I'm walkin' down the street
> Some pretty mama starts breakin' down on me.

Stop breakin' down, please stop breakin' down,

"The stuff I got'll bust your brains out baby, it'll make you lose your mind."

—Robert Johnson, "Stop Breaking Down," 1937

The quoted statement is intended to exemplify the conduct that is complained of, which consists of accosting the performer with sexual overtures.

break 'em down

People come from miles around

Get on Wabash, break 'em down.

—Blind Blake, "Wabash Rag," 1926

A variant of *break down*, meaning to dance riotously (see *break down*). *Break 'em down* also served as a euphemism for sexual relations:

Now give me another kiss, we'll have some fun

We'll break 'em down, an' then we'll run.

—Papa Charlie Jackson, "Mama Don't Allow It (And She Ain't Gonna Have It Here),"

1925

break one's neck

Way down South you oughta see the women Shimmy and shake

Got a new way a-wiggle, make a weak man break his neck.

—Blind Lemon Jefferson, "Southern Woman Blues," 1928

To marry, in Southern slang (WD).

bred and born

Way down in Mis'ippi, where I'se bred an' born

? bein' my native home.

—Kid Bailey, "Mississippi Bottom Blues," 1929

The obsolete forerunner of *born and bred*, a once-popular construction dating to the 1870s and recorded by Partridge as a cliché (DC). The earlier form appears in 1614: "A wench that has been bred and born in an alley" (cf. OED, at *bear*), and in Shakespeare's *Twelfth Night* (1601): "'. . . I was bred and born/ Not three hours' travel from this very place.'" It still survives among some African Americans: "My mother was bred and born in Rock Hill, S.C." (Renatha Saunders, 2008 correspondence with author).

Bridewell

Well you're a pretty good woman and livin' in a nice neighborhood

But I think one hundred and costs and thirty days in the Bridewell will do you good.

—"Funny Paper" Smith, "Tell It To The Judge, No. 2," 1931

The original and popular name for the Chicago House of Corrections, a penal institution at West 26th Street and California Avenue given over to prisoners convicted of petty offenses, such as drunkenness.

bring home

> *When your woman stops bringin' home partner, railroad is all you know*
> *Just get out on the hot track, and work your hands to the bone.*
> —*Buddy Boy Hawkins, "Workin' On The Railroad," 1927*

To bring earnings home; found in the proverb "Tarry-long brings little home" (Thomas Fuller, *Gnomolgia*, 1732). The above couplet poses male employment as a grim alternative to existing as a *sweetback* (q.v.).

bring one down

> *I feel just like I wanna clown*
> *Give the fiddle player a drink because he's bringin' me down.*
> —*Bessie Smith, "Gimme A Pigfoot," 1933*

Black slang meaning to have a depressing effect on someone, usually applied to persons who are unaware that they are so regarded. This term dates to the early 1930s (cf. Lighter, 1994, whose earliest citation is 1935) and became part of the 1960s youth/drug culture. In the following instance, used with an inanimate object, it meant to lower or diminish:

> *Don't you try to bring my good luck down*
> *Lord they call me "Money Johnson," I can get any gal in this town.*
> —*James "Stump" Johnson, "Money Johnson," 1933*

brogan shoes

> *Going downtown, to spread the news*
> *The State Street women wearin' brogan shoes.*
> —*Ma Rainey, "Shave 'Em Dry Blues," 1924*

A colloquial redundancy for brogans (ADD), or cheap, coarse, square-toed work shoes, customarily made of untanned leather. The above couplet apparently suggests that Chicago streetwalkers are scuffling. Another song, by a rustic, treats such shoes as a desirable item:

> *Sewed a hole in my pocket so my change won't lose*
> *Gonna buy my baby, some brogan shoes.*
> —*Skip James, "Illinois Blues," 1931*

Brogans are still manufactured, primarily in emulation of Civil War army footwear.

brother

> *Passin' by the jail this mornin'*
> *Heard a hard-luck brother moan:*
> *"I'm in here right where I don't belong*
> *I never did no wrong."*
> —*Clara Smith, "Waitin' For The Evenin' Mail," 1923*

A black male, as perceived by a fellow black person. The feminine form is not found in early blues, while the former usage is a rare occurrence. The sense of racial fellowship embodied by these expressions derived from church use (see *brothers*) and came to the fore in the 1960s civil rights era.

brothers

> *Elder Green's in town, and he's goin' around*
> *An' he's tellin' all the sisters an' the brothers he meets he's Alabama*
> > *bound.*
> —*Papa Charlie Jackson, "I'm Alabama Bound," 1925*

Male church members; a colloquial variant of *brethren,* the once-conventional clerical address to church members that appears in the New Testament and Book of Common Prayer. These terms are meant to suggest that the communicants are brothers in Christ. See *sister.*

brown (n. 1)

> *Can't keep no brown, got ways like a child*
> *Aw she take the blues, she don't care what train she ride.*
> —*Sam Butler, "You Can't Keep No Brown," 1926*

A brown-complexioned African American, particularly one deployed as a girlfriend; blues or barrelhouse slang, inaccurately given by Lighter as black English for "a young brown-skinned black person" (1994). Although *brown* as a term for a person of brown complexion is standard English (OED), it was rarely, if ever, used by white Americans to describe blacks. Male blues singers appear to have been eager to publicize their associations with *browns,* perhaps because women of this complexion were less attainable to male contemporaries than darker females. With few exceptions (such as given below), the term did not appear in female blues:

> *I called a gypsy, the gypsy said to me:*
> *"He may be a good brown, but you must let him be."*
> —*Monette Moore, "Put Me In The Alley Blues," 1924*

brown (n. 2)

> *It seems cloudy, brown, I believe it's going to rain*
> *Goin' back to my regular, 'cause she got everything.*
> —*Barbecue Bob, "Cloudy Sky Blues," 1927*

An impudent or disrespectful form of address to a brown-complexioned female.

brown Betties

> *She's a kitchen mechanic that's her regular trade*
> *She got the best brown Betties that ever was made.*
> —*Blind Blake, "I Was Afraid Of That," 1929*

An eccentric variant of *brown Betty,* a pudding made of baked apples and bread crumbs; perhaps intended as a double entendre.

brownie

Brownie brownie, what's on your worried mind?
Aw you keep my poor heart achin', worried all the time.
—Seth Richards, "Lonely Seth Blues," 1928

A diminutive of *brown*, used interchangeably with it, or as a synonym of *child*, an underworld connotation of the term (cf. ATS). In general speech, *brownies* were emblematic elf-like figures that gave rise to the schoolgirl organization and an emblem of the St. Louis Browns baseball team; this popular image may have influenced the blues application.

brownskin (a.)

My mama told me, papa tol' me, too:
"Some brownskin woman gonna be the death of you."
—Barbecue Bob, "Barbecue Blues," 1927

Brown-skinned; a standard complexion designation in Southern black speech of the blues era.

brownskin (n.)

High yellow's evil, so is a black woman, too
So glad I'm a brownskin I don't know what to do.
—Tarter and Gay, "Brownie Blues," 1928

A brown-skinned African American; perhaps formed by analogy with *redskin*, a term of colonial vintage. This term occurs in Harlem dialogue depicted by Van Vechten (1926): "You're not going back to that cheap brown-skin again, are you?"

Brown's coal mine, Joe

The longest train, I ever seen
Run around Joe Brown's coal mine.
—Peg Leg Howell, "Rolling Mill Blues," 1928

A Dade County, Georgia, coal mine operated in the 1880s by Joseph Emerson Brown (1821–94), the state governor during the Civil War and, afterward, U.S. senator. In keeping with a Southern practice of the era, Brown (widely known as "Joe Brown") enhanced his profits by using unpaid convict labor.

bug juice

Love my bug juice, just as crazy about it as I can be
. . . Lord I'm 'fraid it's gonna poison me.
—(Kid) Prince Moore, "Bug Juice Blues," 1936

A colloquial American term for bad or cheap whiskey, first recorded in 1863 (cf. Lighter, 1994).

buggish

> *Now, asked sweet mama to let me be her kid*
> *She says I might get buggish I couldn't keep it hid.*
> —Sleepy John Estes, "Milk Cow Blues," 1930

? An apparent black variant of *buggy*, meaning crazy or foolish in early-20th-century slang (cf. Lighter, 1994). In 19th-century English dialect, *buggish* meant terrifying (cf. Davies, 1881).

buggy ride

> *I heard him talkin' in his sleep, I cried and cried:*
> *'Cause he kept on saying: "Thanks for the buggy ride."*
> —Monette Moore, "Somebody's Been Lovin' My Baby," 1926

An act of coition.

'buke

> *Say: "You remember on last Sunday*
> *Twenty-fifth day of May?*
> *You 'buked me an' you cursed me*
> *Oh baby all that day."*
> —Charlie Patton, "Frankie and Albert," 1929

Rebuke. In this instance, where rebuking accompanies verbal abuse, the term is seemingly invoked in the obsolete sense of *to beat*, last documented by the OED as occurring in written English of 1611.

bull-doose

> *I'm goin' where I never get bull-doosed*
> *I'm goin' where I never get bull-doosed.*
> —Henry Thomas, "Bull Doze Blues," 1928

A corruption of *bulldose*, a Southern colloquialism meaning to bullwhip a black person, or to intimidate through threats of violence. The OED cites an 1881 reference: "To 'bull-dose' a Negro in the Southern states means to flog him to death, or nearly to death."

bullfrogs on one's mind, to have

> *Did you ever wake up with them*
> *Bullfrogs on your, bullfrogs on your, I mean mind?*
> *Did you ever wake up with them bullfrogs on your mind?*
> —William Harris, "Bull Frog Blues," 1928

? An obscure idiom that likely stands for restlessness, the subject perhaps feeling "jumpy" and eager to depart.

bull jive (v.)

> *Look here baby what is you tryin' to do?*
> *Waste all my money an' bull jive me too.*
> —Bill Gaither, "That Will Never Do," 1941

Bullshit; cf. *jive.*

bulls

> *Gonna drink my whiskey, gonna drink my tomcat gin*
> *Gonna mess around, till the bulls break in.*
> —Bobby Leecan and Robert Cooksey, "Whiskey And Gin Blues," 1926

Police or private security personnel employed by railroads, a term that ultimately derives from *bulldog*, 17th-century British slang for a sheriff's officer (F&H, 1890).

bullyin'

> *Tell me friend, ever since that bullyin'* Stack *been made*
> *Kansas City Missouri has been her regular trade.*
> —Robert Wilkins, "Alabama Blues," 1928

A variant of *bully-boat*, a superlative first recorded in 1894: " . . . a bully-boat means a boat that beats everything on those [Mississippi] waters" (quoted in OED). This term evolved into the general superlative *bully,* which survives in Theodore Roosevelt's storied description of the White House as a "bully pulpit."

bum (v.)

> *I don't bum, an' I sure God don't beg*
> *I just keep my eyes open, an' work my head.*
> —Ramblin' Thomas, "New Way Of Living Blues," 1928

To live as a tramp; to loaf (DAS). See *on a bum.*

burnin' hell

> *Ain't no heaven, say there ain't no burnin' hell*
> *Where I'm goin' when I die can't nobody tell.*
> —Son House, "My Black Mama, Part One," 1930

An embellishment of *hell,* designed to emphasize its imagined terrors; presumably a clerical invention. "De good Lord sho punishes folks for deir sins on dis earth and dat old man what put dat spell on me died and went down to burnin' hell . . ." (Nicey Kinney, as quoted in *Born in Slavery*)

burn one's coal and wood

> *I got a range in my kitchen, it don't mean me no good*
> *Gonna get a New York woman, to burn my coal and wood.*
> —William Harris, "Kitchen Range Blues," 1928

A blues variant of *to have one's ashes hauled.* This reference reflects the penury of Southern black life; while coal and wood had been used to fire 19th-century kitchen stoves, gas and kerosene ranges became standard around the turn of the 20th century.

burying ground

> *Followed sweet mama, to the buryin' ground*
> *I didn't know I loved her, till they eased her down.*
> —Charlie Patton, "Devil Sent The Rain Blues," 1929

A colloquial term for graveyard dating in print to 1808 (DARE).

bury that thing

> *. . . Some doctor from Tennessee*
> *Has a way of buryin' things on the q.t.*
> *He was buryin' that thing; he was buryin' that thing*
> *Keeps on the transom, he was buryin' that thing.*
> —James "Stump" Johnson, "Transom Blues," 1929

To fornicate; *to bury it* has referred to sexual intercourse since the 1860s (Partridge). See *shake that thing.*

business (1)

> *Some joker learned my baby, how to shift gear on a Cadillac-8*
> *And ever since that happened I can't keep my business straight.*
> —Blind Lemon Jefferson, "Booger Rooger Blues," 1926

Sexual affairs. *Business* is an archaic euphemism for sexual intercourse (cf. OED, which cites examples from 1630 and 1654).

business (2)

> *I said squat low papa, let your mama see*
> *I wanna see that old business, keeps on worryin' me.*
> —Geeshie Wiley, "Eagles On A Half," 1930

A black euphemism for penis.

business fixed, to have one's

> *. . . I wanna get me a Super-6*
> *I'm always ramblin' the ladies, and I like to have my business fixed.*
> —Blind Lemon Jefferson, "D B Blues," 1928

In this context, to obtain sexual gratification; see *get it fixed.* The same phrase was eccentrically employed by a slave in regards to a spiritual transaction: "She always told us that she had her business fixed with the Lord and that when she take sick, it wouldn' be long." (Laura Shelton, as quoted in *Born in Slavery*)

business, pork-grindin'

> *Lord I woke up this mornin' with my pork-grindin' business in my hand*
> *Now if you can't send me no woman, please send me a sissy man.*
> —Kokomo Arnold, "Sissy Man Blues," 1935

Penis, apparently used with reference to *pigmeat* and *hogmeat* (q.v.).

bust

> Some draws a check babe, some draw nothin' at all
> When they don't draw nothin' their husbands bust them in the jaw.
> —"Hi" Henry Brown, "Nut Factory Blues," 1932

To punch forcefully, a slang idiom the OED inadvertently renders as "[t]o burst; to break" (see 1918 and 1919 citations for *bust*, v.2). It may derive from the 19th-century Scottish *bust*, to beat (see OED at *bust*, v.1). "I done bus' 'er on de jaw so pow'ful hahd hit lif' her feet offen de flo'..." ("Uncle Dave," as quoted in *Born in Slavery*).

bust a jug

> Don't bust it no more; don't bust it no more
> I mean pretty papa don't you bust that jug no more.
> —Blind Roosevelt Graves, "Bustin' The Jug," 1929

To drink liquor immoderately; from *bust*, a slang term of 19th-century vintage meaning "to engage in a drinking bout or spree" (Lighter, 1994).

bust one's (own) head, to

> I stood on the corner, and I almost bust my head
> I couldn't earn enough money, to buy me a loaf of bread.
> —Blind Lemon Jefferson, "Tin Cup Blues," 1929

To become too exhausted to think; the forerunner of *bust one's conk*, a synonymous black idiom (cf. Major, 1970). The above couplet remarks on unprofitable street singing.

butter and egg man

> Why don't you take me pretty mama, make something out of poor me?
> I'm just a butter and egg man, just as soft as I can be.
> —Papa Charlie Jackson, "Butter And Egg Man Blues," 1926

A disparaging Jazz Age term for a small-time businessman playing the role of a free-spending playboy, particularly on jaunts to cabarets. This meaning is not evident in the above song; nor is it evident that the singer actually understood the phrase, one of the few fashionable slang terms to trickle down into blues recording.

by

> Now it's by me bein' a bachelor, travelin' through this world all alone
> Well you know (I) got to find, me another home.
> —Son Bonds, "Old Bachelor Blues," 1938

Because of, on account of; construed as standard English by the OED, but doubtfully so in 20th-century American speech. Nonetheless, this sense was common in Southern black speech of the blues era.

by and by

> *The good book tell you: "Reap just what you sow."*
> *Don't reap it now, baby reap it by and by.*
> —*Tommy Johnson, "Bye Bye Blues," 1928*

Soon, presently; though still regarded as standard English by the OED, this is a bygone phrase.

by degree

> *The blues is an achin' old heart disease*
> *Like consumption, killin' me by degree.*
> —*Robert Johnson, "Preachin' Blues," 1936*

Little by little, by steps; usually pluralized, as in *Othello* (1604): "What wound did ever heale but by degrees?" This term may have been essentially outmoded, the last OED cite dating to 1853.

cack

> *Alla you cack women, you better put on the walk*
> *'Cause I'm gonna get drunk an' do my dirty talk.*
> —*Lucille Bogan, "Shave 'Em Dry," 1935*

Respectable or refined. This term was circulated among blacks (DAS) and was also associated with tramp and criminal slang (ATS), thus making its origin moot.

cackleberries

> *"I asked that lady about them chickens; she said*
> *she had none. Cackleberries—had none."*
> —*Blind Willie McTell, "Atlanta Strut," 1929*

An American colloquialism for eggs dating to the late 19th century (cf. Partridge).

Cadillac

> *These here women what call theirself a Cadillac oughta be a T-Model Ford*
> *You know they got the shape all right, but they can't carry no heavy load.*
> —*Walter Roland, "T Model Blues," 1933*

A superlative based on the then-reigning position of the Cadillac as the most luxurious and expensive car. In criminal slang, *Cadillac* similarly connoted "[t]he best of anything" (Dalzell).

Cadillac squad

> *This way of livin' sure is hard*
> *Duckin' an' dodgin' the Cadillac squad.*
> —*Lucille Bogan, "They Ain't Walking No More," 1930*

Presumably, the vice squad, as the above song relates the tribulations of a streetwalker.

cake

> *Sometimes these dreams, just like bein' awake*
> *I saw another man eating up my chocolate cake.*
> —*Emery Glen, "Back Door Blues," 1927*

A black expression for vagina, as well as a racially nondescript term for a pretty girl (DAS).

cake-eater

> *If you don't believe that woman's bread is sweet*
> *Ask all them cake-eaters, hangs out in Queens Street.*
> —*(Kid) Prince Moore, "Sally Long," 1938*

A 1920s slang term for a woman-chaser (DAS).

call one down

> *She was the meanest gal for miles around*
> *She made me love her then she call me down.*
> —*Alec Johnson, "Sundown Blues," 1928*

To reprimand; a colloquial term of late-19th-century vintage (OED).

call one's name

> *I got a woman, good little woman, she ain't a thing but a stavin' Chain'*
> *She's a married woman and I'm scared to call her name.*
> —*Ishman Bracey, "Woman Woman Blues," 1930*

To refer to by name; a Southern colloquialism (cf. DARE; Major [1994], on the other hand, treats it as black slang).

call oneself

> *"I went out yesterday evening; I called myself 'out visiting.'*
> *The ladies invited me over to dinner."*
> —*Papa Charlie Jackson, "I'm Looking For A Woman Who Knows How To*
> *Treat Me Right," 1928*

An ironic disclaimer in black speech (usually couched in the first person) to suggest that the phrase it refers to is open to question. Cf. Smitherman (2000) and ADD (1944), which defines it as "[t]o think that one (is doing something);

also to pretend that one (is doing something). . . ." In white colloquial speech, this term simply means to consider oneself (DARE). See *if you call that gone*.

camp

> *Down by the levee, down on camp number nine*
> *If you pass my door, you will hear me cryin'.*
> —Charley Lincoln, "Gamblin' Charley," 1928

In the Deep South, a makeshift settlement consisting of tent housing and a mess to accommodate itinerant black laborers engaged in levee building, logging, or road construction, notable from the 1880s to the early 1920s. As applied to temporary housing for miners or loggers, *camp* dates in print to 1836 (DAH). Colloquial terms for logging and road camps occur below:

> *When I leave from here, goin' out on the Q*
> *I don't find no log camp, I'll find a gravel camp sho'.*
> —Lewis Black, "Gravel Camp Blues," 1927

candy man

> *Well all you ladies all gather around*
> *That good sweet candy man's in town*
> *It's the candy man; it's the candy man.*
> —Mississippi John Hurt, "Candy Man Blues," 1928

A variant of *candy kid*, slang for a ladies' man (DAS), the latter fostered by the 1909 pop song "Oh, You Candy Kid."

canned heat

> *I give my woman a dollar, to get herself somethin' to eat*
> *She spent a dime for neckbones, an' ninety cents for that old canned heat.*
> —Will Shade, "You Better Let That Stuff Alone," 1928

A trade name for Sterno, a commercial product introduced around 1900 that retails as a heating or cooking gel. Desperate or derelict alcoholics would squeeze and strain the gel through a cloth to extract its denatured alcohol base, and mix the latter with water or some other liquid to create a toxic confection known simply as "canned heat."

cannon

> *I got a dirty mistreater, she's mean as she can be*
> *I hadn't figured that she was so mean till she dropped that cannon on me.*
> —Blind Lemon Jefferson, "Lemon's Cannon Ball Moan," 1928

An underworld term for a pistol dating to the turn of the 20th century, and still current in 1931 (Irwin).

cannon ball

> *I'm long and tall, like a cannon ball*
> *Take a long tall man, make a good gal, make a good gal squall.*
> —Willie Baker, "No No Blues," 1929

A hobo and railroad expression for a fast express or freight train, dating in print to 1894 (cf. Lighter, 1994).

captain

> Says "Good mornin' captain," said: "Good mornin', shine"
> "'Tain't nothin' the matter, captain but I just ain't gwine."
> —Tom Dickson, "Labor Blues," 1928

A subservient form of address applied to whites (particularly foremen) in the Jim Crow era. Baker noted in 1908: "The old term of slavery, the use of the word 'master,' has wholly disappeared, and in its place has arisen . . . the round term 'Boss,' or sometimes 'Cap,' or 'Cap'n.'"

carbox

> I got a freight train, I got a carbox on my mind
> I'm goin' away but I'll be back some old time.
> —Reese DuPree, "Long Ago Blues," 1923

Metathetic for boxcar, replacing the former term in Southern black speech of the blues era. *Carbox* may have been of white Southern origin (cf. DARE); similarly, *hoppergrass* was recorded in 1829 as a Southern "vulgarism" for grasshopper (cf. Mathews, 1931), and survived in recent black speech (cf. Major, 1970). See *friend-girl*.

careless love

> I wanna show you women what careless love have done
> Caused a man like me to, steal away from home.
> —Blind Lemon Jefferson, "Broke And Hungry Blues," 1926

Carefree love, an expression popularized, if not originated by, Ravenscroft's 1673 drama *Careless Lovers,* in which a character named Careless Love personifies its traits. The term became enshrined in black song by virtue of the ballad of that name, which was current in the 1890s.

carry

> Goin' home in the mornin' Lord I sure can't carry you
> Ain't nothin' down there Lord a monkey woman can do.
> —Will Weldon, "Turpentine Blues," 1927

To take, chauffeur; obsolete standard English as applied to persons (cf. OED). It appears in Daniel Defoe's *Moll Flanders* (1722): " . . . 'I never designed to go to Ireland at all, much less to have carried you thither. . . .'"

carry a cub

> Let me tell you men what these married women will do:
> She will get your money, she will carry a cub to you.
> —Blind Willie Reynolds, "Married Man Blues," 1930

A dealer's method of cheating at Georgia Skin by concealing the three cards that match his own at the bottom of a deck, so that they will not be dealt to other players (Jones). It occurs in Zora Neale Hurston's *De Turkey and de Law: A Comedy in Three Acts* (1930): "Y'all carried de cub to us dat time." The expression perhaps derives from the use of *cub* in 18th-century British cant to mean a novice gambler (Grose, 1796). See *cub*.

carry a handcuff

> *Gambled all over Missouri,*
> *Gambled through Tennessee, babe*
> *Soon as I reached old Georgia*
> *The niggers carried a handcuff to me.*
> —Peg Leg Howell, "Skin Game Blues," 1928

Evidently, to render one helpless. Fisher (1928) lists to *put the locks on* as Harlem slang meaning "[t]o handcuff. Hence to render helpless. Most frequently heard in reference to some form of gambling...."

carry (one) down

> *But I just keep on a-drinkin', yes I keep on drinkin'*
> *Yeah I just keep on a-drinkin', till good liquor carry me down.*
> —Big Bill Broonzy, "Good Liquor Gonna Carry Me Down," 1935

To kill one by natural causes; an apparent black invention derived from *carry off*, itself a dated idiom appearing in Ben Franklin's 1771 autobiography: "My distemper was a pleurisy, which very nearly carried me off."

carry ___ on

> *That's the doggondest disease, ever heard since I been born*
> *Feel numb in the front of your body, you can't carry any lovin' on.*
> —Ishmon Bracey, "Jake Liquor Blues," 1930

A black variant of the standard English *carry on*, meaning to keep up or prevent from stopping (cf. OED at *carry*, v.52b). In black usage, the object of the verb is interspersed between "carry" and "on":

> *Dinner got on an' she kissed me some,*
> *Now you know we carryin' the good work on.*
> —Bo Carter, "Dinner Blues," 1936

cash money

> *I don't see why white folks don't have no blues*
> *They got our cash money, an' brownskin women, too.*
> —T. C. Johnson, "JC Johnson's Blues," 1928

A redundant Southern term for cash (i.e., coins and bills) dating in print to 1900 (cf. DARE).

cat

> *Now the black cat told the white cat: "Let's go on across town and clown."*
> *And the white cat told the black cat: "You sit your black self down."*
> —Ben Curry, "Boodle-De-Bum-Bum," 1931

Guy; a black slang term that became incorporated into white speech by virtue of jazz and rock and roll aficionados.

cat juice

> *"All right boys, say play that piano loud and*
> *bring me some of that cat juice there."*
> —*Peg Leg Howell, "Chittlin' Supper," 1929*

? Seemingly, a variant of *catgut*, an uncommon term for cheap liquor dating to the 1920s (DAS), but possibly derived from a common 19th-century term for gin, *cat's water* (F&H, 1891).

catch

> *"Aw sho' baby it's gettin' good as gin"*
> *Aw, I can catch it when*
> *I'm, back in town again*
> —*Charlie Patton, "Hang It On The Wall," 1934*

"To reach, get to (a person or thing before it moves away)" (OED at *catch*, v.7b). The above reference is to *pussy*. "Nowadays I gets something to eat when I can catch it" (Andrew Simms, as quoted in *Born in Slavery*).

c.c. pills

> *Hey hey mama, what you want me to do?*
> *Take c.c. pills, pass away for you.*
> —*Blind Blake, "C.C. Pill Blues," 1928*

Conventional slang for laxative tablets, formally known as compound cathartic pills (ATS).

cell (v.)

> *I beefed to the judge it's a kangaroo court, how she had framed and left*
> *   me flat*
> *An' the old chump I was cellin' with cracked: "Big boy, they can't do that."*
> —*Pine Top Smith, "Big Boy, They Can't Do That," 1929*

To share a prison cell; convict slang (DAUL).

Central

> *Hello Central, the matter with your line?*
> *"Come a storm last night, tore the wire down."*
> —*Charlie Patton, "Pony Blues," 1929*

A dated colloquialism for the operator at a telephone exchange (or the exchange itself); now used in restricted settings, such as police communications. "Hello, Central" was once a stock phrase of telephone dialogue, mentioned in Twain's *A Connecticut Yankee in King Arthur's Court* (1889): "I used to wake ... and say 'Hello, Central!' just to hear the dear [operator's] voice ..." (quoted in DAH). Its popularity in blues song may have been fostered by the 1901 Tin Pan Alley hit, "Hello Central, Give Me Heaven."

Champagne Charley

Champagne Charley is my name, by golly
An' roguin' an' stealin' is my game.
—Blind Blake, "Champagne Charlie Is My Name," 1932

A 19th-century British slang term for a dissipated person, suggested by a popular 1868 music hall song of the same name (Partridge).

Chaney

Said: "All the passengers, you better keep yourself hid;
Naturally gonna shake it like Chaney did."
—Furry Lewis, "Kassie Jones, Part One," 1928

A reference to *Stavin' Chain' (Chan')* (q.v.).

change one's luck

I'm gonna get me a mama, I mean with lots of bucks
I want you to begone mama, so I can change my luck.
—Blind Lemon Jefferson, "Change My Luck Blues," 1928

To improve one's fortunes by acquiring a sex partner whose qualities appear radically different from one's current or usual one; used semi-facetiously. This idiom usually referred to interracial intercourse on the part of white males: "Ah met an ofay wanted to change his luck. He gimme a tenner" (Van Vechten, 1926).

changin' clothes

Lord my woman has quit me, she done throwed my cap outdoor
Lord she taken all-a my money, an' I ain't got changin' clothes.
—Walter Davis, "I Ain't Got Changing Clothes," 1937

A black term for a second set of clothes, suitable for a clothes change. It appears in Zora Neale Hurston's *Jonah's Gourd Vine* (1934): "De nex' time, us buy de chillun some changin' clohes."

cheap

Well Frankie went down to Albert's house:
"How late Albert been here?"
Oh Albert's sittin' on some cheap gal's lap
Buyin' some cheap gal beer.
—Charlie Patton, "Frankie And Albert," 1929

A dated pejorative applied to promiscuous women (DAS), formed by extension from the standard English sense of *cheap* as meaning common or worthless.

cherry ball

Don't give my baby no more cherry ball
Know she may get drunk Lord an' show her Santy Claus.
—Mississippi Bracey, "Cherry Ball," 1930

Cherry wine or brandy; from the use of *ball* to mean "[a] glass of (Irish) malt whiskey" (OED), occurring in Crane's *Bowery Tales* of 1894: "'...th' only thing I really needs is a ball ... But as I can't get a ball, why, th' next bes' thing is breakfast ...'" The expression was corrupted by Skip James to denote an attractive female:

> *I love cherry ball, better than I do myself*
> *An' if she don't have me she won't have nobody else.*
> —*"Cherry Ball Blues," 1931*

chib

> *When I get drunk I'm evil, I don't know what to do*
> *Guess I'll get my good chib, and get somethin' good from you.*
> —*Edith North Johnson, "Good Chib Blues," 1929*

Knife; a term of apparent black origin, now unaccountably surviving in Scottish slang (OED).

chick

> *The food you cook, the hound dog's sick*
> *Woman I swear you'se a no-good chick.*
> —*Springback James, "Poor Coal Passer," 1936*

Slang for young female, ascribed to Harlem "jive" talk in the DAS but of more general circulation (as the above lyric indicates). Although associated with black speech, it dates to turn-of-the-20th-century white slang (cf. Lighter, 1994). A parent term, *chick-a-biddy*, was current in 18th-century England and applied to "a chicken, and figuratively a young woman" (Grose, 1796).

Chicken Wing

> *Now it ain't no Charleston, ain't no Chicken Wing*
> *All you got to do is shake that thing.*
> —*Papa Charlie Jackson, "Shake That Thing," 1925*

An antebellum dance, perhaps synonymous with the Pigeon Wing. "Sometimes we has de fiddle and de banjo and does we do dat chicken wing and de shuffle" (Albert Hill, as quoted in *Born in Slavery*).

chief police

> *Yes I'm goin' uptown an' tell the chief police*
> *You siccin' your dogs on me.*
> —*Bukka White, "Sic 'Em Dogs On," 1939 (LC)*

Police chief, in black parlance.

chifforobe

> *If you was a chifforobe, baby, I'd ramble all through your drawers*
> *I'd just keep on rambling, till I'd find us an old Santa Claus.*
> —*Charley Jordan, "Chifferobe," 1937*

A wardrobe and chest of drawers (hence the pun); the term itself dates in print to 1908 (OED).

child, chile

> If I mistreat you I sure don't mean no harm
> I'm a motherless child an' I don't know right from wrong.
> —Barbecue Bob, "Motherless Chile Blues," 1927

Person, irrespective of age. This conventional figure of black speech was derived from the English dialect *chiel*, "[a] familiar term of address to adults as well as children" (EDD), used in the second person. By 1850 it had passed into general American colloquial speech (Partridge); Bartlett (1877) treats it (in the form of *this child*, meaning myself) as Western slang.

chinch, chinch bug (1)

> I wonder if the chinches bite in Beaumont, like they do in Beale Street town
> The first night I stayed in Memphis, chinch bugs turned my bed around.
> —Blind Lemon Jefferson, "Chinch Bug Blues," 1927

Bedbug; although the standard English *chinch* dates to 1625 (OED), this term was regarded as a Southernism by Clapin (c. 1902) and others, and is misconstrued as an African retention by DeSalvo (2006).

chinch bug (2)

> Oh, that must be the bedbug you know a chinch don't bite that hard
> Asked my sugar for fifty cents, she said: "Lemon ain't a dime in the yard."
> —Blind Lemon Jefferson, "Black Snake Moan," 1927

A body louse (DARE). In this sense it occurs in Zora Neale Hurston's *De Turkey and de Law: A Comedy in Three Acts* (1930): "You got just as many bed-bugs and chinches as anybody else. . . ." The following reference is probably to the same creature:

> I got a brown in Texas, one in Tennessee
> But that brown in Chicago have put that chinch bug on me.
> —Blind Lemon Jefferson, "Rambler Blues," 1927

chinkypin

> Now me and my gal went chinkypin huntin'
> She fell down and I found somethin'.
> —Peg Leg Howell, "Turkey Buzzard Blues," 1928

A variant of *chinquapin*, a Southern term for chestnuts (cf. DARE).

chitlins

> Now some people say chitlins are good to eat
> I'll never eat chitlins long as a hog got feet.
> —Papa Charlie Jackson, "Mama, Don't You Think I Know?," 1925

The small intestines of a pig; a term now associated with blacks that originated as a common English dialect variant of *chitterlings*, first recorded in 1886. An 1888 British glossary observed that they were "usually fried as a great delicacy amongst the poor" (cf. OED).

chitlin supper

I had a chitlin supper, at home last Saturday night
Some house-rent party, it was a low-down sight.
—*Sylvester Weaver, "Chittlin' Rag Blues," 1927*

A house frolic, also called a *supper, chitlin function*, or *chitlin strut*, advertising the fact that food as well as drink were sold on the premises. These terms still survive among some Southern speakers (cf. DARE). See *function*.

chocolate drop

Aw she's a dark brownskin, we always call her a chocolate drop
Got this old-fashioned lovin', man it just won't stop.
—*Blind Lemon Jefferson, "Long Lastin' Lovin'," 1928*

A term for a black person dating to at least 1900, when it was college slang signifying "a young negress" (cf. DARE). Although considered derogatory by DARE and DAS, it is used with no such intent in the above context.

chocolate to the bone

So glad I'm a brownskin, chocolate to the bone
An' I got what it takes to make a monkey man leave his home.
—*Barbecue Bob, "Chocolate To The Bone," 1928*

A once-common description of a very dark-skinned Negro (ATS), generally used by whites.

chop

I feel like choppin', chips flyin' everywhere
I been to the Nation, oh Lord but I couldn't stay there.
—*Charlie Patton, "Down The Dirt Road Blues," 1929*

To fell and trim timber; associated with land clearing (DAH) and, presumably, lumber camps.

chopping block

Don't you remember when my door was locked?
I had your mama on the choppin' block.
—*Kokomo Arnold, "Busy Bootin'," 1935*

Evidently, a variant of *killing floor* (q.v.).

citizen('s) clothes

Never will forget that day when they taken my clothes
Taken my citizen clothes an' throwed 'em away.
—*Bukka White, "When Can I Change My Clothes," 1940*

A black term for civilian clothes, exchanged in the above song for prison stripes. "General Sherman called all the Indian Chiefs together and asked them why they rebelled against the agency, and they told him they weren't going to wear citizen's clothes." (George Conrad, Jr., as quoted in *Born in Slavery*).

clean out

I drank some hootch, Lord it sure was good

It made me clean out the whole neighborhood.

—The Hokum Boys, "Went To His Head," 1929

To thrash, vanquish; a 19th-century slang phrase rendered as *clean* since the 1880s (cf. cites in Lighter, 1994).

clock

Hold me in your lovin' arms

Squeeze me till my clock alarms.

—The Hokum Boys, "Put Your Mind On It," 1929

A double entendre with a vernacular basis in the 19th-century expression *to wind up the clock*, a masculine phrase for having intercourse (F&H, 1904). In the above context, *alarm* = to have an orgasm. *To wind up the clock* is implicit in the following, applied to a female:

Turned my face to the wall an' my baby made an awful moan

"Well I needs my daddy 'cause my clock has run down at home."

—Blind Lemon Jefferson, "Big Night Blues," 1929

close-made

You got plenty-a money, it ain't no doubt

You got one-way pockets an' it won't come out.

You'se a close-made papa; close-made papa . . .

—Kansas City Kitty and Georgia Tom, "Close Made Papa," 1931

Stingy, cheap; a black variant of the synonymous standard English *close-fisted* (OED) or the colloquial comparison *close as wax* (F&H, 1891).

clown (n. 1)

Peach orchard mama, don't turn your papa down

Because when I gets mad, I act just like a clown.

—Blind Lemon Jefferson, "Peach Orchard Mama," 1928

A black pejorative applied to someone who picks a fight (verbal or physical) or "will talk all out of his head" (Hill).

clown (n. 2)

I went downtown this mornin' with my hat on upside down

Everybody looked at me like they thought I was a country clown.

—Peetie Wheatstraw, "Crazy With The Blues," 1937

An obsolete term for a rustic or bumpkin dating to the 18th century (OED).

clown (v.)

Now you Saturday night women, you love to ape an' clown
You won't do nothin' but tear a good man's reputation down.
—Robert Johnson, "Stop Breakin' Down Blues," 1937

In black speech, to act demonstratively, particularly toward the opposite sex; to show off, usually in an obnoxious manner (cf. Calt and Wardlow, 1989). The latter meaning is probably intended in the following lyric:

I'm a long tall mama they call me chocolate brown
Give me two drinks of whiskey and you can see me clown.
—Lucille Bogan, "That's What My Baby Likes," 1935

cock (n.)

My back is made of whalebone,
And my cock is made of brass,
And my fuckin' is made for working mens' two dollars,
Great God, 'round to kiss my ass.
—Lucille Bogan, "Shave 'Em Dry," 1935 (unissued)

The conventional Southern term for the female genitals. It is not known how *cock* (which has stood for penis since c. 1600; cf. F&H, 1891) acquired its altered gender meaning.

cock (v.)

Now you can cock it you can break it you can hang it on the wall
Throw it out the window, see if you can catch it 'fore it falls
—Louise Johnson, "On The Wall," 1930

To fornicate; an obsolete term associated with feminine sexual activity (F&H, 1891).

coffee-grindin' mama

It's so doggone good until it'll make you bite your tongue
An' I'm a coffee-grindin' mama, won't you let me grind you some?
—Lucille Bogan, "Coffee Grindin' Blues," 1929

A prostitute; from *coffee grinder,* a conventional slang term for prostitute (DAS). The expression probably derives from *coffee house,* an 18th- to 19th-century term for vagina (F&H, 1891; Partridge).

coke-headed

Did you ever . . . get clipped by a coke-headed dip
At the time you ain't got no dough?
—Pine Top Smith, "Big Boy, They Can't Do That," 1929

Stupid, a pejorative drawn from conventional slang term *coke head,* in vogue before its association with drug use (DAS). The latter derives from *cokes,* an archaic expression for a simpleton that became obsolete by 1700 (Partridge).

cold chills

She is a little queen of spades, and the mens will not let her be

Everytime she makes a spread, cold chills just runs all over me.

—Robert Johnson, "Little Queen of Spades," 1937

A Southern colloquialism in which the modifier "cold" is redundant. It appears in Opie Read's dialect novel *An Arkansas Traveler* (1896): "Her husband held out his waxen hand, and when I took it I shuddered with the cold chill it sent through me."

cold in hand

Aw did you dream lucky, an' wake up cold in hand?

Then you wanna see some good gal, aw ain't got no man.

—Bo Weavil Jackson, "Some Scream High Yellow," 1926

Penniless; a stock 1920s blues expression probably derived from the synonymous British term *to have a bad cold,* which was "[s]aid of one who keeps his door closed against all comers for fear of duns" (F&H, 1891). In blues song *cold in hand* is invariably coupled with the idea of "dreaming lucky," a connection that likely arose from the popularity of "lucky dream books" among black policy players.

coldest stuff in town, to have the

Oh, where my Third Street woman gone?

. . . Way she treat me that's the coldest stuff in town.

—Blind Willie Reynolds, "Third Street Woman Blues," 1930

A pejorative catchphrase, likely of barrelhouse origin, denoting unwelcome conduct.

color

I ain't gonna state no color, but her front teeth is crowned with gold

She got a mortage on my body now, an' a lien on my soul.

—Robert Johnson, "Traveling Riverside Blues," 1937

Complexion, in African American speech of the antebellum/blues era; generally regarded as red, yellow, brown, or black. "There was a light brownskin boy around there and they give him anything he wanted. But they didn't like my mother and me—on account of my color" (Mary Estes Peters, as quoted in *Born in Slavery*).

come

Somebody's comin' an' I wonder who could it be?

But I ain't gonna let you come mama, until you come with me.

—Walter Davis, "Carpenter Man," 1936

To experience an orgasm. Though this term dates to at least c. 1650 (OED), its taboo nature limited its printed circulation, the OED recording but six instances of its use from 1714 to 1928.

come down

Took my baby, go meet the mornin' train
An' the blues come down, baby like showers of rain.
—*Charlie Patton, "Pony Blues," 1929*

To surge, usually within one; said of both mournfulness and sexual desire. See *love come down, to have one's*. This expression was also applied in black English to luck (cf. Lighter, 1994).

come down (at, on)

Let me tell you, what those women will do
They will take a man from you, and then come down at you.
—*Sam Butler, "Jefferson County Blues," 1926*

A variant of the still-surviving 19th-century colloquialism to *come down upon*, meaning to berate (F&H, 1891) or harass. Skip James and Gary Davis, however, regarded it as an allusion to oral sex, the latter remarking: "That means, you talkin' about changin' ends . . . with the way God have it."

come home to

Oh, it may be a week and it may be a month or two
But the day you quit me honey, it's coming home to you.
—*Bessie Smith, "Downhearted Blues," 1923*

To return to one's doorstep; said of one's alleged misdeeds.

come on home

Please don't stop when you hear me groan
Don't you know I'm comin' on home?
—*Lil Johnson, "Take It Easy Greasy No. 2," 1937*

An embellishment of *come*.

come out

Policy man if my numbers come out, don't fool around on the street
Just cut across St. Lawrence Avenue, and bring my money home to me.
—*Bo Carter, "Policy Blues," 1940*

To form the winning number or combination of numbers in *policy*; still used by participants in this game. It occurs in Van Vechten's Harlem dialogue of 1926: "Nummer come out. Drew sixty-seven bucks."

common women

Gonna show you common women, how I feel
Gonna get me 'nother woman, 'fore I leave.
—*Charlie Patton, "Going To Move To Alabama," 1929*

Prostitutes. As a term for prostitute, *common woman* dates to 1794 in written English ("Your insinuation that Mary Magdalene was a common woman"; OED).

confidencing

> *You can jive me baby, but I don't believe a thing you say*
> *You just a confidencing woman, and wants to have your way.*
> —*Clifford Gibson, "Jive Me Blues," 1929*

Deceitful, glib; an obscure adjective issuing from *confidence* (to swindle by means of a confidence trick) or *confidence man,* American terms dating in print to 1875 and 1849, respectively (cf. OED).

conjure dust

> *I'm gonna get me some bullfrog hips, get me some conjure dust*
> *I'm gonna mix it all up an' make a poison pie*
> *I'm gonna feed it to your bo' hog I mean he just got to die.*
> —*Arnold Wiley, "Rootin' Bo' Hog Blues," 1931*

Evidently, *goofer dust* (q.v.). In the above song, *bo' hog* refers to a boyfriend.

consolate

> *Now I can't walk the streets now to consolate my mind*
> *Some pretty mama she starts breakin' down.*
> —*Robert Johnson, "Stop Breakin' Down Blues," 1937*

Obsolete standard English for *console,* the term that has replaced it (cf. OED, which gives 1773 as its most recent citation). It appears in Zora Neale Hurston's *Jonah's Gourd Vine* (1934): "'You jes' consolate 'em by word uh mouf and fill 'em full uh melody.'"

consumption

> *I want all you women, to listen to my tale of woe*
> *I've got consumption of the heart, I feel myself sinking slow.*
> —*Sara Martin, "Death Sting Me Blues," 1928*

A standard English term that stood for any wasting disease but was generally applied to tuberculosis when the latter was a dreaded ailment:

> *Now, some said it was beans, some said it was greens*
> *But it's a slow consumption killin' you by degree.*
> —*Sleepy John Estes, "Milk Cow Blues," 1929*

It was ordinarily modified by *fast, galloping* (OED) or *quick* (DARE 4), in regard to its progression; the designation *slow consumption* is undocumented.

cookie

> *Papa wants a cookie, papa wants a cookie*
> *Papa wants a cookie right now now now now*
> *Papa wants a cookie, papa needs a cookie*
> *Papa's gonna get it somehow.*
> —*Leroy Carr, "Papa Wants A Cookie," 1930*

A black slang term for the female genitals (DAS).

cooling board

Well I packed my suitcase, bundled up my clothes
When I got there she was layin' on a coolin' board.
—*Sunny Boy And His Pals, "France Blues," 1927*

A colloquial term for a board on which a corpse was placed prior to a funeral. An ex-slave noted: "A coolin' board was made out of a long straight plank raised a little at de head and had legs fixed to make it set straight" (Yetman). The term reflected burial customs of the 19th century, when funerals awaited the construction of a coffin by a local tradesman, and were preceded by wakes in which the deceased (covered with a sheet) would be draped out on such a board. The practice of packing the corpse on ice during this period no doubt gave rise to the expression *cooling board,* which was first recorded in 1855 (DAH) and was generally obsolete by the turn of the 20th century, when Clapin (c. 1902) noted it as "a ghastly name given in Pennsylvania and Maryland to the board or slab upon which a dead body is laid out."

coon

Folks lemme tell you 'bout a travelin' coon his home was down in
*   Tennessee*
He made his livin' stealin' people's chickens, and everything he see.
—*Luke Jordan, "Travelin' Man," 1927*

A dehumanizing term for a black male that originally meant a person in American speech. Its use was first noted in 1839: "In the Western States … they use the abbreviation 'coon when speaking of people …" (Marryat, quoted in Mathews, 1931). By 1860 it had taken on the meaning of "a sly, knowing fellow" (OED). As a term of racial identification, it became nationally popular in the 1890s through its association with a genre of pop songs that came into vogue with Paul Allen's "New Coon In Town" (1888). By c. 1902 Clapin could designate it as "a common term for a negro," and it remained so throughout (and beyond) the "coon song" era, which faded around World War I.

coon-can

My baby gimme some money, just to play coon-can
I didn't win no money, but I sure Lord played my hand.
—*Dad Nelson, "Coon Can Blues," 1926*

A popular barrelhouse card game involving two players, each of whom was dealt ten or (more often) eleven cards. The object of the game was to "get out"; i.e., dispose of one's cards by putting them in combinations. Permissible combinations included a straight flush of ten cards, two four of a kind, and one two (or three) of a kind, or straights of three or more cards in the same suit. The player laid his combinations face up and could draw cards from the remaining deck in order to complete them, discarding one of his own cards as he did so. His opponent could use any discarded card for his own combinations or could "hit" the other player's combinations with his own matching cards, which entitled him to dispose of another card. The first player to dispose of his entire hand won the game; if neither player "got out" after going through the deck, the outcome was called a *tab,* in which case the game would continue with the stakes doubled (Jones). The game originated in Mexico and was first noted in America in 1889 (OED).

Coonjine

> *Coonjine my lady Coonjine*
> *Mama don't allow me to Coonjine*
> —*The Black Hillbillies, "Kunjine Baby," 1929*

An obsolete dance enshrined in the eight-bar ditty of the same or like name. The musical theme associated with it was excerpted in Gottschalk's *Bamboula* (1847) and printed in Allen, Ware, and Garrison's *Slave Songs of the United States* (1867) as one of four Louisiana plantation tunes "for a simple dance, a sort of minuet, called the *Coonjai'* ..." By 1910 it had become a black children's dance and beginner's piano piece current in the South. Its original or prevalent name is in doubt; Little Brother Montgomery, who learned it in 1910, stated that the dance/song was actually *Coon Giant.* As *Kunjine,* it received its first recorded treatment, by Anton Lada in 1921. Puckett, who described it in 1925 as "a sort of Negro dance" done in Louisiana, rendered it as *Counjai*; while Bessie Jones (of the Georgia Sea Islands) and Skip James recalled it as *Coonshine.* Cf. DARE, which relates it solely to a swaying gait.

coon one's hand

> *I was sittin' down, playin' some coon-can*
> *I lose all my money but one little lousy dime.*
> *Studyin' about my woman, could hardly coon my hand*
> *Studyin' about my woman could hardly coon my hand.*
> —*Charlie Patton, "Jim Lee Blues, Part One," 1929*

Evidently, to dispose of one's cards in coon-can.

Cootie Crawl

> *An' when that unjust judge an' that no-good broad*
> *[are] stood on a red-hot coal an' burned to a fat*
> *I wanna be a snitcher for the devil so I can jump up,*
> *Shimmy-She-Wobble, Cut-Out, Charleston, Cootie*
> *Crawl, Mess Around an' Ball the Jack an' crack:*
> *"Big boy they can't do that."*
> —*Pine Top Smith, "Big Boy, They Can't Do That," 1929*

A black dance that arose in the wake of World War I, improbably inspired by the movements of lice on soldiers in the trenches. An item in a black-oriented Ohio newspaper of 1921 gives the following explanation:

"The Cootie Crawl"
. . . At the annual celebration
Of the military ball
Some couples were a gliding,
a stopping and a sliding
In a splendid imitation
Of the famous "Cootie Crawl"

Delicately dedicated to our darling
darling darlings in fond memory of
the gallant heroes who furnished sustenance
to the thousands of dear little cooties, who
clung so lovingly in the trenches "Over There."
—Union *of 8/13/1921*

cooze

I went out and looked around
Somebody yelled: "There's a cooze in town!"
—Blind Blake, "Diddie Wa Diddie," 1929

A black term for both the male and female sex organs derived from *caze*, a 19th-century term for vagina (Partridge). It gave rise to the prison use of *coozey* for loose women, prostitutes, and homosexuals (DAUL), and the general slang terms *couzy* and *cuzzy*, the former meaning girl, the latter, vagina.

corn

Twenty-five cents will buy a half a pint of my corn
You ain't never tasted no liquor like this, since you been born.
—Papa Charlie Jackson, "Corn Liquor Blues," 1928

Corn whiskey, the only available alcoholic drink in much of the South during the blues era.

cornder

I was standin' on the cornder, 'tween 35th and Main
That's where a blind man seed my woman, an' a dumb man called her
* name.*
—Arthur (Big Boy) Crudup, "Standing At The Corner," 1942

Corner, in black dialect; found in *Uncle Remus* (1880).

corn dodger

I worked six months for the rascal
To him I'm "What's his name?"

He fed me on corn dodgers
They was hard as any rock.
—Henry Thomas, "Arkansas," 1927

A hard cornmeal cake first noted in 1834 (DAH) and popular in the South until around the turn of the 20th century. "Our main meal was corn bread and milk and grits with milk. That was a little coarser than meal. The way we used to cook it and the best flavored is to cook it out-of-doors in a Dutch oven. We called it corn dodgers" (Bob Kinchlow, as quoted in *Born in Slavery*).

countryman

I says he's a countryman, but that fool done moved in town
He really done sold his cotton, an' now he's walkin' 'round.
—Bo Carter, "Country Fool," 1938

One who lives in the country; a farmer (which in black usage would connote a sharecropper). As standard English, this term was essentially outmoded at the time of the above recording; the last OED reference dates to 1860: "The words 'countryman, rustic, clown . . . ,' still signify a rude and untaught person."

county farm

Down South when you do anything that's wrong
They'll sure put you down on the county farm.
—Son House, "Mississippi County Farm," 1930

County prison farm. On Southern county prison farms, black persons convicted of misdemeanors (typically vagrancy) performed plantation work under harsh conditions. An Arkansas resident opined in 1937: "Out there at the county farm, they bust you open. They bust you up till you can't work" (Henry Blake, as quoted in *Born in Slavery*).

county road

The judge found me guilty, the clerk he wrote it down
I'm just a poor gal in trouble, I know I'm county road bound.
—Ma Rainey, "Chain Gang Blues," 1926

Colloquial for prison road camp, a county penal institution housing misdemeanants who perform road work. See *road.*

cow

If you see my milk cow tell her: "Hurry home!"
I ain't had no milk since that cow been gone.
—Son House, "My Black Mama, Part One," 1930

A conventional blues term for a female, used with no pejorative overtones, as was the case when *cow* originated as a figurative expression in 17th-century English (cf. F&H, 1891; OED). See the related *heifer.*

crack

The women went to the doctor, doctor said:
"Crackin' them things is gonna kill you dead."
We gonna crack them things (2)
Says we really break the record when you come to crackin' them things.
—*The Mississippi Sheiks, "Crackin' Them Things," 1930*

To penetrate a female sexually (Skip James); an apparent extension of *crack* as a term for deflowering (F&H, 1891).

crave (n.)

Now a married woman, has always been my crave
Now a married woman gonna carry me to my grave.
—*Sleepy John Estes, "Diving Duck Blues," 1929*

Craving; of this word, the OED reports: "Not in general use."

crawfish, ways like a

... Your ways is like a crawfish
You'll get all you can an' doodle back in your hole.
—*Bo Carter, "Ways Like A Crawfish," 1938*

A comparison based on the slang use of *crawfish* as a verb meaning to renege, which dates to c. 1850 (DAS).

crawl

Get way back, hug your girl
Get way back and crawl.
—*Andrew and Jim Baxter, "The Georgia Crawl," 1927*

To dance. As a general slang term for a dance, the noun *crawl* dates in print to 1921 (cf. Lighter, 1994), and likely gave rise to *Cootie Crawl* and *Georgia Crawl*.

creampuff

I'm a hard-workin'; man, have been for many long years I know
And some creampuff's usin' my money, but that'll never be no more.
—*Robert Johnson, "I'm A Steady Rollin' Man," 1937*

A pejorative term for a male consort, derided as soft with the implication that he doesn't work. Gary Davis defined the expression as referring to "a kind of picked-up person . . . usually there ain't nothin' else no closer." As a term for weakling, it dates to c. 1913 (Lighter, 1994) and was associated with black "jive talk" of the 1940s (cf. OED).

credit (v.)

I credit one man, it was to my sorrow
It's cash today, credit tomorrow.
—*Lucille Bogan, "Stew Meat Blues," 1935*

To extend credit to. The above couplet refers to a commercial sex transaction.

creep (n.)

> She keeps a rabbit foot in her hand, at night when she goes to sleep
> She keeps it with her so I won't make a midnight creep.
> —Papa Charlie Jackson, "Bad Luck Woman Blues," 1926

A surreptitious departure attendant to infidelity, always modified by *midnight* or *'fore day* in blues song. As a term for a sneak theft, *creep* dates to the 16th and 17th centuries (Partridge).

creep (v.)

> I got a girl for Mondays, Tuesdays, Wednesdays, Thursdays, Friday, too
> I'm gonna creep up on a Saturday, what the women through the week
>   gonna do?
> —Blind Lemon Jefferson, "Chock House Blues," 1926

To make a *creep*; Folb records the term as current among black teenagers of the 1960s and 1970s, meaning to "cheat on one's mate." See *steal* and *tip*.

creeper

> I saw the creepers and sisters turn around an' begin to grin
> "Lord I believe I'll go back to barrelhousin' again."
> —Frank Stokes, "Mr. Crump Don't Like It," 1927

Someone engaged in an illicit relationship requiring *creeping*. Van Vechten (1926) defines it as: "[a] man who invades another's marital rights." In the above lyric, the performer uses it to take a sideswipe at male church members.

crepe, hang (pin) on one's door

> Lord I'm goin', I'm goin', pin a black crepe on your door
> Gal your man ain't dead he ain't comin' back no more.
> —Frank Stokes, "Frank Stokes' Dream," 1928

An arrogant blues catchphrase suggesting that a singer will be mourned by the female he is deserting, drawing its imagery from the then-traditional custom of fastening crepe on the door of a household where death had recently occurred.

crib

> Now they entered me into that crib of misery
> down in dear old county jail
> —Pine Top Smith, "Big Boy, They Can't Do That," 1929

Bed; derived from English thieves' slang of the early 19th century (F&H, 1891) or from the older use of the word to mean lodgings.

crooked as a barrel of snakes

> They're some men you know they're straight
> Some crooked as a barrel of snakes
> —Bo Carter, "Your Biscuits Are Big Enough For Me," 1936

Completely crooked; a Southern expression applied to one who cannot be trusted in any matter, however small (WD). The same comparison figures in Callison's short story *Bill Jones of Paradise Valley* (1914), set in the Southwest: "I met one of the most crooked real estate agents in Alpine I ever saw in my life. . . . He had a barrel of snakes beat a country block." This expression is a mangled metaphor, inasmuch as it is the snakes rather than the barrel containing them that would appear crooked.

'cross the water

> *Aw listen fair brown, don't you want to go?*
> *Going to take you 'cross the water where a brownskin man can't go.*
> —*Blind Lemon Jefferson, "Shuckin' Sugar Blues," 1926*

Europe; an apparent slave idiom: "She cums fum cross de watah" (Sara Gudger, as quoted in *Born in Slavery*).

crow to pick with one, to have a

> *"I got a crow to pick with you."*
> —*Eliza Brown, "Stop Layin' That Stuff On Me," 1929*

To have a bone to pick, an argument to settle, etc.; dated standard English usually rendered as a *crow to pluck* or *pull*. Cf. OED, which offers 1668 and 1849 as its most recent cites (both involving "pluck").

crow jane

> *Crow jane, crow jane, what makes you hold your head so high?*
> *Oughta just remember, you got to live so long and die.*
> —*Bo Weavil Jackson, "Pistol Blues," 1926*

A black term for a female, with varying connotations. While Gary Davis took *crow jane* to mean "a high-steppin' woman . . . make your mouth water and your teeth grit," the recording team of Foster and Harris portrayed her as a black-complexioned female, or one whose spiteful conduct resembled that commonly ascribed to such women:

> *They will wake up in the mornin' if they don't feel right*
> *Cut up your clothes, just for spite . . .*
> *Want you to listen good to what I'm sayin':*
> *You don't have to be dark to be a real crow jane*
> *A brown is nice-lookin', she needs no repair*
> *A crow jane is ugly, she needs some false hair.*
> —*"Crow Jane Alley," 1928*

As denoting a black-complexioned female, it also appears as follows:

> *Now a yellow gal is like a frigid zone, brownskin's about the same*
> *You want some good lovin', get yourself an old crow jane.*
> —*Frankie "Half Pint" Jaxon, "It's Heated," 1929*

Depending on its original meaning, the phrase was suggested by the varying use of *crow* as synonyms for a black person (DAS; Lighter, 1994), an unattractive female (ATS; Lighter, 1994), or "[a] rather attractive girl" (a c. 1900 connotation cited by Lighter, 1994). See *jane*.

crucify

A nickel's worth a sugar, a dime's worth of rice
I'm gonna crucify my woman, I'm gonna beat her up nice.
—*Clifford Gibson, "Tired Of Being Mistreated, Part One," 1929*

To torture, inflict pain upon; an obsolete sense of the term (OED). "Right after de war dey sent colored teachers through de South to teach colored people and child, do you know, dem white folks just crucified most of 'em" (Lula Chambers, as quoted in *Born in Slavery*).

cruel

She came from the country the other day
Some cruel kind daddy stole her heart away.
—*Papa Charlie Jackson, "Mama Don't Allow It," 1925*

Very; a dated intensifier that was standard English from the 16th through 19th centuries (Partridge). According to Clapin (c. 1902), it was transmitted to America in the early 17th century and was "much affected by uneducated people" at the turn of the 20th.

Crump, Mister

Now Mister Crump don't like it, ain't gonna have it here
No barrelhouse women, God drinkin' no beer
Mister Crump don't like it, ain't gon' have it here.
—*Frank Stokes, "Mister Crump Don't Like It," 1927*

A reference to Edward Hull Crump, a powerful Memphis political boss whose bid for the mayor's office in 1909 involved a pledge to close the city's clubs (the subject of the above lyric) at a time when saloons, brothels, and gambling were all legal there. In 1916 he was ousted from office for letting saloons operate. A widely publicized claim by W. C. Handy that he authored the above song, which (as "Memphis Blues" of 1912) is generally considered the first published blues, is without compelling merit.

crying shame

The way I love my black woman, Lord it's a cryin' shame
I don't want no yellow woman, to even call my name.
—*Lee Green, "Sealskin Black Woman," 1937*

An exceedingly lamentable occurrence, used ironically in the above instance. Cf. DAS 3.

cub

> *Says I bought a cub, man, don't play no three givers on me*
> *'Cause after I fall, the jack I'm bound to see.*
> —Bo Carter, "Skin Ball Blues," 1935

? Presumably, a marked deck of cards, facilitating cheating by *carrying a cub* (q.v.). As explained by Jelly Roll Morton in a 1938 Library of Congress interview, *cub* denoted an act of cheating by *carrying a cub*: ". . . A cub is something where you have three cards where it's impossible for this card [i.e., a matching card] to come out of the deck. And of course these cards are in the party's hands, that's playin' the other card. And in that game, you can never lose. But of course it's very dangerous if you're not able to get the cards back into the deck" (*The Georgia Skin Game*, Riverside RLP 9005).

cunning

> *She's a spare-made woman an' she's cunnin' as a squirrel*
> *When she starts to lovin', man it's out the world.*
> —Blind Lemon Jefferson, "Long Lastin' Lovin'," 1928

An American colloquialism for pretty, dating in print to 1844 (cf. OED; Thornton, 1912).

curl one's hair

> *Nice new furniture, a brand-new chair*
> *When I get home I'm gonna curl your hair.*
> —Clifford Gibson, "Tired Of Being Mistreated, Part Two," 1929

To upbraid, vituperate; a 19th-century colloquial expression (Partridge) used with strange effect in the above couplet since the hair of black people is normally curly.

cut

> *I throws a five pound-axe an' I cut two different ways*
> *An' I cut for the women, both night and day.*
> —Charlie Patton, "Jersey Bull Blues," 1934

To have intercourse; said of males. This term may have been of black origin (cf. 1927 dialect citation in Lighter, 1994).

cut a figure

> *Get off my money, an' don't get funny*
> *'Cause I'm a nigger, don't cut no figure.*
> —Luke Jordan, "Pick Poor Robin Clean," 1927

To make an impression; standard English (OED).

cut down

> *Went gaycattin' with another sealskin brown*
> *Rambled till the butcher cut him down.*
> —Maggie Jones, "Undertaker's Blues," 1925

To kill. An ex-slave held: "The Man above . . . going to cut them [sinners] down" (Elizabeth Hines, as quoted in *Born in Slavery*). The OED (which defines *cut down* as "[t]o lay low or kill with the sword or the like") offers two citations, from 1821 and 1874, both referring to combat. In the above couplet, the meaning of *butcher* is obscure.

cut one's own grass

> *Well I'm so glad, the law has passed*
> *You uptown gals got to cut your own grass.*
> —Luke Jordan, "Won't You Be Kind," 1929

A 19th-century prison term meaning to make one's own living (F&H, 1891). The above couplet, by a Virginia performer, refers to an anti-vagrancy or prostitution ordinance.

cut-out

> *Who's that comin', hey with his motor so strong?*
> *It's Lemon in his D.B., people thinks he's got his cut-out on.*
> —Blind Lemon Jefferson, "D B Blues," 1928

A 1920s term for a car muffler: "[i]n them days the cars had cut-outs on 'em, cut-outs that they could shut it off, open it up; you get on the road, racin', open up that cut-out . . ." (Tom Shaw).

daddy

> *Crawled across the fireplace, an' stopped in the middle of the floor*
> *Say: "Mama ain't that your second daddy, standin' there in the door?"*
> —Blind Lemon Jefferson, "That Crawlin' Baby Blues," 1929

A black term applied to either boyfriend or husband (cf. Van Vechten, 1926), and most commonly used by females, with respect to their own romantic companions.

Dago Hill

> *Oh had a, had a notion, Lord I believe I will*
> *I'm gonna go 'cross the river, stop at Dago Hill.*
> —Charlie Patton, "Jersey Bull Blues," 1934

The local name for a fifty-block Italian neighborhood on the south side of St. Louis, dating to the 1880s and known as "the Hill" since the 1960s.

daisy

She can love so good,

Aw she's a daisy, when she loves so good.

—Lovin' Sam Theard, "She Can Love So Good," 1930

A genteel slang term of 19th-century vintage for an attractive young woman (cf. Lighter, 1994), used to describe the original *Kate Adams:* "She's a daisy, and no mistake!" (*Arkansas City Journal*, 12/3/1882).

Daniel

Lord my good girl says she don't want me no more

But she's on my Daniel Lord everywhere I go.

—Furry Lewis, "Good Looking Girl Blues," 1927

Ass, according to the above performer; Mezzrow (1946) notes it as a black term for buttocks.

dark

An' the sun goin' down boy, dark gonna catch me here

I haven't got no lovin' sweet woman, love an' feel my care.

—Robert Johnson, "Cross Road Blues," 1936

Nightfall; a Southern colloquialism found in Faulkner's *The Mansion* (1955): "... if dark catches me alone in this room with them and no guard handy, I'll never see light again" (reflection of Mink Snopes, a "poor white" convict). The OED construes it as standard English, but lists no post-1865 citations.

Darktown

Black Bottom, it's got 'em, down in Atlanta, on Decatur Street

Everyone you meet in Darktown, shakin' their feet and bustin' around.

—Sadie Jackson, "Original Black Bottom Dance," 1926

A working-class black section of Atlanta located between Courtland and Jackson Streets, near the center of the city. The same term was casually applied to any black residential district by local whites, and enshrined in the pop hit "Darktown Strutter's Ball" (1917).

dead

I wanna go home, that train has done gone dead

I done lost my wife and my three little children, an' my mother's sick in bed.

—King Solomon Hill, "The Gone Dead Train," 1932

In regard to a train, standing still; from the railroad expression *dead one* (ATS).

dead and gone

"Babe I don't care where you bury my body
when I'm dead an' gone."
—Robert Johnson, "Me And The Devil Blues," 1937

A clichéd expression, used "with a connotation of 'long dead' . . ." (DC).

dead cat on the line

Says I'm not jokin', ain't gonna change my mind
The way you treat me mama it's a dead cat on the line.
—Blind Boy Fuller, "I'm A Good Stem Winder," 1935

Something untoward in the background or past that creates or explains a present anomaly or difficulty. In the above instance, the *dead cat on the line* is presumed to be a competing love interest. The example given by the Reverend J. M. Gates (in a best-selling recorded sermon of 1929 that popularized this catchphrase among both races) involves presumed adultery: "If a child is no way like its father, there's a dead cat on the line" ("Dead Cat On The Line"). The phrase still survives in the South and among blacks, but has taken on the meaning of a mere suspicious occurrence (cf. DARE; Smitherman, 2000). It has been claimed, on no likely evidence, that *dead cat on the line* originally referred to dead catfish on fishing lines; *cat* is more likely to refer to a polecat (skunk). Gates provided his own neat etymology for it: "They tell me that once upon a time they had some trouble tryin' to send a message over the telegram [*sic*] line. The company sent a man out to inspect the line. In makin' his report he say he found that a cat had gone up the telegraph pole and died."

death-bell

Hey hey, the death-bell's in my ear
It t'ain't gonna be long 'fore they gonna, ring me 'way from here.
—Tom Dickson, "Death Bell Blues," 1928

"[A] sound in the ears like that of a bell, supposed by the superstitious to portend a death" (OED, which cites a single usage, in Jamaica from 1807). This term was also given white Southern circulation (cf. DARE 2, which gives it a false American pedigree). The underlying reference is to the bygone *passing bell*, rung in churches to signify a local death.

death wagon

When the death wagon rolled up with a rumblin' sound
Says you know by that my gal was graveyard bound.
—Edward Thompson, "Seven Sisters Blues," 1929

A variant of *dead wagon*, a colloquial term for a hearse (cf. DARE 2). See *rumblin'*.

Delta, the

> *They rode in the Delta, kept on easin' by*
> *Know I feel just like she said her last "good-bye."*
> *—Robert Wilkins, "Long Train Blues," 1928*

A provincial term for the Mississippi Delta, referring to the flat, alluvial fertile land of northwestern Mississippi, distinguished in the blues era by its large cotton plantations and primarily black population.

devil, catch the

> *I been to the Nation, from there to the Territo'*
> *An' I'm a hard-luck child, catch the devil everywhere I go.*
> *—Skip James, "Hard Luck Child," 1931*

A euphemism for *catch hell* (q.v.). "If that nigger on his mule got too fur ahead so old doctor couldn't see de light he sho' catch the devil from that old doctor." (Anthony Dawson, as quoted in *Born in Slavery*).

devilment

> *She's got devilment, little girl you got devilment all on your mind*
> *Now I got to leave this mornin', with my arm fold up and cryin'.*
> *—Robert Johnson, "Rambling On My Mind," 1936*

Mischief; a standard English term (OED) recorded in DARE 2 despite its British pedigree and construed by Major (1994) as meaning "evil."

diddy-wah-diddy

> *There's a great big mystery*
> *And it sure is worryin' me*
> *This diddy-wah-diddy (2)*
> *I wish somebody would tell me what diddy-wah-diddy means . . .*
> *Met a little girl about four feet four*
> *She said: "Come on papa won't you give me some more*
> *Of your diddy-wah-diddy?" (2)*
> *I wish somebody would tell me what diddy-wah-diddy means.*
> *—Blind Blake, "Diddie Wa Diddie," 1927*

Dick, a double entendre with no apparent vernacular basis coyly circulated in the above song. Of itself, Diddy-Wah-Diddy was a mystical paradise recounted by rustic blacks in Florida, the native state of the above performer: "It is said 'Everybody would live in Diddy-Wah-Diddy if it wasn't so hard to find and so hard to get to after you even know the way'" (Botkin, 1944). The association between this paradise ("a place of no work and no worry") and pleasure may account for its utility as a sexual reference, and the term itself may derive from the English dialect *diddy,* for breast (EDD). There seems to be no basis for the claim in DARE 2 that *diddy-wah-diddy* was "[u]sed as a substitute or a word or name one does not want to use; hence as the name of an imaginary place.

. . ." It apparently became a metaphor for a remote area, noted by Zora Neale Hurston (1942) as a Harlem term for "a far place, a measure of distance" and used thusly in her *Spunk* (1935): "I bet you I'll send it to Diddy-wah-Diddy!" A "Diddie Wa Diddie" recorded by Bo Diddley in 1958 treats it as an unspecified place ("Ain't no town, ain't no city"), without a sexual component.

ding-dong

> *Early in the mornin', good true kind captain,*
> *when the ding-dong ring*
> *Go look on the long old table, oh my God*
> *an' find the same ol' thing.*
> —Ben Covington, *"Mule Skinner Moan,"* 1932

Bell; in this instance, a bell used to summon levee or logging camp workers to a mess table. The term also occurs, as a bell summoning convicts, in "Midnight Special":

> *You get up in the mornin', hear the ding-dong ring*
> *Go marchin' to the table, you see the same ol' thing.*
> —Sam Collins, *"Midnight Special Blues,"* 1927

dip

> *Did you ever . . . get clipped by a coke-headed dip*
> *At the time you ain't got no dough?*
> —Pine Top Smith, *"Big Boy, They Can't Do That,"* 1929

A conventional slang term for pickpocket (cf. Lighter, 1994).

dip snuff

> *Rooster chew tobacco and the hen dip snuff*
> *Biddy can't do it but he struts his stuff.*
> —Blind Willie McTell, *"Kind Mama,"* 1931

To dip into a snuff box and place the extracted snuff in the mouth; a practice first reported in 1830: "They [females in Raleigh, Virginia] do not snuff it up the nose, but take it into the mouth—they call it dipping. . . . It is simply dipping a small wooden brush, a little stick (bruised or chewed at one end) into a common box of snuff and rubbing the teeth . . ." (Mathews, 1931)

directly

> *"That's my gal—get away from him. 'Cause I'm gonna*
> *grab him directly an' I'm gonna shake him every way but loose."*
> —Blind Blake, *"Southern Rag,"* 1927

Immediately or in short order; in the former sense it was standard English (despite DARE 2, which treats it as an Americanism; cf. OED).

doopididy

> *Now lookey here mama what's goin' on wrong?*
> *The reason I can't get in my happy home*

You must be doin' the doopididy (3)

Just because the stuff is here.

—Kokomo Arnold, "Doin' The Doopididy," 1935

? An obscure term for sexual relations, perhaps invoking the name of a contemporary dance.

do-right

I'm a do-right woman, can't no lovin' man refuse

Whenever I'm around, the women screamin' "do-right blues."

—Rosa Henderson, "Do Right Blues," 1924

Law-abiding, upright; underworld slang (cf. Lighter, 1994).

do that thing

You can't sing,

But you don't have to when you do that thing.

—Rosa Henderson, "Do That Thing," 1924

A black catchphrase used as an encouragement to dancers that appears in Van Vechten's *Nigger Heaven* (1926): "Hey! Hey! Do that thing!"

dog, to be one's

Says my blues fell this mornin' and my love come fallin' down

Says I'll be your low-down dog mama but please don't dog me around.

—Kokomo Arnold, "Milk Cow Blues," 1934

To be an abused figure. The comparison between a maltreated lover and household dog is of ancient lineage, appearing in Shakespeare's *A Midsummer-Night's Dream* (1595): "'What worser place can I beg in your love . . . Than to be used as you use your dog.'"

dog (v.)

Says I'll be your monkey baby, sure won't be your dog

Says 'fore I'll stand your doggin' I'll sleep in a hollow log.

—Charlie Patton, "Joe Kirby," 1929

To harass or abuse; a still-surviving slang term dating in print to 1896 (cf. Lighter, 1994).

Dog

I'm goin' where the Southern 'cross the Dog (3)

—Charlie Patton, "Green River Blues," 1929

The customary name given to the Yazoo and Mississippi Valley Railroad line, a subsidiary of the Illinois Central chartered in 1882 that serviced large portions of Mississippi, including the entire Delta region, until the early 1930s. The term arose from conventional railroad slang: ". . . on little draggletail branches of larger roads . . . '[d]og' with or without adjectives is a favorite epithet for crawlers made up of cast-off equipment of the parent road, and covering only a few miles daily, there and back" (Botkin and Harlow). Perhaps artificially, the *Dog* was termed the *Yellow Dog* in W. C. Handy's 1916 Tin Pan Alley composition "Yellow Dog Blues."

dog one around

> *Girl if you don't love me, please don't dog me around*
> *If you dog me around I know you'll put me down.*
> —Blind Lemon Jefferson, "Shuckin' Sugar," 1926

To follow one everywhere, as if smitten; an extension of the standard English *dog*, meaning to follow (cf. OED).

dogs

> *Now her dogs are swollen, and she got one eye*
> *She looks like a wreck, that happened last July.*
> —Memphis Slim, "Jasper's Gal," 1941

General slang for feet, dating in print to 1913 (Lighter, 1994).

done

> *See see rider, see what you done done*
> *Made me love you, now your friend has come.*
> —Blind Lemon Jefferson, "See See Rider," 1926

Recorded in 1829 as "[a] prevalent vulgarism in the *Southern states*; as 'done gone,' 'What have you done do?' Only heard among the lowest classes; probably obtained from Ireland" (quoted in Mathews, 1931).

doney

> *I don't want no woman, wants any downtown man she meet*
> *She's a no-good doney, they shouldn't allow her on the street.*
> —Robert Johnson, "I Believe I'll Dust My Broom," 1936

A variant of *dona*, a 19th-century British slang term for woman (also occurring as *doner, donna,* and *donny*) associated with Cockney and circus use and regarded as vulgar by Farmer and Henley, although it derives from the Italian, Spanish, or Portuguese term of respect for a lady. (The standard English *dame* and *prima donna* both arose from the same source.) In Southern white speech it connoted "[a] sweetheart, girlfriend," the definition put forth by DARE 2. In black speech, however, it simply meant a woman (Moore) and had a pejorative overtone, thus leading Son House (who spelled it "donay") to define it as meaning "no-good woman." In rustic white song, the term occurs as early as 1910, when "Doney Gal" was collected by John Lomax; in black song, it figures in a slave composition, "Off To Richmond," cited by Talley:

> *I'se off from Richmon' sooner in de mornin'*
> *I'se off from Richmond befo' de break o' day.*
> *I slips off from Mosser [Master] widout pass an' warnin'*
> *For I mus' see my Donie wharever she may stay.*

don't get funny

Get off my money, an' don't get funny

'Cause I'm a nigger, don't cut no figure.

—Luke Jordan, "Pick Poor Robin Clean," 1927

A 1920s catchphrase given by Martens (1923) as meaning "do not take liberties."

don't mean a thing

I got a bird to whistle, and I have a bird to sing

I got a woman that I'm lovin', boy but she don't mean a thing.

—Robert Johnson, "Stones In My Passway," 1937

Is utterly inconsequential (to the speaker). This expression was most often applied to sexual consorts: ". . . the sailor who was with me didn't mean a thing—" (Feminine dialogue in Charles Willeford's *Pick-Up*, 1955). Less commonly, it was applied to a group:

Vampires see her comin', they all look an' frown

They don't mean a thing when she's around.

—Irene Wiley, "This Sweet Reedie Brown," 1931

It was also used to downplay any imputation of significance, as in the 1932 Duke Ellington composition "It Don't Mean A Thing (If It Ain't Got That Swing)," where it referred to music.

doodle (n., v.), doodle hole

Sometimes a little doodle, pretty hard to get

Keep on twistin' and you will find it.

Just doin' the doodle-do-do

I like to take my straw, go play in the doodle hole.

—Charley Lincoln, "Doodle Hole Blues," 1930

Double entendres based on the Southern colloquial use of *doodlebug* to mean "[a] yellow beetle that lives in the ground and shows its presence by the hole it makes. It is caught by children who put a straw in the hole . . ." (1909 Arkansas attestation cited in DARE 2). The above song also employs *doodle* as a verb for sexual intercourse:

I knowed a little girl, she was very very nice

She got to doodle once and she wanted it twice.

doodle it back

My gal stayed out till half past three

Come wakin' me up, start worryin' me

About doodle it back, she wants doodle it back . . .

—Sam Theard, "Doodle It Back," 1929

Sexual intercourse; an apparent embellishment of *doodle*. As with various sexual terms, it ostensibly referred to a dance:

Everybody down my way, goin' insane
About that dance ain't got no name
It's called Doodle It Back . . .
Don't you never let me catch you, doin' that Doodle It Back.

doodley-squat

My gal got a house an' a lot
Poor me ain't got doodley-squat.
—Blind Willie McTell, "Hillbilly Willie's Blues," 1935

A black euphemism for *shit*, used as an expression of negative value. As a synonym for "nothing," it has been (along with the more prevalent *squat*) a general American colloquialism since the 1960s (cf. OED). The original figurative sense is conveyed in Zora Neale Hurston's *Jonah's Gourd Vine* (1934): "She never had nothin'—not eben doodly-squat."

Dooga

I'm feelin' sad, lonely and blue
There's only one thing I like to do
Come on, let's do the Dooga . . .
—Kitty Gray and her Wampus Cats, "Doing The Dooga," 1938

An obscure swing-era dance, perhaps limited to pockets of Louisiana (the above performer's home state).

door

Oh I remember one mornin', stand in my rider's door
"You know what she tol' me?"
"Looka here papa Charlie I, don't want you no more."
—Charlie Patton, "Bird Nest Bound," 1930

Doorway; standard English found in Shakespeare's *Merry Wives of Windsor* ("'They . . . met the jealous knave their Master in the doore . . .'") that was obsolete by the 20th century but occurs frequently in blues song.

dough roller

Now don't your house look lonesome, your dough roller gone?
Lord in your kitchen now, cookin' till she come home.
—Sleepy John Estes, "The Girl I Love, She Got Long Curly Hair," 1929

A live-in female companion, apprehended as a food and sex provider. As a Southern expression for wife, the probable parent term *dough beater* dates in print to 1911 (Lighter, 1994).

down (a.)

Went down for stealin' 'cause I didn't have a dime
Nothing will release me but the thing called Father Time.
—Sara Martin, "The Prisoner's Blues," 1926

In prison; contemporary underworld slang (cf. Lighter, 1994).

down (adv. 1)

When you were down, sick down on your bed
Know Bobbie brought you your medicine, also brought you bread.
—Barbecue Bob, "She's Gone Blues," 1928

Prostrate with illness; dated standard English (cf. OED). *Sick down* may have been a black idiom, along with the converse: "... dere was a gal name Penny what had been down sick a long time" (Uncle Tom Baker, as quoted in *Born in Slavery*). See *taken down*.

down (adv. 2)

You quit me mama when I was in your town
You told your friends you'se glad, I was down.
—Charley Lincoln, "Mama Don't Rush Me," 1930

In low spirits; dejected. Although the OED classifies this sense as colloquial, it offers citations from Samuel Johnson and Henry David Thoreau, the former reading: "When I prest your hand at parting I was rather down" (cf. OED at *down*, adv.8).

down (n.)

He got to rob he got to steal, don't he got to leave outta this man's town
No he say he goin' back to the country an' gonna, sow some more country
    down.
—Bo Carter, Country Fool," 1938

An open expanse of elevated land (OED); not associated with American farms.

down (v.)

Some people doubt me, most talk about me
Just to down my name.
—Ethel Waters, "Kind Lovin' Blues," 1922

To denigrate; disparage (cf. Lighter, 1994).

downhearted

What's the matter baby, you look so downhearted and sad
When you look that way, make your daddy feel so bad.
—George Allison and Willie White, "How I Feel My Love," 1929

Discouraged, depressed; an uncommon locution, the OED offering three citations (from c. 1774–1869).

down home

You oughta have seen my baby, when I first brought her from down home
Why she looked just like a rag-doll, hair looked like it had never been
    touched with a comb.
—Guy Smith, "Sad Story Blues," 1929

In black parlance, the South or one's former Southern neighborhood, from a Northern vantage point.

down on

> *... I'm tired of bein' mistreated, an' the way you do*
> *Won't you tell everybody, that I'm down on you?*
> —*Clifford Gibson, "Tired Of Being Mistreated," 1929*

Against, disdainful of; an American colloquialism of mid-19th-century origin (cf. OED).

down the country

> *Elder Greene is gone*
> *Gone way down the country,*
> *with his long clothes on.*
> —*Charlie Patton, "Elder Greene Blues," 1929*

In or into a rural area; a Southern colloquialism (cf. DARE 2, which offers a 1967 example as its earliest citation). This expression implies a southward direction and is contrasted with *up the country* in an 1815 letter: "I am uncertain whether I am to ... go *up* or *down* the country" (TT). See *up the country*.

down the line, get on

> *Get your hat get your coat get shakin' on down the line. (3)*
> —*Henry Thomas, "Texas Worried Blues," 1928*

An apparent variant of *go down the line,* meaning to go carousing in a red-light district. Cf. Lighter (1997).

down to the bricks

> *"Aw, beat 'em boy!*
> *Beat 'em down to the bricks."*
> —*Lucille Bogan, "Baking Powder Blues," 1933*

Down to the pavement. The phrase *beat 'em down to the bricks* occurs above as a directive to a pianist to "assault" his instrument and was an apparent barrelhouse catchphrase. A variant, "Whup that thing down to the bricks, boys!" occurs as a vocal aside on Madlyn Davis's "Too Black Bad" (1928).

down yonder

> *Way down yonder in Arkansas*
> *Where you find a turkey in the straw.*
> —*Hambone Willie Newbern, "Way Down In Arkansas," 1929*

Down South (DAS 3).

dozen(s), play the

> *I don't play the dozen and neither the ten*
> *'Course if you keep on talkin' I'll ease you in.*
> —*Little Hat Jones, "Kentucky Blues," 1930*

To hurl stylized taunts consisting of obscene reflections on one's mother, a favorite pastime of boisterous black youths. Although associated with males, they are portrayed in one song as a pastime of prostitutes who abounded in a popular Memphis barrelhouse operated by *Jim Kinnane:*

> They drink beer whiskey; drink they coke and gin
> When you don't play the dozen they will ease you in.
> —*Robert Wilkins, "Old Jim Canaan," 1935*

A sign reading "No Dozens Allowed" once commonly adorned Mississippi Delta barrelhouses (Willie Moore). The term itself is of obscure origin and may have arisen from the expression "to talk nineteen to the dozen" (to talk rapidly). See *ease (one) in.*

drag one down

> My last man, tried to drag me down
> But he was one good man to have around.
> —*Maggie Jones, "You Can't Do What My Last Man Did," 1923*

To have a negative effect on a social or romantic companion; a still-current slang expression, presumably of black origin.

dreadful

> Now now now your days so lonesome, mama your nights so dreadful
>   long . . .
> Well well been so many lonesome days, whooh-well since I been gone.
> —*Peetie Wheatstraw, "Police Station Blues," 1932*

Very; a dated colloquialism. Bartlett (1877) notes that it was "indiscriminately used by uneducated people for the purpose of giving emphasis to an expression."

drink so much whiskey, I stagger in my sleep

> I drink so much whiskey, I stagger in my sleep
> My brains is dark and cloudy, my mind's goin' to my feet.
> —*Blind Willie McTell, "Dark Night Blues," 1927*

A black catchphrase (cf. Hughes and Bontemps).

drivers

> "Put on your water, put on your coal
> Put your head out the window, see my drivers roll."
> —*Furry Lewis, "Kassie Jones, Part One," 1928*

Driving-wheels; see *driving-wheel.*

driving-wheel

> Feel like a broke down engine, ain't got no drivin'-wheel
> You ever been down an' lonesome, you know how a poor boy feel.
> —*Blind Willie McTell, "Broke Down Engine Blues," 1931*

A large wheel of a train engine, to which power is transmitted (OED).

drop down

Now drop down baby, let your daddy see
I know just what you're tryin' to pull on me.
—Sleepy John Estes, "Drop Down Mama," 1935

A seeming misapplication of *drop down to one*, a slang term of British under-world origin meaning to discover a person's character or designs (cf. F&H, 1891; Lighter, 1994). In the above couplet, it is the singer rather than his girlfriend who "drops down" in this sense.

dry long so

I ain't got no wife, I ain't got no child to school
Reason I'm hangin' 'round here, man: I'm stickin' here dry long so.
—Blind Lemon Jefferson, "Rambler Blues," 1927

A black idiom meaning for no good reason; "without a cause" (Skip James). Willie Moore reported: "...Just like I come up and do something to you, an' you hasn't done nothin' to me: now I done it 'dry long so.'" It arose from or gave rise to *dry so*, a less common term of like meaning recorded in white Southern speech by 1896 (cf. DARE 2). *Dry long so* evolved into a Harlem catchphrase; Calloway (1939) defines it as "fate, or 'that's life' or 'just like that,'" the latter of which appears to correspond with the variant *dry just long so* appearing below:

Listen here ... everybody got to go [i.e., die]
But it's too sad when you lose one of your best friends,
you have to take it dry just long so.
—King Solomon Hill, "My Buddy Blind Papa Lemon," 1932

In present-day black parlance, *drylongso* is used to mean "ordinary."

duckins

When you see me comin' with my dirty dirty duckins on
You know my man's in trouble, there's got to be some hustlin' done.
—Moanin' Bernice Edwards, "Hard Hustling Blues," 1928

Overalls, work clothes, or other garments made of duck; a colloquialism often rendered as *duckin* and associated with Texas, the home state of the above performer (cf. DARE 2).

dummy

Now when I got on the dummy, didn't have no fare
The police asked me, what was I doin' on there?
—Bessie Tucker, "The Dummy," 1928

A colloquial term dating to the late 19th century for a short train (or branch line) generally used to transport loggers or other laborers (cf. DARE 2; Lighter, 1994).

dust one's broom

> *And I believe, I believe I'll dust my broom*
> *So some of you low-down rounders, Lord you can have my room.*
> —Kokomo Arnold, *"Sagefield Woman Blues,"* 1934

To leave hurriedly. Although Burley's *Handbook of Harlem Jive* (c. 1944) lists *dust your broom* as a Harlem "jive" phrase, its earlier occurrence in the above lyric and in Robert Johnson's "I Believe I'll Dust My Broom" (1936) indicate a Southern origin. The expression is a semantic blending of two conventional slang synonyms. *To broom* meant to run away in 19th-century slang; to *get up and dust* meant to depart hastily in American slang of the same vintage (F&H, 1891). Previously, in the 17th and 18th centuries, *dust* was standard English for depart (Partridge), suggested by the admonition of Matthew 10:14: "And whosoever shall not receive you, nor hear your words, when ye depart out of that house or city, shake off the dust off your feet." Bartlett (1877) records its use in American speech, which gradually dwindled to the point of surviving only in convict slang (DAUL).

Dye, Aunt Caroline

> *I'm going to Newport News just to see Aunt Caroline Dye*
> *She's a fortune-tellin' woman, oh Lord she don't tell no lie.*
> —Memphis Jug Band, *"Aunt Caroline Dyer Blues,"* 1930

A well-known conjurer who kept a hotel in Newport, Arkansas, also commemorated in W. C. Handy's "Sundown Blues" (1923). An ex-slave recounted in 1936: ". . . Mother Dye. You all know she's a hoodoo doctor who lived at Newport . . . Mother Dye is dead now . . ." (Angelina Thompson, as quoted in *Born in Slavery*).

eagle

> *Eagle been here, start a nest an' gone*
> *An' you know by that I ain't gonna be here long.*
> —Charlie Patton, *"Circle Round The Moon,"* 1929

An allusion to money based on the prevalence of the eagle on bills and half-dollars. The term itself once stood for a ten-dollar gold piece (DAH).

Eagle Rock

> Eagle Rock me mama, Sally Long it, too
> Ain't nobody in town, can Eagle Rock like you.
> —Furry Lewis, "Black Gypsy Blues," 1929

A passé dance or arm motion associated with the age of the *Turkey Trot*, but described by the above performer as meaning (along with *Sally Long*) "just good fucking." As a dance maneuver involving the spreading of arms in wing-like fashion, it was incorporated into *Balling the Jack* as delineated by Chris Smith in the 1913 hit:

> Stretch your lovin' arms straight out in space
> Then you do the Eagle Rock with style and grace
> Swing your foot way 'round, then bring it back:
> Now that's what I call Ballin' the Jack.

ease

> Don't a man act funny, when a single woman ease in town?
> He stay out all night, he throw his home girl down.
> —Sleepy John Estes, "You Shouldn't Do That," 1941

To move quietly or unobtrusively (DARE 2); a Southern colloquialism. In the near-synonymous, standard English sense of moving gently or gradually, it appears in:

> There's a brown across town, an' she's tall as a sycamore tree
> That gal'd walk through the rain and snow, for to ease that thing on me.
> —Blind Lemon Jefferson, "Deceitful Brownskin Woman," 1927
> Followed sweet mama, to the buryin' ground
> I didn't know I loved her, till they eased her down.
> —Charlie Patton, "Devil Sent The Rain Blues," 1929

(Cf. OED at *ease*, v.7b, citing Mark Twain from c. 1875: "I eased the gravestone down till it rested on the ground.")

ease one in

> Don't ease, don't you ease
> Don't you ease me in
> Says all night Cunningham,
> Don't ease me in.
> —Henry Thomas, "Don't Ease Me In," 1928

To entice or provoke one into *playing the dozens* by means of preliminary banter (Skip James). This phrase is an extension of *ease in*, standard English meaning "to break in gently" (OED at *ease*, v.4d).

eastman

> *I left Memphis, to spread the news*
> *Memphis women don't wear no shoe*
> *Had it written in the back of my shirt:*
> *"Natural-born eastman, don't have to work."*
> —Furry Lewis, "Kassie Jones, Part Two," 1928

A black term for pimp, also applied to gigolos; defined by Van Vechten (1926) as "a man who lives on women."

easy (1)

> *Mama I feel like jumpin' through the keyhole of your door*
> *I can jump so easy your man will never know.*
> —Furry Lewis, "Falling Down Blues," 1927

Quiet; a standard English connotation of the word (cf. OED). This sense is found in:

> *Make me down, a pallet on your floor*
> *Make it calm an' easy, make it down by your door.*
> —Blind Lemon Jefferson, "Stocking Feet Blues," 1926

easy (2)

> *If you wanna live easy, pack your clothes and 'bye' (2)*
> —Tommy Johnson, "Lonesome Home Blues," 1930

Unburdened; a standard English connotation (OED).

easy rider

> *I wonder where my easy rider's gone*
> *Easy ridin' women, always in the wrong.*
> —Blind Lemon Jefferson, "Easy Rider," 1927

"Easy rider's just some gal that's pretty good in the bed" (Tom Shaw). Ordinarily applied to females, it also figured in the rhetoric of female blues singers:

> *You'll find your easy rider, with a high yellow or his brown*
> *That's why he don't want you, always to hang around.*
> —Kansas City Kitty, "Mistreatin' Easy Rider," 1930

Although *easy rider* almost certainly lost most of its 1920s currency in black speech, it was nevertheless recorded by Folb as a 1960s/1970s black teenage term denoting a "sexually promiscuous female." As slang for a sexually forward or promiscuous female, *easy* dates to the turn of the 18th century (cf. Lighter, 1994).

easy roll (n., v.)

> *Take Alcorub, (tearin' about?) my soul*
> *Because brownskin woman, don't do the easy roll.*
> —Tommy Johnson, "Canned Heat Blues," 1928

? Most likely, an act of prostitution, the term apparently bearing a suggestion that sex or prostitution is easy work, *roll* (q.v.) having signified both labor and sex. As a verb, it appears as follows:

> *Would go to Bougalusa, but it's too low-down*
> *Them Bougalusie women now, they just easy roll.*
> —Tommy Johnson, untitled Paramount blues, 1930

easy roller

> *Now don't you wish your easy roller, partner was little an' cute like mine?*
> *Boy every time she walks, Lord she sure bring that jack to town.*
> —Memphis Jug Band, "Memphis Jug Blues," 1927

Evidently, a prostitute.

eat (one) out

> *He will eat your chicken, he will eat your pie*
> *He will eat your wife out on the sly.*
> —Kansas Joe, "Preacher's Blues," 1931

To perform oral sex on a female; despite its familiarity, this term has no documented history prior to its appearance in the above couplet.

eatless days

> *I'm gonna get a job up there in Mr. Ford's place*
> *Stop these eatless days from starin' me in the face.*
> —Blind Blake, "Detroit Bound Blues," 1928

A humorous or ironic play on *meatless and wheatless days.*

elder

> *"Come in elder, please shut my door*
> *Want you to preach the same text for me, preached the night before."*
> —"Hi" Henry Brown, "Preacher Blues," 1932

A term of 18th-century origin for a preacher or minister, employed by Baptists (among others); cf. DAH.

Elder Green

> *Elder Green told the deacon: "Let's go down in prayer,"*
> *There's a big 'ssociation in New Orleans, come an' let's go there."*
> —Charlie Patton, "Elder Greene Blues," 1929

Most likely, the personification of a preacher or lay preacher, deriving from *green-apron,* a term for a lay preacher of 17th-century vintage (F&H, 1893) or *lady green,* a thieves' term for a clergyman (F&H, 1896).

eleven twenty-nine

> *When I got arrested, what you reckon was my fine?*
> *They give all coons, 'leven twenty-nine.*
> —*Charlie Patton, "Jim Lee Blues, Part Two," 1929*

A jail term of eleven months and twenty-nine days, or essentially the maximum sentence for a misdemeanor. The above couplet calls attention to excessive punishment doled out to Mississippi blacks for petty offenses, such as vagrancy.

Elgin Movements

> *She got Elgin Movements, a twenty-year guarantee*
> *I bet you my last dollar, she done put that jinx on me.*
> —*Blind Blake, "Panther Squall Blues," 1928*

Literally, the component of an Elgin watch containing its moving parts. Before the 1920s, particular watch movements were customarily selected by customers, who would then have a jeweler pair them with the desired watch face. This method of purchasing is implicit in the following vaudeville blues lyric:

> *He ain't no Ingersoll, he got no Elgin movement*
> *There's nothin' about him needs improvement.*
> —*Dorothy Jenkins, "Sister, It's Too Bad," 1925*

To characterize a female as having "Elgin Movements" would likely constitute a comment on her solid or sturdy build or body, or remark on her reliability. This expression also appears as a nebulous superlative applied by Blind Lemon Jefferson:

> *She got Elgin Movements from her head down to her toe*
> *An' she can brake in on a dollar, man most anywhere she go.*
> —*"Change My Luck Blues," 1928*

evening

> *In the evening, in the evening, mama when the sun goes down*
> *Well ain't it lonesome, ain't it lonesome baby,*
> *When your lover's not around?*
> —*Leroy Carr, "When The Sun Goes Down," 1934*

A Southern term for afternoon (ADD), apparently derived from British dialect (cf. OED). It appears in Ray Charles's "Hallelujah, I Love Her So" (1956): "In the evening when the sun goes down . . ."

every dog has his day

> *Ball on baby, you can have your way*
> *Each an' every dog, sure must have his day.*
> —*Charlie Patton, "Hammer Blues," 1929*

A proverbial saying first recorded in 1550 and recounted in *Hamlet* (1602) as: "The Cat will Mew, and Dogge will haue his day."

evil (a.)

> *I don't want no jet-black woman Lord to cook no pie for me*
> *'Cause black is evil I'm scared she might pizin' me.*
> —Will Weldon, *"Turpentine Blues,"* 1927

Ill-tempered, spiteful, unpleasant; a black colloquialism likely derived from *evil tongue*, archaic English for a malicious speaker (cf. OED). This term is still current in black speech(Smitherman, 2000).

evil (n.)

> *Beatrice got a phonograph, an' it won't say a lonesome word*
> *What evil have I done, what evil has the poor girl heard?*
> —Robert Johnson, *"Phonograph Blues,"* 1936

Obsolete standard English for a wrong-doing, sin, or crime (OED). The above utterance may have been a rhetorical catchphrase; it occurs in Zora Neale Hurston and Dorothy Waring's *Polk County* (1944): "But, Pudding-Pie, what evil have I done?"

evil spirit

> *You may bury my body, down by the highway-side*
> *So my old evil spirit, can get a Greyhound bus and ride.*
> —Robert Johnson, *"Me And The Devil Blues,"* 1937

In Southern black mythology of the antebellum/blues era, the restless ghost of an apostate: "Ha'nts ain't nothin' but somebody died outten Christ an' his sper't ain't at rest. Jes' in a wandrin' condition in de world. Dis is de evil sper't what de Bible tells about when hit say a person has got two sper't, a good one an' a evil one. De good sper't goes to a place of happiness an' rest, an' you doan see hit no mo', but dis evil sper't ain't got no place to go" (Ank Bishop, as quoted in *Born in Slavery*).

face full of frowns, to have one's

> *Oh where were you now babe, Clarksdale mill burned down?*
> *"I was way down Sunflower with my face all fulla frowns."*
> —Charlie Patton, *"Moon Going Down,"* 1930

To frown conspicuously; a colloquialism used in a black field worker's 1937 description of an ex-slave: "With a face full of frowns, 'Parson' tells of a white

man persuading his mother to let him tie her to show that he was master"
(Rachel Austin, as quoted in *Born in Slavery*).

fade

> *Oh no fast-fadin' papa, you're fadin' too fast for me*
> *Listen here gal can't I love you, I can love you passionately.*
> —*Butterbeans and Susie, "Fast Fadin' Papa," 1928*

To lose sexual potency.

fade away

> *Be easy mama, don't you fade away*
> *I'm goin' where the Southern cross the Yellow Dog.*
> —*Sam Collins, "Yellow Dog Blues," 1927*

To vanish or disappear gradually; though construed as African American slang (cf. Major, 1994), this was a standard English expression, employed by Washington Irving in 1820 (cf. OED) and in the famous saying of General MacArthur: "Old soldiers never die, they just fade away."

fair

> *I said: "Ticket agent, how long has your train been gone?"*
> *Say: "Yon go the train that your fair brown left here on."*
> —*Blind Lemon Jefferson, "Booster Blues," 1926*

Beautiful (Skip James); an archaic modifier (OED) that is reserved in blues song for brown-complexioned females. In the following, *fair* means light:

> *She don't chew tobacco, swear she don't dip no snuff*
> *She ain't no high yellow woman, she's fair brown enough.*
> —*Luke Jordan, "If I Call You Mama," 1929*

fairo

> *I love my fairo, tell the world I do*
> *What makes me love her, you will come an' love her too.*
> —*Charlie Patton, "Magnolia Blues," 1929*

A barrelhouse term that "just means a woman" (Willie Moore). It may have been derived from *fair roebuck*, an 18th-century slang expression for a woman in the bloom of her beauty (Partridge), from *farrow*, obsolete standard English for a young pig (OED), or from *fairy* (see *fairy*). A suggestion by DeSalvo (2006) that the term was actually *pharoah* distorts the blues sensibility, in which females are distinctly subordinate and are anything but ruling figures; the above performer was himself notorious for beating female companions (cf. Calt and Wardlow, 1989).

fairy

> *I got a lovn' sweet fairy, she treats me nice and kind*
> *She treats me so lovin', she satisfies my mind.*
> —*Peg Leg Howell, "Fairy Blues," 1928*

A slang term for a female dating to the mid-19th century (Lighter, 1994) that seems to have originated as a colloquialism for a small, graceful woman (cf. OED, which dates it to 1838).

fall (1)

> My jelly, my roll
> Sweet mama don't you let it fall.
> —Charlie Patton, "Shake It And Break It (But Don't Let It Fall)," 1929

Become limp; applied to an erection.

fall (2)

> The reason I like the game, the game you call Georgia Skin
> Because when you fall, you can really take out again.
> —Memphis Minnie, "Georgia Skin," 1930

To be defeated by another card at *Georgia Skin*; from the same term as meaning "[t]o be captured (by a higher card)" (OED at *fall*, v.23e). It occurs in Zora Neale Hurston's *Cold Keener* (1930): "Nearly all you nigger biddies done fell—pay off."

falling down

> She caught the rumblin', I caught the fallin' down
> But I never see her, I never turn around.
> —Furry Lewis, "Falling Down Blues," 1927

? An inexplicable ailment recorded in a 1982 DARE file note: "Blacks in Memphis used to speak of friends who had the 'falling downs,' . . ." (DARE 2). The above performer was likewise from Memphis.

Fallin' Off A Log

> Takes a long-tail monkey, short-tail dog
> To do that dance they call Fallin' Off A Log.
> —Papa Charlie Jackson, "Mama, Don't You Think I Know?," 1925

A popular 1920s barrelhouse dance, also called Fall Off The Log (Skip James).

fanfoot

> You drink your whiskey, run around
> Get out in the street now like a fanfoot clown.
> —Blind Willie McTell, "Your Time To Worry," 1933

A black pejorative for an indiscriminately promiscuous female, who "don't care who she's with, long as she get what she wants [sex]" (Skip James). Gary Davis defined *fanfoot* as a woman who "gets drunk, falls down in the street . . . don't care who get on her; don't even know half the time," and distinguished *fanfoots* from other promiscuous women by virtue of their physical dirtiness. This term is misrendered by DARE 2 as signifying a "woman who openly seeks sexual relations." The prefix *fan* likely derives from *fen*, an archaic British slang term for "a common prostitute" (Grose, 1796) or from its original standard English meaning of mud or filth (OED). The suffix may have a similarly archaic basis in either *foot*, a term for an act of copulation dating to Shakespeare (SB), or *footy*, a term Grose (1796) cites as meaning despicable, and the EDD (1898) as obscene or base. The latter gave rise to *footer*, recorded by the EDD as "a term of the deepest contempt," which is almost certainly related to *fanfoot*.

fare thee well

> Told me in the fall, you didn't have no man at all
> Fare thee, sweet mama, fare thee well . . .
> Now you got more men than a two-ton truck can haul.
> —Joe Calicott, "Fare Thee Blues," 1929

A stereotyped parting address in blues rhetoric that is a carryover of archaic English, occurring in Shakespeare's *As You Like It* (1599): "'But fare thee well; thou art a gallant youth.'" It appears in the chorus of "Polly Wolly Doodle" (a popular minstrel song of the 1840s), by which time it was already obsolete as a conversational phrase.

fatmouth

> I was raised in Texas, schooled in Tennessee
> An' sugar you can't make no fatmouth outta me.
> —Blind Lemon Jefferson, "Got The Blues," 1926

A stock blues pejorative for a man who gives money to a female (Skip James), the implication being that he is being outwitted by a hustler.

Tom Shaw held: "'Fatmouth' is a man that a woman can do any kind of way, and there's nothin' he can do about it." The term was also current with female blues singers:

> He said: "Come here Dorothy, sit down on my knee
> You done took all my money, made a fatmouth outta me."
> —Dorothy Everetts, "Fatmouth Blues," 1930

fattening frogs for snakes

> The gals around here, are just like leeches
> They tarry in your orchard and steal your peaches
> I wish these women would let my man be
> Every man I get, they take him 'way from me
> So now, I'm tired of fattenin' frogs for snakes.
> —Virginia Liston, "I'm Sick Of Fattening Frogs For Snakes," 1925

Lavishing care on lovers who wind up with other partners, a catchphrase used to suggest that such is the inevitable result of efforts made on behalf of the opposite sex. This metaphor has a faulty basis, as it is hogs rather than frogs that are kept and fattened for consumption.

feed your friend with a long-handled spoon

> *Yes my mother always taught me: "Son, feed your friend with a long-*
> *handled spoon."*
> *She said: "Son if you feed them with these short ones, Lord, they will soon*
> *be no friends to you.*
> —Memphis Jug Band, *"Feed Your Friend With A Long-Handled Spoon,"*
> *1929*

A proverbial admonition to trust no one and keep one's seeming friends at arm's length. This saying is applied to eating with the devil in Shakespeare's *Comedy of Errors* ("'He must have a long spoon that must eat with the devil'") and *The Tempest* ("'This is a devil, and no monster: I will leave him; I have no long spoon'"). Parrish (1942) quotes a black speaker remarking on a "double-crosser": "My ole gran'mother use t'say: 'Them's the kind you gotta feed with a long spoon.'"

A similar proverbial sentiment is embodied in the following lyric:

> *... I may be right or wrong*
> *Watch your close friend, baby, then your enemies can't do you no harm.*
> —Robert Johnson, *"When You Got A Good Friend,"* 1936

As expressed by an ex-slave: "Remember, your closest friend is your worst enemy" (Marshal Butler, as quoted in *Born in Slavery*).

fever, the

> *My gal's got the fever, baby got the whoopin' cough*
> *Doggone a man let a woman be his boss.*
> —Peg Leg Howell, *"Monkey Man Blues,"* 1928

A Southern colloquialism for any illness marked by a fever (cf. DARE 2). In the above instance, the reference is probably to malaria.

fever gauge

> *Doctor get your fever gauge an' put it under my tongue*
> *Doctor said: "All you need, your lover in your arms."*
> —Bukka White, *"High Fever Blues,"* 1940

Thermometer; despite having the ring of a colloquialism, this term has no known standing as such.

fiddle (v.)

> *"Fiddle it, boy!"*
> —Charley Jordan, *"Starvation Blues,"* 1931

To play guitar in a spirited or expert fashion: "... oh, man—you're talkin' about how Skip did some *fiddlin'* then" (Skip James, as quoted in Calt).

field

> *The white man will go to the college, and the nigro to the field*
> *The white man will learn to read and write and the nigger will learn to*
> *steal.*
> —Bo Chatman, *"Good Old Turnip Greens," 1928*

Cotton field.

fine (a.)

> *Now Delilah she was a woman, fine an' fair*
> *Had pleasant looks and coal-black hair.*
> —Blind Willie Johnson, *"If I Had My Way," 1927*

Remarkably good-looking; dated standard English (OED) that is misconstrued as black English by Lighter (1994). The same sense is conveyed in the following:

> *Don't look for me on Sunday I wanna take pigmeat to Sunday school*
> *She's a fine-lookin' fair brown but she ain't never learned Lemon's rule.*
> —Blind Lemon Jefferson, *"Chock House Blues," 1926*

Another dated connotation of *fine,* applied to dress, appears in:

> *Somebody stole her, just ought to be mine*
> *She ain't so good-lookin', but she do dress fine.*
> —Ed Bell, *"Mamlish Blues," 1927*

In this sense *fine* means showy; smart (OED). "In de morning everybody dress up fine and go to the house whar de body is and stand around in de yard outside de house and don't go in" (Lucinda Davis, as quoted in *Born in Slavery*).

fine (n.)

> *When I got arrested, what you reckon was my fine?*
> *They give all coons, 'leven twenty-nine.*
> —Charlie Patton, *"Jim Lee Blues, Part Two," 1929*

Punishment or prison time; obsolete criminal slang dating to the 17th century (F&H, 1891). In modern parlance, *fine* means only a monetary penalty imposed by a court.

fireman

> *Engineer blew the whistle and the fireman he rung the bell*
> *An' my woman's on board, she was wavin' back "Fare you well."*
> —Son House, *"Depot Blues," 1942 (LC)*

"One who attends to a furnace or the fire of a steam-engine" (OED). This term has become obsolete since the passing of steam-powered locomotives in the 1940s.

first thing smokin'

> You can go to Memphis, find me there
> Catch the first thing smokin', find me on the road somewhere.
> —Sam Collins, "My Road Is Rough And Rocky," 1931

A still-used black term signifying a train; cf. Hurston (1942).

fish

> I runs a fish house, get my fish down by the sea
> You got a new kind of fish, sure do taste good to me.
> —Kansas City Kitty and Georgia Tom, "Fish House Blues," 1930

A slang term for vagina dating to around 1850 (Partridge).

fish house

See *fish*. A probable term for brothel, *fish market* (in British vogue c. 1850–1910) having stood for same (Partridge).

Fish Tail

> "I thought you told me you didn't know how to do that Fish Tail."
> —Romeo Nelson, "Head Rag Hop," 1929

A contemporary black dance, evidently involving various other dances, as indicated by the following description:

> Shake both your shoulders, move around slow
> Do a wicked dance an' Shimmy right on to the floor.
> Now rise up slow an' throw your hands into the air
> Count your money an' get it from everywhere.
> An' you get way back an' you Ball the Jack
> Do a Black Bottom, then you have got 'em
> You don't need no help to do that Fish Tail dance,
> You can do the Fish Tail by yourself.
> —Hociel Thomas, "Fish Tail Dance," 1925

fixin' to

> I'm lookin' funny in my eyes an' I believe I'm fixin' to die
> I know I was born to die but I hate to leave my children cryin'.
> —Bukka White, "Fixin' To Die Blues," 1940

About to, to be ready to or preparing to; a Southern colloquialism dating in print to c. 1854: "Aunt Lizy is just fixin' to go to church" (TT). Though noted in Spears (2006) as "Hospital jocular, cruel word play," *fixing to die* is also Southern: "I was able to tell him his brother was fixin' to die" (North Carolina speaker on "Coast to Coast A.M." radio program, 3/3/2008).

flag one's train

> Man if that's your lover, you better pin her to your side
> If she flag my train, papa Lemon's gon' let her ride.
> —Blind Lemon Jefferson, "Match Box Blues," 1927

To accost another sexually or indicate one's own sexual availability; said of females. This expression originated as white slang meaning "to catch the attention of" (cf. Lighter [1994] at *flag someone's train*).

flop-house

> *Clothes is gettin' shabby, shoes won't stand fixin' any more*
> *Now if things don't get no better, to the flop-house another poor scuffler*
>   *will go.*
> —Leroy Henderson, "Good Scuffler Blues," 1935

A commercial dormitory offering cheap sleeping accommodations to unregistered transients on a nightly basis. They were described thusly in a 1923 study of the homeless: "'Flop-houses' are nearly all alike. Guests sleep on the floor or in bare, wooden bunks. The only privilege they buy is the privilege to lie down somewhere in a warm room" (Anderson, 1923). Such establishments ceased to exist in the 1940s or 1950s; their modern equivalent, the *homeless shelter,* is operated by the state and does not charge admission.

flowery

> *Canned heat ain't no good, boy, keep you with a flowery mind* ·
> *Jailhouse doors open, an' you got a ramblin' mind.*
> —Arthur Pettis, "Good Boy Blues," 1928

A slang term for jailhouse (ATS).

folkses

> *Let me tell you folkses, how he treated me*
> *Well he put me in a cell it was dark as it could be.*
> —Charlie Patton, "High Sheriff Blues," 1934

A Southern variant of *folks,* first recorded in 17th-century Virginia (ADD). It occurs in Langston Hughes and Zora Neale Hurston's *The Mule-Bone* (1931): "Wait till I come back, folkses."

fool about (a)

> *I remember the time just before the war*
> *Colored man used to hunt about chips and straw.*
> *But now bless God old Master's dead*
> *Colored man plum fool about the feather bed.*
> —Cannon's Jug Stompers, "Feather Bed," 1928

Enamored of, to the point of obstinacy. (Skip James: "I was young, and I was a fool, too. A fool about my 'protection' [weaponry].") Cf. DARE 2 at *fool,* n. 3.

fool about (v.)

> *Hangin' around and foolin' about'll*
> *Sure get you down (2)*

If you hangin' 'round and foolin' about too long.
—*Ollis Martin, "Police And High Sheriff Come Ridin' Down," 1927*

A variant of to *fool (a)round,* "to 'hang about' aimlessly" (OED).

fool around

St. Louis is on a-fire, Chicago is burnin' down
I am sick an' tired, of my baby foolin' 'round.
—*Jack Kelly, "I Believe I'll Go Back Home," 1933*

General slang of 1920s vintage meaning "to engage in casual, extramarital, or non-coital sexual activity" (OED, draft addition, December 2007). See *run around.*

fool with

I fooled with women till I lost everything I own
It was a married woman, caused me to lose my home.
—*Clifford Gibson, "Hard-Headed Blues," 1929*

To involve oneself with; perhaps short for *fool around with.* (See *fool around.*)

for

If I don't go crazy, I'm sure gonna lose my mind
'Cause I can't sleep for dreamin', sure can't stay awoke for cryin'.
—*Ramblin' Thomas, "Sawmill Moan," 1928*

Used to denote an obstacle (OED), as in Samuel Richardson's *Pamela* (1740): "Mrs. Jervis could not speak for crying." This idiom seems to have survived in black speech after becoming passé in standard English; the narrator of Ralph Ellison's *Invisible Man* (1952) notes: "I could hardly get to sleep for dreaming of revenge."

for days

When a man get down, his trouble last always
Your gal will leave you an' be gone for days and days.
—*Willie Baker, "Crooked Woman Blues," 1929*

For an extended period of time; cf. Folb, who recounts it as an idiom of black urban youth from the 1960s and 1970s.

'fore day

I'm gonna buy me a bulldog, watch my old lady whilest I sleep
'Cause women these days, is so doggone crooked,
till they might make a 'fore day creep.
—*Blind Joe Reynolds, "Outside Woman Blues," 1930*

According to Clapin (c. 1902), an oft-heard idiom for "[t]he period of time immediately before sunrise." In black speech, the expression persists, less precisely, to indicate an unspecified period before daybreak (cf. Smitherman, 2000, who renders it as *foe day*).

'fore day prayer

> *I take my daily*
> *"Daily 'fore day prayer"*
> *I didn't have me nobody, speakin' Bible here.*
> *—Charlie Patton, "When Your Way Gets Dark," 1929*

A black Fundamentalist term for a prayer said upon rising, called a *morning prayer* in white Biblical rhetoric.

'fore God

> *... Blue the whole night long*
> *Oh I swear 'fore God the man I love is in the wrong.*
> *—Louise Johnson, "All Night Long Blues," 1930*

Given by Bartlett (1877) as "a negro asservation." Morgan quotes a black Virginian from 1676: "Here! Shoot me, foregod ..." It endured in Harlem dialogue appearing in Chester Himes's 1959 novel *The Real Cool Killers:* "Boss, listen, I beg you, I swear 'fore God."

forty

> *Bo weevil told his wife: "Let's take this forty here," Lordie!*
> *—Charlie Patton, "Mississippi Bo Weavil Blues," 1929*

Forty acres; a conventional plot of farm land amounting to a quarter of a square mile (cf. DARE 2).

Four, Big

> *And the Big Four, Big Four, it's a mean old train to ride*
> *She took my babe away and left me dissatisfied.*
> *—Charley Jordan, "Big Four Blues," 1930*

A popular nickname dating to the 1890s for the Cleveland, Cincinnati, Chicago, and St. Louis rail line (ATS), absorbed by the New York Central in 1930.

four-eleven forty-four (4–11–44)

> *"Mister Man, Mister Man, please open the door*
> *I wanna play four-eleven forty-four."*
> *—Papa Charlie Jackson, "Four Eleven Forty Four," 1926*

A synonym of *policy* dating to the 1890s, when it appeared on the cover of *Aunt Sally's Policy Playing Dream Book.* Its prominence among blacks, who were said to regard it as a lucky numbers bet, likely arose from a black bettor's having won a considerable sum by playing it. In the 1980s, *4–11–44* surfaced as a black term for penis (cf. DCS).

frazzling

> *Penitentiara, penitentiara, ain't a frazzlin' thing*
> *I been mistreated, it ain't a frazzlin' thing.*
> *—Bessie Tucker, "Whistling Woman Blues," 1929*

A Southern term for trifling, measly; cf. DARE 2.

freakish

> She called me a freakish man, what more was there to do?
> Just 'cause she said I was strange, that did not make it true.
> —George Hannah, "Freakish Man Blues," 1930

Black slang for "an effeminate man or a mannish woman" (*Sunday News* article on Harlem speakeasy speech, 11/3/1929).

free-hearted

> Talk about free-hearted I declare I'm an honest man
> Give my woman money, broke her apron-strings.
> —Furry Lewis, "I Will Turn Your Money Green," 1928

Generous; a largely Southern colloquialism (cf. DARE 2, WD).

freeze to

> Aw freeze to me mama, please don't let me roam
> Freeze to me mama, with both skin and bone
> Freeze to me mama, before I go home.
> —Barbecue Bob, "Freeze To Me Mama," 1929

To cling or hold tight to; a colloquialism dating in print to 1851 (cf. DARE 2 at *freeze on to*).

friend-boy, friend-girl

> You can run, you can run, tell my friend-boy Willie Brown
> Lord that I'm standin' at the crossroad babe, I believe I'm sinkin' down.
> —Robert Johnson, "Cross Road Blues," 1936

Male or female friend; an inversion in the manner of *carbox* that bears no romantic or sexual connotations. A variant, *friend-woman*, appears on one blues:

> Girls if you got a good man and don't want him taken away from you
> Don't ever tell your friend-woman how your man can do.
> —Ida Cox, "Fore Day Creep," 1927

friends have to part

> Did you get that letter now, mailed in your back yard?
> It 'twas sad word(s) to say but the best o' friends have to part.
> —Kid Bailey, "Rowdy Blues," 1929

A proverb originally published as "Farewell and be hanged! Friends must part" in Dr. Thomas Fuller's *Gnomolgia* (1732). In the above song it is cynically invoked by an apparent *back door man* who has initiated a break-up.

from sun to sun

> These here women, they want these men to act like them oxen done
> Grab a pick and shovel and roll from sun to sun.
> —Blind Lemon Jefferson, "Chockhouse Blues," 1927

From sunup to sundown, also known as "can to can't" (i.e., can see to can't see). Both terms were used by blacks with regard to plantation labor: "We wuked from sun to sun" (Andrew Boone, as quoted in *Born in Slavery*).

front door

If you go to the butcher, if you go to the butcher
To get . . . your sausage grind
If he can't get it in the front door, he don't want it behind.
—*Kokomo Arnold, "Let Your Money Talk," 1935*

A corollary of *back door,* referring to the vaginal orifice (cf. Lighter, 1994).

fucked out

Say you know says come here woman, said an' lay your black self down
You know I'm gonna fuck you, right there till you're plum fucked out.
—*Walter Roland, "I'm Gonna Shave You Dry" (unissued), 1935*

Sexually exhausted from intercourse, an expression that dates in print to 1866 (Lighter, 1994).

function

"We gonna have a function here tonight."
—*Cow Cow Davenport, "Mooch Piddle," 1929*

A black term for a house party, drawn from the standard English use of the word in reference to a formal social gathering (cf. OED). A variant, *chitlin function,* called attention to the food sold at such affairs:

"...hello Buddy, where you goin'?"
"Well, I'm goin' to that chitlin function."
—*Buddy Burton/Irene Sanders, "New Block And Tackle," 1936*

funny

Says I like your mama, sister too
I did like your papa but your papa wouldn't do.
I met your papa on the corner the other day
I soon found out that he was funny that-a-way.
—*Kokomo Arnold, "The Twelves (The Dirty Dozen)," 1935*

Sexually off-kilter; applied to homosexuals. In the latter sense this term survived in black teenage speech of the 1960s and 1970s (cf. Folb).

fuss (n. 1)

Tell all you men somethin', don't you raise no fuss
'Cause most of these here women won't do to trust.
—*Willie Baker, "Ain't It A Good Thing?," 1929*

A loud disturbance or racket; a Southern colloquialism, as is the following use of the term (cf. DARE 2).

fuss (n. 2)

> *Lord me an' my black gal had a fuss last night*
> *Will you let me tell you what it was all about?*
> —*Charlie Pickett, "Crazy 'Bout My Black Gal," 1937*

A quarrel or argument (cf. DARE 2).

fuss an' fight

> *I love to fuss an' fight (2)*
> *Lord an' get sloppy drunk offa bottle an' bond*
> *And walk the streets all night.*
> —*Charlie Patton, "Elder Greene Blues," 1929*

A black embellishment of *fuss* (i.e., to argue vociferously or pick quarrels; cf. DARE 2). "So many married folks don't do nothin but fuss an' fight." (George Morrison, as quoted in *Born in Slavery*)

gal in the white folks' yard, a

> *I got a gal in the white folks' yard*
> *She brings me meat an' she brings me lard.*
> —*Luke Jordan, "Cocaine Blues," 1927*

A cook employed by a white family. Such figures were known for catering to gigolo musicians: "Those boys I used to sing with were really tough babies.... They were sweet-back men ... these boys used to all have a sweet mama—I guess I will have to tell it as it is—they was what I would call, maybe a fifth-class whore. They got something when they could and when they couldn't, they worked in the white people's yard" (Jelly Roll Morton, as quoted in Lomax). See *yard*.

gallinipper

> *I would say gallinippers, them gallinippers bite too hard*
> *I sat back in my kitchen, and just sprayed it up in my back yard.*
> —*Blind Lemon Jefferson, "Mosquito Moan," 1929*

A Southern term for a large variety of mosquito (cf. DARE 2).

gamblin' man

> *Kind Stella was a good gal, known to be a good man's friend*
> *She take money from her husband, give it to her gamblin' men.*
> —Lucille Bogan, "Kind Stella Blues," 1927

One who ostensibly lives by gambling. In black speech of the blues era, such gender-based formations often replaced predicate nouns as descriptions of people engaged in various activities. Thus, *gamblin' man* = gambler; *hustlin' woman* = hustler; *lyin' man* = liar; *ramblin' woman* = rambler; *woman man* = womanizer. See *traveling man*.

game-fish

> *Some low-down scroundrel been fishin' all in my pond*
> .... *Catchin' all my game-fish and grindin' up the bone.*
> —Bo Carter, "Old Devil," 1938

Literally, a standard English term for "a fish which affords sport to the angler in its capture" (OED). In actuality, such fish would inhabit streams or oceans rather than ponds.

gang

> *Tore the railroad down, so that Sunshine Special can't run*
> *I got a gang of women, they ride from sun to sun.*
> —Blind Lemon Jefferson, "Sunshine Special," 1927

A large amount; associated with black speech (cf. Major, 1970; DARE 2).

Gatlin' gun

> *Babe when I walk to town*
> *With my razor an' Gatlin' gun*
> *I'll cut you if you stand, and shoot you if you run.*
> —Casey Bill, "Sold My Soul To The Devil," 1937

A blues misnomer for submachine gun, the Gatling gun having been a multi-barreled machine gun invented during the Civil War and used as a battlefield weapon.

gauge

> *I started blowing my gauge, and I was having my fun*
> *I spied the police, and I started to run.*
> —Lil Green, "Knockin' Myself Out," 1941

Black slang of early 1930s vintage for marijuana (cf. Lighter, 1994); from the archaic 17th-century British slang term *gage*, meaning a pipeful of tobacco (cf. OED at *gage*, n.2.). See *get one's gauge up*.

gay cat (v.)

> *"Hey man, I went out gay cattin' last night,*
> *an' my gal, she threw a party for me."*
> —Blind Lemon Jefferson, "Maltese Cat Blues," 1928

According to Mayo Williams, "gay cattin' was just playin' around." More specifically, it meant to chase women. The term was derived from the noun *gay cat*, 20th-century hobo slang for a tramp who "hangs about for women" (Partridge), which itself evolved from the 18th-century phrase *gay man* (F&H, 1893). Altogether, F&H records nine 19th-century expressions in which *gay* is indicative of sexual activity or immorality; its present-day association with homosexuality marks a relatively recent development.

gay catter

> *. . . Soon as you get on your feet*
> *A gang of gay catters you sure can meet*
> *But it's mighty strange without a doubt*
> *Nobody knows you when you're down and out . . .*
> —Pine Top Smith, "Nobody Knows You When You're Down And Out," 1929

A playboy; woman-chaser.

geechie

> *"Go on old geechie, I ain't studyin' about you . . .*
> *Now we gonna do the dance now we call the geechie dance . . .*
> *I'm gonna give you some music you call the geechie music now."*
> —Blind Blake, "Southern Rag," 1927

An African American native of the low country of Georgia and South Carolina, a people named for their proximity to the Ogeechee River in Georgia and known for their distinctive culture, which had more African aspects than was evident among other blacks of the early 20th century.

Georgia Crawl

> *Feel like a broke-down engine, ain't got no drivers at all*
> *What makes me love my woman: she can really do the Georgia Crawl.*
> —Blind Willie McTell, "Broke Down Engine Blues," 1931

A dance of late 1920s vintage that may have been a regional variant of the *Cootie Crawl*.

Georgia grind

> *Some like it slow, some like it fast*
> *But I like my Georgia grind, half an' half*
> *Pass my house an' hear me sighin':*
> *"Great God, daddy, won't you take your time?"*
> *'Cause I'm crazy about my Georgia, I love my Georgia grind*
> —Lucille Bogan, "My Georgia Grind," 1930

Sexual intercourse. This term arose as a name for a dance that itself was probably likened to sex, and dated to at least 1915, when the ragtime piano instrumental "Georgia Grind" was written by Ford T. Dabney. See *grind*.

Georgia ham

> *She don't dress shabby, and wears a tam*
> *Legs look as nice, as Georgia ham*
> —Memphis Jug Band, "Everybody's Talking About Sadie Green," 1930

A black term for watermelon.

Georgia rub

> *I'm goin' down Market Street*
> *Where the men and women all do meet*
> *That's where the men do the Georgia rub*
> *Women fall in line with a big washtub.*
> —Tampa Red, "The Duck Yas Yas Yas," 1929

? Evidently, a term for sexual intercourse, with *washtub* serving as a song euphemism for female genitalia (see *rub*).

Georgia Skin

> *The reason I like the game, the game you call Georgia Skin*
> *Because when you fall, you can really take out again.*
> —Memphis Minnie, "Georgia Skin," 1930

A black card game fashionable among levee, lumber, and turpentine workers, perhaps because such figures were periodically flush with money. In a prevalent version of Georgia Skin, the dealer charges the other players an arbitrary amount to draw a single card from his deck. After the players bet various sums, the dealer turns a card; if none of the previously dealt cards (known as "fall cards") match it, the dealer wins the bets. Jelly Roll Morton said of it: "Of all the games I've ever seen, no game has so many cheats right in front of your eyes . . ." (Morton, as quoted in Lomax). The second element of its name undoubtedly derived from a gambling term (not connoting cheating) recorded in 1812 by Vaux: "To strip a man of all his money at play, is termed *skinning* him" (quoted in OED).

get

> *Aw the rollin' mill, sure Lord burned down last night*
> *I can't get that, brown in this town today.*
> —Bo Weavil Jackson, "Some Scream High Yellow," 1926

With respect to females, to possess carnally, *get* being equivalent to *have* (q.v.).

get down (1)

> *Some folks say a preacher won't steal*
> *I caught three in my cornfield.*
> *One had a yellow, one had a brown*
> *Looked over in the meadow one was gettin' down.*
> —Kansas Joe, "Preacher's Blues," 1931

To have sexual intercourse; black-originated slang. This term still survives with assorted meanings, including to have intercourse and to dance (UD).

get down (2)

> So please get down big boy, man you big enough to walk
> And when I tell you about a job, ooh Lord you say you don't want to talk.
> —Washboard Sam, "Get Down Brother," 1941

"[T]o get down to business; apply oneself in earnest; get busy" (Lighter [1994] at *down*); a slang phrase of probable black origin.

get in

> You stay out all night, drink your gin
> When you come home now, you won't get in.
> —Kansas City Kitty and Georgia Tom, "Close Made Papa," 1931

To enter a female sexually.

get it fixed

> A girl with a Ford and a guy named Jim
> He liked her and she liked him
> Ford broke down in a quiet park
> Didn't get home 'till after dark
> But they got it fixed, ain't no doubt
> Nobody knows what it's all about
> Too bad that the news got out
> But they got it fixed right on.
> —Tampa Red and Georgia Tom, "But They Got It Fixed Right On," 1930

A song double entendre based on *get fixed*, a slang expression meaning to engage in sexual intercourse (cf. Lighter [1997], which traces it to 1948).

get off

> I know a man by the name of Jack Frost,
> Originated the dance they call "Gettin' Off."
> Every night about half past twelve,
> You can hear all the pretty gals yell:
> "Get off with me, honey, bend your knee!
> Don't get too strong, 'cause you can't last long
> Gettin' off with me!"
> —Coot Grant, "Get Off With Me," 1931

To attain orgasm; slang of 19th-century vintage (cf. Lighter, 1994). The above performer's attempt to provide a verbal fig leaf for a vulgar expression by fabricating a dance of the same name is similarly at work in *boogie woogie*. *doodle it back*, *scronch*, and *shake that thing* (q.v.).

get one's gauge up

> *Let's get our gauge up papa, let our love come down*
> *Get leapin' drunk, an' leave this low-down town.*
> —*Bertha Henderson, "Let Your Love Come Down," 1928*

To reach a level of peak excitement, usually from marijuana. This phrase is of moot racial origin; it survived as criminal slang into the 1950s, meaning "to achieve peak marijuana stimulation" (DAUL at *gage*).

get one told

> *Grandpa got, grandma told*
> *He says her jelly roll was most too old.*
> —*Ma Rainey, "Hear Me Talkin' To You," 1928*

To tell someone off; a black colloquialism (cf. DARE 2 at *get someone told*).

get over to

> *Trouble an' worry, have killed more people than anything else*
> *An' if it get over to you, don't blame nobody else but yourself.*
> —*Buddy Boy Hawkins, "Yellow Woman Blues," 1927*

Reach.

get shut of

> *Now I changed my pants, changed my shirt*
> *I changed baby to get shut of the dirt.*
> —*Sleepy John Estes, "Everybody Oughta Make A Change," 1938*

Get rid of; a dated colloquialism based on an obsolete meaning of *shut* (OED). It appears in Faulkner's *Go Down, Moses* (1942) as a plantation ledger entry in reference to a bothersome slave: "Mar 23th 1856 . . . Get shut of him."

get to

> *I lay down last night . . . tried to take my rest*
> *My mind got to ramblin', like a wild geese in the west.*
> —*Skip James, "Devil Got My Woman," 1931*

To begin; a black colloquialism used with -ing verbs: ["]I got to rambling trying to get better" (Emmett Augusta Byrd, as quoted in *Born in Slavery*). "Those guys on those camps, would even get to squabblin' and fightin' at the dinner table . . ." (James, as quoted in Calt and Wardlow, 1989).

get to the place

> *Canned heat's just like morphine, it crawls all through your bones*
> *An' if you keep on usin' canned heat mama, you*
> *get to the place you just won't leave it alone.*
> —*Will Shade, "You Better Let That Stuff Alone," 1928*

Reach the point; a black colloquialism found in Zora Neale Hurston's *Spunk* (1935): "It got to the place where I had done tasted all the food in the world."

ghost woman

Had a ghost woman, sure do keep me thin
Take the money I get, from the L&N.
—George Carter, "Ghost Woman Blues," 1929

Black parlance for a female ghost, identified by gender on invisible grounds. An ex-slave reported of one: " . . . the ghost woman thinks I is too old to dig" (Yetman).

gig

I says: "Go on, mister writer, that gig ain't comin' out."
He said: "You better get on it, I know what I'm talkin' about."
—Bumble Bee Slim, "Policy Dream Blues," 1935

A three-number policy combination, as opposed to a *saddle* (two-number combination) or *horse* (four-number combination), both of which were seemingly outmoded during the blues era. For these terms, cf. Bartlett (1877).

gill (jill)

He don't work, he call himself a "smart gill"
He don't care nothin' about nobody, no he just out for himself.
—Roosevelt Sykes, "Papa Sweetback Blues," 1930

Fellow; an underworld term of 18th-century British vintage that survived in 20th-century (chiefly circus) speech (cf. Lighter, 1994).

girl

When I stay at home baby, you don't treat me right
Say best time I have, girl, when you're outta my sight.
—Cannon's Jug Stompers, "Heart-Breakin' Blues," 1928

Among blacks, a still-common familiar term of address for an adult female.

give

Aw, baby how can it be?
You will give everybody, but you won't give me.
—Clifford Gibson, "Sunshine Moan," 1929

Give *pussy* to.

give down

I walked 61 Highway, till I give down in my knees
Lookin' for that M&O, but she came on that Santa Fe.
—Will Batts, "Highway No. 61 Blues," 1933

To give out, become exhausted (ADD, which lists a single citation, from Kentucky in 1938).

give one the air

You went to Memphis, found a butter an' egg man there
And now you're trying to, give your regular man the air.
—Charlie Spand, "Ain't Gonna Stand For That," 1929

To reject; then-current American slang (OED) that probably arose from the vaudeville expression *to get the air,* meaning to be canceled (see "The Argot of Vaudeville," *New York Times,* 12/30/1917).

glad hands, shake

> *I'm gonna shake glad hands I say, Lord of your lovin' boy*
> *Fixin' to eat my breakfast in, Shelby, Illinois.*
> *—Charlie Patton, "Rattlesnake Blues," 1929*

A variant of *to glad hand,* to proffer a ceremoniously friendly handshake (often masking antipathy in the process); conventional slang dating to the late 19th century (cf. Lighter, 1994). The expression probably arose from the rote phrase "Glad to meet you."

go (1)

> *Early this mornin', when you knocked upon my door*
> *An' I said: "Hello Satan, I believe it's time to go."*
> *—Robert Johnson, "Me And The Devil Blues," 1937*

To die; standard English (OED). The euphemistic *gone* rarely occurs in blues:

> *When I die, you may bury me in a Stetson hat*
> *Tell my good gal I'm gone when I'm still a-standin' pat.*
> *—Blind Lemon Jefferson, "Pneumonia Blues," 1929*

go (2)

> *My black mama stays apart of this town*
> *Can't nothin' go when the poor girl is around.*
> *—Son House, "My Black Mama, Part Two," 1930*

Go on; happen. The above couplet indicates that the presence of the "black mama" causes others to restrict their social activities, out of distaste for her complexion. See *go down (1).*

go, to have no place to

> *Brown I ain't got no money, and got me no place to go*
> *But if you take me back baby I'll never do wrong no more.*
> *—Seth Richards, "Lonely Seth Blues," 1928*

To be homeless; to have nowhere to sleep.

go dead

> *"Oh doctor, doctor, what can a good man do?"*
> *Say: "Your girl ain't dyin', but she done gone dead on you."*
> *—Blind Lemon Jefferson, "Gone Dead On You Blues," 1928*

To die; an American colloquialism (ADD).

go down (1)

> *You better let the deal go down*
> *Skin game comin' to a close*

An' you better let the deal go down.

—Peg Leg Howell, "Skin Game Blues," 1928)

Occur; happen. This expression, of apparent black origin, seems to have arisen in conjunction with gambling. In the following song, *deal* is likely figurative:

It's the last fair deal, goin' down, good Lord

On that Gulport Island road.

—Robert Johnson, "Last Fair Deal Gone Down," 1936

By 1946, it had become general slang (cf. OED).

go down (2)

I done had my fun, if I don't get well no more

Lord my health is failin' me, and I believe I'm goin' down slow.

—St. Louis Jimmy, "Going Down Slow," 1941

To decline in health, deteriorate; standard English (OED). As used in the past tense on race records, it is equivalent to *died*:

When I'm dead and gone, and six feet in the ground

You can only say, there's a good man has gone down.

—Leroy Carr, "Take a Walk Around the Corner," 1934

go head on

I go head on, and do the best I can

I know every woman in the world, love her outside man.

—Big Boy Crudup, "She's Gone," 1945

To go about one's ordinary business (Skip James); a black colloquialism found in Zora Neale Hurston's *Woofing* (1931): "Aw, go head on, woman, and leave me be!" In standard English, *head on* = head first (OED).

go one's bail

When you hear the captain callin' you: "Men, let's move that rail."

An' if you don't do what he says you'll have to, get someone else to go your bail.

—Buddy Boy Hawkins, "Workin' On The Railroad," 1927

To post bail on behalf of an arrested person; common blues terminology that seemingly originated with Southern blacks. The above couplet remarks on the practice of white bosses of bailing out favored black laborers for petty crimes.

go to

The white man will go to the college, and the nigro to the field

The white man will learn to read and write and the nigger will learn to steal.

—Bo Chatman, "Good Old Turnip Greens," 1928

A standard English phrase "used to imply the additional notion of entering on a mode of life, employment, or the like, which is associated with it; e.g., in **to go to college, to the university, to prison**, etc." (OED). In this instance, *going to the field* implies a dismal field hand's life marked by petty theft.

go to France

> *Lord he likes it slow, when he goes to dance*
> *He likes it slow, when he goes to France.*
> —*Trixie Smith, "He Likes It Slow," 1925*

To engage in oral sex; from the verb *French,* dating in print to 1923 (for the latter, cf. Lighter, 1994).

go to the bushes

> *Aw Mister Charlie, you had better watch your men*
> *They all goin' to the bushes, and they all goin' in.*
> —*Jack Kelly, "Red Ripe Tomatoes," 1933*

To relieve oneself outdoors; a Southern colloquialism occurring in Faulkner's *The Mansion* (1959): "'Durn it, let me out on that bridge. I ain't been to the bushes this morning.'"

god-dog

> *Now I got two little women, you can't tell 'em apart*
> *Said one is my livin', and the other one is my heart, god-dog it.*
> —*Bo Carter, "My Little Mind," 1940*

A black euphemism for *god-damn* found in Ellison's *Invisible Man* (1952): "'Oh, goddog, daddy-o,' he said with a sudden bluster."

goggle-eyed perch

> *I got dead shrimp here, someone fishin' in my pond*
> *Catchin' my goggle-eyed perches, an' they barbecuin' the bone.*
> —*Robert Johnson, "Dead Shrimp Blues," 1937*

A Southern term for a rock bass (DARE 2), the first element deriving from a standard English adjective for prominent, staring eyes (cf. OED). As with *game-fish* (q.v.), the above couplet refers to girlfriends.

goo-goo eyes

> *Now could you blame the colored man for makin' them goo-goo eyes?*
> *When he sat down the President's table he began to smile.*
> —*Gus Cannon, "Can You Blame The Colored Man?," 1927*

A term for amorous glances dating to 1900 (OED) that has survived into the 21st century, and is often used to suggest idiotic infatuation. In the above work, it is employed to denigrate Booker T. Washington, whose 1901 visit to the White House (the subject of the song) created a storm of white Southern vituperation.

good

> *My babe, my babe, certainly was good to me*
> *She tore up my trouble, broke up my misery.*
> *. . . She made from one to five dollars every day*
> *I didn't have to do nothin' but lay around an' throw it away.*
> —Kansas Joe, "My Babe Blues," 1935

Generous to a gigolo. See *good gal, good girl.*

good book, the

> *I cried last night an' I ain't gonna cry anymore*
> *'Cause that good book tells us you've got to reap just what you sow.*
> —Charlie Patton, "Pea Vine Blues," 1929

The Bible, a dated Southern colloquialism used with the implication that there are no other good books. It appears in Opie Read's *Len Gansett* (1888), based on white Arkansas dialect: "'The good book may say that man e'rns whut he eats by the sweat of his brow, but it oughter say by the sweat uv his wife's brow.'"

good common sense

> *You know I bought the groceries, an' I pay the rent*
> *She try to make me wash her clothes but I got good common sense.*
> —Richard "Rabbit" Brown, "James Alley Blues," 1927

A colloquial or black embellishment of *good sense,* standard English for "[n]ative soundness of judgement, esp. in the ordinary affairs of life" (OED). Cf. Gwaltney (1980): ". . . I have good common sense, so I don't sit here like a fool and believe everything I see on this TV."

good friend

> *I've often sit an' wondered, mama who could my good friend be?*
> *Now I got myself a mama, means everything to me.*
> —Walter Davis, "Just Wondering," 1936

A black colloquial term for a romantic partner.

good gal, good girl

> *Aw did you dream lucky, an' wake up cold in hand?*
> *Then you wanna see some good gal, aw ain't got no man.*
> —Bo Weavil Jackson, "Some Scream High Yellow," 1926

A soft touch; applied to a female (frequently a prostitute) who can be counted on to ease the lot of a gigolo:

> *Kind Stella was a good gal, known to be a good man's friend*
> *She take money from her husband, give it to her gamblin' men.*
> —Lucille Bogan, "Kind Stella Blues," 1927

Frankie was a good ol' gal, everybody know
She paid one half a hundred, for the makin' of her man's clothes.
—Charlie Patton, "Frankie And Albert," 1929

A relatively ingenuous understanding of this term was offered by Tom Shaw: "'Good gal' means some gal that's really good to you and will go for whatever you want...." Gary Davis similarly said: "That's a woman, you understand, she's very interested in your affairs ... she always looks out for you...."

good hair

I will tell you girls one thing, you know it really is true
Baby you know you got good hair, but you bought it from the Jew.
—Charley Jordan, "Tight Haired Mama Blues," 1931

Straight hair, reminiscent of that of Caucasians or Native Americans.

good ol' boy

Windstorm come, an' it blowed my house away
I'm a good ol' boy, but I ain't got nowhere to stay.
—Furry Lewis, "Dry Land Blues," 1928

A Southern term of general approbation for males, mistakenly construed by the OED as applying only to "[a] white male of the rural southern United States..." and by DARE 2 as "[a] man who embodies the traditional values of the White, rural South...." A feminine equivalent, perhaps exclusive to blacks, appears on this blues recording:

Well I walked up close I looked down in her face
Good ol' gal, you got to lay here till Judgement Day.
—Son House, "My Black Mama, Part Two," 1930

good provider

I wakes up every mornin' with a jinx all 'round my bed
I have been a good provider but I believe I have been misled.
—Charlie Patton, "Revenue Man Blues," 1934

A husband whose family is free from want, thanks to his efforts as a breadwinner. It appears in Thomas Wolfe's *Look Homeward, Angel* (1929): "... he could not bear to be thought incapable of the support of his family—one of his most frequent boasts was that he was 'a good provider.'" By itself, *provider* stood for "A husband, or mate" (Clapin, c. 1902).

good road

So many wagons, they have cut the good road down
And the gal I love, her mama don't want me around.
—Blind Lemon Jefferson, "Chockhouse Blues," 1926

A road deemed suitable for automobile traffic by virtue of being topped with gravel or asphalt, particularly (in the South) one paved as a result of the Shackleford Good Roads Bill (a federal program enacted in 1917).

good scout

> We can be buddies, you are a good scout
> But the road you are traveling, is done played out.
> —Washboard Sam, "I'm Not The Lad," 1941

A good person; slang dating in print to 1933 (cf. OED at *scout*).

good (old) time, in (the)

> I went down to Huntsville, I did not go to stay
> I just got there in the good ol' time, to wear that ball and chain.
> —Henry Thomas, "Run, Mollie, Run," 1927

At the right moment; archaic English appearing in Shakespeare's *Comedy of Errors* (1594): "'Learne to iest [jest] in good time, there's a time for any thing.'" The most recent OED citation for this phrase is 1639.

good-time flat

> I'm the good-time rounder, I runs a good-time flat
> Sometimes for two or three weeks my mama don't know where I'm at.
> —Barbecue Bob, "Good Time Rounder," 1929

An apartment where liquor or sex is sold; Jelly Roll Morton recalled of an associate: "Game Kid played the piano all day long ... moving around from one girl's house to another—what we called the 'good-time' houses ..." (Morton, as quoted in Lomax).

good-time rounder

See *good-time flat*. A pimp or gigolo; synonymous with *sweet back* (q.v.). Gary Davis said of this figure: "He's a 'play-about' boy.... Make a woman buy him a suit of clothes.... He's called a 'good-time boy.' ... He don't do nothin' but walk around all dressed up, you know; he ain't gonna work nowhere.... More than apt to be with some woman older than he is, 'cause he can't fool no younger one."

good-time women

> I'm gonna build me a heaven of my own. (3)
> I'm gonna give all good-time women a home. (3)
> —Henry Thomas, "Texas Worried Blues," 1928

Prostitutes, most likely those who worked in "good-time" establishments.

good work, the

> I asked the good girl to kiss me some
> She says: "Wait until my dinner get on."
> Dinner got on an' she kissed me some,
> Now you know we carryin' the good work on.
> —Bo Carter, "Dinner Blues," 1936

Sexual activity. For other correlations between sex and work, see *roll, do one's work, working,* and *workin' woman*.

goofer dust

> *I'm gonna sprinkle a little goofer dust, all around your nappy head*
> *You wake up some of these mornin's, find your own self dead.*
> —*Charlie Spand, "Big Fat Mama Blues," 1929*

A concoction, said to consist of graveyard dust, used in malevolent black witchcraft. Puckett (1925) reported: "Some hoodoos burn a kind of powder called 'goopher dust,' which represents the person being hoodooed, who is perhaps miles away at the time. This causes the conjured individual to lose his personality and to become sick or insane." Hurston (1935) wrote: "It will be noted that frequently graveyard dust is required in the practice of hoodoo, goofer dust as it is often called." The term *goofer* is of African origin and has been linked to a Kikongo word, *kufwa*, to die (cf. OED).

gown

> *I laid at my window this mornin', watchin' the mornin' sun go down*
> *I was thinkin' about my pretty mama, I had to walk in my mornin' gown.*
> —*Texas Bill Day, "Good Mornin' Blues," 1929*

Loose-fitting male attire, a sense of the word that is quite obsolete, though not given as such by the OED. See *mornin' gown*.

grab

> *My daddy got no shoe, partner it's done got cold*
> *I'm gonna grab me somebody, if I don't make myself some dough.*
> —*Memphis Minnie, "Hustlin' Woman Blues," 1935*

Rob. In 19th-century American slang, a *grab* stood for a robbery, while the verb meant to steal (cf. F&H, 1893).

graveyard love

> *Did you ever love a girl and she do not care for you?*
> *Still, you tried to treat her nice, no matter what she say or do*
> *That's love, that graveyard love.*
> —*Bertha Idaho, "Graveyard Love," 1928*

A love affair that culminates (or is sure to culminate) in homicide. A variant expression, *graveyard talk*, appears in the following:

> *I've got a lovin' disposition, but here's where I balk*
> *For that ol' quittin' stuff you doin', is graveyard talk.*
> —*Biddy Paine and "Popo" Warfield, "Not Today, Sweet Cookie," 1926*

graveyard, start a

> *I'm gonna start a graveyard of my own*
> *If that man don't leave my gal alone*
> —*Jim Jackson, "I'm Gonna Start Me A Graveyard Of My Own," 1928*

To commit or foster a slew of murders, or (as in the above) commit the first of numerous murders; a black idiom of 19th-century vintage. "... 'Listen white folks, you is gwine start a graveyard if you come round here teachin' niggers to sass white folks'" (Will Adams, as quoted in *Born in Slavery*).

great long

> *Come here mama, let me speak my mind*
> *To cure these blues gonna take a great long time.*
> —George Carter, "Rising River Blues," 1929

Very long; a Southern colloquialism (DARE 2). The above couplet is a sexual proposition.

greenback dollar bill

> *Said I went down to the little crap game*
> *Lord that was against my will*
> *I lost every penny that I had in my pocket*
> *But a greenback dollar bill.*
> —Frank Stokes, "I Got Mine," 1928

A seeming redundancy, perhaps born of the use of script to pay black laborers in the Jim Crow South. The same term figures in Ray Charles's mid-1950s R & B tune "Greenbacks." "De palm of my hand sho' begin to itch for dat greenback money" (Ned Walker, as quoted in *Born in Slavery*).

grind

> *Steady grindin' now, you can't come in*
> *Take the key outta the hole because it's too bad Jim.*
> —Dorothy Baker, "Steady Grinding Blues," 1930

To copulate (F&H, 1893).

grinder

> *"Don't you know I got a little grinder?*
> *She lives in St. Louis."*
> —Milton Sparks, "Grinder Blues," 1935

A sex partner; suggested by *grind*.

guitar king

> *I'm a guitar king, sing the blues everywhere I go*
> *I'm gonna sing these blues, till I get back to Indian Territo'*
> —Tommy McClennan, "I'm A Guitar King," 1939

A top-notch guitarist, regardless of sex; hence, Willie Moore said of Memphis Minnie: "She's a guitar king." This term was likely formed by analogy with such accolades as *cotton king*, applied to outstanding farm laborers by patronizing whites: "All de white folks liked me and still likes me and called me 'cotton king'" (Bert Luster, as quoted in *Born in Slavery*). In the 1930s, Son House was similarly known as "tractor king" (conversation with author). See *jelly roll king*.

gumbo

> *Down in Lake County, in that gumbo mud*
> *Where the mosquito bills, keep a-biting through her tub.*
> —Sleepy John Estes, "Mary Come On Home," 1940

A colloquial term for thick, sticky mud (DARE 2).

gypsy

> *No gypsy woman, can fry no meat for me*
> *I ain't scared I'm skittish, she might pizin me.*
> —Sam Butler, "Devil And My Brown Blues," 1926

"A contemptuous term for a woman, as being cunning, deceitful, fickle, or the like . . ." (OED). This sense of the word, which was in vogue in 17th- and 18th-century English, draws on the once-popular perception of gypsies as an underhanded or quasi-criminal element.

habits on, have one's

> *Bring me another two-bit pint*
> *'Cause I got my habits on, I'm going to wreck this j'int.*
> —Lucille Bogan, "Sloppy Drunk Blues," 1930

To be in the grip of habitual desires or inclinations, particularly in regard to immoderate drinking (as in the above song) or lust (as in the following):

> *Daddy, you really knows your stuff when you take me for a buggy ride*
> *I like you when you got your habits on, you can shift your gear with so much pride.*
> —Bessie Smith, "Take Me For A Buggy Ride," 1933

A variant term for sexual desire is used by Smith:

> *I've got my wantin' habits on*
> *I've had 'em on since this morn'.*
> —"If You Don't I Know Who Will," 1923

The expression originated in reference to opium addiction, as in "I feel my habit coming on" (1914 citation given in Lighter [1997] at *habit*). Without reference to specific conduct, it appears in Zora Neale Hurston's *Jonah's Gourd Vine* (1934): "Much up de young folks and you got somebody tuh strain wid dem old rams when dey git dey habits on."

hack

>*Rubber tired buggy, two-seated hack,*
>*Took Delia to the graveyard, never brought her back*
>*—Blind Willie McTell, "Delia," 1940 (LC)*

A colloquial term for a horse-drawn hearse, also applied to any horse-drawn vehicle (cf. DARE 2).

hail, to fall like

>*I got to keep movin', I got to keep movin', blues fallin' down like hail . . .*
>*An' the day keeps on 'mind me, there's a hellhound on my trail . . .*
>*—Robert Johnson, "Hell Hound On My Trail," 1937*

A variant of a conventional 19th-century simile, *to fall like hailstones* (DAP).

hair like drops of rain

>*I don't like no woman got hair like drops of rain*
>*Oh the girl I like got hair like a horse's mane.*
>*—Jim Thompkins, "Bedside Blues," 1930*

Nappy, kinky hair (Skip James), a black colloquialism probably suggested by the sparkling appearance of such hair in sunlight. The idiom appears in Zora Neale Hurston and Dorothy Waring's *Polk County* (1944): "They own [hair] looked like horse's mane, and mine looks like drops of rain."

half in two

>*I'm low an' onery, don't care what I do*
>*Feel like cuttin' my man half in two.*
>*—Maggie Jones, "Dangerous Blues," 1925*

In half; in two; a black colloquialism (cf. Hurston, 1935).

hambone (n., v.)

>*I left Memphis Tennessee, on my way back to dear old Marked Tree*
>*I think I'll hambone my baby says: "Jam up above the knee."*
>*—Hambone Willie Newbern, "Shelby County Workhouse Blues," 1929*

As a noun, penis; see *hambone boiled, get (one's)*. As a verb, to have intercourse with a female.

hambone boiled, get (one's)

>*I ain't got nobody but I'm gonna get my hambone boiled, oh daddy*
>*I'm gonna take it down home, 'cause these Northern men will let it spoil.*
>*—Virginia Liston, "I Never Knew What The Blues Were (Until You Went Away)," 1924*

To obtain sexual gratification. As applied to females, *hambone* does not appear to refer to a sex organ; the male singers who subsequently trafficked in the above couplet almost certainly employed it as a term for penis:

I got to move to Cincinnati, for to get my hambone boiled

Women in Alabama gon' let my hambone spoil.

—Ed Bell, Ham Bone Blues, 1927

hamfatchit

I want all you hamfatchit people, listen at my hamfatchit blues

I'm gettin' so doggone hamfatchit lonesome, I don't know what to do.

—Buddie Burton, "Ham Fatchet Blues, Part One," 1928

? Apparently, a euphemistic or nonsensical expletive on the order of *fetched* or *fetchtaked:* "I reckon that is the reason he stayed so fetched mean" (Annie Hawkins, as quoted in *Born in Slavery*); ". . . whyn't yer drive that fetchtaked dog out?" (Opie Read, *Len Gansett*, 1888). In one conversational aside on a Chicago blues, it is applied, perhaps facetiously, to a dance step:

"Here's a couple doin' the Hamfatchit!"

—The Hokum Boys and Jane Lucas, "Hokum Stomp," 1930

hammer

Drove so many piles, my hammer's all worn out

That's when I do my driving, and I begin to shout.

—Kansas Joe, "Pile Drivin' Blues," 1931

Literally in the above context, a *pile hammer*, i.e., "a device or machine for driving piles into the ground . . ." (OED), also called a *pile driver*. As a slang term for penis (the connotation of the above lyric), *hammer* dates to the turn of the 18th century and is now associated with blacks (cf. Lighter, 1997). See *pile*.

hand

Said I went to the gypsy, to get me a hand

Seen my gal walkin' with another man

—Papa Charlie Jackson, "Drop That Sack," 1925

A charm or conjure object. The word derives from the synonymous archaic English expression *hand of glory.* The latter was originally used to describe the mandrake root (Shipley), which had an ancient association with magic and good fortune. In black usage, *hand* also connoted a medicinal cure (sometimes called a *curing hand*), as noted in a 1902 dialect novel: "Her child, Jesse, followed her in all her jaunts through forest and swamp in search of herbs or insects, or small wild things to be used for 'hands' or 'cures'" (Martha Young, *Plantation Bird Legends*). In black song, *hand* almost invariably appears as part of the redundant phrases *hoodoo hand* and *mojo hand.* A conjuring hand is depicted in Zora Neale Hurston and Dorothy Waring's *Polk County* (1944) as "a small bundle about three inches long sewed up in red flannel. . . ." An ex-slave's recitation, *Hoo-doism*, held: "Den git a hand which is a bag, Hoo-doo; Made uv any sort uv rag, Hoo-doo . . ." (Mamie Hanberry, as quoted in *Born in*

Slavery). Another former slave recounted: "... he say ifen I git up five doller he make me a hand—you know, what collored folks calls a jack. Dat be a charm what will keep de witches away.... You take a little pinch o' dried snakeskin an some graveyard dirt, an some red pepper an' a lock o' your hair wrapped roun' some black rooster feathers. Den you spit whiskey on em an wrop em in red flannel an sew it into a ball.... Den you hang it under your right armpit" (Josephine Anderson, as quoted in *Born in Slavery*).

handful of "Gimme," mouthful of "Much obliged", a

> *Some of these here women sure make me tired*
> *Got a handfulla "Gimme," mouthfulla "Much obliged."*
> *—Charlie Patton, "Going To Move To Alabama," 1929*

A black catchphrase lampooning a transparent mooch. It occurs in Van Vechten's Harlem dialogue (vintage 1926): "Han' full o' gimme, mouf full o' much oblige, mused the Creeper."

hand in hand

> *When you see two women, both runnin' hand in hand*
> *Bet your life, one's got the other one's man.*
> *—Willie Baker, "Weak-Minded Blues," 1929*

Side by side, a standard English figure of speech (OED).

hand me down

> *The woman I love's 'bout five feet from the ground ...*
> *She's a tailor-made woman, she ain't no hand me down.*
> *—Blind Lemon Jefferson, "Bad Luck Blues," 1927*

A facetious black term for a lover or mate who was discarded by his or her previous companion.

handsome

> *Said she's long and tall, and handsome, sweet as she can be*
> *To satisfy that woman takes more than a bumble bee.*
> *—Big Bill, "Long Tall Mama," 1932*

A once-conventional description of attractive females, e.g.: "... a whore if handsome makes a wife for some rich planter" (17th-century English soldier quoted in Jordan and Walsh).

hanging crime

> *I've killed no man and I've robbed no train*
> *And I've done no hangin' crime.*
> *—Peg Leg Howell, "Rolling Mill Blues," 1929*

A now-outmoded black expression for a crime punishable by hanging; found in Zora Neale Hurston's *Spunk* (1935): "I ain't done no hanging crime."

ha'nt

Well late last night I heard somethin' talkin' on my telephone

It musta been that ha'nt, because it was nobody home alone.

—Memphis Minnie, "Haunted Blues," 1936

A black variant of *haunt,* a provincial British and American term for ghost the OED traces to 1878. It occurs in *Uncle Remus* (1880): "dem wuz ha'nts"; though obsolete, the term (which rhymes with "can't") survives among black "seniors" (cf. Smitherman, 2000, which renders it as *haints*).

happy-tapping

So now I'm gone, an' I won't be back no more

I'm so tired of you bull-headed women, happy-tappin' with my dough.

—Kokomo Arnold, "Bull-Headed Woman Blues," 1936

? Evidently, partying; perhaps an extension of the same term as signifying dancing.

hard

District Attorney, sure is hard on a man

He will take a woman's man and leave her cold in hand.

—Bukka White, "District Attorney Blues," 1940

Harsh, severe (with others); a standard English term (cf. OED at *hard,* a. (n.) 12.a, which offers citations from 1682 [by Swift], 1738, and 1862 [by Trollope]). "My master was my father; he was kind to me but hard on the field hands who worked in the fields" (James Calhart James, as quoted in *Born in Slavery*).

hard-down

I love my baby, I makes him do what's right

I ain't never told him, a hard-down lie in my life.

—Memphis Minnie, "Hard Down Lie," 1931

Pure, unadulterated; an obscure Southern colloquialism (cf. ADD, which offers a single citation, from Arkansas in 1938).

hard-headed

Woman, you is hard-headed as can be

I want someone to make a fuss over me.

—Biddy Paine and "Popo" Warfield, "Not Today, Sweet Cookie," 1926

Stubborn; although regarded as archaic standard English by OED (whose most recent citation is 1642), this sense of the term survives in American colloquial speech. Presently, *hard-headed* more often connotes an absence of sentimentality: "Those closest to her will give her a hard-headed analysis ..." (Tim Russert, *NBC Nightly News,* 5/7/2008). The related race synonym *to have a hard head* has no known precedent:

Let me tell you boys, don't you have no hard, hard head
If you do you will be hellbound, just as soon as your mother is dead.
—Charley Jordan, "Hellbound Boy," 1932

hard-luck (a.)

I been to the Nation, from there to the Territo'
And I'm a hard-luck child, catch the devil everywhere I go.
—Skip James, "Hard Luck Child," 1931

Plagued by misfortune, a modifier dating in print to 1899 (Lighter, 1997).

hard road

I'm gonna find my baby, don't think she can be found
Gonna walk this hard road, till my mustache drag the ground.
—Blind Blake, "Hard Road Blues," 1927

A paved road (DARE 2).

hard times

Hard times boy, an' it's hard times everywhere I go
These people keep cryin' about hard times, and there's work to do.
—Lane Hardin, "Hard Times Blues," 1935

A prevalent topical term for the Great Depression of 1929–38 to which the above song refers; applied in previous eras to any period of high unemployment and privation.

hat, to have one's in one's hand

Got up this mornin', my hat in my hand
Didn't have no woman, have no man.
—Charlie Patton, "Going To Move To Alabama," 1929

To be obsequious; a clichéd 19th-century figure of speech (DC).

have, to

Mama mama have you forgot
When I had you in the vacant lot?
—Seth Richards, "Skoodle Um Skoo," 1928

To possess carnally (cf. F&H, 1893).

have a fit

"Have a fit, baby! Have a fit!"
—Charlie Patton on Louise Johnson, "Long Ways From Home," 1930

A spectator's catchphrase directed at jukehouse musicians, appearing in Zora Neale Hurston and Dorothy Waring's *Polk County* (1944): "Do that thing, My Honey! Have a fit!"

have a man on, to

That's the way, that's the way, these barefooted soul[s]'ll do
They will get your money an' they'll have a man on you.
—Ed Bell, "Ham Bone Blues," 1927

Of women, to cuckold. An embellishment of this expression occurs in Charlie Patton's *It Won't Be Long* (1929):

> She's got a man on her man, got a kid on her kid . . .
> She done got so bold, Lord she won't keep it hid.

'hay, just won't

> I got the Maxwell Street blues, mama and they just won't 'hay
> Those Maxwell Street women, gonna carry me to my grave.
> —Papa Charlie Jackson, "Maxwell Street Blues," 1925

Just won't behave, a blues catchphrase suggesting that something or someone has gotten out of hand.

head

> My mother's gettin' old, head is turnin' gray
> Don't you know it'll break her heart know, my livin' this a-way?
> —Charlie Patton, "Screaming and Hollering The Blues," 1929

The hair on one's head (cf. DARE 2).

headache stick

> "In a few minutes here come the man with the headache stick."
> —Cannon's Jug Stompers, "Madison Street Rag," 1928

A policeman's or prison guard's night stick, apparently used with the implication that it is freely wielded by its possessor. This term may have been of prison origin (cf. examples given in Lighter, 1997).

head-board

> On my head-board write my name
> I left a-many girls' hearts in pain.
> —Blind Willie McTell, "Lay Some Flowers On My Grave," 1935

A wooden board serving as the equivalent of a headstone (cf. OED); perhaps an emblem of pauperdom. The second line of the above is advanced as an epitaph.

headknocker

> Three barrels of your whiskey, mama four barrels of gin
> "There's a headknocker home, daddy an' you can't come in."
> —Papa Charlie Jackson, "Coffee Pot Blues," 1925

A black slang term for penis (Hill); used in the above couplet as fanciful dialogue on the part of a female entertaining a male lover. It derives from *knocker*, an obsolete slang term for penis dating to the 18th century (Partridge).

head rag hop

> "Come on, take me down to that head rag hop."
> —Romeo Nelson, "Head Rag Hop," 1929

Evidently, a vogue name for a party at which a dance of the same name was performed. The latter is invoked on the same recording: "Aw, you doin' the

Head Rag Hop now." As a slang or colloquial term for a dance, *hop* is of 18th-century vintage (OED), and survived into the rock and roll era via such songs as "At the Hop" (1957). For *head rag*, see *rag*.

hear me talkin' to you, now don't you

> *"Now don't you hear me talkin' to you!"*
> —Lil Johnson, "House Rent Scuffle," 1929

A black or barrelhouse catchphrase of the blues era, ordinarily occurring in blues song with reference to sung rather than spoken words.

hearing (n.)

> *Backwater risin', Southern people can't make no time*
> *An' I can't get no hearing, from that Memphis gal of mine.*
> —Blind Lemon Jefferson, "Rising High Water Blues," 1927

A Southern term for a letter or reply (ADD).

heart-string

> *Pearlie Mae you is my heart-string, you is my destiny*
> *And you rolls across my mind, each an' every day.*
> —Robert Johnson, "Honeymoon Blues," 1937

A misnomer for *heart-strings*, a rather outmoded word denoting one's deepest feelings or affections (cf. OED).

heifer

> *If you've got a good bullcow you oughta, feed that cow good at home*
> *There may come along a young heifer an' just, tow your bull from home.*
> —Charlie Patton, "Jersey Bull Blues," 1934

A colloquialism for a girl or woman dating to about 1830 (DAS). Clapin (c. 1902) notes it as "not uncommon in the West for 'wife,' and used with all kindness and respect." *Heifer* survives as a semi-humorous term for a hefty female: "We're such heifers, it's disgusting!" (teenage dialogue in Bill Murray's 2005 movie *Broken Flowers*). *Bullcow*, the male counterpart of *heifer* appearing in blues song, has no discernable basis in colloquial speech.

hell, catch

> *Now these blues, blues ain't nothin' Lord but a doggone hungry spell*
> *Got no money in your pocket and you surely catchin' hell.*
> —Ishmon Bracey, "Woman Woman Blues," 1930

A slang term of mid-19th-century vintage meaning to get a thrashing or a scolding (cf. Lighter, 1997). It is evidently a variant of *catch it*, a synonymous British colloquialism the OED dates to 1835. "I sho' caught hell after dem Yanks comes" (Bert Luster, as quoted in *Born in Slavery*).

hellhound

I takes time when I'm prowlin', and wash my tracks out with my tail
Get off and get blue and start howlin', and the hellhound gets on my trail.
—*"Funny Paper" Smith, "Howling Wolf Blues, Part Three," 1931*

In Southern black mythology, a manifestation of Satan who visits the irreligious, either as a dog or by sending a pack of such animals. One Black Belt youth reported in 1941: "I saw the Devil when I was praying to get religion. He stuck my track, and he ran me in the field. He looked like an old hound dog..." (Johnson, 1941). The "Devil and devils [were] imagined as shaggy like beasts in archaic English expressions" (OED, at *ragged*). The notion of a hellhound dates to Greek mythology and was later fanned in Christendom by Martin Luther; a dog-like Satan is depicted in Albrecht Dürer's famous engraving *Knight, Death, and the Devil (1513).*

help I got, the

My hook's in the water, an' my cork's on top
How can I lose, Lord with the help I got?
—*Charlie Patton, "Banty Rooster Blues," 1929*

An idiomatic reference to one's sexual assets, occurring in Zora Neale Hurston's *Cold Keener* (1930): "She can't beat my time. (Wiggles her fat hips with her hand.) Not wid de help I got." The same author elsewhere uses the expression to refer to the assistance afforded by hoodoo charms: "...she combed her hair and under-braided the piece of John-de-conquerer root in her stiff back hair. 'Dey can't move me—not wid the help Ah got,' she gloated..." (*Jonah's Gourd Vine*, 1934). In the above song, the reference to fishing is a double entendre.

henry

I don't know, mama but I expect I will
Catch a long jumpin' henry, go on 'cross the hill.
—*Bo Weavil Jackson, "You Can't Keep No Brown," 1926*

Black slang for a train, invoked in Zora Neale Hurston's *Jonah's Gourd Vine* (1934):

"Where you bound fuh?" John asked.
"Tuh ketch me a high henry."
"Whuss dat?"
"Uh railroad train, man..."

Otherwise, *Henry* was a slang term for a Ford automobile, used in reference to Henry Ford and dating to around 1918 (cf. Lighter, 1997). The latter meaning may obtain in the above couplet; see *jumpin' Judy.*

high

I bought my gal, a hobble skirt
Boy she's dressed up like a black crow bird...

I said: "Lookey here black gal, now, don't you get smart"
She better stop to walkin' 'round me dressed so high
—Buddy Boy Hawkins, "Snatch It And Grab It," 1929

Luxuriously, to excess; standard English (OED).

high brown (a.)

Well the blues come to Texas, lopin' like a mule
You take a high brown woman, man she's hard to rule.
—Blind Lemon Jefferson, "Got The Blues," 1926

Light brown in complexion; a term applied to females and formed by analogy with *high yellow*. The only adjectival reference I have encountered beyond blues song (where it abounds) is in Martha Young's *Plantation Bird Legends*, a 1902 dialect novel: "She drew up her little high brown shoulders. . . ."

high brown (n.)

If I was a jaybird flyin' in the air
I'd build my nest in some of these high browns' hair.
—William Harris, "Kansas City Blues," 1928

An African American female with a light brown complexion: "That's a real light brownskin gal; good-lookin'" (Tom Shaw).

high-powered

High-powered mama, keep hittin' on all four
You make your daddy happy, I couldn't ask for more.
—Monroe Walker, "High Powered Mama," 1930

A black slang term meaning "[u]p-to-date, nice-looking" (Burley, c. 1944). It apparently arose from descriptions of 1920s automobiles; in the above song, *all four* means all four cylinders.

high sheriff

Police and the high sheriff, come a-ridin' down
An' you know you don't want to go.
—Ollis Martin, "Police And High Sheriff Came Riding Down," 1927

In Southern counties, an elected sheriff, as distinguished from a deputy sheriff.

high-stepper

My friend picked up a new girl in a dance hall
He used to be a high-stepper but now he can't dance at all.
—Hokum Boys, "Somebody's Been Using That Thing," 1929

A slang term of 19th-century vintage applied to one perceived as proud, fashionable, or spirited (cf. Lighter, 1997). The above couplet appears to invoke it as a term for an avid dancer, a figure who (it is intimated) has contracted a debilitating social disease.

high-steppin'

Lord heavy-hipped mama, she done moved to the piney woods
She's a high-steppin' mama she don't mean no man no good.
—Blind Lemon Jefferson, "Piney Woods Money Mama," 1928

? A black pejorative applied to show-offs; cf. DCS. It is uncertain that this (rather than the meaning attached to *high-stepper*) is the connotation of the above lyric.

high yeller (yellow)

"Aw, play it till I turn high yeller!"
—Willie Harris, "West Side Blues," 1929

Of African Americans, light-complexioned to the point of bearing pronounced white ancestry; a term often used by whites. It is likely that *high* in this context originally meant "[s]howing pride, self-exaltation, resentment, or the like; haughty, pretentious, arrogant, overbearing . . ." (OED at *high*, a. and n.2 at 14.a.). See *hold one's head high.*

highway (v.)

Do you want your friend to be "bad" like Jesse James?
Get two six-shooters, highway some passenger train.
—Blind Lemon Jefferson, "One Dime Blues," 1927

To rob; an obscure expression formed from *highwayman*, a dated term for a criminal who waylaid travelers on roadways.

highway-side

You may bury my body, down by the highway-side
So my old evil spirit, can get a Greyhound bus and ride.
—Robert Johnson, "Me And The Devil Blues," 1937

The side of a highway; an archaic formulation for which the OED gives a single example, dating to 1669.

hill

Bo weevil meet his wife: "We can sit down on the hill," Lordie!
—Charlie Patton, "Mississippi Bo Weavil Blues," 1929

A Southern farm term, usually pluralized, for the ridge on which a cotton plant is grown (cf. Brown, 1938).

hilly country

Lord the water done rushed over, down old Jackson Road
I'm goin' back to the hilly country, won't be worried no more.
—Charlie Patton, "High Water Everywhere, Part One," 1929

The relatively elevated land girding the Mississippi Delta to the north, east, and south, usually referred to as simply *the hills* by resident blacks and the *hill country* by Delta planters.

hincty

Two old maids, over forty
Two old maids, hot and haughty
They got the nerve to be hincty and haughty
Talkin' about the maids in a bed.
—Monette Moore, "Two Old Maids In A Folding Bed," 1936

Stuck up, snooty; a broadly based and still-used black slang term.

Hindenberg Line

Crossin' that ol' desert mama, just like breakin' the Hindenberg Line
Now if you get discharged from that freight train, you know that will be
the end of the line.
—Lane Hardin, "California Desert Blues," 1935

The heavily fortified line of trenches extending from the North Sea to Switzerland that served as the western front for the German army after the Battle of the Marne in 1914, ultimately broken by the Allied offensive three years later, and so named for the supreme commander of the German forces.

hit

When I first met the woman, I figure I hadn't made no hit
She got this old-fashioned lovin', man it just won't quit.
—Blind Lemon Jefferson, "Long Lastin' Lovin'," 1929

A highly favorable impression; drawn from the original sense of the word, usually involving the effect of a performance upon an audience (cf. OED, which traces the related *hit record* to 1918 and *Broadway hits* to 1908).

hit and run

Hit an' run, ain't no fun.
—Louise Vant, "The Man I Love Is Oh! So Good To Me," 1926

An act of casual sex followed by hasty departure on the part of the male; a still-current slang expression (cf. UD), perhaps of black origin.

hit the ground

You might go uptown an' have me 'rested have me put in jail
Some hotshot's got money, come an' go my bail.
Soon as I get out, hit the ground
Your southern can is worth two dollars an' a half a pound.
—Blind Willie McTell, "Southern Can Mama," 1933

Prison slang meaning to be released from custody; cf. Lighter (1994) at *ground*.

hobble skirt

I saw the deacon looked around, said: "Sister why in the world don't
you hush?
I'd rather see you drunk than wear these hobble-skirt(s)."
—Frank Stokes, "Mister Crump Don't Like It," 1927

A style of tight-fitting skirt that came into fashion in 1911; it fell between the ankles and knees, crimping one's movements (hence the term *hobble*).

hobo (v.)

> *Well, I believe I'll get drunk, tear this old barrelhouse down*
> *Folks I don't got no money, but I can hobo on outta town.*
> —*Memphis Minnie, "Drunken Barrelhouse Blues," 1934*

To make one's way in hobo fashion, by stealing rides on freight trains.

hog-head

> *Mister conductor man, one thing I want to know:*
> *How far do that hog-head, drive this engine go?*
> —*Lucille Bogan, "Forty-Two Hundred Blues," 1933*

Railroad slang for train engineer, dating in print to 1907 (OED).

hogmeat

> *Some likes pigmeat, hogmeat's what I crave*
> *I believe they sure gonna, carry me to my grave.*
> —*Willie Baker, "Bad Luck Moan," 1929*

A black slang term for a supposedly old woman (reckoned at forty or more years of age by Tom Dorsey), contrasted with *pigmeat* (Hill). *Hogmeat* was otherwise used by blacks to signify fleshy portions of a pig: ". . . dey won't eat no hog meat 'cept hams an' shoulders . . ." (Charlie Barbour, as quoted in *Born in Slavery*).

hokum

> *Now you want to know just what we've got*
> *Got good hokum and serve it hot.*
> —*Famous Hokum Boys, "Eagle Riding Papa," 1930*

A vaudeville term applied to comedy acts, defined by the *New York Times* (in a 12/13/1917, article, "The Argot of Vaudeville") as "a brand of fun bordering on vulgarity and quite obvious." As such, it was descriptive of material by the popular recording group billed as the Hokum Boys (Tampa Red and Georgia Tom Dorsey), whose songs were frivolous and sexually suggestive. In race recording, the musical approach *hokum* embodies was fostered by Papa Charlie Jackson's 1925 hit "Shake That Thing" (q.v.).

hold one's head high

> *Crow jane, crow jane, what makes you hold your head so high?*
> *Oughta just remember, you got to live so long and die.*
> —*Bo Weavil Jackson, "Pistol Blues," 1926*

To be haughty or excessively proud; a proverbial figure of 19th-century American speech (DAP). In explaining the above couplet, which he sang as the title verse of "Crow Jane," Skip James said: ". . . That was deferrin' to some . . . 'ristocratic, onery girlfriend . . . live above you and hold her head up above you."

holdover

> *It's too late, too late, too late too late too late*
>
> *I'm on my way to the holdover, and I cannot hesitate.*
>
> —Charley Jordan, "Raidin' Squad Blues," 1930

A jailhouse (Hill); an obscure slang term perhaps originating in Missouri, where the above performer lived. Cf. DAH, which offers a Missouri newspaper citation dating to 1888 and defines the term as a prison "where persons awaiting trial are kept."

hole

> *If you don't believe I'm sinkin' look what a hole I'm in*
>
> *If you don't believe I love you look what a fool I been.*
>
> —Henry Thomas, "Bull Doze Blues," 1928

Fix or difficulty; a colloquialism of 18th-century origin (F&H, 1893).

Hole In The Wall, The

> *No matter where you go you'll found*
>
> *Find somewhere in every town*
>
> *A place where nighthawks hang around*
>
> *It's dark an' small*
>
> *An' they always call it "The Hole In The Wall."*
>
> —Sara Martin, "Hole In The Wall," 1928

A proper name given to certain barrelhouses, from *hole in the wall* as "(an originally disparaging term for) any small, obscure place; *spec.* in the U.S., a place where alcoholic drinks are sold illegally" (OED).

holler

> *"Play it, Mister Kokomo! Now get ready*
>
> *To pick it up there an' holler a while."*
>
> —Kokomo Arnold, "Back To The Woods," 1934

To sing at full volume in a loud voice; a term dating to slave English: "I used to holler a heap . . . but after I let it down, all dat leave me" (Hector Smith, as quoted in *Born in Slavery*). It is occasionally used in blues songs to introduce verses:

> *Hollerin' little girl, what kind of little ol' girl are you?*
>
> *Says you actin' so funny, what do you want your papa to do?*
>
> —Kokomo Arnold, "Traveling Rambler Blues," 1935

holler murder

> *I would holler murder, but the fakin' town's too small*
>
> *Woman quit me, throwed my trunk outdoors.*
>
> —Furry Lewis, "I Will Turn Your Money Green," 1928

To holler or cry out in a manner suggesting that a catastrophe akin to murder has just taken place; an expression dating in print to 1847 (cf. Lighter, 1997, at *murder*).

home girl

Don't a man act funny, when a single woman ease in town?
He stay out all night, he throw his home girl down.
—Sleepy John Estes, "You Shouldn't Do That," 1941

A girl from one's own neighborhood or home town; a colloquialism of apparent 1930s vintage that (with *home boy, home slice,* etc.) is now a virtual badge of black English (cf. DARE 2).

honkies

I met your mama in the alley way
She's catchin' honkies both night and day.
—Kokomo Arnold, "Busy Bootin'," 1935

White people, a term sometimes said to have originated from the automobile honking by white Johns in black districts (the situation implied above). This idiom only surfaced in the mid-1960s, when it was used as a term of racial abuse by black militants (cf. *hunkie tunkie*).

hoodoo (a.)

I'm getting so that I can't rest
You almost ruined me, with that low-down hoodoo mess.
—Freddie Nicholson, "You Gonna Miss Me Blues," 1930

Conjuring; in this instance, by means of black (destructive) magic.

hoodoo (n.)

Aw she went to the hoodoo, she went there all alone
'Cause everytime I leave her I have to hurry back home.
—Charley Lincoln, "Mojoe Blues," 1927

Conjurer, sometimes referred to as a *hoodoo doctor*. Both terms date in print to 1875 (DAH).

horn

An' my bull's got a horn baby, long as my right arm
My bull got a horn, longly as my arm.
—Charlie Patton, "Jersey Bull Blues," 1934

A slang expression for erect penis (F&H, 1893).

horse pistol

Captain got a big horse pistol, an' he thinks he's "bad"
I'm gonna take it this mornin', if he make me mad.
—Bessie Tucker, "Key To The Bushes," 1929

"[A] large pistol carried at the pommel of the saddle when on horseback" (OED, which offers two British citations, from 1704 and 1814).

hot (adv.)

> *An' I know she want it hot, babe, sure don't want it cold*
> *It would break my heart if you ever say you can't use me no more.*
> —Charlie Patton, "Love My Stuff," 1934

Passionately; in a sexually arousing fashion; a term of ancient lineage appearing in *The Canterbury Tales* (1383): "So hote he loved . . ." (cf. F&H).

house

> *They'se a house over yonder, painted all over green*
> *Some of the finest young women that a man most ever seen.*
> —Charlie Patton, "Moon Going Down," 1930

A barrelhouse doubling as a whorehouse, a sense conveyed in:

> *An' it ain't but the one thing, Lordie worries my mind*
> *That's a house fulla women, none in there was mine.*
> —Kid Bailey, "Mississippi Bottom Blues," 1929

As a term for a whorehouse, *house* dates to the mid-19th century (DAH; Lighter, 1997).

house lady

> *Says house lady I been playin', for you the whole night long*
> *And I says you is not even given me, just one drink of corn.*
> —Walter Roland, "House Lady Blues," 1933

The proprietress of a house frolic, an all-night Friday and Saturday night affair organized for profit at which alcohol and food were sold, and gambling and dancing occurred on the premises (usually outdoors). The blues performers who serenaded there were given free drinks, hence the complaint of the above performer. A male who put on such affairs, typically a bootlegger, was similarly termed the *house man*, as was the manager of a barrelhouse.

house-rent man

> *Don't a woman look real funny, when she wakes up cold in hand?*
> *And the broad ain't got a dollar, to give the house-rent man.*
> —Lucille Bogan, "Drinking Blues," 1934

Rent collector.

house-rent party

> *I had a chitlin supper, at home last Saturday night*
> *Some house-rent party, it was a low-down sight.*
> —Sylvester Weaver, "Chittlin' Rag Blues," 1927

A house frolic. This term was transferred to the northern ghettos of Chicago and New York, where it connoted an indoor apartment party featuring liquor and music, ostensibly organized in the interests of raising rent money. Regarding the latter, Van Vechten (1926) noted Harlem's "modest rent-parties, to which little groups were invited to dance to the music of the phonograph in somebody's small apartment, individual contributions of fifty cents helping to defray the occupant's exorbitant rent." The customary practice, however, was to charge for food and drink in the fashion of juke joints.

"How 'bout it?"

> *An' I asked her: "How 'bout it?" Lord and she said: "All right."*
> *But she never showed up, at the shack last night.*
> —*Willie Brown, "M&O Blues," 1930*

A sexual proposition, used by either sex:

> *I asked him: "How 'bout it?" and he said: "All right."*
> *I asked him: "How long?" and he said: "All night."*
> —*Mattie Delaney, "Down The Big Road Blues," 1930*

It occurs as part of a prostitute's dialogue in David Goodis's *Down There* (1956):

> *... "How's about it?"*
> *"Not tonight."*
> *"You broke?"*
> *He nodded. ... She said, "You want it on credit?"*

A variant proposition, *What about it?*, appears below in rhetorical blues song banter between a female and her mate, the former expressing a desire have her picture posted in a barrelhouse in the fashion of a prostitute:

> *"Oh take my picture, hang it up in Jackson's Wall."*
> *"If anybody asks you: 'What about it?' tell 'im: 'That's all, that's all.'"*
> —*Charlie Patton, "Banty Rooster Blues," 1929*

howl

> *I'm the man that rolls, when icicles hangin' on the tree*
> *And now you hear me howlin' baby, down on my bended knee.*
> —*Robert Johnson, "I'm A Steady Rollin' Man," 1937*

To yell or complain; a standard English figure of speech that had become a Southern colloquialism by the time it appeared in Erskine Caldwell's *God's Little Acre* (1933): "'Nobody ought to howl about just one tiny little bit when nobody is getting hurt.'"

hump in one's back, to have a

> *I knew a man once, who got up on the doodle track*
> *He doodled so much he got a hump in his back.*
> —*Charley Lincoln, "Doodle Hole Blues," 1930*

A black expression applied to males engaged in sexual intercourse (Smitherman, 2000), either underlying the above observation, or suggested by same.

hunkie tunkie, monkey hunkie tunkie

> *Well it's everybody talkin' about your hunkie tunkie blues*
> *Well it's everybody talkin' about your monkey hunkie tunkie blues.*
> *Well it's everybody talkin' about your hunkie tunkie baby*
> *You oughta seed that curly-headed monkey head*
> *'Cause his head is curly, baby and bushy, too.*
> —*Charley Jordan, "Hunkie Tunkie Blues," 1930*

? Obscure phrases that likely stood for interracial hanky-panky, the above lyric plainly referring to miscegenation. Of itself, *hunky* was a contemporary slang term for blacks (Fisher, 1928).

hush one's fuss

> *Now mama ashes to ashes an' it's dust to dust*
> *Corn liquor daddy done hushed his fuss.*
> —*Lewis Black, "Corn Liquor Blues," 1927*

In the above context, to die; a still-used black colloquialism also meaning to fall silent.

hustle (1)

> *. . . Where my Third Street woman gone?*
> *Believe to my soul she will hustle everywhere but home.*
> —*Blind Willie Reynolds, "Third Street Woman Blues," 1930*

To work as a prostitute, an extension of the 19th-century use of *hustle* as a slang equivalent of "copulate" (F&H, 1893). As such it appears in both Faulkner's *Sanctuary* ("'I'll take you back to Memphis Sunday. You can go to hustling again'") and Edmund Wilson's diaristic description of a New Orleans prostitute: ("—Worked in a store in Atlanta, then was in Macon hustlin'").

hustle (2)

> *Dice jumped to hustlin', I swear my money won't lose*
> *I got to win tonight and buy this baking powder man some shoes.*
> —*Lucille Bogan, "Baking Powder Blues," 1933*

To cheat. The above passage indicates that the performer has substituted a pair of crooked dice in a crap game.

hustlin' woman

> *She's a big fat mama with the meat shake on the bones*
> *An' every time she shakes it Lord a hustlin' woman lose her home.*
> —*Blind Willie Reynolds, "Third Street Woman Blues," 1930*

A prostitute.

If I live

I been gone, sixteen years
I'll be home, some of these days
If I live, don't get killed.
—Henry Thomas, "The Fox And Hounds," 1927

A fatalistic black catchphrase, once constituting such a badge of negritude as to betray a light-complexioned employee attempting to pass for white in an incident recounted in W. C. Handy's *Father of the Blues.* When the latter answered his boss's admonition to arrive at work the following day by stating: "If I live, an' nothin' happens," the boss "spotted him for what he was from this remark, and he was fired immediately" (cf. Handy, 1941).

if you call that gone

Now good-bye honey if you call that gone
I'm gonna take a ride in my high brown's arms.
—"Funny Paper" Smith, "Honey Blues," 1931

A black catchphrase based on to *call oneself* (q.v.) and the black proverbial saying: "Every good-bye ain't gone" (for keeps). A variant expression appears in:

I leave this time, hang crepe on your door
I don't call that gone baby, ain't comin' back no more.
—Skip James, "Yola My Blues Away," 1931

in a barrel

Hard luck done come here, caught me in a barrel
I even got no friend, or even got no gal.
—Joe Evans, "Shook It This Morning Blues," 1931

Broke; a black slang term usually expressed as *in the barrel* (cf. DAS 3). This phrase arose from the stock image of a barrel as a broke man's only attire.

in front

Some folks may try to come back an' pay
I must get mine in front.
—Barrel House Annie, "Must Get Mine In Front," 1937

In advance; a black slang term usually applied to money, dating to the 1920s and superseded in the 1960s by *up front* (cf. Lighter, 1994).

in one's whiskey

> *When I'm in my whiskey, I don't care what I say*
> *'Cause me and my whiskey, we going to have our way.*
> —Barbecue Bob, "Me And My Whiskey," 1929

Intoxicated; perhaps suggested by the genteel equivalent, *in one's cups*. The above is one of the few instances of blues-era black slang for drunkenness.

in so'

> *I been shootin' craps and gamblin', mama an' I done got broke*
> *I done pawned my pistol mama an' my best clothes in so.'*
> —Blind Willie McTell, "Broke Down Engine," 1931

In soak, meaning in pawn; from the 19th-century colloquialism *to put in soak* (F&H, 1903). See *soak*.

Indian Territo'

> *I'm a guitar king, sing the blues everywhere I go*
> *I'm gonna sing these blues, till I get back to Indian Territo'.*
> —Tommy McClennan, "I'm A Guitar King," 1939

Indian Territory, the official name for land held by Native Americans that lay beyond the boundaries of states, used in a historic judicial pronounce-ment: "The Indian Territory is admitted to compose part of the United States" (1831 ruling of Justice Marshall in *Cherokee Nation v. State of Georgia*). From 1854–90, this territory consisted of what is now Oklahoma, given over to five major tribes. In 1890, it was reduced to eastern Oklahoma for the sake of accommodating white settlers, and abolished completely in 1907 when Okla-homa became a state. Numerous blues songs (such as the above) continued to treat *Indian Territory* as though it was a current entity.

it

> *Now mama mama, hurry an' bring it back to me*
> *You were so crazy for ever leavin' me.*
> —Barbecue Bob, "Hurry And Bring It Back Home," 1928

A conventional term for pudenda (F&H, 1896) that was also applied to the male equivalent:

> *Now don't you hear me talkin' to you,*
> *I don't bite my tongue*
> *You want to be my man you got to bring it with you when you come.*
> —Ma Rainey, "Hear Me Talkin' To You," 1928

it's a long lane ain't got no end

> *It's a long lane ain't got no end*
> *And it's a bad wind don't never change.*
> —Blind Lemon Jefferson, "See That My Grave Is Kept Clean," 1927

A corruption of a 19th-century expression, "It's a long lane that has no turn in it," which appears in Bessie Smith's "Devil Gonna Git You" (1928) as "It's a long lane that has no turning." The second half of the above couplet is a paraphrase of another such saying, "It's an ill wind that blows nowhere" (cf. DAP).

jack (1)

> *Number three can go but he'll come back . . .*
> *'Cause I always carry plenty of jack in the old sack.*
> —*Ethel Ridley, "I Don't Let No One Man Worry Me," 1923*

Conventional slang for money (cf. Lighter, 1997).

jack (2)

> *It's a mean jack cat Lordie, crawlin' on my door*
> *I'm goin' down to Louisiana where I won't, hear him whine no more.*
> —*Charlie Patton, "Mean Black Cat Blues," 1929*

A derogatory term for a black person (Spears, 2001).

jackleg preacher

> *Says I'm gonna get religion, goin' back an' j'in the church*
> *You know I'm gonna be a jackleg preacher, for then I won't have to work.*
> —*Walter Roland, "Worn Out Man Blues," 1935*

A still-employed black colloquialism for an unordained minister, an itinerant preacher with no regular congregation, an apprentice or substitute preacher who fills in for a congregation's regular pastor, or a minister whose motive for preaching is financial (Evans). It is in the last and probably most common sense that this term is likely applied by the above performer. As a pejorative adjective implying a lack of training or professional standing, *jackleg* (initially applied to lawyers) dates to at least 1850 in Southern white speech, and is still so used (cf. OED and DARE 3); thus a *jackleg musician* is one without sight-reading ability or formal knowledge of chords. In English dialect, *jackleg* (also *jockteleg*) was the parent term of *jack knife*; perhaps the negative connotations of the American term arose through unfavorable comparisons between jack knives and conventional ones.

jack stropper

> Some jack strop', some jacker have stole my gal
> Yes you know you can tell by that, boys you know I don't feel so well.
> —Lightnin' Hopkins, "Jackstropper Blues," 1947

Black slang for "some guy that's tryin' to steal your gal" (Tom Shaw). It derives from *jack stripper,* a gambling expression for a jack trimmed around the edges for purposes of cheating (ATS), which in turn was derived from *strippers,* a late-19th-century term for trimmed cards (Partridge).

jake

> I drink so much jake, it have settled down in my knee
> I retched for my lovin', my baby turned her back on me.
> —Ishmon Bracey, "Jake Liquor Blues," 1930

Conventional slang for any alcoholic drink created with Jamaica Ginger Extract, an alcohol-based remedy for headaches, indigestion, and the like that remained legal during Prohibition, when it was commonly sold in drugstores. Bootleggers who adulterated their jake-based product in 1930 with the toxic additive triorthocresyl phosphate as a cost-cutting device created an epidemic of paralytic injuries among lower-class consumers, such as are noted in the above song. See *limber leg.*

jambooger

> I'm gonna buy me a mattress, pillow to lay my head
> I don't want to lay, where you and jambooger lay.
> —Barbecue Bob, "Jambooger Blues," 1930

A derogatory black slang term for a black male, equivalent to *nigger* (anonymous black informant, New York, 1971), and a likely offshoot of *booger,* a more common derogatory term for blacks. It gave rise to the synonymous *scambooger:* "I said: 'Lord, I want you to give me the strength, the power, the know-how to kill that scambooger'" (Joe Frazier's prayer before facing Muhammad Ali, recounted in the 2008 documentary *Thrilla In Manilla*). *Jambooger* and *scambooger* may have been euphemisms for "damn nigger."

jane

> I'm going to get a black spider, put him in the bottom of your shoe.
> That's the only way I can get rid of a jane like you.
> —Sylvester Weaver, "Black Spider Blues," 1927

A slang term for a female or girlfriend, dating in print to 1906 (Lighter, 1997), that attained widespread youth and student use in the 1920s.

jaw (n.)

> *She's a long tall woman, she got relatives in Arkansas*
> *She ain't so good-lookin' but Lord them dimples are on her jaw.*
> —*Blind Lemon Jefferson, "Booger Rooger Blues," 1926*

A black misnomer for cheek. "They say to me 'Why don't you have your hair straightened' but I say 'I've got along this far without painted jaws and straight hair'" (Mary Williams, as quoted in *Born in Slavery*).

jaw (v.)

> *That's where my great grandma*
> *First met up with great grandpa*
> *Where they settled down together*
> *How they jaw with each other*
> *Way down in Arkansas.*
> —*Hambone Willie Newbern, "Way Down In Arkansas," 1929*

Talk; regarded by the OED as "[a] vulgar, contemptuous, or hostile equivalent for *speak*."

jelly, jelly roll

> *I got a sweet jelly, a lovin' sweet jelly roll*
> *If you taste my jelly, it'll satisfy your worried soul.*
> —*Peg Leg Howell And His Gang, "New Jelly Roll Blues," 1927*

Stock blues expressions for the male and female genitals (and, by extension, sexual discharges), derived from the dated colloquial term *jelly,* signifying semen as early as the 17th century (when it appeared in one of John Donne's poems), and *jelly bag,* a term of like vintage for the vagina and scrotum (F&H, 1896). In black speech, *jelly* had probably lost currency by the time of the blues era, and could thus serve as a euphemism for the blunter *cock* (but see Folb, who lists it as a black teenage 1960s/1970s term for "genitalia"). As with other sexual terms, *jelly roll* was also applied to a female perceived as a sexual object:

> *You can take my money, I mean you can wear my best clothes*
> *Lemon won't kill you no quicker, if you bother with my jelly roll.*
> —*Blind Lemon Jefferson, "Fence Breakin' Yellen' Blues," 1929*

jellybean

> *Down on Franklin Avenue, jellybeans standin' to an' fro*
> *Well you hear one jellybean ask the other one:*
> *"Which a-way did my good girl go?"*
> —*"Hi" Henry Brown, "Nut Factory Blues," 1932*

A moron or simpleton. As an ex-employee of the St. Louis factory that was the subject of the above song put it: "'Jellybean' means you half-cracked. . . . If I call you a 'jellybean' that mean you a simple-crack guy. . . . If a guy call me a 'jellybean' direct to my face, he callin' me somethin' ignorant . . ." (Sylvester Grant, 1970 interview with author). As a general pejorative, the term dates to about 1915 (DAS); it appears in Faulkner's *The Sound and the Fury* (1929).

jelly rollin'

> *Who's gonna do your sweet jelly rollin' . . . when I'm gone?*
> *Who's gonna do our old-fashioned lovin' . . . from now on?*
> —*Whistlin' Rufus, "Sweet Jelly Rollin'," 1933*

Lovemaking.

jelly roll king

> *Now old Uncle Jack, the jelly roll king*
> *He just got back from shakin' that thing.*
> —*Papa Charlie Jackson, "Shake That Thing," 1925*

? Most likely, a name given to someone with a stable of women.

jet

> *Mary had a little lamb,*
> *His fleece was black as jet.*
> *I went home with Mary last night*
> *An' I ain't quit scratchin' yet.*
> —*Winston Holmes and Charlie Turner, "Skinner," 1929*

A variety of coal (OED). The above lyric is a reference to catching crabs.

jet-black

> *Brownskin woman is like somethin' fit to eat*
> *Oh but a jet-black woman, don't put your hand on me.*
> —*Charlie Patton, "Pony Blues," 1929*

Glossy black. Although a standard English term, it appears to have been relatively uncommon in white usage; the OED lists four citations from c. 1475–1875, a number that is at least equaled in recorded blues from 1927–30.

Jewtown

> *"If I got what you want, come on over in Jewtown*
> *and get it sweet mama, you're perfectly welcome to."*
> —*Papa Charlie Jackson, "If I Got What You Want," 1934*

A name given to the Jewish neighborhood in and around Maxwell Street on Chicago's west side, where the above performer was discovered performing on the street in 1924. See *Maxwell Street market.*

jimmy-john

> *Stand around, stand around the jimmy-john (2)*
> —*Leadbelly, "Green Corn," 1935 (LC)*

A Southern colloquial term for liquor jug that first appeared in print in 1884 as black dialect rendered by Joel Chandler Harris (cf. DARE 3).

jive (n., v.)

>*Did you ever have a woman with a real sweet line of jive?*
>*Sometimes you thought, she oughta be buried alive.*
>—*Blind Blake, "Sweet Jivin' Mama," 1929*

Empty, deceptive talk, bullshit; black slang derived from the British dialect term *gyve*, meaning to banter or jibe (EDD). Like the latter, it was used as a verb:

>*Beef to me baby, me an' pork chops do not agree*
>*I love you but I don't like that way that you are jivin' me.*
>—*Teddy Darby, "Deceiving Blues," 1931*

By the mid-1930s, it had lost its pejorative connotations and became a vogue term for the fashionable speech of Harlem youth, commemorated in Dan Burley's *Original Handbook of Harlem Jive* (c. 1944) and eventually transmitted to whites.

join the church

>*Oh I'm gonna get religion, I'm gonna join the Baptist church*
>*I'm gonna be a Baptist preacher an' I sure won't have to work.*
>—*Son House, "Preachin' Blues, Part One," 1930*

To become a church member; a Southern colloquialism originally noted in 1829 (Mathews, 1931) that frequently figures in the WPA slave narratives of 1936–38. In actuality, one joins a congregation, not a church.

joker

>*I feel like fallin', from a treetop to the ground*
>*My rider's got a mean joker, an' he don't 'low me around.*
>—*Blind Lemon Jefferson, "Mean Jumper Blues," 1928*

Slang for a black person (Fisher, 1928).

jomo

>*It must be a black cat bone, jomo can't work that hard*
>*Every time I wake up, Jim Tampa's in my yard.*
>—*Lucille Bogan, "Jim Tampa Blues," 1927*

A synonym of *mojo*, formed by transposition. The suggestion of the above couplet is that it is less effective than a *black cat bone* in preventing a desirable partner from straying.

jomo sack

>*You know I let that woman tote my money, Lord in a jomo sack*
>*And you know it's gonna be some hell raisin',*
>*Lord if she don't bring some of my money back.*
>—*Walter Roland, "Penniless Blues," 1935*

A seemingly eccentric term for a *mojo* bag, used as a purse.

juke (v.)

> *Bill an' Oscar shootin' dice the other night*
> *Oscar win the money an' he started to fight*
> *Bill tried to hit him, he was too fast*
> *Took his knife an' juked him on his yas-yas-yas.*
> *Now he's a jukin' mistreater, a robber an' a cheater . . .*
> —Ben Curry, "The New Dirty Dozen," 1931

In Southern black speech of the blues era, to dance or to fight (Skip James; Willie Moore). The word itself was borrowed from a Scottish dialect term (variously spelled "juke," "jook," and "jouk") dating to the 15th century and expressing assorted types of motion; among its meanings was to spring aside, to shift (John Jamieson's *Scottish Dictionary* of 1825, EDD), and to bend the body adroitly (OED), which sense would have an obvious application to black dancing. As an ex-slave from Alabama put it in a 1937 interview: "We used to call figgers on dancing. . . . None of this twisting and turning. Jus' can't stand all that juking, just won't look at it" (Ellen King, as quoted in *Born in Slavery*).

The plasticity of this word is further indicated by the title of a 1933 piano instrumental by Walter Roland, "Jookit Jookit" (anticipated by the English dialect *joukit* [EDD]). The same is true of the only other apparent occurrence of *juke* in race recording, where it applies to a bending motion:

> *Well juke down mama let your daddy see*
> *You got somethin' just worryin' me.*
> —Big Joe Williams, "Little Leg Woman," 1936

As a term meaning to dodge, *juke* entered 19th-century American speech as a racially nondescript colloquialism (cf. ADD), and became football slang by the 1960s, "used as shorthand for the move where a runner fakes in one direction, forcing the defender to commit, then quickly cuts back the other way" (David Hinckley, *New York Daily News* columnist, 2007 correspondence with author).

In black Mississippi speech, *juke* was also used as a noun, meaning a dance: ". . . there wasn't no clubs [to play music in]; they'd have their jukes and parties in private homes" (Skip James). *Juke, juke house,* and *juke joint* were conventional Southern black terms for a commercial establishment, typically a plantation shack, offering a combination of live dance music, whiskey, and gambling to patrons on Friday and Saturday nights, misconstrued by the OED as "[a] roadhouse or brothel; *spec.* a cheap roadside establishment providing food and drinks, and music for dancing" (cf. OED at *juke*). In this context the term *juke* was something of a misnomer, as such establishments were operated by bootleggers for the sake of dispensing their product, which was generally the main attraction. There is no evidence that the term represented "[a] place where prostitutes ply their trade" (DARE 3, which renders it as *jook house* and *jook joint*).

The coin-operated automatic record players that began to displace live music in black Southern cafes and the like in the mid-1930s became known as *juke boxes* (i.e., dance boxes), a term dating in print to 1939 (OED) that quickly became standard English. In assessing the latter, dictionaries mistakenly treat the term *juke* as being of African origin; see Lydia Parrish's *Slave Songs of the Georgia Sea Islands* (1942), which related the noun *juke* to *dzug,* an African word meaning to misconduct oneself. This faulty etymology arose from the illogical premise that because black housewives whose husbands patronized *jukes* (dance joints) regarded such places negatively, the term itself therefore had a negative connotation. Similarly, Turner (whose research informed Parrish) arrived at the same etymology on the basis of wrongfully defining *juke* as meaning "infamous, disorderly" and having no cognizance of its existence as a verb.

jump (1)

> Blues jumped a rabbit, run him one solid mile
> This rabbit fell down, cryin' like a natural child.
> —Blind Lemon Jefferson, "Rabbit Foot Blues," 1926

"To cause (game) to start; to 'spring'" (OED); a sporting idiom of 19th-century vintage, found in slave speech: "Now and den, a crowd of Niggers would jump a rabbit when no dogs was 'round. Dey would throw rocks at him and run him in a hollow log" (Charlie Hudson, as quoted in *Born in Slavery*).

jump (2)

> Now when jump steady [daddy] start to jumpin', he does it slow
> He goes from the top, down to the floor
> Oh, just can't let him go
> 'Cause he jump better than any man that I know.
> —Lucille Bogan, "Jump Steady Daddy," 1935

To have sex or to thrust sexually; perhaps an extension of the same term as referring to dancing. (For the former, cf. DAS 3; for the latter, cf. Burley, c. 1944). Dance parties attended by Son House were termed *jump ups*. See *jump steady, keyhole.*

jump a rattler

> I jumped that fast mail rattler, an' I almost went a-flyin'
> "Hurry engineerman for my pigmeat mama is dyin'."
> —Blind Lemon Jefferson, "Gone Dead On You Blues," 1928

To board a train without paying; used as dialogue in a 1936 novel: "'Well sir, for last year you certainly paid your fare on the railways.' 'I've never jumped the 'rattler' in my life'" (quoted at *rattler* in OED, which does not recognize the expression in toto). Irwin's dictionary of tramp slang (1931) defines *jump* as "to ride on a train" and *nail a rattler* as meaning to "jump a fast train in motion." See *rattler*.

jump down

> *I'd rather hear the screws in my coffin sound*
> *Than to hear my good gal says: "I'm jumpin' down."*
> —Furry Lewis, "Furry's Blues," 1928

To terminate a relationship. According to the above performer, *jumpin' down* "just means leavin' me. . . . I could have said: . . . '[H]ear my good gal say: "I'm gonna put you down,"' . . . but that's the first thing that come to my damn mind, [so] I just say it." The same expression occurs below:

> *Sweet woman I ain't going to stand no quittin', I ain't going to stand no jumpin'*
> *down*
> *Before I let you quit me baby, I'm going to burn half Chicago down.*
> —James "Boodle It" Wiggins, "Got To Shave 'Em Dry," 1930

jump steady

> *Jump steady daddy, please take your time*
> *You've got a year and a day, to satisfy my mind.*
> —Lucille Bogan, "Jump Steady Daddy," 1935

In this context, to thrust regularly or persistently in intercourse. The primary meaning of this term was probably dancing, as indicated by its use in Johnny Mercer's "Conversation While Dancing" (1944): "We could both jump steady." The suggestion that *jump steady* (as used by Bogan) was a "command to be honest and regular in a love relationship" (Major, 1994) is unwarranted. See *steady*.

jumpin' Judy

> *I got a notion, woman I believe I will*
> *Catch a long jumpin' Judy, go on 'cross the hill.*
> —Bo Weavil Jackson, "Some Scream High Yellow," 1926

Black slang for "a woman who takes care of more than one man" (Evans) or "a gal, you can make good [have sex] with whensoever you find her" (Davis). The term is an elaboration on *judy*, which signified a female, and particularly a promiscuous one, in 19th-century slang (F&H, 1896). The above lyric may be a humorous reference to an oft-ridden car, based on the connotation of promiscuity attached to *jumpin' Judy*; an elderly black female in Birmingham (the hometown of the above performer) recalled that her boyfriend "would tell her to get ready cuz he was coming over in ol' 'Jumpin Judy' to take her dancing" (recounted in *The Jalopy Journal*, www.jalopyjournal.com).

Kate Adams

Well the big Kate Adams, *she got ways like a man*
She'll steal a woman baby, anywhere she lands.
—Mooch Richardson, "Big Kate Adams," 1928

The name of a well-known Mississippi steamboat, existing in three ill-fated models. The first, a luxury liner, operated between Memphis and Arkansas City from 1882 to 1888, when it caught fire near Commerce, Mississippi. The second *Kate* became a dance hall for blacks after running afoul of a sandbar near Helena, Arkansas, around 1919 (Willie Moore); its successor burned on the Memphis wharf in 1926.

keep it up

Now twenty-five cents a saucer, seventy-five cents a cup
But it's extra dollar papa if you mean to keep it up.
—Hattie Hart, "Won't You Be Kind," 1928

To prolong a debauch; an archaic slang phrase recorded by Grose (1796). The above couplet refers to a commercial sex transaction.

keyhole

I feel like jumpin' through the keyhole in your door
"If you jump this time baby, you won't jump no more."
—Blind Lemon Jefferson, "Broke And Hungry Blues," 1926

A term for vagina dating to the 19th century (F&H, 1896). Jefferson's protégé Tom Shaw gave the above verse a literal interpretation, casting it in terms of a dialogue between a quarreling couple: "She stole his money and he tracks her down.... She's at home, won't open the door for him.... He done told her, he feel like jumpin' through the keyhole of her door; she told him, if he jump this time, he won't jump no more, 'cause she's standin' there with a yokie-yoke [pistol]. Boom boom! ... Happens every day." Other blues performers evince a figurative sexual understanding of *keyhole*:

Mama I feel like jumpin' through the keyhole of your door
I can jump so easy your man will never know.
—Furry Lewis, "Falling Down Blues," 1927

key to the highway, to have the

> I got the key to the highway, and I'm billed out and bound to go
> I'm gonna leave here runnin' 'cause walkin' is most too slow.
> —Big Bill, "Key To The Highway," 1941

Evidently, to be homeless; *to have the key of the street* stood for the same condition in 19th-century speech (F&H, 1896). A variant expression, *key to the bushes*, appears in the following:

> I got the key to the bushes, and I'm rarin' to go
> I ought to leave here runnin', 'cause footpath's most too slow.
> —Bessie Tucker, "Key To The Bushes Blues," 1929

kick it

> When I have it I can hardly talk
> When I kick it I can hardly walk
> —Kansas City Kitty, "Gym's Too Much For Me," 1930

To engage in sexual intercourse; in current black slang, the expression means to socialize.

kick one's heels up

> I got me two or three bottles of homebrew, three or four quarts of rye
> Stuck my head out in the alley and kicked my heels up high.
> —Lillie Mae, "Wise Like That," 1930

A black slang term meaning to carouse: "... he didn't do all this ramblin' and drinkin' corn whiskey and 'kickin' up heels' and things" (Son House, quoted in Calt and Wardlow, 1989).

kid, kid gal, kid man

> Now you tell me mama, do you think that's right?
> With your kid all day an' run to me at night.
> —Ishman Bracey, "Saturday Blues," 1928

A once-common black expression for a surreptitious sex partner taken in addition to one's customary companion. As explained by Gary Davis, a *kid gal* is "a person ... she's not your regular gal; she's fine if you want her sometimes. ... You don't care who else got her, you understand you'll always have her. ... Maybe in a late hour you might catch her sometime: 'Gal, I'd like to have you tonight, what about it?' Boom." The term probably originated with the popular vaudeville song of 1909, "I Love My Wife, But Oh, You Kid!"

kill one dead

> If I catch you in my bed
> Mama I'm gonna kill you dead.
> —Kansas City Kitty, "Leave My Man Alone," 1934

A redundant expression found in several blues and in the speech of an exslave ("The news killed her dead," cf. Botkin, 1945).

killing floor

Come on in sweet mama, I can't fool around no more

Aw get yourself ready, gonna rush you to that killing floor.

—Georgia Tom in Kansas City Kitty, "Killing Floor Blues," 1930

A black slang term, still current among teenagers of the 1960s and 1970s, denoting "any place used to engage in sexual intercourse" (Folb). Recently, it has been applied to school playgrounds with a rigid social hierarchy and to schools that teem with violence (UD). The term itself derives from slaughter-houses, the spoken introduction of the above song stating: "My man works at a stockyard, cleanin' chitlins, up on that killin' floor." Although given short shrift by lexicographers, the latter is standard English: ". . . the once-silent workers of Agriprocessors now tell of a host of abusive practices, of rampant injuries and of exhausted children as young as 13 wielding knives on the killing floor" (*New York Times* editorial, 8/1/2008).

killing floor, on the

The dry spell blues have caused me, to drift from door to door

The dry spell blues have put everybody, on the killing floor.

—Son House, "Dry Spell Blues, Part One," 1930

In a state of extreme privation from which there is no apparent escape.

kind-hearted woman

I got a kind-hearted woman, do most anything in the world for me

But they'se evil-hearted women, an' they will not let me be.

—Robert Johnson, "Kind Hearted Woman Blues," 1936

A woman who caters to a gigolo in exchange for sexual fidelity. This idiom was apparently drawn from a perverse understanding of "kind," as reflected in the following:

Kind Stella was a good gal, known to be a good man's friend

She take money from her husband, give it to her gamblin' men.

—Lucille Bogan, "Kind Stella Blues," 1927

I believe sweet mama, sure was kind to me, baby

She is up at night, like a police on his beat.

—Charlie Patton, "It Won't Be Long," 1929

(The latter lyric refers to female prostitution.) Whereas *kind-hearted* (in standard English) signifies "having naturally a kind disposition" (OED), the *kind-hearted woman* of blues/gigolo lore is taken as a vengeful companion in response to a sexual betrayal:

She's a kind-hearted woman, she studies evil all the time

You wish to kill me, else to have it on your mind.

—Robert Johnson, "Kind Hearted Woman Blues," 1936

Kinnane, Jim

Have you ever been to Memphis an' you stopped at Uncle Jim Kinnane?
He will pay more for a woman, any farmer pay for land.
—Roosevelt Sykes, "Roosevelt's Blues," 1929

A barrelhouse operated by Jim Kinnane, a gangsterish figure known as the crime czar of Memphis. His establishments flourished from the 1890s until around 1915, when civic reform shuttered the city's drinking and gambling joints. The club most readily identified with him (probably referred to in the above couplet) stood at 340 Beale Street and was known as the Monarch Club; it contained a first-floor gambling hall and a second-floor dance hall, where blues pianists held court.

kitchenette

She got a kitchenette, an apartment too
She don't do nothin' but ballyhoo.
—Kokomo Arnold, "Sister Jane Cross The Hall," 1937

A black term dating to at least the 1920s for an apartment given over to numerous paying boarders, confined to a single subdivided room. Chester Himes's Harlem-based *The Real Cool Killers* (1959) takes note of them: "... the houses had been split up into bed-size one-room kitchenettes, renting for $25 weekly, at the disposal of frantic couples who wanted to shack up for a season." The standard English *kitchenette* denoted a small room containing a kitchen and pantry (OED).

kitchen mechanic

She's a kitchen mechanic that's her regular trade
She got the best brown Betties that ever was made.
—Blind Blake, "I Was Afraid Of That," 1929

Cook, a slang expression first recorded in 1887 (New Orleans): "A ... dirty looking kitchen mechanic called Maggie Howard" (cf. OED).

knock

Excuse us stranger for bein' bold and strong
But will you knock a jug band another drink-a corn?
—Memphis Jug Band, "Fourth Street Mess Around," 1930

Black slang meaning to obtain; this term, recorded by Calloway (1939), apparently migrated northward to become fashionable in Harlem.

knocked out

Oh the revenue man is ridin', boy you'd better watch out
If he hollers you don't stop you will, likely be knocked out.
—Charlie Patton, "Revenue Man Blues," 1934

Arrested (DAUL). *Knock* was in vogue among youthful black street criminals of the mid-1980s: "'People think they ain't going to get paid, nine out of ten times, they get knocked'—arrested" (*New York Magazine*, 6/3/1985).

know what it's all about, to not

> *When I reach old Los Angeles, California, you oughta hear me jump an'*
>> *shout*
>
> *Now the people in Los Angel', they didn't know what it's all about.*
> —Lane Hardin, "California Desert Blues," 1935

To lack a sense of awareness; a catchphrase noted in Edmund Wilson's diary of 1929 under "Slang and Songs: 'doesn't know what it's all about.'" It likely originated with antebellum blacks: "Us da'kies didn' know whut it wah all bout" (Sarah Gudger, as quoted in *Born in Slavery*).

know your stuff, to

> *You're my bumble bee, an' you know your stuff*
> *Oh sting me bumble bee, until I get enough.*
> —Memphis Minnie, "Bumble Bee," 1930

To be competent and alert; contemporary slang (cf. Partridge) that still receives occasional use.

lane

> *Don't be no rascal an' don't be no lane*
> *Don't let these women leave your heart insane.*
> —Blind Willie McTell, "Warm It Up To Me," 1933

A fool or sucker; contemporary slang of apparent convict origin that gained appreciable black currency (cf. Lighter, 1997).

last go-round, on one's

> *I believe, I believe, I'm on my last go-round*
> *Lord all-a my money gone, I feel myself sinkin' down.*
> —Roosevelt Sykes, "Last Go Round Blues," 1930

Approaching death; a still-used black idiom derived from *go-round*, a standard English term for a fight or experience (OED) that never appears in blues song. One can experience one's *last go-round* without going anywhere: "This is the song that this boy sings when he was on his way to the chair to die.

It ever was a time that a body would tell the truth and would talk plain for himself it's the time when he's makin' his last go-round" (Blind Gary Davis, "Bad Company Brought Me Here," 1963).

law

> Lord the police 'rest me, carried me 'fore the jury
> Well the laws talked so fast didn't have the time to say not nary a word.
> —Hambone Willie Newbern, "Shelby County Workhouse Blues," 1929

In Southern black speech, a policeman. "Didn't no laws or nothin' fool with him in these little towns: he'd put his pistol on him and walk the streets" (Sam Chatmon on his brother Ferdinand).

lay around

> She had an' old job, makin' four dollars a day
> I didn't have to do nothin' but lay around and throw it away.
> —Kansas Joe McCoy, "My Babe My Babe," 1935

To loaf; an expression of apparent black origin that occurs in Roark Bradford's *John Henry* (1931): "'I'm a man and I'm tired er layin' around, so I'm huntin' a job….'" A related noun for a habitual loafer, *layabout,* dates to 1932 (OED).

lay it on (one)

> Mama let me lay it on you (2)
> I'll give you anything in this whole round world
> Let me lay it on you.
> —Blind Boy Fuller, "Mama Let Me Lay It On You," 1936

To give or impart something to someone; black slang (cf. Lighter, 1997, at *lay on*) that is given a sexual connotation in the above lyric.

leaping drunk

> Let's get our gauge up papa, let our love come down
> Get leapin' drunk, an' leave this low-down town.
> —Bertha Henderson, "Let Your Love Come Down," 1928

Apparently, intoxicated with drugs, *leaping* having had mid-1920s currency as a term for being "under the influence of dope" (cf. Lighter, 1997, 1925 citation at *leaping*).

Lee, Jim

> I was way up the river, some forty miles or more
> I thought I heard the big Jim Lee when it blowed.
> —Charlie Patton, "Jim Lee Blues, Part Two," 1929

The name generally given to the *James Lee II,* a Mississippi steamboat named for the founder of the Memphis-based Lee Line and operated between 1898 and 1917. Another Lee steamer, the *Robert Lee Junior,* running from St. Louis to Vicksburg, operated from 1912 to 1913 and was invoked as follows:

I was way up Red River, crawlin' on a log

I think I heard the Bob Lee boat when it (moaned).

—Charlie Patton, "Hammer Blues," 1929

Like the trains that succeeded them, such boats were recognizable by their distinctive whistles. See *Stack*.

left, get

I started once to write, but I believe I'll go myself

'Cause a letter's too slow then a telegram may get left.

—George Torey, "Married Woman Blues," 1937

To fail (F&H, 1896).

'leven light city

Oh, baby don't you wanna go?

Back to the 'leven light city, sweet old Kokomo.

—Kokomo Arnold, "Old Original Kokomo Blues," 1934

A blues equivalent of *one-horse town*, a municipality conspicuous for its small population, *light* connoting stop or traffic light.

light

If a black gal makes it thunder, a brownskin makes it pour down rain

An' a real light woman, will make your heart pain.

—Bill Gaither, "Racket Blues," 1939

Light-complexioned; said of such African Americans. A black narrator in Gwaltney (1980) recounted a job interview: "She wanted a waitress and she asked me over the phone, 'Are you light?'"

light, to turn out one's

I been a bad boy, didn't treat nobody right

They wanna give me thirty-five years, someone'll turn out my light.

—Barefoot Bill, "Bad Boy," 1930

To kill; a figure of speech that likely originated with the climactic murder speech in *Othello*: "... she must die, else she betray more men. —Put out the light, and then put out the light ..." It was used by a biker questioned in the Manson murder investigation of 1969: "I've got no balls for puttin' anybody's lights out" (Vincent Bugliosi, *Helter Skelter*, 1974), and by a detective referring to the "BTK killer" in 2005: "I'd like to be the one to put him in his cell and turn his lights out" (MSNBC documentary). In slightly altered form it appears in the following lyric:

Now you know I'm gonna get you, I mean without a doubt

Baby an' put your tail-light out.

—Irene Scruggs, "Itching Heel," 1930

like that

> *It's tight like that, beedle um bum*
> *Don't you hear me talkin' to you?*
> *Know it's tight like that.*
> —Tampa Red and Georgia Tom, "Tight Like That," 1928

A still-employed black catchphrase indicating the possession "of whatever quality is suggested by the preceding statement" (Smitherman, 2000). "'I'll take the homers when I can get them,' said Easley. 'I'm kind of streaky like that'" (*New York Daily News*, 5/14/2007). See *tight like that*.

like the flowers that comes in May

> *You're havin' a good time now, you're like the flowers that comes in May*
> *You're havin' a good time now, but you got to die some day.*
> —Henry Townsend, "She's Got A Mean Disposition," 1935

Fleeting; destined to die. This simile dates at least to Thomas Durfey's *Pills to Purge Melancholy* of 1681:

> *The pleasures of youth are flowers but of May*
> *Our Life's but a Vapour, our body's but clay.*

like to

> *Now scaredest I ever been in my life:*
> *Uncle Bud like to caught me kissin' his wife.*
> —Papa Charlie Jackson, "Salty Dog Blues," 1924

Nearly; a still-common black colloquialism (Smitherman, 2000).

limber

> *Aunt Jane she come a-runnin', tellin' everybody in the neighborhood:*
> *"That man a-mine got the limber trouble, an' his lovin' can't do me any good."*
> —Ishman Bracey, "Jake Liquor Blues," 1930

Limp; flaccid; obsolete English as pertaining to "things which are properly firm" (OED). The above reference is to the male sex organ, rendered limber by *jake*.

limber leg, the

> *I drink so much a-jake, till it done give me the limber leg*
> *If I don't quit drinkin' it sure gonna kill me dead.*
> —Tommy Johnson, "Alcohol And Jake Blues," 1930

An impaired walk (sometimes permanent) as a result of drinking adulterated *jake*, an effect also known as *jake leg* or *jake walk*.

line

> *Put your make-up on baby, go see what you can find*
> *You can't tell what's for you, till you get out on the line.*
> —*Gene Campbell, "Main Papa's Blues," 1931*

A red-light district or area where prostitutes congregate (cf. Lighter, 1997).

line, off the

> *Look a-here black gal, why don't you get off the line?*
> *What you tryin' to sell, it ain't nobody buyin'.*
> —*Memphis Minnie, "You Can't Give It Away," 1935*

The converse of *on the line*, criminal slang meaning to be engaged in street-walking or brothel work (DAUL).

linen

> *You show your linen to any man*
> *An' that is something mama that I just can't stand.*
> —*Walter Davis, "I Can Tell By The Way You Smell," 1935*

Undergarments; a standard English connotation of the word (cf. OED).

little bitty

> *Lord I'm a little bitty mama, baby an' I ain't built for speed*
> *I got everything that a little bitty mama need.*
> —*Geeshie Wiley, "Skinny Leg Blues," 1930*

Tiny, petite; a Southern colloquialism dating in print to 1905 (cf. ADD), but occurring in the speech of an ex-slave born a half-century earlier: "He plant little bitty patches close to the house . . ." (Botkin, 1945). The modifier (miscon-strued in Major [1994] as *little biddie*, meaning a small female) likely derives from *little bit*: "'You are but a little bit of a lad.' . . ." (Thackeray, *The History of Henry Esmond*, 1852). In current black slang, *lil bit* is an affectionate term for diminutive women (Smitherman, 2000).

load

> *. . . in your front yard is where I got my load*
> *Well you talk like you like my hoppin', why don't you keep me for your*
>   *little toad?*
> —*"Funny Paper" Smith, "Hoppin' Toad Blues," 1931*

Conventional slang for ejaculated semen (cf. Lighter 2, 1997). The rest of the above couplet ("front yard," etc.) is figurative.

long

> It was early one mornin', just about the break of day
>
> An' my long brownskin come in here and throwed me 'way.
>
> —Garfield Akers, "Cottonfield Blues, Part One," 1929

Tall; an uncommon colloquialism of British origin (cf. OED; DARE 3). "Her marry a big, long nigger name Saul Griffin" (Charlie Robinson, as quoted in *Born in Slavery*).

long and tall, long-tall

> I'm long and tall, like a cannon ball
>
> Take a long-tall man, make a kid gal, make a kid gal squall.
>
> —Willie Baker, "No No Blues," 1929

A redundant expression, oft-used in blues.

long as one's arm

> An' my bull's got a horn baby, long as my right arm
>
> My bull got a horn, longly as my arm.
>
> —Charlie Patton, "Jersey Bull Blues," 1934

Unusually or notably long; a colloquial comparison dating to the 19th century and conventionally rendered *as long as one's arm* (cf. Partridge). "He had a beard long as your arm" (Henry F. Pyles, as quoted in *Born in Slavery*).

Long Lincoln Land

> I got a gal in Oak Cliff, Highland Park and Long Lincoln Land, too
>
> I'm not livin' as no musician, what these meal-ticket women gonna do?
>
> —Blind Lemon Jefferson, "Booger Rooger Blues," 1926

A section of Dallas described by Tom Shaw as "kind of a hot neighborhood, where bunch of high-class whores and everybody hung out."

Sally Long (v.)

> "Oh, Sally Long, Sally Long your fanny, gal,
>
> Sally Long that thing, Sally it, shake your fat fanny."
>
> —Jim Clarke, "Fat Fanny Stomp," 1929

To shake in a manner associated with the Sally Long, a black dance apparently named for the renowned dancer who starred in the Ziegfeld Follies in the early 1920s and subsequently forged a film career.

lookey here

> I says lookey here mama what in the world is you tryin'-a do?
>
> You gonna make me love you, you gonna break my heart in two.
>
> —Garfield Akers, "Cottonfield Blues, Part One," 1929

Look here, in colloquial (particularly Southern) speech (ADD). *Look'ee* is given by Partridge as "[a] low coll. [colloquial] form of *look you!* (C. 18–20) = mind this!" The variant *looka here* also appears in blues song:

Oh I remember one mornin', stand in my rider's door
"You know what she tol' me?"
"Looka here papa Charlie I, don't want you no more."
—*Charlie Patton, "Bird Nest Bound," 1930*

The latter is colloquial usage, found in Frank Norris's *McTeague* (1899): "'Looka here, Mac.'"

love (v.)

Now ain't it hard to love someone who's married?
You can't get her when you wanna have to use her when you can.
—*Sleepy John Estes, "Diving Duck Blues," 1929*

To have sexual contact with.

love come down, to have one's

Now my love come down and I'm all alone
I want the kind of lovin' that'll make me moan.
—*Irene Scruggs, "You've Got What I Want," 1929*

To feel amorous or to become sexually aroused; black slang misrendered by Major (1994) and Spears (2001) as a term for orgasm or ejaculation. It is conventionally invoked in blues rhetoric by females but applies to either sex:

I need lovin' when my love come down
The womens I got all runnin' around.
—*Georgia Tom on Kansas City Kitty's "Do It By Myself," 1930*

It appears in Zora Neale Hurston and Dorothy Waring's *Polk County* (1944): "Is that what they say when they want to shack up with a gal? When they feel they love come down?" Though passé, it figured in the opening verse of Wilson Pickett's "In The Midnight Hour" (1965): "I'm gonna wait till the midnight hour/That's when my love comes tumblin' down." In the following variant, *love* means lust:

It's all about a man who always kicked and dogged me 'round
And when I try to kill him that's when my love for him comes down.
—*Bessie Smith, "Please Help Me Get Him Off My Mind," 1928*

See *come down*.

love, that game you call

My poor father died an' left me an' my mother done the best that she
  could
Every man loves that game you call love but it don't mean no man no
  good.
—*Robert Johnson, "Drunken Hearted Man," 1937*

A dated lower-class expression of disillusionment, harking back to Defoe's *Moll Flanders* (1722): "I had been tricked once by that cheat called love, but the game was over...."

lovin' (a.)

> *I'm gonna run 'cross town catch that southbound Santa Fe . . .*
> *. . . Be on my way to what you call lovin' Tennessee.*
> —Blind Lemon Jefferson, "Bad Luck Blues," 1927

Damned; construed in Lighter (1997), which dates it in print to 1944 as a probable euphemism for *fucking*.

lovin' (n.)

> *Where it ain't no lovin', sure ain't no gettin' along*
> *'Cause you'll have more trouble, honey than the day is long.*
> —Bo Weavil Jackson, "You Can't Keep No Brown," 1926

Lovemaking; like the latter, a euphemism for sex.

low (a. 1)

> *Now she little an' she's low, right down on the ground*
> *I guess the reason I love her, she ain't no hand me down.*
> —Charlie Spand, "Back To The Woods," 1929

Of persons, short; standard English (OED), but more customary as a Southern colloquialism (cf. ADD).

low (a. 2)

> *You called me a low rider, I'm goin' back to Tennessee*
> *An' mama there's no reason why, baby you should mistreat poor me.*
> —Blind Willie McTell, "Low Rider's Blues," 1931

A standard English pejorative, variously meaning "[a]bject, base, mean," "[d]egraded, dissolute," and "coarse, vulgar, not socially respectable" (OED), senses conveyed by *low-down*, an Americanism of later (19th-century) coinage (cf. DARE 3). The claim that *low rider* as used above was a black slang term for a pimp or inconstant lover (found in Lighter, 1997) is unfounded.

low black

> *She not a high yellow, she not a low black*
> *You meet her just once she bound to come back.*
> —Barbecue Bob, "She Moves It Just Right," 1929

? An obscure complexion designation, analogous to *low brown*, the latter recounted in Hurston (1942) as representing a shade lighter than dark brown in Harlem speech.

low-down

> *It's a low, it's a low, low-down dirty shame*
> *I got a brownskin man and I'm scared to call his name.*
> —Geeshie Wiley, "Eagles On A Half," 1930

In the above instance, an intensifier. In some contexts, it apparently serves as a euphemism for a stronger pejorative:

I wish I hadda died, mama when I was young
I would not a-had, this low-down race to run.
—*Furry Lewis, "Cannon Ball Blues," 1928*

low-down, to play it

"Play it low-down!"
—*Blind Willie McTell, "Love-Changing Blues," 1929*

Apparently, to play an accompaniment in a manner that bears no suggestion of refinement, the directive to do so implying that such is the most appealing musical attack.

machine

Bo weevil told that farmer: "Buy no Ford machine," Lordie mama!
"'Cause we're gonna take this earth, can't buy no gasoline."
—*Sam Butler, "Devil And My Brown," 1926*

A slang term for automobile, dating to at least 1901 (OED).

mad dog (a.)

Got a red-eyed captain, got a squabblin' boss
Got a mad dog sergeant, honey an' he won't knock off.
—*Blind Lemon Jefferson, "Prison Cell Blues," 1928*

A term of American origin, first recorded in 1904, meaning "wild, reckless, or hare-brained, esp. dangerously so" (OED).

made

Put you down in a ditch with a great long spade
Wish to God that you had never been made.
—*Son House, "Mississippi County Farm," 1942 (LC)*

Born, created; similarly, the phrase *to make a baby* is associated with African American speech (for the latter, cf. OED).

make a crop

Now my mother often taught me: "Son, quit playin' a box.
Go somewhere, settle down an' make a crop."
—*Sleepy John Estes, "Floating Bridge," 1937*

To raise a crop; a Southern idiom (ADD).

make a panther squall

> *I got a sweet mama, she ain't long or tall*
> *She got the kind of lovin', will make a panther squall.*
> —Blind Blake, "Panther Squall Blues," 1927

In regard to lovemaking, to be remarkably exciting. This compliment is misplaced, inasmuch as panthers were proverbially noted for their loud squalling under any circumstances; DAP records the 19th-century expression "A-squallin' wusser than a painter [panther]." The association between panthers and powerful squalling was perhaps overdrawn, William Byrd remarking of the panther in the *History of the Dividing Line* (1728): "... it must be confessed his voice is a little contemptible for a monarch of the forest, being not a great deal louder nor more awful than the mewing of a household cat."

make it

> *Mama I'm havin' bad luck, and bad luck I can't understand*
> *Got me out here scufflin' mama, tryin' to make it if I can.*
> —Walter Davis, "Jacksonville, Part Two," 1936

To succeed. This expression, which became fashionable in the 1960s, dates to at least 1906, when it was used in the context of theatrical success (cf. Lighter, 1997, at *ham*.)

make one tired

> *Some of these here women sure make me tired*
> *Got a handfulla "Gimme," mouthfulla "Much obliged."*
> —Charlie Patton, "Going To Move To Alabama," 1929

To bore or annoy; a late-19th-century catchphrase generally expressed as *You make me tired* (DC).

makin' whoopee

> *Undertaker been here an' gone, I give him your heights an' size*
> *You'll be makin' whoopee with the devil, in hell tomorrow night.*
> —King Solomon Hill, "Whoopee Blues," 1932

A 1920s vogue term for carousing, particularly at parties and with the opposite sex, popularized among white youth by the Gus Kahn and Walter Donaldson Tin Pan Alley hit, "Makin' Whoopee" (1928). It was afterward associated with gossip columnist Walter Winchell, who claimed to have coined it.

malted milk

> *I keep drinkin' malted milk, trying to drive my blues away*
> *Baby you just as welcome to my lovin', as the flowers is in May.*
> —Robert Johnson, "Malted Milk Blues," 1937

A term for beer (Willie Moore); as slang for whiskey or beer, *milk* dates to the mid-19th century (cf. Lighter, 1997).

mama

> *Have mercy, mama, sit on your daddy's knee*
> *Said tell your sweet papa, what may your troubles be?*
> —*Peg Leg Howell, "Rock And Gravel Blues," 1928*

A favorite blues term of address for a girlfriend that is also applied to any adult female. Despite the prevalence of this term, which was more common in black than in white colloquial speech, it is not used in any sense peculiar to blues singers or blacks on race recording. It likely trickled down to blacks from its 19th-century use in white speech; the OED notes: "[i]n the 19th cent. its use was much extended, and among the lower middle classes was a mark of 'gentility.' . . ."

mamlish

> *"Yes folks, these are my mamlish blues. I'm gonna*
> *tell you just what they mean."*
> *Used to be my sugar but you ain't sweet no mamlish more*
> *'Cause you mistreat me an' you drove me from your door.*
> —*Ed Bell, "Mamlish Blues," 1927*

? A vogue term of unknown meaning that figured in half a dozen blues recordings between 1927 and 1930, including this eccentric variant:

> *Got the bull frog blues mama, can't be satis- can't be satis- mamlishfied*
> *Got the bull frog blues, can't be satisfied.*
> —*William Harris, "Bull Frog Blues," 1928*

It may have been facetiously nonsensical, an intensifier, or a euphemistic expletive, perhaps deriving from *mamesh,* a Yiddish word meaning "really, truly, literally" (Wex), *Ma'alish!* a World War I expression used by British troops meaning "Never mind!" (STY), or (less likely) *mamish,* recorded by Davies (1881) as apparently meaning "foolish, effeminate, mammyish."

man, the (1)

> *I'd rather be sloppy drunk, sitting in the can*
> *Than to be out in the streets, runnin' from the man.*
> —*Leroy Carr, "Sloppy Drunk Blues," 1930*

The police, individually or collectively; a seeming black modification of the 19th-century slang phrase *the man in blue* (F&H, 1896), which became general convict slang (DAUL).

man, the (2)

> *Tell you women, how to keep your husbands at home*
> *Get you a job, an' roll for the man, an' try to carry your labor home.*
> —*Blind Joe Reynolds, "Outside Woman Blues," 1930*

As used by blacks in the Jim Crow South, any white employer.

manager

Oh mama, who may your manager be?

Reason I ask so many questions, can't you make arrangements for me?

—Blind Lemon Jefferson, "Match Box Blues," 1927

Pimp. This term (used by a Texas performer) was extant in white Texas underworld circles of the 1960s and probably originated with criminals (cf. Thompson, 1976); the related *sporting-girls' manager* was noted as general underworld slang in 1950 (DAUL). It unaccountably surfaced in the 1983 Tom Cruise movie *Risky Business*.

master

Aw the bossman may come here, we better not run

Old master got a pistol, he got a great big gun.

—Bessie Tucker, "Mean Old Master," 1929

The conventional antebellum term for slave owner or (if a slave) one's particular owner, used in the above context to imply that (in the Jim Crow South) the difference between a white boss and slave master was negligible.

Maxwell Street market

Lord I'm talkin' 'bout the wagon, talkin' 'bout the pushcart too

'Cause Maxwell Street's so crowded, on a Sunday you can hardly pass through.

Says Maxwell Street market, South Water Street market too

If you ain't got no money, the women got nothing for you to do.

—Papa Charlie Jackson, "Maxwell Street Blues," 1925

The open-air market given over to pushcart peddlers on Maxwell Street, a small street on the west side of Chicago. The performer of the above song was a denizen of the area who was discovered while singing on a local street, probably Maxwell Street itself, which became a mecca for Chicago blues singers after World War II. The market was in existence between 1871 and 1994, when it was demolished (cf. Wikipedia, http://en.wikipedia.org/wiki/Maxwell_Street).

meal

The farmer went to the merchant, says: "I want meat an' meal," Lordie mama!

The merchant screamed: "Lord no, the bo weevil's in your field."

—Sam Butler, "Devil And My Brown Blues," 1926

Cornmeal, a staple of sharecroppers' diet. The above couplet refers to the standard plantation practice of obtaining goods on credit during cotton-growing season.

meal-ticket (rider, woman)

I got a gal in Oak Cliff, Highland Park and Long Lincoln Land, too
I'm not livin' as no musician, what these meal-ticket women gonna do?
—*Blind Lemon Jefferson, "Booger Rooger Blues," 1926*

A female provider; used with the implication that such is her chief utility. "A meal-ticket woman means some woman that takes care of you. You don't wanna lose your meal-ticket, 'cause she'll stand by you when things get tough" (Tom Shaw). As a term for a provider, irrespective of gender, *meal-ticket* dates to the turn of the 20th century (cf. DARE 3).

mean

Take a mighty crooked woman, treat a good man wrong
Take a mighty mean man, take another man, take another man's whore.
—*Willie Baker, "No No Blues," 1929*

As this term is applied to men who successfully impinge on a blues singer's sexual territory, it is likely employed as a synonym for disreputable (ADD), or to indicate ignobility or a lack of moral dignity (cf. OED at *mean,* a1.5.a.). For other examples, see the following:

I feel like jumpin' from a treetop to the ground
My rider's got a mean joker, an' he don't 'low me 'round.
—*Blind Lemon Jefferson, "Mean Jumper Blues," 1928*

It was late one night, I tried so hard to sleep
When a mean ol' tomcat, started on his midnight creep.
—*Freddie Spruell, "Tom Cat Blues," 1928*

It's a mean black cat, Lordie, crawlin' on my bed
I'm gonna get up some mornin', kill that black cat dead.
—*Charlie Patton, "Mean Black Cat," 1929*

measure, to take one's

If the blues gonna kill me, take my measure, take my measure now
If the blues gonna kill me baby, take my measure now.
—*Eli Framer, "Framer's Blues," 1929*

To measure one's height and width, done in the above instance to determine coffin size. *To take one's measure* (to make measurements, especially for clothes) is obsolete standard English (cf. OED), while the same sense of *measure* was retained in Ozark speech: ". . . the first thing that will be done for him after he gets what he's entitled to," Jim replied, "will be the sending of his measure to a coffin maker" (Opie Read, *An Arkansas Planter,* 1896).

meat

> *She's hot as mustard, sly as a fox*
> *And she likes plenty of meat, in her ice box.*
> —*Pigmeat Pete and Catjuice Charlie, "She Shakes A Mean Ash Can," 1931*

Conventional slang for male or female sex organs (F&H, 1896).

meatless and wheatless days

> *Baby tell me somethin' about those meatless and wheatless days*
> *"This not bein' my home I don't think I should stay."*
> —*Blind Lemon Jefferson, "Rabbit Foot Blues," 1926*

A short-lived catchphrase referring to the voluntary wartime food rationing program proposed by Secretary of Commerce Herbert Hoover in a speech on 1/26/1918. It entailed eating one meatless and wheatless meal per day, and observing one meatless and wheatless day per week. Presumably, the term *meatless and wheatless days* referred to the latter regime.

Mecca Flat woman

> *Mecca Flat woman, stings like a stingaree*
> *Mecca Flat woman, take your teeth outta me.*
> —*Priscilla Stewart, "Mecca Flat Blues," 1924*

In the above context, a prostitute affiliated with the well-known Chicago brothel located in Mecca Flats (Mayo Williams), a four-story apartment complex at 3338–3360 South State Street. The latter was constructed as a showpiece of fine housing in 1893 and demolished around 1950, decades after deteriorating into a slum.

meet up with

> *"I was goin' down to Merritt Street the other night; met up with a gang of*
> *stags."*
> —*Blind Willie McTell, "Atlanta Strut," 1930*

To encounter, particularly by accident; a black or Southern colloquialism. "On de road I meet up with two boys, so we go on" (John Eubanks, as quoted in *Born in Slavery*).

mellow

> *I'm goin' sing this verse, and then I will decline*
> *For I'm goin' to St. Louis, to that low mellow gal of mine.*
> —*Teddy Darby, "Low Mellow," 1933*

A black superlative meaning "all right, fine" (Calloway, 1939).

mess

> *Too tight, it's a mess*
> *Too tight, it's the best*
> *Too tight, this rag of mine.*
> —*Blind Blake, "Too Tight," 1926*

A still-used black superlative of possible 19th-century vintage (see Della Harris quote) recounted by Calloway (1939) as meaning *wonderful*. Major (1970) reports that "to say to someone 'You're a mess,' is to imply that he or she is remarkable or puzzling." "Men gwine say, Miss Sue, where in the devil do you get this stuff? Gal, you are a mess" (Mrs. Della Harris, as quoted in *Born in Slavery*).

Mess Around

> *The stompin' dance gained world renown*
> *This dance is a scream in every town*
> *Down in Georgia, Carolina*
> *Where they do that Mess Around.*
> —Sara Martin, "That Dance Called Messin' Around," 1926

A black dance of limited 1920s popularity, despite the above lyric, described thusly in one song:

> *Why, anyone can learn the knack,*
> *Hands on your hips and nearly break your back,*
> *Stand on one spot, hold it tight,*
> *Twist to the left, and jive to the right,*
> *And believe me, you are Messin' Around!*
> —Ethel Waters, "Ev'rybody Mess Aroun'," 1926

Although long obsolete, it was treated as a current-day sensation in Ray Charles's "Mess Around" (1953) and Chubby Checker's "The Mess Around" (1961).

mess, strew one's

> *There's time for everything, so the good book say*
> *The best time to strew it is a while 'fore day*
> *Then you strew your mess. . . .*
> *In the cool of the morning, Lord you can strew your mess.*
> —Billie McKenzie and Jesse Crump, "Strewin' Your Mess," 1929

To engage in sex; a black slang term drawn from the sense of *mess* as meaning excrement, or "stuff" (cf. Lighter, 1997).

midnight woman

> *I don't want no midnight woman, knockin' on my door*
> *'Cause I got me a pigmeat woman I cannot, use her berry no more.*
> —Blind Boy Fuller, "Black And Tan," 1936

? A black-complexioned woman. The reference to *berry* appears to invoke the black proverb: "The blacker the berry the sweeter the juice."

milk cow

> *If you see my milk cow tell her: "Hurry home!"*
> *I ain't had no milk since that cow been gone.*
> —Son House, "My Black Mama, Part One," 1930

A blues term for a woman, likely suggested by the conventional colloquial synonym *cow*, which dates to the 17th century (F&H). It was used in contrast to *bullcow*, which has no discernable basis in vernacular speech.

mind (n. 1)

> *If I hadda listened, to my second mind*
> *I don't believe I'd-a been here, wringin' my hand and cryin'.*
> —Blind Lemon Jefferson, "Corrina Blues," 1926

A black idiom for "a presentiment, an intention, an idea or notion" found both in America and in the Caribbean (OED). In the above, *second mind* may constitute a separate idiom (cf. OED, which lists the example *first mind*).

mind (n. 2)

> *You don't know, sure don't know my mind*
> *I don't show you my ticket now you, don't know where I'm gwine.*
> —Charlie Patton, "Devil Sent The Rain," 1929

"The way in which a person feels, or the attitude a person has, towards another; disposition or intention towards others" (OED).

mind (v.)

> *I got to keep movin', I got to keep movin', blues fallin' down like hail . . .*
> *An' the day keeps on mind me, there's a hellhound on my trail . . .*
> —Robert Johnson, "Hell Hound On My Trail," 1937

To remind one; standard English now associated with Scottish speech (OED).

missed meal cramps

> *My body feels so weary 'cause I got the missed meal cramps*
> *Right now I could eat more than a whole carload of tramps.*
> —Alec Johnson, "Miss Meal Cramp Blues," 1928

A black term for hunger pangs resulting from "missed" meals, also rendered as *missing meal cramps*: ". . . I do know those missing-meal cramps" (Gwaltney, 1980).

Mister Charlie

> *Aw Mister Charlie, you had better watch your men*
> *They-all goin' to the bushes, and they all goin' in.*
> —Jack Kelly, "Red Ripe Tomatoes," 1933

Among blacks, a generic term for a white man that became nationally familiar during the 1960s civil rights era, when it was used derisively to indicate the perceived interchangeability of whites. In blues song it is used in direct address:

Oh Mister Charlie, why don't you leave my gal alone?
Well you keep on kicking her, you bound to break up my happy home.
—Kokomo Arnold, "Mister Charlie," 1936

Mister Man

Black man is evil, brownskin man is too
But a yellow man is conceited an' he'll make a fool outta you.
Mister Man, Mister Man, Mister Man.
—Ida Cox, "Mister Man, Part One," 1925

A form of address to strangers; of a Memphis blues audience that attended one of his appearances in 1909, W. C. Handy recalled: "Now and again one [listener] got happy and shouted, 'Aw, do it, Mister Man'" (*Father of the Blues*, 1941). The same term is used generically for white people (particularly plantation owners) in Martha Young's dialect novel *Plantation Bird Legends* (1902): "'. . . he take 'n' drap dat corn in Mister Man's new plowed fiel'.'"

Mister So and So

Baby baby, I ain't gonna worry with you no more
Lord I'm goin' down the country, let you have Mister So and So.
—Walter Davis, "Jacksonville, Part Two," 1936

A blues embellishment of the standard English *so-and-so* as "a term of abuse for a person" (OED), also used in the sense of "a substitute for an expression or name not exactly remembered or not requiring to be explicitly stated" (OED).

Mister Williams

"It done got good to Mister Williams."
—Blind Blake, "Dry Bone Shuffle," 1927

A reference to J. Mayo Williams, the Chicago-based recording director for Paramount Records between 1923 and 1928, and discoverer of the above guitarist, who thereby suggests that his music has been having an effect on Williams in the recording studio.

mistreater

I got a dirty mistreater, she's mean as she can be
I hadn't figured that she was so mean till she dropped that cannon on me.
—Blind Lemon Jefferson, "Lemon's Cannon Ball Moan," 1928

A black-originated colloquialism for one who mistreats others, particularly a partner in a romantic/sexual relationship; used with the implication that such is that person's defining characteristic.

moan (n.)

It's a mean black moan, an' a, black moan my God
An' the strike in Chicago, Lord it just won't stop.
—Charlie Patton, "Mean Black Moan," 1929

An archaic term for a lamentation or complaint, given by the OED as "now chiefly Sc. [Scottish]." In blues, however, *moan* is a common substitute for the term *blues* as a song label, as in "Levee Camp Moan." (The two terms are so intertwined as to be nearly synonymous.) Son House (a crony of the above performer) took the phrase *mean black moan* to represent a dirge on behalf of a dead loved one.

mojo

My rider's got a mojo, she's tryin' to keep it hid
But papa's got somethin' for to find that mojo with.
—Blind Lemon Jefferson, "Low Down Mojo Blues," 1928

A *hand* concocted in the form of a small cloth bag that was sometimes worn between the legs, thus giving rise to the above couplet, which gives the term a sexual twist. It was held to bring luck to gamblers and to prevent infidelity. "Lotta gamblin' peoples got 'em," Willie Moore noted. "Lotta peoples got 'em that play cards." Although the era in which blacks embraced such items has long passed, the term *mojo* has become a pretentious media vogue word for one's power, influence, aura of success, and the like, thanks to its prominence in the *Austin Powers* films. *Mojo* is one of the few blues locutions with an apparent African pedigree; the similar *moco,* a Gullah term for witchcraft and magic, was derived from a Fula term (*moco'o*) for medicine man (Turner).

Mollie

Run, Mollie, run; run, Mollie, run
Run, Mollie, run, let us have some fun.
—Henry Thomas, "Run, Mollie, Run," 1927

A reference to Miss Mollie McCarthy, a California racehorse whose celebrated 1878 Louisville contest with a horse named Ten Broeck sparked various ballads. In the above square dance tune, *Mollie* is not identified as a horse, and is invoked only in the chorus of a song about criminality.

money men

It have been so dry, you can make a powder-house outta the world
An' all the money men, like a rattlesnake in his curl.
—Son House, "Dry Spell Blues, Part Two," 1930

Wealthy men (House); used here as an oblique criticism of uncharitable Delta planters.

monkey

Says I'll be your monkey baby, sure won't be your dog
Says 'fore I stand your doggin' I'll sleep in a hollow log.
—Charlie Patton, "Joe Kirby," 1929

See *monkey man*.

monkey doodle

Monkey doodle, monkey doodle doo
Try to make a monkey outta me, I'll make a baboon outta you.
—Barbecue Bob, "The Monkey And The Baboon," 1930

Foolishness, nonsense; a slang term (ATS) that figured in the title "The Monkey Doodle-Doo," a 1925 pop instrumental by Ted Lewis and his Band. It likely originated with "Monkey Doodle Dandy," a frivolous pop song of 1909: "Monkey Doodle, Doodle Dandy, that's a very funny name."

monkey man

I want all you women to strictly understand:
When God made me he didn't make no monkey man.
—Peg Leg Howell, "Monkey Man Blues," 1928

A man who will "let a woman make a monkey outta him" (House) by capitulating to her in a relationship. Skip James said contemptuously of the monkey man: "He's always grateful to touch the hem of her [a female's] garment." This term was the supreme pejorative in the blues vocabulary, and the blues singer took pains to distinguish himself from the *monkey man* by advertising his detachment from women, except as creatures of convenience:

My love's like water, it turns off an' on
When you think I'm lovin' I done turned off an' gone.
—Edward Thompson, "Seven Sisters Blues," 1929

It is likely that in barrelhouse-prostitution circles, a *monkey man* was regarded as a mark to be exploited, as indicated in the following songs:

I'm goin' now, find my monkey man
I'll get all he's got, then find my regular man.
—Lottie Beaman, "Regular Man Blues," 1924

My woman's got a new way of loving, a monkey man can't catch on
When he knows anything, she done got his dollar and gone.
—Jake Jones, "Monkeyin' Around," 1929

The expression arose from the standard English *to make a monkey out of*, meaning to deceive or make a fool of, which dates in print to 1767 (OED). With moot accuracy, Fisher (1928) records it as meaning "cake-eater" (woman chaser) in Harlem, while in Zora Neale Hurston's *De Turkey and de Law: A Comedy in Three Acts* (1930), it signifies a suitor used for convenience: "You know you love Dave. I'm your monkey-man." Coincidentally, a *monkey* in criminal slang signified "[a] victim of a con game" (Dalzell).

monkey woman

> *I'll hold your head when you are feeling bad*
> *Sing and dance for you when you are sad*
> *I'll love you in the morning, also at night*
> *Even stand for you to fuss an' fight*
> *So what more can a monkey woman do?*
> —Sara Martin, "What More Can A Monkey Woman Do?," 1925

An overly obliging or compliant female; an extension of *monkey man* rarely used in blues song (and presumably, in black speech).

mooch it

> *"Come on, let's mooch it, mama—I say: 'Mooch it!'*
> *Don't mooch it up an' down—mooch it 'round an' round.*
> *Now that's the way to do it; now you moochin' it."*
> —Cow Cow Davenport, "Mootch Piddle," 1929

To move one's hips in a manner associated with the Mooch, a dance for which Bert Williams became celebrated in 1903.

morning gown

> *You can tear the good road down*
> *But you can't raise, the morning gown.*
> —Skip James, "Illinois Blues," 1931

? A black equivalent of nightgown; also heard on Leadbelly's "See See Rider" (1935):

> *I was lookin' right at her, when the sun went down...*
> *She was standin' in the kitchen, in her mornin' gown.*

morrow

> *Standin' at the station, waitin' for my train to come*
> *Singin' "Hurry up moonlight, let the morrow come."*
> —Charley Lincoln, "Depot Blues," 1928

Morning, a sense of the word regarded as rare by the OED. Of itself, the use of *morrow* as a synonym of *tomorrow* is construed as literary, archaic, or regional English.

most too

> *The walk you got baby, is most too bad*
> *When I see you do it, it nearly makes me mad.*
> —John Harris, "Glad And Sorry Blues," 1929

A black modifier in which *most* is apparently equivalent to *much*.

motherfuyer

> *I met another man, asked me for a dollar*
> *Might have heard that motherfuyer holler:*
> *"Let's go down in the alley*
> *You can get your business fixed all right."*
> —Memphis Minnie, "Down In The Alley," 1937

A recording euphemism for "motherfucker," a term that the above performer (described as a "burrhead" by Sam Chatmon) habitually applied to males in ordinary conversation (Ted Bogan).

Mother Hubbard

> *When the news retched town Casey Jones was dead*
> *Women dressin' up an' outed out in red.*
> *Slippin' and slidin' across the street*
> *In their loose Mother Hubbard and their stocking feet.*
> —Jesse James, "Southern Casey Blues," 1936

A loose-fitting, long-sleeved, and nearly floor-length type of dress regarded as an emblem of feminine modesty and worn primarily by rural females. Introduced around 1884, they remained popular through the early years of the 20th century, and are still worn by members of the Amish sect.

motherless dollar, to lack a

> *Did you dream lucky, an' wake up cold in hand?*
> *And didn't have a motherless dollar, to give your house-rent man.*
> —Frank Stokes, "Frank Stokes' Dream," 1929

? To be dead broke. The expression *dead motherless broke* is cited by the OED as Australian slang (dating to 1898) for being completely broke. As an adjectival term of abuse, *motherless* is recorded by Lighter (1997) as meaning *godamned*, which may apply to the above.

mountain jack

> *If I could holler, like a mountain jack*
> *I'd go up on the mountain, call my baby back.*
> —Leroy Carr, "How Long Blues," 1928

An embellishment (presumably black, or Southern) of *jack*, short for jackass (male ass). For the latter, cf. OED at *Jack*, n.1, which offers three citations, from George Washington, Washington Irving, and Longfellow.

mouth

> *Now don't think you are smart, because you got a lotta mouth*
> *For the line you are carryin' is done played out.*
> —Washboard Sam, "I'm Not The Lad," 1941

A facility for talking; generally used pejoratively: "... gals dese days is got too much mouf" ("Aunt Irene" of Alabama, as quoted in *Born in Slavery*). It was said of the famous blues singer Charlie Patton: "Charlie Patton had a whole lotta mouth..." (Calt and Wardlow, 1989).

mouth stuck out, to have one's

> *Everything I do you got your mouth stuck out*
> *An' the hole where I used to fish you got me posted out.*
> —Robert Johnson, "Dead Shrimp Blues," 1937

To display a disapproving frown, a black colloquialism occurring in Langston Hughes and Zora Neale Hurston's *The Mule-Bone* (1931): "Got your mouth stuck out jus' because some one is enjoying theyselves."

mud-kicker

> *Now they entered me into that crib of misery, down in dear old county jail*
> *They helt me there for ten long days, and my mud-kicker didn't send no*
>   *mail.*
> —Pine Top Smith, "Big Boy, They Can't Do That," 1929

An uncommon slang term for a prostitute (DAS).

muddy water, to look through and spy dry land

> *I can look through muddy water, baby and spy dry land*
> *If you don't want me, honey, let's shake hand in hand.*
> —Furry Lewis, "Dry Land Blues," 1928

A black catchphrase applied to one who possesses uncanny ability, or the power to achieve improbable results. A conjurer in Zora Neale Hurston's *Spunk* (1935) is said to act as though he "can peep through muddy water and see dry land." Figuratively, muddy water = turmoil and danger; dry land = safety and serenity.

mule kickin' in one's stall, to have a

> *Oh, what's the matter now?*
> *There's a black mule baby, kickin' in my stall.*
> —Henry Thomas, "Texas Easy Street Blues," 1928

To be cuckolded; a blues catchphrase likely drawn from black colloquial speech. An overt sexual twist is given to the expression in Margaret Thornton's "Jockey Blues" (1927):

> *Men don't like me because I'm young and tall*
> *Don't believe I'm a jockey, back your mule in my stall.*

mumble-peg

> *My mama told me, when I'se a boy playin' mumble-peg*
> *"Don't drink no black cow's milk, don't you eat no black hen's egg."*
> —Blind Willie McTell, "Talkin' To Myself," 1931

An informal children's game, dating in print to 1627, which tests the ability of the participants to make a thrown knife blade stick in the ground (or some other surface). It derives its name (rendered in England as *mumblety-peg*) from the proverbial penalty for the loser, who must pull a peg from the ground with his teeth (cf. OED and DARE 3, which misconstrues the term/game as simply American).

mumsie

> *Oh mumsie, mumsie, papa do double do love you*
> *Honey babe; babe, oh babe*
> *Your popsie loves you, don't care what you do.*
> —*Charlie Jackson, "Mumsy Mumsy Blues," 1926*

Mother, in British domestic and nursery parlance (Partridge); perhaps used in the above song as a humorous affectation. In America the term received some society use, lending an air of gentility or refinement to mundane conversation, as in Margaret Ayer Barnes's novel *Years of Grace* (1930): "'Come on, Mumsy, Albert and Dad are waiting.'"

murder

> *Every day, seem like murder here*
> *I'm gonna leave tomorrow, I know you don't bid my care.*
> —*Charlie Patton, "Down The Dirt Road Blues," 1929*

A slang term of 19th-century origin for something insufferable, unbearable, unmanageable, etc.(Lighter, 1997). In the above couplet it is applied to a detested domestic situation.

must-I-holler

> *Must I holler, or must I shake 'em on down?*
> *Aw don't stop hollerin' mama, must I shake 'em on down?*
> —*Bukka White, "Shake 'Em On Down," 1937*

? As the subject of the above song is sex, *must-I-holler* may be used in the sense indicated by Major (1994), as a black term for vagina, the latter being of reported 1980s vintage.

my stomach thinks my throat's been cut

> *Am I hungry? I ain't nothin' but*
> *Stomach's empty, thinks my throat is cut.*
> —*Maggie Jones, "Western Union Blues," 1924*

A black catchphrase denoting severe hunger. Incongruously, it appeared as dialogue in a 1990 Tom Selleck Western, *Quigley Down Under*: "I don't know about you, but my stomach thinks my throat's been cut."

nail one to the wall

> *Lord I'm so heartbroken, girls, I cannot cry at all*
> *But if I find my man, girls, I'm-a nail him to the wall.*
> —Rosie Mae Moore, "Stranger Blues," 1928

To punish severely; treated as current slang by DCS.

nappy

> *Your head is nappy, your feets so mamlish long*
> *An' you like a turkey, comin' through the mamlish corn.*
> —Bobby Grant, "Nappy Head Blues," 1927

The prevalent black adjectival term for the head hair of blacks, derived from the archaic standard English sense of *nappy* to mean wooly and used to describe cloth (cf. OED).

Naptown

> *When you get lonesome, and want to have some fun*
> *You just grab a train, and try old Naptown some.*
> —Leroy Carr, "Naptown Blues," 1929

A black term for Indianapolis.

nary

> *Lord the police 'rest me, carried me 'fore the jury*
> *Well the laws talked so fast didn't have the time to say not nary a word.*
> —Hambone Willie Newbern, "Shelby County Workhouse Blues," 1929

Not even, not a single, a term that entered American colonial speech (where it was first recorded in New England, in 1746) from provincial British speech, and ultimately descended into dialect (cf. OED). In blues it is preceded by a gratuitous *not*, and comes with an alternative form, *nar'*:

> *Nickel is a nickel, dime is a dime*
> *Got a house fulla children not nar' a one mine.*
> —King Solomon Hill, "Tell Me Baby," 1932

nasty

> *So the next daddy I get, I'm gonna take him to a restaurant*
> *Ain't gonna have him . . . eatin' biscuits, made up with your nasty hands.*
> —Memphis Minnie, "Good Biscuits," 1938

Filthy or dirty to the point of being repulsive; also applied figuratively to lewd conduct or language. Once standard English, this term has been largely the province of blacks and Southern whites since the late 19th century (cf. OED; DARE 3).

Nation

I been to the Nation, from there to the Territo'
An' I'm a hard-luck child, catch the devil everywhere I go.
—Skip James, "Hard Luck Child," 1931

Properly, the land within Indian Territory occupied by one of the Native American tribes designated as Nations. Of itself, *nation* was used as an informal designation for various Native American people, dating to early colonial times (cf. OED). During the 19th century, the federal government recognized five "civilized" Indian nations that were granted a measure of self-government: the Cherokee, Creek, Choctaw, Seminole, and Chickasaw people, all of whom were settled in Oklahoma (the *Territo'* of the above reference). Blues songs commonly refer to the Nation, but in the faulty sense of a region, rather than people, as found in the following reference by an ex-slave: "They took my mother to her nation in Oklahoma" (Robert Solomon, as quoted in *Born in Slavery*). See *Indian Territo'*.

'nation sack

Aw she's gone, I know she won't come back
I taken the last nickel, out of her 'nation sack.
—Robert Johnson, "Come On In My Kitchen," 1936

A pouch worn by jukehouse proprietors to collect proceeds from food and drink, hence its formal name, *donation sack* (Skip James). It was also applied to any carryall: "You put money in a 'nation sack, you can put anything in it . . . whiskey or a gun, anything; they'd fasten it around your waist" (Willie Moore). One lyric contains a pun on the expression:

Been to the Nation, an' I just got back
Didn't get no money, but I brought the sack.
—Andrew and Jim Baxter, "Bamalong Blues," 1927

As a term for pocketbook, *sack* dates to at least 1888 (Thornton 1912).

natural

Well I tell you buddy this natural fact:
Whenever you quit me I ain't gonna take you back.
—William Harris, "Hot Time Blues," 1928

True, indisputable, absolute (cf. Lighter, 1997, at *natural-born,* with which it is essentially synonymous).

natural-born

> Had it written in the back of my shirt:
> "Natural-born eastman, don't have to work."
> —Furry Lewis, "Kassie Jones, Part Two," 1928

Of personal qualities, present at birth, and thus presumably unalterable; a standard English formulation dating in print to 1835 (OED) that is now associated with black speech (cf. Lighter, 1997). "Dem pickaninnies dey had de natural born art ob twistin' dey body any way dey wish" (Dora Roberts, as quoted in *Born in Slavery*).

nearabout

> I was so cold, my face was nearabout froze
> I didn't have a penny, I couldn't find no place to go.
> —Memphis Minnie, "Outdoor Blues," 1932

Nearly, in (chiefly Southern) colloquial speech, dating to the 18th century (DARE 3).

never drive a stranger from your door

> Said brown don't you never, drive a stranger 'way from your door
> It may be your best friend, honey you don't know.
> —Barbecue Bob, "Good Time Rounder," 1928

An opportunistic blues bromide based on the biblical admonition: "Be not forgetful to entertain strangers: for thereby some have entertained angels unawares" (Hebrews: 13:2). The singers who advanced such counsel were interested in receiving the benefits of charity, not dispensing it.

nickel-plated

> Had the blues all of '28, Lord and again in '29
> Tell me New York Central is a nickel-plated line.
> —Furry Lewis, "Black Gypsy Blues," 1929

First-class; a slang term of late-19th-century vintage (cf. Lighter, 1997). The New York, St. Louis, and Chicago railroad referred to above was nicknamed *The Nickel Plate*.

nigger

> I went to my window, my window was cracked
> I went to my door, my door was locked.
> I stepped right back, I shook my head
> A big black nigger in my foldin' bed.
> I shot through the window, I broke the glass
> I never seen a little nigger run so fast.
> —Memphis Jug Band, "On The Road Again," 1928

In the above instance, a worthless or contemptible black male, a sense also evident in the following:

Gonna grab me a freight train, ride the lonesome rail
Nigger stole my baby, she's in the lonesome jail.
—*Blind Willie McTell, "Stole Rider Blues," 1927*
And I went on the mountain. I looked down in the sea
Niggers had my woman, Lord and the blues had me.
—*Sleepy John Estes, "Stack O' Dollars," 1930*

The notion that "nigger" served as a figurative term for a contemptible person of either race appears disingenuous, as this epithet appears to have been applied only to blacks in actual practice. Nonetheless, Skip James held that a "[m]ean disposition and dirty ideas" rather than racial identity were the defining characteristics of a "nigger" (see also Lighter, 1997, at *nigger*, sense 3). Regardless of connotation, the term rarely occurs in blues lyrics, which suggests that it was considered unseemly by blacks of the Jim Crow era, despite assertions that it was (and is) used freely among African Americans, with no pejorative overtones.

nigger hounds

Have chickens on my back, nigger hounds on my track
I dropped my head an' I couldn't stop look back . . .
—*Sam Collins, "My Road Is Rough And Rocky," 1931*

Bloodhounds, deployed in pursuit of escaped slaves in antebellum days and, in the Jim Crow era, in pursuit of black fugitives. The term was of antebellum derivation, an ex-slave reporting of a slaver: "He had nigger hounds and he made money a-huntin' runaway niggers" (Yetman). Such dogs had no other function: ". . . he said that on most plantations were kept squirrel dogs, 'possum dogs, snake dogs, rabbit dogs, an' 'nigger' dogs" (account of interview with George Patterson, as quoted in *Born in Slavery*).

nigh

Oh liquor liquor liquor, gimme liquor till I die
An' I'm always happy, when I've got my liquor nigh.
—*Barbecue Bob, "Blind Pig Blues," 1928*

Near; once standard English, but associated with provincial speech in the 20th century (cf. OED).

nighthawk

No matter where you go you'll found
Find somewhere in every town
A place where nighthawks hang around
—*Sara Martin, "Hole In The Wall," 1928*

"A person who is active at night, esp. for a nefarious purpose" (Lighter, 1997).

ninety-nine

I'm goin' down South wear ninety-nine pair a-shoes
I'm gonna keep on walkin', till I lose these blues.
—Peg Leg Howell, "Walkin' Blues," 1929

Damaged or dilapidated shoes; a salesman's term (DAS).

ninety-nine degree

I gave my baby now, the ninety-nine degree
She jumped up and throwed a pistol down on me.
—Robert Johnson, "Stop Breaking Down Blues," 1937

? Most likely, black slang for severe physical abuse: "We all hated what they called the 'nine ninety-nine,' usually a flogging until [a slave] fell over, unconscious or begging for mercy" (Dennis Simms, as quoted in *Born in Slavery*).

no-'count

Now I'm goin' to Detroit, to find me an angel man
"I don't know about that angel man, but he ain't no-'count."
—Bessie Mae Smith, "St. Louis Daddy," 1929, with spoken asides by Wesley
    Wallace

Aphetic for *no-account*, a colloquialism meaning worthless and dating in print to 1845 (DARE 3). Clapin (c. 1902) reports the latter as "much used in the South and South-west." It occurs in Faulkner's *The Sound and the Fury* (1929): "'Every other no-count nigger in town eats in my kitchen.'" As *no count*, it is recorded as a current black expression in Smitherman (2000).

no-good weed

When I was a little boy Lord, my stepfather didn't 'low me around
He's a no-good weed mama, the cows gonna mow him down.
—Big Joe Williams, "Stepfather Blues," 1935

A black expression for a worthless person, derived from the 19th-century use of *weed* as "[g]eneric for sorriness or worthlessness" (F&H, 1904), specifically applied to horses.

Norah's dove

If I had wings like Norah's turtle dove
I would rise and fly, light on the one I love.
—Peg Leg Howell, "Turtle Dove Blues," 1928

A reference to the dove Noah sent from his ark "to see if the waters were abated" after resting three months on Mount Ararat (Genesis: 8:7).

not for mine

New York's a good town, but it's not for mine
Goin' back to Avalon, there where I have a pretty mama all the time.
—Mississippi John Hurt, "Avalon Blues," 1928

An apparent colloquial variant of *not for me*, occurring as shopgirl dialogue in O. Henry's *The Trimmed Lamp* (1906): "'Him?' said Nancy . . . 'not for mine. I saw him drive up outside . . . give me the real thing or nothing, if you please.'" The preceding couplet may be a rejoinder to a 1909 pop song, "New York Town For Mine, Boys."

notoriety

> *I got a notoriety woman, she 'bout to drive me wild*
> *Besides that woman, the devil('s) meek an' mild . . .*
> —Blind Blake, "Notoriety Woman Blues," 1928

In black speech, someone who is notoriously disreputable; a known criminal or hell-raiser. Gary Davis defined *notoriety* as "a person that has a outstandin' [police] record or a bad reputation; a great long court record. Just don't care what they say or where they say it at or what they do or where they do it at." As applied to a female: "She ain't nothin' but noise: she'll do anything, say anything" (Hill).

notoriety talk

> *Say all you dicty folks, you better take a walk*
> *'Cause I'm a notoriety boy, with some notoriety talk.*
> —Sam Theard, "Three Sixes," 1930

Speech consisting of *dozens* (Skip James).

occupation

> *I got ways like the devil, sleep in a lion's den*
> *And my chief occupation: takin' women from the monkey men.*
> —Papa Charlie Jackson, "The Cat's Got The Measles," 1924

Activity; standard English (OED) put to an unusual context.

old black dog

> *Lord, "Old black dog," honey when I'm gone*
> *Come in with my money an' it's "Where you been so long?"*
> —Edward Thompson, "West Virginia Blues," 1929

An antebellum epithet, used with racial overtones: "I called one of the white girls "old black dog" and they pretended they would tell their mother (my mistress) about it" (Mattie Hartman, as quoted in *Born in Slavery*).

old shoe

It's some other low-down scoundrel, been had his foot in my shoe
'Cause it don't feel good to me sweet baby, a-honey like it used to do.
—Bo Carter, "Old Shoe Blues," 1935

A double entendre with a colloquial basis in the obsolete 19th-century expression *to ride in another man's old shoes,* meaning to maintain or marry someone else's mistress (F&H, 1903).

old woman's darling or a young woman's slave, an

I'd rather be dead, and sleepin' down in my grave
Than to be an old woman's darling, or to be a young woman's slave.
—Papa Charlie Jackson, "Papa Do Do Do Blues," 1929

A play on the 19th-century saying "Better an old man's darling than a young man's slave," applied to females. The latter was an updated version of a proverb recorded by John Heywood in 1546: "Better an old man's darling/Than a young man's warling."

on a bum

Well look here mama what you done done
Took my money, put me on a bum.
—Jed Davenport and His Beale Street Jug Band, "You Oughta Move Out of
    Town," 1932

A variant of *on the bum,* slang dating to the 1890s for surviving by panhandling, or going homeless (cf. Lighter, 1994, at *bum*; DAUL).

on a sly

I whip my black woman, tell you the reason why
Black woman's evil, do things on a sly.
—Memphis Jug Band, "On The Road Again," 1928

Surreptitiously; a variant of *on the sly,* a standard English expression (OED).

on a wander

Lord I hate to hear the little Katy blow
Puts me on a wander, mama makes me wanna go.
—Little Brother Montgomery, "No Special Rider," 1930

In the grip of wanderlust; a black colloquialism.

on a wonder

Everybody's on a wonder, what's the matter with my milk cow today?
Long as she give that sweet milk an' butter . . . she sure can't drive me
    away.
—Kokomo Arnold, "Milk Cow Blues No. 3," 1935

Wondering, likely formed by misapprehending *on a wander.*

on the 'count of

> *I'm worried and bothered, don't know what to do*
> *Reason I'm worried an' bothered, it's all on the 'count of you.*
> —Blind Lemon Jefferson, "Rambler Blues," 1927

A black variant of *on account of,* a Southern colloquialism meaning *because of* (for the latter, cf. ADD).

on the hog

> *I was down in Cincinnati, baby on the hog*
> *I'm drinkin' muddy water, sleep in a hollow log.*
> —Peg Leg Howell, "Away From Home," 1929

Broke, living as a tramp; a slang term of late-19th-century vintage in which *hog* refers to *hog-train* (cf. Lighter, 1997).

on the road again

> *Your friend come to your house, wife asks him to rest his hat*
> *The next thing he wanna know: "Where's your husband at?"*
> *She says: "I don't know, he's on his way to the pen."*
> *"Come on mama, let's get on the road again."*
> —Memphis Jug Band, "On The Road Again," 1928

? Engaged in a resumed (in this instance, sexual) activity; an apparent catch-phrase.

on the road somewhere

> *On the road somewhere (2)*
> *You can find highway robber, on the road some. . . .*
> —Charlie Patton, "Elder Greene Blues," 1929

Leading a rootless existence; lacking a home. It appears in Zora Neale Hurston and Dorothy Waring's *Polk County* (1944): "I won't have no home no more. Be like I done before. Just on the road somewhere."

on the shelf

> *I ain't trustin' nobody, I'm 'fraid of myself*
> *I been too low-down, Liza put me on the shelf.*
> —Peg Leg Howell, "Low Down Rounder Blues," 1928

Laid aside; a common 19th-century colloquialism applied to both persons and objects (F&H, 1903).

on the square

> *Now when you've got a man, don't never be on the square*
> *'Cause if you do he'll have a woman everywhere.*
> —Ida Cox, "Wild Women Don't Have The Blues," 1924

Honest; above board.

one-night stand

> *I'm one woman, who can't use a no-good man*
> *Because a man like him, is only good for a one-night stand.*
> —Trixie Smith, "No Good Man," 1939

A sexual relationship of one night's duration; a now-standard English phrase first recorded in 1937 (cf. Lighter, 1997).

one-way (gal, woman)

> *This gal of mine she's one-way all the time*
> *She takes the blues away and satisfies my mind.*
> —William Moore, "One Way Gal," 1928

Honest; a contemporary slang term associated with underworld and prison use (cf. Lighter, 1997). In regard to a female, it connotes a faithful consort; as Gary Davis put it: "That one-way gal is a woman that puts up with one man." See *two-way*.

ooze

> *Now listen here good people, about three weeks ago*
> *I caught a train an' I oozed down here . . .*
> —Milton Locke, "Oozing Daddy," 1934 (LC)

A catchall verb of motion, particularly stealthy motion (DAS) that (in the expression *to ooze out*) originated as a student term that came into vogue before 1910, meaning to sneak out (STY).

oughta could

> *Now come along boys, I'm gonna say to you*
> *I really know somethin' that you oughta could do.*
> —Bo Carter, "I've Got A Case Of Mashin' It," 1931

Ought to be able to; of presumable black (and perhaps antebellum) origin: ". . . dey say I been born wid veil over my face en if anybody could see spirits, I ought to could" (Julia Woodberry, as quoted in *Born in Slavery*). This expression was also used by white Mississippians, as evidenced in a Eudora Welty short story of 1941: "Her husband ought to could make her behave" (quoted in WD). See *used to could*.

out (v.)

> *When the news retched town Casey Jones was dead*
> *Women dressin' up an' outed out in red.*
> —Jesse James, "Southern Casey Blues," 1936

To go out, especially on a pleasure excursion; usage now considered rare by the OED.

out and down

Lovin' babe I'm all out an' down

I'm layin' close to the ground.

—Henry Thomas, "Lovin' Babe," 1929

A variant of *down and out*, an American slang term for being utterly destitute that dates in print to 1899 (Lighter, 1994). Although less common than the latter, it still figured in colloquial speech, as seen from an exchange in Jim Tully's hobo novel *Beggars of Life* (1924):

"So you're broke, huh kid?" she asked.

"Yes, mum, I'm all out and down."

Out means out of money or luck.

outside loving

If papa has outside loving, mama has outside loving, too

If papa done done some cheatin', mama done done some cheatin', too.

—Eliza Brown, "If Papa Has Outside Lovin'," 1929

Sexual relations with someone other than one's spouse or live-in companion; see *outside man, woman*.

outside man, woman

You can't watch your wife, an' your outside women, too

While you're off with your woman, your wife could be at home, beatin'
*   you doin', buddy what you're tryin' to do.*

—Blind Joe Reynolds, "Outside Woman Blues," 1930

Black slang for the lover of a married male or female, *outside* connoting outside of the home. The offspring of such pairings were termed *outside children*: "My mother had three outside chilluns, and we each had a different father" (Isiah Jefferies, as quoted in *Born in Slavery*). The synonymous *outside kid* still survives in black speech (cf. Smitherman, 2000).

outta sight

Way you doin' me mama, says it's outta sight

Says anything your kid man do, well it be's all right.

—Joe Calicott, "Traveling Mama Blues," 1930

A 19th-century lower-class superlative that figures in Stephen Crane's 1893 novel *Maggie: A Girl of the Streets* ("Say Mag, I'm stuck on yer shape. It's outasight . . .") and Frank Norris's *McTeague* (1899). Although the term was never associated with black speech, the hippies who adopted it in the 1960s likely acquired it from blacks.

overcome

I'm down on ol' Parchman Farm an' I sure wanna go back home

But I hope some day I will overcome.

—Bukka White, "Parchman Farm Blues," 1940

"To surmount (a difficulty or obstacle); to recover from (a blow, disaster, etc.)" (OED at *overcome*, v.4). In the above and the black spiritual "I'll Overcome Someday" (published in 1901 and credited to C. A. Tindley), *overcome* is used without taking an object, as also occurs in the famous civil rights anthem of 1940s vintage, "We Shall Overcome."

pain (v.)

> *My heart did pain when my baby got on the train*
> *My heart struck sorrow, it felt like drops of rain.*
> —Ruth Day, "Painful Blues," 1931

To suffer emotional or physical pain; regarded as archaic and rare by the OED.

paling

> *I'm gonna jerk me a paling, from-a your back fence*
> *I'm gonna start whuppin', learn the good girl some sense.*
> —Joe Calicott, "Traveling Mama Blues," 1930

A stake driven into the ground and used to build a fence (OED).

pallet

> *Make me down, a pallet on your floor*
> *Make it calm an' easy, make it down by your door.*
> —Blind Lemon Jefferson, "Stocking Feet Blues," 1926

A Southern term for improvised bedding, consisting of clothes or rags spread on a floor (OED).

Palmer's Skin Success

> *Now if you want your woman to look like she's redish*
> *You buy high brown powder, Palmer's Skin Success.*
> —Ishman Bracey, "Saturday Blues," 1928

The trade name of a still-popular skin bleach originally manufactured by the Morgan Drug Company of Brooklyn, New York, offering blacks of the blues era the prospect of becoming "one shade lighter" by applying a thirty-five or seventy-five cent ointment to the face at night, and washing it away the following morning with a thirty-five cent soap product.

papa

> I take a long look, right smack down in your mind
> An' I see poor papa, come a-hobblin' down the line.
> —Bertha Lee, "Mind Reader Blues," 1934

A feminine and predominately black term for a male lover or husband, dating to the late 19th century (cf. OED).

partner

> I'm gonna shake hands with my partner, ask him how come he's here
> "I had a ruckus with my family, they gonna send me to the 'lectric chair."
> —Blind Lemon Jefferson, "Electric Chair Blues," 1928

Cell mate. In other blues recordings, *partner* simply means associate, male or female.

partnership man

> Now there's one thing daddy, that I can't understand
> If you are lovin' me, I don't want no partnership man.
> —Pearl Dickson, "Twelve Pound Daddy," 1927

Black slang for a man who is shared by two females (Hill).

pass (n.)

> My enemies have betrayed me, have overtaken poor Bob at last
> And there's one thing certain: they have stones all in my pass.
> —Robert Johnson, "Stones In My Passway," 1937

Literally, "a way through or across an area where passage is limited by natural impediments, such as trees, marshes, or hills" (OED). The above couplet is a complaint that various rivals have prevented the performer from having sexual success with a coveted female. See *stones in my passway.*

pass (v.)

> If you don't quit bettin' boys, them dice won't pass
> It's gon' send you home on your yas-yas-yas.
> —Sleepy John Estes, "Someday Baby Blues," 1935

Win; obsolete standard English used in connection with the dice game of Passage (OED), and evidently applied by blacks to craps.

passway

> ... You laid the passway for me, now what are you tryin' to do?
> I'm cryin': "Please, please let us be friends."
> And when you hear me howlin' in my passway rider
> Please open your door an' let me in.
> —Robert Johnson, "Stones In My Passway," 1937

In the above instance, a double entendre in which *passway* is a figurative route to *pussy.* In standard English, a *passway* is "a means of passing; a course, road, or route through" (OED).

pay no mind

> *What's the need-a me hollerin', what's the need-a me cryin'?*
> *Woman I love, she don't pay me no mind.*
> —*Furry Lewis, "I Will Turn Your Money Green," 1928*

To pay no attention to; a Southern colloquialism (cf. DARE 3 at *mind*, B2).

peaches

> *Have you ever seen peaches, grow on a sweet potato vine?*
> *Just step in my back yard, and take a look at mine.*
> —*Trixie Smith, "Sorrowful Blues," 1924*

Breasts, a term that (in the above instance) predates most recording double entendres and may thus have a basis in black vernacular speech. In the familiar couplet below, *peaches* has no express sexual meaning, the singer ordering a female not to pursue him absent a sexual interest or attraction:

> *Well if you don't like my peaches don't shake my tree*
> *Gal stay outta my orchard an' let my peaches be.*
> —*William Harris, "Hot Time Blues," 1928*

peg, don't move a

> *"When I say: 'Stop!' don't move a peg."*
> —*Pine Top Smith, "Pine Top's Boogie Woogie," 1928*

An admonition to remain motionless, based on the Southern expression *not to move a peg* (cf. DARE 4 at *peg*).

pencil

> *Lead in my pencil, babe it's done gone bad*
> *An' that's the worst old feelin', I most ever had.*
> —*Johnnie Temple, "Lead Pencil Blues," 1935*

A slang term for penis dating to the late 19th century (Partridge). The use of *lead* as an indicator of "pencil" potency dates in print to 1925 (cf. Lighter, 1997, at *have lead in (one's) pencil*). Of the occurrence of this phrase in a 1970s Walter Vinson blues song, Sam Chatmon wryly commented: "Everytime he get up there [on stage] the same thing: 'Well here's a little piece I put out: "the lead's gone, the old pencil won't write." I say: 'I know it's gone and the other folks they know it, too.'"

penitentiary crime

> *I was walkin' around in Memphis, until my foots got thin as a dime*
> *Don't be for President Roosevelt, I would have done a penitentiary crime.*
> —*Jack Kelly, "President Blues," 1933*

A felony, as opposed to a misdemeanor that would merit jail rather than prison time.

one's people(s)

> *I'm goin' to town an' hurry back, you salty dog*
>
> *I'm gonna show your peoples how to Ball the Jack, you salty dog.*
>
> —Sam Collins, "New Salty Dog," 1931

Family, relatives; a Southern colloquialism, the plural form of which is associated with black speech (cf. DARE 4).

percolate

> *"Say boy, how you percolatin' now?"*
>
> *"Boy, I ain't percolatin' . . ."*
>
> —William Harris, "I'm Leavin' Town," 1927

A mid-1920s term meaning to think or act efficiently, commonly (in the latter sense) applied to automobiles (DAS).

p.i.

> *Once upon a time, a p.i. could get most anything*
>
> *Now the streets are crowded, a p.i. can't even get spendin' change.*
>
> —Bill Gaither, "Racket Blues," 1939

Slang for a pimp (DAS 3 at PI). The above couplet remarks on the proliferation of promiscuous women.

pick (1)

> *"I can't pick it, I'm just learnin' how, but I will go head on an' boot it."*
>
> —Little Hat Jones, "Corpus Blues," 1929

In blues parlance, to pluck individual strings of a guitar, as opposed to less accomplished strumming (known as *rapping*).

pick (2)

> *"I don't feel like pickin' so much piano, man."*
>
> —Lee Green, "Pork Chop Stomp," 1929

An eccentric extension of *pick* as meaning to play a stringed instrument, in no particular manner; for the latter, cf. OED.

pick (3)

> *I've done got evil, and I've done got mean*
>
> *And when I start to stealing, I'm going to pick the rounders clean.*
>
> —Leroy Carr, "Tight Time Blues," 1934

To pilfer, a term that dates to Chaucer (ca. 1400) and gave rise to *pick-pocket* (F&H, 1902). See *poor robbin*.

pigmeat

> *Mailman done brought misery to my head*
>
> *I got a letter this mornin', my pigmeat mama was dead.*
>
> —Blind Lemon Jefferson, "Gone Dead On You Blues," 1928

A black term for a young female, or virgin (Hill), based on the standard English use of *pig* to signify a young hog, or piglet (cf. OED). *Pigmeat* is misconstrued by the OED as "coarse slang" signifying "sexual intercourse or gratification; a woman or girl regarded as a sexual object." There is no evidence that this term signified a sexually loose woman or prostitute, as Spears (2001) has it. By extension, *pigmeat* was applied in one blues song to a youthful or inexperienced male sex partner:

> *Pigmeat's all right, but pigmeat soon gives out*
> *I'd much rather have my big bo' hog, he knows what it's all about.*
> —Irene Wiley, "Rootin' Bo Hog Blues," 1931

As denoting a virgin, the term occurs in Zora Neale Hurston's *Cold Keener* (1930): "She ain't no pig-meat. That's a married 'oman."

Piggly-Wiggly

> *My name is Piggly-Wiggly, and I swear you can help yourself*
> *And I've got to have your greenback, and it don't take nothin' else.*
> —Lucille Bogan, "Groceries On The Shelf," 1933

A reference to a still-existing Southern grocery chain noted for introducing (in 1916) the concept of retail self-service, which the above performer uses as the basis of a song about prostitution.

piggy-wiggy

> *What did that old piggy-wiggy, say to the great big cow?*
> *"Mama turn over on your side, I wanna milk you right now."*
> —Ben Curry, "Boodle-De-Bum-Bum," 1931

A pet pig (Partridge).

pile

> *Drove so many piles, my hammer's all worn out*
> *That's when I do my driving, and I begin to shout.*
> —Kansas Joe, "Pile Driver Blues," 1931

A standard English term for a heavy post "driven vertically into a riverbed, the sea, or marshy ground to support the foundations of a superstructure such as a house, a bridge, a pier, etc. . . ." (OED); used in the above context as a far-fetched double entendre.

pile stones

> *When I leave the Seven Sisters, I'll pile stones all round*
> *An' go to my baby, and tell her there's another Seven Sister man in town.*
> —"Funny Paper" Smith, "The Seven Sisters Blues, Part One," 1931

Part of a hoodoo ritual, said to be effected to "mark one's kingdom" or signify territory (Evans).

pimp (v.)

> *Now listen here brother, you may can understand*
> *I might would pimp a woman, but I will never pimp a man.*
> —Washboard Sam, "Get Down Brother," 1941

To exploit or live off another; slang otherwise expressed as *pimp on* or *off*, in which form it was first recorded in 1928 (cf. OED at *pimp, v.4.a*).

pinchback

> *Yes, get a working man when you marry*
> *Let all these pinchbacks be*
> *Child, it takes money to run a business*
> *And with me I know you surely will agree.*
> —*Bessie Smith, "Pinchbacks—Take 'Em Away," 1924*

A colloquial term for cheapskate (F&H, 1902), regarded by the OED as "now U.S. and rare."

piney woods

> *Big mama owns, everything in her neighborhood*
> *But when she makin' money, is when she lives in the piney woods.*
> —*Blind Lemon Jefferson, "Piney Woods Money Mama," 1928*

"Southern for any land with pines, especially in the low country" (Bartlett, 1877). By itself, "piney" is now construed as standard English.

pistol

> *I'm gonna slap her face, gonna drink that woman's rye*
> *Gonna kill that whiskey pour the pistol dry.*
> —*Bo Weavil Jackson, "Pistol Blues," 1926*

A flask. This term is a black modification of *pocket-pistol*, an old English synonym of flask used by Falstaff in Shakespeare's *Henry IV* (1597) and still current in 19th-century British speech (F&H, 1902). An untimely use of *pistol* by the blues singer Son House almost resulted in his death at the hands of police in Rochester, New York, in the 1950s. Arrested for drunkenness, he reached under his pillow and said: "Hold it! Let me get my pistol" (conversation with author).

pizin (pizen)

> *No gypsy woman, can fry no meat for me*
> *I ain't scared I'm skittish, she might pizin me.*
> —*Sam Butler, "Devil And My Brown Blues," 1926*

A 19th-century variant of *poison* (DAP) that survives in Southern dialect. According to one lexicographer, *pizen* is "a pronunciation that the South's early aristocrats borrowed from upper-class English speech" (WD).

plank walk

> *Says I been down to that long plank walk*
> *An' I'm on my way back home.*
> —*Sam Collins, "Lonesome Road Blues," 1931*

A walkway paved with planks; formed by analogy with *plank road*, given by the OED as "chiefly *N. Amer.* (now *hist.*) a road made of a flooring of planks laid transversely on timbers."

"Our home was on Alvis's Hill and a long plank walk had been built from the bank of the Ohio River to the Alvis home" (Betty Jones, as quoted in *Born in Slavery*).

play in one's yard

Man you can take my woman, but you ain't done nothin' smart
For I got more than one woman playin' in my back yard.
—Furry Lewis, "Dry Land Blues," 1928

To cavort with; a catchphrase applied to females that occurs in O. Henry's *The Cop and the Anthem* (1904): "He made eyes at her ... and went through the contemptible litany of the 'masher.' ... 'Ah there, Bedelia! Don't you want to come and play in my yard?'" It probably derived from a 1900 pop tune by H. W. Petrie, "I Don't Want To Play In Your Yard."

play the numbers

Some play the numbers, some read your mind
They all got a racket of some kind
—Hezekiah Jenkins, "The Panic Is On," 1931

To place a *policy* bet, involving betting on one number or a combination of two or three numbers. This expression, which may have been of black origin, apparently gave rise to *numbers* as a synonym of policy.

plumb good

I'm a poor ol' boy, an' a long ways from home
An' she causin' me to leave my plumb good home.
—Charlie Patton, "Jim Lee Blues, Part Two," 1929

A black superlative of pre-blues (if not antebellum) origin: "Dem mangy hogs what our marster give us the first year was plum good hogs after we grease dem. ..." (Jenny Proctor, as quoted in *Born in Slavery*). Of itself, *plumb* is a Southern intensifier; cf. DARE 4 at *plumb*, 1966–70, Inf TN23.

police

I was walkin' down Morgan, stopped on Maxwell Street
I asked the desk sergeant: "What police brought my gal offa the street?"
—Papa Charlie Jackson, "Maxwell Street Blues," 1925

Policeman, in black parlance.

police dog

Guess I'll travel an' I guess I'll let her be
Before she sics her police dog on me.
—Blind Blake, "Police Dog Blues," 1928

A popular 1920s term for a German shepherd.

policy

> *So policy is all I hear today*
> *What good is it, when you don't know what [number] to play?*
> —Papa Charlie Jackson, "Four Eleven Forty Four," 1926

The illegal daily lotto patronized by blacks to the extent of becoming popularly identified with them in the 1920s, when they were its chief customers. In its familiar form, policy dates to at least 1830, the name arising from *policy* as a term for a conditional promissory note (OED). Various anti-gaming statutes enacted in the first decade of the 20th century proscribed policy, and largely eliminated its white clientele in the process. Despite the advent of state-sponsored lotteries in the mid-1970s, policy (now better known as *numbers*) remains a fixture in many neighborhoods.

policy-writin' man

> *Hey, I wonder where is that policy-writin' man at now?*
> *I done losed all my money shootin' craps and I can't win no money nohow.*
> —Bo Carter, "Policy Blues," 1940

A policy writer or numbers runner, the figure to whom one transmits policy bets and who is responsible for paying out appropriate sums to winners. This position was described in an 1892 account of policy in New York retail stores: "...the man who keeps the game...is called the 'writer.' He is not the proprietor, but simply a clerk on a salary, and his duties are to copy the slips handed up by the players, mark them with the amount of money paid, and watch to see that no fraud is practiced" (Thomas Knox, *Darkness and Daylight; or, Lights and Shadows of New York Life*).

Polack town

> *Down the alley, to the levee, then to Polack town pretty mama*
> *I am sorry, that I can't take you*
> *You don't know how to gamble, nothin' else for you to do.*
> —Clifford Gibson, "Levee Camp Moan," 1929

A name given to a black section of East St. Louis, Illinois, formerly settled by Polish immigrants.

pond

> *Come here pretty mama, gonna take you far across the pond*
> *I'm gonna make my stop in Italy where these monkey men don't belong.*
> —Blind Lemon Jefferson, "Teddy Bear Blues," 1927

Ocean; standard English once associated with sailors (cf. OED).

pony

> Well I'm goin' to the race track to see my pony run
> He ain't the best in the world but he's a runnin' son of a gun.
> —Son House, "My Black Mama, Part One," 1930

Slang for a racehorse, dating in print to 1900 (OED).

poor

> I'm a poor boy I'm a long ways from home
> . . . Look where the sun done gone.
> —Henry Thomas, "Red River Blues," 1928

In blues recording, this term is always used to mean unfortunate rather than impoverished, a distinction that facilitated the utility of early blues as a means of soliciting sympathetic female sponsors.

pork chop

> If you good men wanna keep her outta town at night
> Just feed her a little pork chop, suits her appetite.
> —Tom Dickson, "Labor Blues," 1928

Dick, likely colloquial in black speech.

pot hound

> You come here every day lookin' for your stew and beans
> And you have got more nerve than any pot hound I've ever seen.
> —Lucille Bogan, "Pot Hound Blues," 1929

A pejorative for a person who eats large amounts of food at someone else's expense; derived from the colloquial *pot hound* as a term for a dog regarded as good for nothing but consuming food (cf. DARE 4), and perhaps used with reference to *chow hound*, a glutton (OED). (Allusively, pot = food; cf. OED.)

pour-down rain

> I'm gonna get a black gal, take black to ease my pain
> 'Cause a black gal makes the thunder, yellow gal makes the pour-down
>   rain.
> —Rudy Foster, "Black Gal Makes Thunder," 1930

A downpour; sudden, heavy rain (cf. DARE 4). The above couplet advances the notion that a black female is subject to loud, harmless outbursts, while a less demonstrative yellow one will cause prolonged problems in a relationship.

powder-house

> It have been so dry, you can make a powder-house outta the world
> An' all the money men, like a rattlesnake in his curl.
> —Son House, "Dry Spell Blues, Part Two," 1930

A building used to store gunpowder. The term has been obsolete since the demise (due partly to its susceptibility to humidity) of black powder as a burning charge in ammunition, which occurred shortly after the Spanish-American

War. The expression "dry as a powder-house" that prompted the above couplet was a conventional 19th-century figure of American speech (DAP).

power, in

When I was in power, you could hear 'em say: "Here comes Mister So
   and So."
But since I lost my black money, they wouldn't even speak to me no more.
—Leroy Henderson, "Good Scufflin' Blues," 1935

In funds; apparently formed from the expression *money is power*.

praying ground

I even went to my prayin' ground, dropped down on bended knee
I ain't cryin' for no religion Lordie, give me back my good gal please.
—Blind Willie McTell, "Broke Down Engine," 1933

In rural black speech, a secluded outdoors place where supplicants could pray in solitude, referred to in Zora Neale Hurston's *Jonah's Gourd Vine* (1934): "... he found a tiny clearing hidden by trees. 'Dis is uh prayin' ground,' he said to himself." Also known as *prayer grounds*, these havens originated during slavery and were employed to avoid intrusive whites (cf. Yetman).

preach

Walk with my good girl in the daytime, walk with her at night
Says I'm tryin' to preach' an' tell her, how to treat a good man right.
—Joe Calicott, "Traveling Mama Blues," 1930

To harp on a subject in the interests of educating or correcting; now usually given a negative connotation (OED).

prison, in

When I was in prison, it ain't no use of screamin' an' cryin'
Mister Purvis' the onliest man can ease that pain o'mine.
—Charlie Patton, "High Sheriff Blues," 1934

"Originally: the condition of being kept in captivity or confinement; forcible deprivation of personal liberty; imprisonment" (OED at *prison*). The above song refers to incarceration in a town jailhouse.

professor

On a Monday morning, first thing sad news:
"Listen here professor, play for me those blues."
—Barbecue Bob, "Hurry And Bring It Back Home," 1929

"... [A] grandiose title or mock title: assumed by or applied to professional teachers and exponents of various popular arts and activities, as dancing, performing, etc." (OED). In American speech, this term was "[a]pplied indiscriminately to any one who makes a profession of anything" (Clapin, c. 1902). Similarly pretentious terms for professional blues guitarists (employed by Skip James) were *music philosopher* or *music physicianer*.

project

> *Workin' on the project, my gal spendin' all my dough*
> *Now I have waked up on her, ooh-well-well I won't be that weak no more.*
> —*Peetie Wheatstraw, "Working On The Project," 1937*

A job created by the Works Projects Administration (WPA), which offered employment (often in the form of road and bridge construction) to persons on relief between 1935 and 1943.

protection

> *You getter go find yourself some good protection*
> *'Cause sweet mama, papa 'bout to get mad.*
> —*Pink Anderson and Simmie Dooley, "Papa's 'Bout To Get Mad," 1928*

A black term for weaponry in the form of a knife or gun (Skip James), the implication being that it is used for self-defense.

prove on

> *They say I do it, ain't nobody caught me*
> *Sure got to prove it on me.*
> —*Ma Rainey, "Prove It On Me Blues," 1928*

To prove against; a dated construction appearing in Defoe's *Moll Flanders* (1722): "I pressed him to go to a magistrate with me, and if anything could be proved on me ... I should willingly submit...."

pull down your blind

> *Now when you see me comin', pull down your window blind*
> *So your next door neighbor, sure can hear you whine.*
> —*Geeshie Wiley, "Skinny Leg Blues," 1930*

A declaration probably arising from *pull down the blind!*, a lower-class British catchphrase dating to around 1880 addressed to couples making love (Partridge).

pull game

> *Know it ain't no tellin' what a Mississippi gal'll do*
> *She will get your money, then pull game at you.*
> —*Tom Dickson, "Labor Blues," 1928*

? Apparently, to cheat on. This expression is a likely forerunner of *to run a game*, black slang of mid-1960s vintage meaning to obtain money by trickery (cf. OED).

put on the walk

> *Alla you cack women, you better put on the walk*
> *'Cause I'm gonna get drunk an' do my dirty talk.*
> —*Lucille Bogan, "Shave 'Em Dry," 1935*

Take a walk; depart.

put one down

I ain't got no job, now you gonna put me down

You gonna quit me baby, for a hard-workin' clown.

—Blind Blake, "No Dough Blues," 1928

To drop as a sexual companion. As a term denoting verbal rejection, it was noted by Burley (c. 1944) as a Harlem "jive" term, and as a "beat" phrase of mid-1950s origin by the DAS. See *throw one down.*

put one's hand on one

Brownskin woman is like, somethin' fit to eat

Oh but a jet-black woman, don't put your hand on me.

—Charlie Patton, "Pony Blues," 1929

To touch one in a familiar or sexual manner. The negative imperative form of the expression used in the above couplet also appears in Faulkner's *Sanctuary* (1931), spoken by a female rebuffing her drunken husband: "'Don't put your hand on me,' she said."

put one out

Because I'm broke, all down an' out

You have done quit me, an' put me out.

—Sam Collins, "I'm Still Sitting On Top Of The World," 1931

To force a live-in lover to seek other accommodations in consequence of a breakup.

put out

Ain't nothin' but muddy water for miles or more

The low-levee women ain't puttin' out no more.

—Barbecue Bob, "Mississippi Low-Levee Blues," 1928

To allow sexual activity, with no pretense of emotional or romantic involvement; said of females. The OED traces this expression, which bulked large in teenage conversation of the 1950s, to 1947.

put the thing on (one)

An' it's T for Texas, T for Tennessee

Lord bless the woman that put the thing on me.

—Willie Brown, "Future Blues," 1930

To yoke in a relationship or impose one's presence (particularly sexual) on another, often by means of conjuring. The latter sense occurs in the following example, as applied to the effects of winter:

Ol' Jack Frost is now ready to put that thing on you

If you don't stop him, bad luck be your "Howdy do."

—Barbecue Bob, "Cold Wave Blues," 1928

A variant expression is:

> *I'm goin' to see you gypsy, beggin' on my bended knees*
> *That man's put somethin' on me, oh take it off, please.*
> —Bessie Smith, "Please Help Me Get Him Off My Mind," 1928

A related expression, to *put it on one*, is given by Fisher (1928) as Harlem slang meaning to injure one deliberately.

quit, (it) just won't

> *"They had a trombone player there just won't quit."*
> —Blind Blake, "Seaboard Stomp," 1927

A black catchphrase of the blues era, generally used as an expression of merit, but applied to anything of remarkable length or duration, as in Langston Hughes and Zora Neale Hurston's *The Mule-Bone* (1931): "...that coarse black hair of hers jes' won't quit!" It is invoked to register exasperation in the following couplet:

> *Next time I met you, you know I made a hit*
> *But you got a new way a-lovin', swear it just won't quit.*
> —Charlie Patton, "Mean Black Cat Blues," 1929

This expression survives in Southern colloquial speech: "...that lady has got a set of legs that don't quit" (white Texan's description of a murder defendant on *48 Hours* television program, "Secrets and Lives on Grapevine Lake," 4/9/2008).

rack it back

> *Hold me close, hold me tight*
> *You gotta rack it back an' tell it right.*
> —Joe Pullum, "Rack It Back And Tell It Right," 1935

"That means really get to it" (Tom Shaw). The expression derives from a dated colloquialism applied to horses, *rack*, which meant to move in a half-trot, half-canter (cf. Thornton [1912], who traced it to 1796). A garbled form appears in a song couplet collected by White (1928) in 1916:

> Las' year I was from Rack-in-sack
> An' dis year I'se er rack-en-back.

Rackensack was "an ancient and derisive name for Arkansas, often encountered in old newspaper files" (Randolph).

rag

> She wake up soon, every mornin' babe wearin' a rag all around her head
> Every time you wanna speak to her she swear she's nearly dead.
> —George Torey, "Married Woman Blues," 1937

"In the South, a common term for any piece of linen or cotton-cloth" (Clapin, c. 1902). The above lyric refers to a piece of wrapped cloth used by black females as a turban, now known as a *do-rag* and additionally worn by males since the 1960s or 1970s. Such apparel was termed a *head rag* in antebellum times: "At the camp meetings the womens pulled off the head rags ... the mammies wore linen head rags freshly laundered" (Botkin, 1945). Initially, they were worn in lieu of hats: "My sun hat was a rag tied on my head" (Fannie Tatum, as quoted in *Born in Slavery*).

raggedy-ass

> Worked all summer bettin' the dice won't pass
> Now winter done caught you in a raggedy—(ass)
> —Casey Bill, "Go Ahead, Buddy," 1934

Ragged, unkempt; a term dating to the 1920s (cf. DARE 4).

rain

> The Lord sent the sunshine, devil he sent the rain
> I'm liable to be there tomorrow, on a money swing.
> —Charlie Patton, "Devil Sent The Rain Blues," 1929

Reversals or unwelcome occurrences, as contrasted with sun or sunshine. The above couplet is based on a proverbial expression appearing in John Bunyon's *The Pilgrim's Progress* (1678): "God sends sometimes rain, and sometimes sunshine...."

raise (one) to (one's) hand

> Take me back baby, raise me to your hand
> Some day honey I'll become a lucky man.
> —Bumble Bee Slim, "I Keep On Drinkin' (To Drive My Blues Away), Part
>   One," 1935

To elevate one as a regular sex partner or romantic companion, perhaps ousting another in the process. This expression was applied to both sexes:

If you got a woman, or raise her to your hand
Keep away from my little woman, Molly 'ham is lonesome Molly Cunningham.
—Charlie Patton, "Elder Greene Blues," 1929

An awkward use of the phrase occurs in the following lyric:

What make a married woman, crazy 'bout a single man
'Cause the husband might lay down an' die, an' raise that fellow to her hand.
—Blind Willie Reynolds, "Married Woman Blues," 1930

raise sand

Can't a woman act funny, quit you for another man?
She ain't gonna look at you straight but she's always raisin' sand.
—Blind Lemon Jefferson, "Got The Blues," 1926

To create a disturbance, slang derived from the British *raise* or *kick up a dust*, given by Grose (1796) as meaning "to make a disturbance or riot." Clapin (c. 1902) records it as a white expression meaning "to get furiously angry"; Tom Shaw (a protégé of the above performer) saw *raisin' sand* as "fussin' and raisin' hell." The survival of this idiom in black speech is indicated by DCS and Smitherman (2000), which (like DAS 3) treat it as exclusively black.

raising the deuce

Oh you got to stop your forkin' an' raisin' the deuce
Else I'll grab you mama an' turn you every way but loose.
—Blind Willie McTell, "Southern Can Is Mine," 1931

A euphemism for raising hell. As a figurative synonym for the devil, *deuce* dates to the 17th century (F&H, 1891).

ram (v.)

I do my ramming at midnight, and I don't be seen in the day
When everything is quiet and easy, mister grinder can have his way.
—Memphis Slim, "Grinder Man Blues," 1940

To have sexual intercourse with a female; cf. F&H (1902).

ramble

I am a rambler an' gamblin' man, I gambled in many a town
I rambled this wide world over, I rambled these women around
—Henry Thomas, "Arkansas," 1927

To wander over, a sense given as rare by the OED. To ramble women (as opposed to an area such as "this wide world") is apparently to accost or sample them sexually in Don Juan fashion, a sense also conveyed in:

...I wanna get me a Super-6
I'm always ramblin' ladies, and I like to have my business fixed.
—Blind Lemon Jefferson, "D B Blues," 1928

ram rod

> *When I get to use my ram rod, I sure Lord takes my time*
> *It ain't no other ram-roddin' daddy can put his load below where I put*
> *   mine.*
> —Bo Carter, "Ram Rod Daddy," 1931

A slang term for penis dating to the mid-19th century (Partridge), superseded by the current-day *rod*.

ramshackled

> *My mind is ramshacked, my heart is full of pain*
> *If money lasts ... my luck is bound to change.*
> —Walter Vinson, "Every Dog Must Have His Day," 1941

Unstable, ready to fall apart; a term invariably applied to such structures as houses but used above in connection with mental turmoil, and similarly by Skip James: "... that feeling has caused your mind to be rambling or ram-shackled" (as quoted in Calt).

range

> *An ol' screw that was walkin' my range cracked:*
> *"Big boy, they can't do that."*
> —Pine Top Smith, "Big Boy, They Can't Do That," 1929

A tier of cells; given by DAUL (1950) as a Western prison term.

rank oneself

> *I used to think you was sweet as any sugar could be*
> *But you done lied so much, you done ranked yourself with me.*
> —Bill Gaither, "You Done Ranked Yourself With Me," 1941

To make oneself objectionable or unacceptable; from *rank*, black slang meaning to insult or put down (for the latter, see DARE 4).

rat

> *When she went to leave me rat stuck to her shoe*
> *Fell down an' broke her little toodle-oo-oo.*
> —Hambone Willie Newbern, "She Could Toodle-oo," 1929

A woman's hairpiece; more commonly, a pad used in hair styling to make hair appear thicker (cf. OED).

rattler

> *I jumped that fast mail rattler, an' I almost went a-flyin'*
> *"Hurry engineerman for my pigmeat mama is dyin'."*
> —Blind Lemon Jefferson, "Gone Dead On You Blues," 1928

A slang term for train, or any rattling conveyance (OED).

rattlesnake, like a

Just like a rattlesnake I stay mama, in a mamlish curl

I ain't gonna have no job mama, rollin' through this world.

—Charlie Patton, "Rattlesnake Blues," 1929

A cheapskate (Son House, who used the expression in "Dry Spell Blues"). This figure of speech may have been facilitated by an idiomatic use of *rattle* in regard to money: "He had two hundred or three hundred dollars then in his pocket to rattle" (Louise Pettis, as quoted in *Born in Slavery*).

Reachin' Pete

If you go to Helena, stop by Cherry Street

I want to show you the man, they-all call "Reachin' Pete."

He's the tallest man, ever walked on Cherry Street

And the "baddest" copper, that ever walked a beat.

—Memphis Minnie, "Reachin' Pete," 1935

The nickname of a storied Helena, Arkansas, sheriff (around 1912), noted for his height and his refusal to fire on fleeing suspects (Moore).

realize

Well I tried to love a sweet woman

But that woman didn't seem to understand

But I know she realizin' trouble since she got another man.

—Little Hat Jones, "Bye Bye Baby Blues," 1930

An Americanism meaning "[t]o have actual experience of" (OED, which offers citations from 1776 and 1791, the latter from correspondence of George Washington).

reap what you sow

Yes I cried last night an' I ain't gonna cry any more

'Cause the good book tells us you've got to reap just what you sow.

—Charlie Patton, "Pea Vine Blues," 1929

A stock blues observation based on Galatians 6:7: "... whatsoever a man soweth that shall he also reap," which in various forms has long been a proverbial saying. "You gotta reap just what you sow 'cause the Good Book says it" (Alice Douglass, as quoted in *Born in Slavery*).

Red Cross store

Said me an' my good girl talked last night, we done talked for an hour

She wanted me to go to the Red Cross store an' get her a sack of that Red Cross flour.

—Walter Roland, "Red Cross Blues," 1933

A topical reference to one of the six free food distribution centers created in 1932 by the Birmingham, Alabama, chapter of the American Red Cross, which thereby assisted some 12,000 families a month and dismantled its program when the federal government began undertaking relief efforts in 1933.

red-eyed

> *Got a red-eyed captain, got a squabblin' boss*
> *Got a mad dog sergeant, honey an' he won't knock off.*
> —*Blind Lemon Jefferson, "Prison Cell Blues," 1928*

Angry (cf. DARE 4).

red-hot

> *Give me just one hour, let me show you what I got*
> *I know you're going to like it, baby 'cause it is red-hot.*
> —*Barbecue Bob, "Beggin' For Love," 1928*

Extraordinarily exciting, sexually; a contemporary embellishment of *hot* usually applied to females.

redish

> *Now if you want your woman to look like she's redish*
> *You buy high brown powder, Palmer's Skin Success.*
> —*Ishman Bracey, "Saturday Blues," 1928*

In black speech, white or light-complexioned to the point of resembling the hue of whites, whose complexion was regarded as red. "I'se often heard my mammy was redish-lookin' wid long, straight, black hair" (Charlie Davenport, as quoted in *Born in Slavery*).

reddished (v.)

> *When the war was on, everybody well, when the war was on*
> *Well they reddished everybody when the war was on.*
> —*Blind Willie Johnson, "When The War Was On," 1929*

A Southern black corruption of "registered," applied to the World War I draft.

regular (n.)

> *It seems cloudy brown, I believe it's going to rain*
> *Goin' back to my regular, 'cause she's got everything.*
> —*Barbecue Bob, "Cloudy Sky Blues," 1927*

One's usual sexual companion.

relief

> *I was workin' on the project, beggin'... relief for shoes*
> *Because the rock and gravel, hoo-well-well, now they givin' my feet the*
> *blues.*
> —*Peetie Wheatstraw, "Working On The Project," 1937*

The Depression-era term for welfare. Relief agencies of the period provided clothing as well as food and cash stipends to the needy, hence the above reference to shoes.

religion, get

Oh I'm gonna get religion, I'm gonna join the Baptist church
I'm gonna be a Baptist preacher an' I sure won't have to work.
—Son House, "Preachin' Blues, Part One," 1930

To be seized by sudden religious transport; to become a convert or religious enthusiast; a largely Southern colloquialism scored by Partridge as a phrase of "insensitive vulgarity." The above couplet remarks on the fact that Southern Baptist congregations (unlike their Methodist and Holiness counterparts) supported a full-time minister, who was not expected to hold down a job beyond the pulpit. "Several of dem got religion right out in de field and would kneel down in the corn-field" ("Aunt" Hannah Allen, as quoted in *Born in Slavery*).

rest content

When I was in Missouri, would not let me be
Wouldn't rest content until I came to Tennessee.
—Furry Lewis, "I Will Turn Your Money Green," 1928

To become satisfied with one's own efforts; a passé colloquialism found in Mayer (1852): "I ordered a general inspection of the slaves, yet where a favorable report was made, I did not rest content. . . ."

rest, take (one's)

I lay down last night . . . tried to take my rest
My mind got to ramblin', like a wild geese in the west.
—Skip James, "Devil Got My Woman," 1931

To sleep; an obsolete expression invoked in Shakespeare's *The Tempest* (1611): "'. . . while you take your rest. . . .'"

revenue man

The bootleggin' man got his bottle in his hand
An' all he need: a little more speed, so he can outrun the revenue man.
—Jim Jackson, "Policy Blues," 1928

Revenue agent; a Southern colloquialism applied to state law enforcement officials traditionally deployed to uphold prohibition statutes.

rheumatism

Old woman got down, a little too fast
Caught the rheumatism in her yes-yes-yes.
—Ben Curry, "The New Dirty Dozen," 1931

A black catchall for assorted ailments, Puckett (1925) reporting: "[R]heumatism is a very inclusive term with the [rural Southern] Negroes, taking in almost every unfamiliar ache from a crick in the neck to tertiary syphilis."

rick

> *She just keeps on rickin',*
> *Now she said she gonna leave, and goin' to some ol' one-horse town.*
> —*Jazz Gillum, "She Keeps On Rickin'," 1936*

? An obscure slang term that seemingly means to lie or mislead, and may thus have arisen from an adjectival standard English sense of the word as "fictitious, sham" (OED at *rick*, n.3).

ride

> *Woman for ridin', you got rough*
> *I been used to, struttin' my stuff.*
> —*Charley Lincoln, "Mama Don't Rush Me," 1930*

To copulate, an old term (usually referring to male activity) dating in print to around 1520 (F&H). In the example below, occurring as female dialogue, *ride* probably means to assume the topmost position in intercourse.

> *Me an' my gal was side by side*
> *She said: "Daddy I would like to ride."*
> —*Barbecue Bob, "Freeze To Me Mama," 1929*

rider

> *See see rider, what you done done*
> *Made me love you, now your friend has come.*
> —*Blind Lemon Jefferson, "See See Rider," 1926*

A sex partner, or as one informant put it, "a fuck" (Hill); usually applied to women. It originally referred to males, and is thus given by Partridge as an obsolete slang term for "an actively amorous man." Although pervasive in blues couplets, *rider* did not occupy a discernable place in black speech, indicating that it was either a "barrelhouse word," or once-fashionable slang that got fastened onto blues song, where it took on an extended life.

riding horse

> *Ain't gonna be your ridin' horse no more*
> *'Cause I been your dog ever since I entered your door.*
> —*Tommy Johnson, "Ridin' Horse," 1930*

A figurative (and perhaps nonce) expression for an agreeable sexual companion or plaything. Literally, a *riding horse* (also called a *pleasure horse*) is a horse bred for riding, as opposed to a work horse; it also represents (in the South and Appalachia) a child's imaginary horse formed from a branch or a see-saw. (For the latter senses, cf. DARE 4 at *ridy-horse*.)

right, live

> *Well I can't live right, ain't going to try no more*
> *This woman's left town, she ain't comin' back no more.*
> —*Blind Lemon Jefferson, "Booster Blues," 1926*

To live in a moral fashion, particularly by church standards; from the standard English sense of *right* (cf. OED at *right*, adv. III.12.a).

righteous

> *I fell in with a woman about fifty-two*
> *I thought she was too old, I'm tellin' you*
> *But she was righteous*
> *She was righteous!*
> *An' she was righteous, righteous Lord Lord Lord.*
> —Blind Blake, "Righteous Blues," 1930

Fine or wonderful, a superlative that was colloquial in British speech by c. 1860 (Partridge) and became associated with black Americans to such an extent that DAS classified it as a "Negro and jazz" term. Calloway (1939) defines it as "splendid or okay"; its use as a 1960s/1970s black teenagers' synonym of "outstanding" is recorded by Folb.

right-hand friend

> *After mother and father's gone, a dollar's your right-hand friend*
> *Then after our last dollar's gone, you're like a road that has no end.*
> —Lonnie Johnson, "Don't Drive Me From Your Door," 1930

Indispensable friend; formed from the standard English *right-hand man*.

right mind

> *Honey I'm so worried, ain't had my right mind today*
> *I got one mind to leave you, an' one mind to stay.*
> —Barbecue Bob, "Good Time Rounder," 1929

One's usual mental faculties; a clear head.

right on

> *A girl with a Ford and a guy named Jim*
> *He liked her and she liked him*
> *Ford broke down in a quiet park*
> *Didn't get home 'till after dark . . .*
> *Too bad that the news got out*
> *But they got it fixed right on*
> —Tampa Red and Georgia Tom, "But They Got It Fixed Right On," 1930

Nevertheless; black slang (Fisher, 1928) that was later associated with Southern white speech (cf. DARE 4). "She's stone blind, but she can have chillum right on" (Hannah Jones, as quoted in *Born in Slavery*).

rise

> *I can tell the wind is risin', the leaves tremblin' on the tree*
> *Oh I need my little sweet woman, for to keep my company*
> —Robert Johnson, "Hell Hound On My Trail," 1937

As applied to wind, to increase in force; somewhat outmoded standard English, the most recent OED cite dating to 1883.

road

> Out on the road, servin' out my time
> An' the Delta women were tryin'-a run me down.
> —Charlie Patton, "Circle Round The Moon," 1929

County road prison camp. "I was on de road three months with a ball and chain on de legs" (Zek Brown, as quoted in *Born in Slavery*).

give one the road

> Stack O'Lee was a bad man, everybody know
> And when they see Stack O'Lee comin', they give him the road.
> —Ma Rainey, "Stack O'Lee Blues," 1926

To give one a wide berth; a figure of speech drawn from automobile driving.

road rider

> Guards an' the road rider, go to carryin' you down
> An' you know you don't want to go.
> —Ollis Martin, "Police And High Sheriff Came Riding Down," 1927

? A term of unknown meaning that apparently refers to a law enforcement official who transports prisoners to the county road.

poor robbin

> I picked poor robbin clean,
> Picked poor robbin clean
> I picked his head an' I picked his feet
> Woulda picked his body but it wasn't fit to eat.
> —Geeshie Wiley and Elvie Thomas, "Pick Poor Robin Clean," 1929

? Most likely, a ragged person, from the 19th-century colloquialism *ragged robbin* (cf. OED). In the above song, the subject is left penniless by a crooked gambler, *clean* signifying completely without funds in criminal slang, and *to clean*, to rob one of everything of value (cf. DAUL). Traditionally, *poor Robin* is a figure from *Mother Goose*.

rock (n., v.)

> "Now we goin' on the old country rock. First thing we do: swing your
> partner. Promenade."
> —Blind Blake, "West Coast Blues," 1926

A square dance or square dance party; by extension, to dance at a square dance:

> Everybody rock; old folk rock; young folk rock. Boys rock! Girls rock! Drop back man
> and let me rock . . . Chillun rock!
> —William Moore, "Old Country Rock," 1928

rock (v. 2)

> *Here come that woman . . . had a hundred in her hand*
> *She had to rock some fatmouth, whose really lookin' for her man.*
> —*Little Hat Jones, "Corpus Blues," 1929*

To have sexual intercourse with, a euphemism that makes for a punning reference in another blues:

> *Let me be your rocker, till your straight chair comes*
> *An' I'll rock you easier than your straight chair ever done.*
> —*Rube Lacy, "Ham Hound Crave," 1928*

As a sexual term, *rock* is customarily applied to female activity:

> *She used to rock me (2)*
> *She used to rock me in the mornin' soon*
> *Lord, she used to rock me, in the mornin' soon*
> *Got another man she don't rock me no more.*
> —*Edward Thompson, "West Virginia Blues," 1929*

> *Rock me mama, rock me slow*
> *Rock me mama, Lord before I go . . .*
> —*Arthur Crudup, "Rock Me Mama," 1944*

In regard to mere motion, *rock* appeared in a recorded spiritual issued around 1910, the product of an anonymous (likely black) Male Quartette:

> *Keep on rockin' and roll me in your arms*
> *Rock an' roll me in your arms (2)*
> *In the arms of Moses.*

The above constitutes the earliest reference to "rock and roll," said to be a euphemism for sex in 1950s rhythm and blues.

rod(s), ride the

> *Just as sure as your train Lord backed up in your yard*
> *I'm gonna see my baby if I have to ride the rod.*
> —*Sam Collins, "Riverside Blues," 1927*

A storied and hazardous method of hoboing effected by lying over the rods located beneath train carriages.

rogue (v.)

> *Champagne Charley is my name, by golly*
> *An' roguin' an' stealin' is my game.*
> —*Blind Blake, "Champagne Charlie Is My Name," 1932*

To commit crimes, to swindle; standard English (cf. OED).

roll (1)

> *These here women, they want these men to act like them oxen done*
> *Grab a pick and shovel and roll from sun to sun.*
> —*Blind Lemon Jefferson, "Chockhouse Blues," 1927*

To work; common in blues songs, and presumably, in black speech of the blues era.

roll (2)

> *She said: "Roll on Jack, daddy do roll on"*
> *"Like the way you rollin', but you ain't gonna roll for so long."*
> —Bo Weavil Jackson, "Pistol Blues," 1926

By extension of (1), to have sexual intercourse. In some instances, the word is given a dual meaning, so as to stand for both working and fornicating:

> *Now you never have told me how you want your rollin' done*
> *I believe you must want me to roll from sun to sun.*
> —Sleepy John Estes, "Diving Duck Blues," 1929
> *I'm a steady rollin' man, I roll both night and day*
> *But I haven't got no sweet woman, boys to be rollin' this-a-way.*
> —Robert Johnson, "I'm A Steady Rollin' Man," 1937

roll (3)

> *I been rollin' and drifting along the road*
> *Just lookin' for my room and board.*
> —Lottie Beaman, "Rollin' Log Blues," 1929

"To wander, roam, travel, or move about" (OED at *roll*, v.2, 13.a). This definition may apply to:

> *I'm gonna put some, wings on my shoe*
> *And I ain't gonna stop rollin' till I kill 'em homeless blues.*
> —Seth Richards, "Lonely Seth Blues," 1928

roll (4)

> *It's a brownskin gal she's rollin' 'cross my mind*
> *And she keeps me worried, I'm bothered all the time.*
> —Skip James, "Four O'Clock Blues," 1931

"To revolve, come around again, in the mind" (OED at *roll*, v.2, 21). This sense is outmoded, the most recent OED citation dating to 1818.

roll and tumble

> *An' I rolled an' I tumbled an' I cried the whole night long*
> *When I rose this mornin' mama I didn't know right from wrong.*
> —Hambone Willie Newbern, "Roll And Tumble Blues," 1929

A colloquial equivalent of *toss and tumble,* the latter a standard English expression for restless motion in bed (cf. OED). Of itself, *roll and tumble* was an outmoded catchphrase applied to motion; it appears in Beaumont and Fletcher's *Wit Without Money* (1616): "My head's a Hogshead still, it rowls and tumbles." Describing an escaped slave, a Mississippian told Olmsted (1859): "'Fore Allen could stop his hoss he'd tumbled and rolled himself 'way out of sight.'"

roll up (1)

> *I ain't gonna tell nobody, thirty-four have done for me*
> *Christmas rolled up, I was broke as I could be.*
> —Charlie Patton, "34 Blues," 1934

To arrive; then-current slang held to be of Australian origin (OED). "... [Y]our time is gonna roll up, just like mine is, and when you come to die, you can't tell me to die for you" (Bukka White).

roll up (2)

> *I'm gonna roll up my ninety, gonna pay my fine an' get goin'*
> *I'm gonna wander back in the Nation, gonna make the Territo' my home.*
> —Bo Carter, "The County Farm Blues," 1940

Accumulate or finish; used in the above with respect to prison time.

roller (1)

> *I ain't no gambler an' I don't play no pool*
> *I'm a ramblin' roller, jelly-bakin', jelly-bakin' fool.*
> —Willie Baker, "No No Blues," 1929

Black slang for "someone who keeps on movin'; keeps on dancin'" (Hill). As a term for one who moves continuously, it survived in latter-day (1980s) black speech (DCS).

roller (2)

> *Lord, it's so easy, can't you see?*
> *Come on, mama, tee roll for me.*
> *Let other rollers understand,*
> *They ain't got a chance to take your man.*
> —Freddie "Redd" Nicholson, "Tee Roller's Rub," 1930

One who steals another's bedmate; a variant of *tee-roller*. This term probably arose from *roller* as meaning a thief. See *tee-roll*.

roller (3)

> *I heard you was a roller, I come to chop your wheel*
> *Know a roller never knows just what a kid man feels.*
> —Walter Vinson, "Rosa Lee Blues," 1941

? An easily available or promiscuous female; perhaps drawn from *easy roll* or *easy roller*. In current-day D.C.-Virginia youth slang, a *roller* connotes "[a] girl that goes from one man to another" (UD).

rollin' ball

> *I went down to Huntsville, I did not go to stay*
> *Just got there in the good ol' time, to wear a rollin' ball.*
> —Henry Thomas, "Run, Mollie, Run," 1927

Ball and chain.

rollin' mill

Aw the rollin' mill, sure Lord burned down last night
I can't get that, brown in this town today.
—*Bo Weavil Jackson, "Some Scream High Yellow," 1926*

A "factory for shaping metal by passing it between a pair of work rolls" (Wikipedia, http://en.wikipedia.org/wiki/Rolling_mill).

rolling stone

Don't care how long she gone don't care how long she stay
She's a rollin' stone she'll roll back home some day.
—*Robert Wilkins, "Rolling Stone, Part One," 1928*

A passé expression for "[a] rambler, a wanderer, a good-for-nothing" dating to the early 17th century (OED). It arose from the couplet of Thomas Tusser's *Five Hundred Points of Good Husbandry* (1573), which became a proverbial sentiment:

The stone that is rolling can gather no moss;
For master and servant oft changing is loss.

In quoting the latter, one song holds that it is better to change residences frequently than to subject oneself to feminine domination:

Old folks say: "Rollin' stone gathers no moss."
But let me tell you boy, never let a woman be your boss.
—*Sylvester Weaver, "Dad's Blues," 1927*

room

I'm gonna get up in the mornin', I believe I will dust my broom
Girlfriend the black man you been lovin', girlfriend can get my room.
—*Robert Johnson, "I Believe I'll Dust My Broom," 1936*

Archaic English for "[a] particular place or spot, without reference to its area" (OED). "He told them when he finished that crop they could have his room" (T. W. Cotton, as quoted in *Born in Slavery*).

root doctor, root man

Mama here come your root man, open the door an' let him in
It is just about time you usin', some of your good roots again.
—*Walter Davis, "Root Man Blues," 1935*

In the above song, a double entendre based on black idioms for one who treated ailments or conjured through the use of roots and herbs. The practice of root-based medicine was customary in colonial America, when roots and herbs were sold by peddlers. Although these expedients were largely displaced by patent medicines in the 1700s, they continued to flourish in the rural South, particularly among blacks. Among slaves, medicinal roots were commonly boiled and dispensed in tea form (cf. *Born in Slavery*). See *snake doctor*.

rough

> This little song it's a little bit rough
> Name of it is "Twistin' Your Stuff."
> —Barbecue Bob, "Twistin' Your Stuff," 1928

Vulgar or coarse in terms of language; a standard English term for which the earliest OED citation is 1958.

rounder

> Workin' man builds up an' the rounders tear him down
> That's the reason, I'm going to leave this town.
> —Sonny Scott, "Working Man Blues," 1933

"A man who won't work" (Skip James). This sense of the term is implicit in most blues references to a *rounder;* the word otherwise signified "one who makes the round of prisons, workhouses, drinking saloons, etc.; a habitual criminal, loafer or drunkard" (OED, which dates it to 1854). Most blues singers were by definition *rounders,* since performing homespun music was not considered legitimate work by anyone of the blues era, the singers themselves included.

rub

> Rub me down on your floor;
> Rub me so your man never know.
> —Henry Thomas, "Lovin' Babe," 1929

To copulate (F&H, 1903); a dated sense of the word seemingly formed from *rub-off,* which stood for an act of copulation between the 17th and early 19th centuries (Partridge).

rumble seat

> I knocked her face to the ground, her cap to the risin' sun
> I jumped in her rumble seat, when she tried to run.
> —Lee Green, "Wash Day And No Soap," 1930

A euphemistic or humorous term for ass, fostered by the position of rumble seats at the rear end of contemporary cars.

rumblin'

> I heard a mighty rumblin' down under the ground
> The boll weevil an' the devil was keepin' somebody's brown.
> —Sam Butler, "Devil And My Brown Blues," 1926

The subterranean sounds made by occupants of hell; a traditional allusion found in John Bunyan's *The Pilgrim's Progress* (1678): "... they also thought that they heard there a rumbling noise, as of fire, and a cry of some tormented; and that they smelt the scent of brimstone. ... The Sheperds told them, [t]his is a by-way to hell...." As a harbinger of death, *rumblin' sound* appears in the following couplet:

When the death wagon rolled up with a rumblin' sound

Says you know by that my gal was graveyard bound.

—*Edward Thompson, "Seven Sisters Blues," 1929*

run (n. 1)

"Listen to this run."

—*Buddy Boy Hawkins, "A Rag Blues," 1929*

A quick succession of notes; a standard English term associated with the 19th century (cf. OED, which quotes an 1876 dictionary: "Except for the purpose of training the voice, runs may be said to be out of fashion").

run (n. 2)

Me an' my girl friend went out for a little run

When she seen my man she told him what I had done.

—*Lil Johnson, "Never Let Your Left Hand Know What Your Right Hand Do,"*
1929

Excursion; standard English (cf. OED). The above couplet refers to sex between females.

run (v. 1)

I sold my gin, I sold it straight

The police run me to my woman's gate

She come to the door, she nod her head

Made me welcome to the foldin' bed.

—*Furry Lewis, "Kassie Jones, Part Two," 1928*

To chase. In this sense, *run* was employed in standard English from the 15th century onward to refer to chasing hunted animals, particularly with dogs (cf. OED and DARE 4, which misconstrues it as an Americanism). It is obvious that this meaning was transferred to blacks during slavery, when dogs were customarily deployed in pursuit of escaped slaves. One ex-slave reported: "Dere was a white man call Henderson had 80 bloodhounds and rented 'em out to run slaves" (Green Cumby, as quoted in *Born in Slavery*). See *run down*. In the following example, *run* means to chase:

Blues jumped a rabbit, run him one solid mile

This rabbit fell down, cryin' like a natural child.

—*Blind Lemon Jefferson, "Rabbit Foot Blues," 1926*

run (v. 2)

Which way, which a-way, do the Red River run?

Which a-way, do the Red River run?

—*Charlie Patton, "Jim Lee Blues, Part One," 1929*

To flow; standard English, but normally applied to the ocean or tides (cf. OED).

run around

That's all right baby, 'bout how you run around

But your heart'll strike sorrow, when Bob gets back to town.

—Barbecue Bob, "Atlanta Moan," 1930

To consort with other males sexually; said of female companions of whom sexual fidelity is expected. This colloquialism, of moot black origin, likely arose from *run around with* as meaning to associate with, in a generally hedonistic fashion: ". . . I never woulda run round wid no Nigger and married him if I hadn't been witched by dat conjur business" (Nicey Kinney, as quoted in *Born in Slavery*).

run down

I got ten little puppies, I got twelve little shaggy hounds

It's gonna take them twenty-two dogs to run my good gal down.

—Blind Lemon Jefferson, "Booger Rooger Blues," 1926

To locate someone, particularly a missing or rootless person. An ex-slave complained of "[y]oung ladies . . . running with bootleggers, and running the hoodlums down . . ." (H. B. Holloway, as quoted in *Born in Slavery*). This term may have originated with regard to the practice of tracking escaped slaves with bloodhounds: ". . . a bunch of men taken they dogs and run me down." ". . . when they had to run 'em down with the nigger dogs, they'd git in bad trouble" (Ex-slaves quoted in Botkin, 1945).

run into

Shakin' her (rumble?) jus' like you shake a sack

She say: "Run into me baby an' make me break my back."

—Walter Davis, "Sweet Sixteen," 1935

A sexually provocative expression used in beckoning catchphrases, as in the following vocal asides:

"Aw, run into me but don't hurt me!"

—Lil Johnson, "Never Let Your Left Hand Know What Your Right Hand Do," 1929

"Aw, run into me an' crush me baby, but don't bruise me!"

—Frankie (Half Pint) Jaxon, "Jive Man Blues," 1929

run wild

He runnin' wild, that mitey boy

That mitey girl, that mitey girl

He runnin' wild.

—Charlie Patton, "Running Wild Blues," 1929

To live with no constraints; a still-current disparaging black idiom typically applied to delinquent youth (cf. Smitherman, 2000), a sense dating at least to the blues era: "I wouldn't know what to think of these young people. Some of them is running wild." (Adelaide J. Vaughn, as quoted in *Born in Slavery*). The expression may have originated with respect to wild horses: "The world is so far gone, it would be the hardest thing to put the bridle on some of the people that's runnin' wild now" (Griffin Myrax, as quoted in *Born in Slavery*).

salting the dog

> *Ain't but two things I jus' like*
> *That's saltin' the dog an' Ballin' the Jack.*
> —Barbecue Bob, "Easy Rider, Don't You Deny My Name," 1927

? Perhaps a term for having sexual intercourse. See *salty dog*.

saltwater

> *A doney love saltwater, she always wants a drink*
> *If they see you with a bottle they will, almost break your neck.*
> —Charlie Patton, "Revenue Man Blues," 1934

? Most likely, urine, the 17th–18th century colloquial meaning of *saltwater*, (Partridge), in which event the waggish intention of the performer is to convey the idea that a *doney* must love to urinate, as she constantly drinks alcohol.

salty, jump

> *Gonna get me some poison, kill myself*
> *'Cause the man I love has put me on the shelf*
> *The dirty old viper jumped salty on me.*
> —Rosetta Howard, "My Man Jumped Salty On Me," 1939

To become angry without warning; a vogue Harlem term of 1930s vintage (cf. Major, 1970).

salty dog

> *Won't you let me be your salty dog?*
> *I don't wanna be your man at all*
> *You salty dog . . .*
> —Papa Charlie Jackson, "Salty Dog Blues," 1924

Apparently, a lecherous companion; an obscure idiom steeped in archaicism, despite the prevalence of the song "Salty Dog" in the blues repertoire. In the 17th and 18th centuries, *salty* referred to a female dog in heat (cf. OED, which offers citations for 1603 and 1796). Grose (1796) defines *salt* as meaning "lecherous," citing the expression *a salt bitch* that is the obvious basis of *salty dog*, itself an obscure term that had lost its meaning when blues singers took up the song of that name in the early 1900s. (Thus Skip James held that *salty dog* was a term for an actual dog with an "unloosable" grip, while Mississippi John Hurt, who similarly performed it, stated that he had no idea what the phrase meant; 1966 conversations with author.) The substitution of "dog" for "bitch" might have been facilitated by the 18th-century *sad dog*, a term for a debauched person (Grose, 1796). Fisher's 1928 listing of *salty dog* as a Harlem intensifier for *dog* ("[a]ny extraordinary person, thing, or event") does not jibe with its use in the song above.

sand

> *I let you burn my biscuits, an' fill my coffee fulla sand*
> *An' now you take my money, and give it to another man.*
> —Charlie Spand, "Ain't Gonna Stand For That," 1929

Sugar; convict and hobo slang dating to around 1915 (DAS).

Santa Claus

> *Don't give my baby no more cherry ball*
> *Know she may get drunk Lord an' show her Santy Claus.*
> —Mississippi Bracey, "Cherry Ball," 1930

Pudenda; suggested by the use of this term in slave English as a synonym for Christmas presents: "Then they'd give us plenty of Sandy Claus and we would go back to our cabins to have fun twel New Year's day" (James Bolton, as quoted in *Born in Slavery*). Perhaps expediently, it was also applied to males:

> *Your auntie and your uncle and your ma's and pa's*
> *They all got drunk and showed their Santa Claus.*
> —Memphis Minnie, "New Dirty Dozen," 1930

Saturday night (a.)

> *Now you Saturday night women, you love to ape an' clown*
> *You won't do nothin' but tear a good man's reputation down.*
> —Robert Johnson, "Stop Breaking Down Blues," 1937

A Mississippi pejorative applied to barrelhouse habitués or hedonists for whom Saturday night was a focal point of existence. A Delta planter (Joe Rice Dockery) recalled: "The hill people weren't your Saturday night, skin-balling, crap-shooting nigger," while a jukehouse proprieteress described blues singers as "them there Saturday night folks . . . good people don't be out with them" (cf. Calt and Wardlow, 1989).

says

> *Says I'll be your monkey baby, sure won't be your dog*
> *Says 'fore I stand your doggin' I'll sleep in a hollow log.*
> —Charlie Patton, "Joe Kirby," 1929

An "unmeaning and silly prefix to [a] sentence" (Tucker, 1921) that is rampant in blues song diction.

Scratchin' Gravel

> Do the Black Snake Wiggle an' the Boston Trot
> Scratchin' Gravel in a vacant lot.
> —Jane Lucas and Georgia Tom, "Come On Mama," 1930

A double entendre based on Scratchin' the Gravel, a black dance that would not have been done in vacant lots.

Scraunch (Scronch), Georgia Scronch

> You wiggles and wobble and you move it around
> Ball the Jack an' you go to town
> And do that Scraunch, aw you does that Scraunch
> Aw you shake it an' you wiggle it
> Honey when you do that Scraunch.
> —Barbecue Bob, "Doin' The Scraunch," 1930

> Oh you talk about your Shuffle, talk about your Raunch
> They got a new dance they call the Georgia Scronch
> Now they Scronchin', oh they Scronchin'...
> —Georgia Tom on Kansas City Kitty, "Scronchin," 1931

Ostensibly, a black dance, noted as "scronch" by Van Vetchen (1926). As with *boogie woogie*, its bona fides as a dance are questionable; Mayo Williams recalled "scronch" as a term for a sex party, while the context of Van Vechten's dialogue invoking it is patently sexual:

> Toly, you sho' is one bardacious scroncher.
> You's goin' git scronched.

The term itself appears to have derived from *scraunch*, a synonym of crunch.

scuffler

> Clothes is gettin' shabby, shoes won't stand fixin' any more
> Now if times don't get no better, to the flophouse another poor scuffler
>   will go.
> —Leroy Henderson, "Good Scufflin' Blues," 1935

One who scuffles, i.e., barely gets by despite strenuous efforts. This term is of likely black origin; *scuffle* itself was first recorded in 1939 (cf. OED).

sealskin black

> Black women may be evil, but they'se all right with me
> I got a sealskin black woman, boy, sweet as she can be.
> —Lee Green, "Sealskin Black Woman," 1937

A probable neologism formed from *sealskin brown* (q.v.), indicating (in the above song) a black-complexioned female with smooth skin.

sealskin brown

> *Some folks say black is evil, but I will tell the world they are wrong*
> *'Cause I'm a sealskin brown, and I've been evil since I was born.*
> —Lucille Bogan, "Pig Iron Sally," 1934

An African American with a medium-brown complexion (Hill).

see

> *I'm goin' down to the courthouse, see the judge an' the chief police*
> *My good gal fell dead an' I sure can't see no peace.*
> —Sam Collins, "The Jail House Blues," 1927

To experience in one's own person, a sense of the word classified as rare by the OED (cf. *see* v.11) that also occurs in the well-known spiritual, "Nobody Knows The Trouble I See."

Seven Sisters

> *The Seven Sisters sent me away happy, 'round the corner I met another*
>   *little girl*
> *She looked at me and smiled and said: "Go devil and destroy the world."*
> —"Funny Paper" Smith, "Seven Sisters Blues," 1931

A legendary conjurer who was said to reside in *Algiers* (Hill).

Seven Up

> *Now the nigger an' the white man playin' Seven Up*
> *The nigger beat the white man, a-scared to pick it up*
> —Tommy McClennan, "Bottle It Up And Go," 1939

A variation of a card game known as All Fours that was played for seven points and was one of the most popular 19th-century Mississippi riverboat gambling games. Thornton (1912) dates the expression to 1856, while Bartlett (1877) classifies it as a Western term. The game itself had no known currency in black barrelhouses during the blues era, and the above performer was a professional gambler whose forte was *coon-can* swindling (David Edwards).

shake (n.)

> *Give your house rent shake on Saturday night*
> *Monday morning you'll hold [rent] collectors good an' tight.*
> —Bessie Smith, "Safety Mama," 1931

A black term for a dance party, used with assorted modifiers. In the 1920s, Chicago house parties were termed *funky shakes* (Mayo Williams).

shake (v.)

> *If you don't shake you won't get no cake*
> *You salty dog.*
> —Sam Collins, "New Salty Dog," 1931

A blues euphemism for engaging in sex. As a term for moving or dancing, without sexual connotations, *shake* appears in a single blues recording:

Get your hat get your coat get shakin' on down the line. (3)
—Henry Thomas, "Texas Worried Blues," 1928

shake (a, one's) shimmy

There's a big fat mama with the meat shakin' on her bone
Every time she shakes a shimmy, another gal loses her home.
—Papa Charlie Jackson, "Mumsy Mumsy Blues," 1926

Literally, to shake the dress known as a shimmy. In white American speech the expression was popularized by Irving Berlin's "You Cannot Make Your Shimmy Shake On Tea" (1919) and had a vaguely risqué connotation; in blues song, it was a euphemism for a female's engaging in sex:

Aunt Dinah rolls her britches way above her knees
She's shakin' her shimmy for who she please.
—Walter Davis, "Sweet Sixteen," 1935

Cf. *shimmy.*

shake it

Aw you shake it an' you wiggle it
Honey when you do that Scraunch.
—Barbecue Bob, "Doin' The Scraunch," 1930

To move one's hips suggestively, if not to engage in actual sex. As a black catchphrase *shake it* dates to slavery, when it occurred as part of a ring dance: "... boys en girls would choose dar partners den weuns sing: 'Ole Brer Rabbit, / Shake it, shake it, / How I love you, / Shake it, shake it'" (Mary Wright, as quoted in *Born in Slavery*).

shake it and break it

You can shake it you can break it you can hang it on the wall
Throw it out the window, catch it 'fore it falls
—Charlie Patton, "Shake It And Break It," 1929

A circus catchphrase dating to around 1890 (Stearns). The phrase *hang it on the wall* appeared in slave song with regard to clothing: "Ole Massa take dat new brown coat, / And hang it on de wall ..." (William Warfield, as quoted in *Born in Slavery*).

shake ... on down

She's low an' squatty, right down on the ground
She's a light-weighted mama, shook her kid man, shook her kid man down.
—Willie Baker, "No No Blues," 1929

? An obscure sexual idiom that likely means to initiate sexual activity. In slightly altered form it became the title phrase of a popular 1930s blues recording:

Must I holler, or must I shake 'em on down?

Aw don't stop hollerin' mama, must I shake 'em on down?

—*Bukka White, "Shake 'Em On Down," 1937*

shake, rattle, and roll

Oh shake shake, Mattie,

Shake, rattle and roll.

—*Kansas Joe, "Shake Mattie," 1931*

A gambling catchphrase referring to throwing dice, apparently from a cup. It appeared as the title of a 1919 Tin Pan Alley tune by a blackface comedian, Al Bernard, who may have derived the expression from blacks. Subsequently, it was used as the nonsensical title phrase and chorus of the 1954 rhythm and blues hit "Shake, Rattle And Roll," a straightforward blues composition by Jesse Stone that helped usher in the age of rock and roll.

shake that thing

Now it ain't no Charleston, ain't no Chicken Wing

All you got to do is to shake that thing

Now shake that thing, aw shake that thing

I'm gettin' sick and tired of tellin' you to shake that thing.

—*Papa Charlie Jackson, "Shake That Thing," 1925*

To engage in sexual intercourse or to evoke its motions while dancing. Taken at face value, *shake that thing* was a dance done (judging from the above song) to fast syncopated music. However, it is doubtful that a dance of that name actually existed when the above performer recorded what became the most influential race record of all time, and was the first commercial hit by a self-accompanied blues performer. (The recording created a new genre of blues songs with choruses, nearly all of which featured sexual double entendres.) Initially, the phrase *shake that thing* was likely a fashionable directive to female dancers at house parties or barrelhouses, *that thing* referring to a dancer's hips and/or ass. As a result of the 1925 recording, *shake that thing* was transformed into a euphemistic slang term for intercourse:

Nothin' but mud an' water, far as I can see

I need some sweet mama, come an' shake that thing with me.

—*Barbecue Bob, "Mississippi Heavy Water Blues," 1927*

A contemporary (1927) issue of the *Journal of Abnormal and Social Psychology* noted: "'Shake it,' 'shake that thing,' etc. Such expressions are very frequent in the blues, ostensibly they refer to dancing, but they are really Negro vulgar expressions relating to coitus." In various renditions of "Shake That Thing," such as Frank Stokes's "Stomp That Thing" (1928), Tampa Joe and Macon Ed's "Wringin' That Thing" (1929), and Walter Coleman's "Smack That Thing" (1936), *that thing = pussy.* The expression *shake that thing* was resurrected as a vague risqué allusion in Ray Charles's "Mess Around" (1953) and "What'd I Say," a best seller of 1960; it is still encountered in black speech, usually in regard to dancing.

shave 'em dry

> *There's one thing I just can't understand*
> *Why a good-lookin' girl likes a workin' man.*
> *Hey hey; daddy let me shave 'em dry.*
> —Ma Rainey, "Shave 'Em Dry Blues," 1924

According to Mayo Williams, the expression "Can I shave 'em dry?" meant "Can I go to bed with you?" and was a black catchphrase at the time of the above recording, which he produced. But see below.

shave (one) dry (1)

> *When I hit Birmingham, you know I was feelin' awful funny*
> *Nest a-crabs on my ass, and the whores had my money*
> *Now you know all I could say: "You know them bitches done*
> *   shaved me dry."*
> —Walter Roland, "I'm Gonna Shave You Dry," 1935 (unissued)

To get another person's money by underhanded means; a black slang term based on the archaic idiom *to dry shave*, recorded in glossaries of the 17th and 18th centuries. A 1620 chronicler of Latin terms defined one expression as meaning "to ridde him of his gold, to drie shaue him," while the author of a 1706 compilation included the term "to *Dry-shave*, to chowse, gull or cheat notoriously" (cf. OED).

shave (one) dry (2)

> *You know said I done so long time you know she said: "Baby, I'm dead."*
> *Now I told her: "No, great God I just shaved you dry."*
> —Walter Roland, "I'm Gonna Shave You Dry," 1935 (unissued)

By extension of (1), to exhaust a sexual partner, perhaps to the point of draining the person's sexual fluid.

sheik

> *His ways an' actions is hard to beat*
> *For he's the sheik, of Desplaines Street.*
> —Papa Charlie Jackson, "Sheik Of Desplaines Street," 1927

Romeo; renowned lover; a vogue term created by Rudolph Valentino's role in *The Sheik* (1921). It was in reference to this film that the popular fiddle-guitar team of Lonnie Chatmon and Walter Vinson dubbed themselves The Mississippi Sheiks (Vinson).

shift gear

Some joker learned my baby, how to shift gear on a Cadillac-8
And ever since that happened I can't keep my business straight.
—Blind Lemon Jefferson, "Booger Rooger Blues," 1926

To have sexual intercourse, perhaps with skillful motions. In blues song this term is invariably applied to females:

Lordy Lordy Lordy I'm gettin' up in years
But mama ain't too old to shift her gears.
—Ida Cox, "Fore Day Creep," 1927

Shim-Sham-Shimmy

Check all your razors and your guns
Do the Shim-Sham-Shimmy till the risin' sun
—Bessie Smith, "Gimme A Pigfoot," 1933

A variant of the *Shimmy-She-Wobble*, recorded by Calloway as "a dance introduced at the Cotton Club in 1930." It probably remarked on the light complexion of Cotton Club dancers, *shims shams* having been a black idiom dating to slavery for "Negroes of mixed blood": "I know some pore white trash . . . de shim shams was nigh 'bout also [trash]" (Clay Bobbit, as quoted in *Born In Slavery*; explanation furnished by interviewer Mary A. Hicks).

shimmy (v. 1)

Turn your lamp down mama, an' keep your window pinned
I might start shimmyin', don't let nobody in.
—Sam Collins, "Slow Mama Slow," 1931

A term for having sexual intercourse drawn from the *Shimmy*, unless the name of the dance arose as a result of its association with sex.

Shimmy (v. 2)

Way down South you oughta see the women Shimmy and shake
Got a new way a-wiggle, make a weak man break his neck.
—Blind Lemon Jefferson, "Southern Woman Blues," [1928]

To dance the Shimmy. This sense of the word is almost never used in blues song.

Shimmy-She

I took a trip out on the ocean, walked the sand of the deep blue sea
I found the crab with a shrimp, tryin' to do the Shimmy-She.
—Blind Willie McTell, "Talkin' To Myself," 1931

See *Shimmy-She-Wobble.*

Shimmy-She-Wobble

Quit Shimmy-She-Wobble, quit shakin' your hips.
—Blind Willie McTell, "Razor Ball," 1931

A basic blues dance of plantation origin, also called the *Shimmy* and the *Shimmy-She*. It was current by 1907, when a locally popular Bolton, Mississippi, blues tune recalled by Walter Vinson began: "If you can't Shimmy, you got no business here" (3). As done by blacks, the *Shimmy* was a bump-and-grind contact dance that was so suggestive as to be prohibited in Mississippi Delta barrelhouses of the blues era. A tepid white version of the dance became a stage hit as performed by Gilda Grey in 1918 and thereafter enjoyed a Jazz Age vogue, largely on the basis of its titillating shaking movements. Sam Chatmon (who recalled the dance from 1907–8) reported: "... The white folks never did *Shimmy* ... just to get with a woman and stand like we used to do and wobblin' upside her like we used to do, I never did see no white folks do that." The etymology of *Shimmy* as a dance term is uncertain; the word itself is known to have been an American corruption of *chemise*, recorded in 1837 (DAH). However, there is no obvious connection between an item of clothing and a provocative dance like the Shimmy. Conceivably, *Shimmy* in black usage was a corruption of *shinny* or *shammy*.

Shimmy-Wobble (v.)

> "Here's how I made the Jackson girls Shimmy-Wobble."
> —Buddy Boy Hawkins, "A Rag Blues," 1929

To dance the Shimmy; the second element may have been introduced to distinguish the activity from sex.

sho'!

> Oh come on mama let us go to the edge of town, aw sho'!
> I know where there's a bird's nest, built down on the ground.
> —Charlie Patton, "Revenue Man Blues," 1934

An American equivalent of *Pshaw!*, the latter "an exclamation expressing contempt, impatience, or disgust" (OED). F&H, which considers it a distinct term (as "*sho*") provides one example, dating to 1851.

short little town

> Boy they tell me the water, done took short little town
> I'm goin' to Vicksburg, over that higher mound.
> —Charlie Patton, "High Water Everywhere, Part One," 1929

A black colloquialism for a town notable only for its insignificant size. Its derivation is indicated by a Leadbelly monologue: "... 'Well I'm way down here in a little place'; the place was so short it didn't have a name, it was so little" (*Leadbelly's Last Session*, Folkways Fa 2941, Volume 1).

shout

> Oh, I want everybody to shout
> I'm gonna do like a prisoner, I'm gonna roll my time on out.
> —Son House: "Preachin' The Blues, Part One," 1930

To make boisterous affirmations of a preacher's exhortations; a mark of black religious fervor dating to antebellum times. It once involved enthusiastic gestures as well as utterances: "He can 'shout' (jumping up and down about a foot and a half from the floor and knocking his heels together)" (comment on "Father" Charles Coates, as quoted in *Born in Slavery*).

show

> *Take me sweet mama, 'low me one more show*
> *I swear to the Lord that I won't do wrong no more.*
> —Peg Leg Howell, "Doin' Wrong," 1927

Chance; an Americanism of mid-19th-century vintage (cf. OED).

show one's shape

> *I told my wife: "If you want me to wait,*
> *You better stop your sister from showin' her shape."*
> —Willie Baker, "Mama, Don't Rush Me Blues," 1929

To wear a form-fitting dress; a still-used black idiom involving 19th-century standards of feminine decorum: "We wore our dresses, down to our ankles in length and my dresses was called mother hubbards. The skirts had about three yards circumference and we wore plenty of clothing under our dress. . . . Folks did not know how we was made. We did not show our shape" (Dina Beard, as quoted in *Born in Slavery*).

shuck it

> *I know she want it hot (babe), sure don't want it cold*
> *"Aw shuck it, mama"*
> *It would break my heart if you ever say you can't use me no more.*
> —Charlie Patton, "Love My Stuff," 1934

Presumably, a directive to remove clothing, *shuck* having been an American colloquialism meaning to undress or peel off clothes, dating in print to 1848 (F&H, 1903).

Shuffle

> *Oh you talk about your Shuffle, talk about your Raunch*
> *They got a new dance they call the Georgia Scronch*
> —Georgia Tom on Kansas City Kitty's, "Scronchin," 1931

The name of a black dance with roots in slavery: "Sometimes we has de fiddle and de banjo and does we do dat chicken wing and de shuffle." (Albert Hill, as quoted in *Born in Slavery*).

side-track

> *Let me be your side-track, mama till your mainline come*
> *I can do more switchin' than your mainline ever done.*
> —Sam Collins, "Dark Cloudy Blues," 1927

A secondary lover to whom one has no abiding attachment; black slang of the blues era.

signify

> *I'm gonna tell everybody, what a signifyin' man will do*
> *He will come to my house an' he tell about you*
> *Go to your house an' he tell about me*
> *But he better learn he ain't gonna signify no more.*
> —*Sam Collins, "Signifying Blues," 1931*

To lie (Willie Moore) or make baseless statements; a black idiom misrendered by the OED as meaning "[t]o boast or brag; to make insulting remarks or insinuations." In the above song *tell* means to tell lies.

sin and a shame, a

> *"Ain't that a sin an' a shame?"*
> —*Kate McTell on Blind Willie McTell, "Mama, Let Me Scoop For You," 1932*

A Southern catchphrase for a deplorable circumstance, occurring in Opie Read's *Len Gansett* (1888): ("'I declare, papa, it is a sin an' a shame for as old a man as you air to carry on this way'") and Zora Neale Hurston's *De Turkey and de Law: A Comedy in Three Acts* (1930): ("I just think it's a sin and a shame . . . de way dese Baptis' niggers is runnin' round here carryin' on").

sing one's blues, to

> *When I first met you baby, you were blind and you could not see*
> *But now I'm quittin' you mama, don't sing your blues unto me.*
> —*Charlie Spand, "Mistreating Blues," 1930*

To bewail one's situation.

single-tree

> *I beat my gal, with a single-tree*
> *She h'ist up the winder, sweet mama, her watch on me.*
> —*Henry Thomas, "Don't Ease Me In," 1928*

A wooden crossbar used in horse or mule-driven ploughs.

sinking down

> *I believe, I believe, I'm on my last go-round*
> *Lord all-a my money gone, I feel myself sinkin' down.*
> —*Roosevelt Sykes, "All My Money Gone Blues," 1929*

Falling prey to misfortune or ill health; a passé expression found in Defoe's *Moll Flanders* (1722) that appears in the 1976 Warren Zevon song "Carmelita": "Carmelita hold me tighter / I think I'm sinking down."

sister

> See that preacher walkin' down the street
>
> Fixin' to mess with every sister he meet.
>
> —"Hi" Henry Brown, "Preacher Blues," 1932

In black Christianity, a female member of a congregation.

sissy

> My man got a sissy, his name is Miss Kate
>
> He shook that thing like jelly on a plate.
>
> —Ma Rainey, "Sissy Blues," 1926

"A derogatory term for a gay male" (Smitherman, 2000) dating to slavery: "Marse Lordnorth was a good man, but he didn't have no use for 'omans—he was a sissy" (Georgia Baker, as quoted in *Born in Slavery*).

Six, Big

> "I don't see how you hungry women carry your feet;
>
> Hey you walk these streets like Big Six on his beat."
>
> —Cow Cow Davenport, "State Street Jive," 1928

The nickname of a storied black policeman who lived at Thirty-first and Lasalle Streets in Chicago and retired in the 1930s (Mayo Williams); so named for his height, which was said to exceed 6'6". The above couplet refers to prostitutes.

Skoodle Do Do, Skeedle Loo Doo, Skoodle Um-Skoo

> I Skoodle Do Do, for my meat
>
> When I don't Skoodle, I don't eat.
>
> —Seth Richards, "Skoodelum Doo," 1928
>
> Skeedle Loo Doo, all night long
>
> Skeedle Loo Doo, all day, too
>
> Skeedle Loo Doo, if you can't . . . I know who can
>
> . . . Now Skeedle Loo Doo, that's all I do.
>
> —Blind Blake, "Skeedle Loo Doo Blues," 1926

References to sexual intercourse drawn from a popular dance among Chicago blacks in the late 1920s (Mayo Williams) given various names:

> ". . . Do you know anything about that new dance they got out now?"
>
> "No, I don't, what is it?"
>
> "It's the dance they call 'Skoodle Um Skoo.'"
>
> —Papa Charlie Jackson, "Skoodle Um Skoo," 1927

The dance or the sexual activity associated with it was first invoked in a 1925 Jimmy O'Bryant jazz instrumental, "Skoodlum Blues." The derivation of the term (which is reminiscent of *beedle um bum*) is unknown.

skeet

> *I've got a head like a freight train, an' I walk just like a grizzly bear*
> *An' I use my skeetin' Garrett, and I skeet my ambeer everywhere.*
> —Lucille Bogan, "Pig Iron Sally," 1934

To spit, particularly between the teeth; regarded as standard English by the OED, but associated with Southern use after 1900. The above lyric refers to spitting tobacco juice.

skeetin' Garrett

See *skeet*. A black term for dipping tobacco (construed as snuff), found in Zora Neale Hurston's *Woofing* (1931): "I took a minute to see if yo' could let me have a little skeeting garret." *Garrett* invokes a well-known brand of chewing tobacco, *Levi Garrett*.

skin game

> *Hangin' around the skin game, sure will get you down*
> *If you hang around the skin game too long.*
> —Ollis Martin, "Police And High Sheriff Came Riding Down," 1927

Georgia Skin game; a term used in Zora Neal Hurston's *Lawing and Jawing* (1931): "I knowed it, one of those skin game jelly-beans robbin' hard workin' men out they money."

skin man

> *Let me tell you, what the skin mens will do:*
> *Well they sell your wife skins an' take her away from you.*
> —"Hi" Henry Brown, "Skin Man," 1932

A peddler of dried and seasoned barbecue skins, retailed in black communities in the 1920s in the form of balls costing ten cents apiece (Skip James). These were commonly eaten as sandwiches, on bread smeared with molasses.

sleep in a hollow log, to drink muddy water and

> *What you gonna do, when they take your man to war?*
> *"I'm gonna drink muddy water, gonna sleep in a hollow log."*
> —Blind Lemon Jefferson, "Wartime Blues," 1927

To live outdoors in the manner of a vagrant (Hill); a semi-proverbial expression in the blues era that likely originated from the example of rabbits, said to be a homeless animal that took shelter in hollow logs. A variant phrase appears as:

> *I'd rather drink muddy water, sleep in a hollow tree*
> *Than to hear my kid gal, say she don't want me.*
> —Charley Lincoln, "Depot Blues," 1928

sling snot

I said get my 'tunia, only thing I love
Make you weep like a willow, sling snot like a turkle dove.
—Jesse James, "Sweet Patuni," 1936

To weep demonstratively, in black colloquial speech. In regard to sanctified preachers, Skip James said: ". . . They all make those long, extensive prayers . . . sling snot, cry. . . ." It was derived from an obscure, archaic British slang expression, *to throw snot about*, recorded by John Ray in *A Collection of English Proverbs* (1678), where it is included among "joculatory, nugatory, and rustic proverbs" and given as meaning "to weep." Grose (1796) uses the phrase in defining *snivel*: "[t]o cry, to throw the snot or snivel about." *Sling snot* still occurs in black speech: "I said: '. . . you can throw rocks, sling snot, cry all you want, but you're coming out'" (Mets' manager Jerry Manuel at post-game press conference, 6/17/2008).

slippin' and (a)-slidin'

Say yon go your mama out across the field
Slippin' and a-slidin' just like an automobile
—Kokomo Arnold, "The Twelves (Dirty Dozens)," 1935

Moving furtively or "sneaking around" (Smitherman, 2000); a still-used black expression that formed the title of a 1956 Little Richard rock and roll song.

sloppy drunk

I'd rather be sloppy drunk, sleepin' in the can
Than to be at home, rollin' with my man.
—Lucille Bogan, "Sloppy Drunk Blues," 1930

Drunk to the point of exhibiting messiness, or soiling one's clothing; said of people who couldn't handle their liquor. (As Sol Henderson recalled of Robert Johnson: "He'd get *sloppy* drunk.") It appears in Richard Wright's *Native Son* of 1940: "'That's enough, now. You don't want to get sloppy drunk.'"

Slow Drag

Give me that old time Slow Drag, it's plenty good enough for me
I mean that old time Slow Drag, it certainly is a mystery.
—Trixie Smith, "Give Me That Old Slow Drag," 1922

The prevalent dance performed to slow blues pieces, dating at least to 1901, when the Scott Joplin–Scott Hayden composition *Sunflower Slow Drag* (billed as a "Ragtime Two-Step") appeared. The Slow Drag was a contact dance described by Johnny Shines as "just dry screwin'"; a chaste version was proffered by Joplin in the 1911 opera *Treemonisha*, containing this instruction: "The Slow Drag must begin on the first beat of each measure. . . . When moving forward, drag the left foot; when moving backward, drag the right foot. . . ." During the 1930s it remained the most popular blues dance (Shines), and served as the inspiration for the 1940s works of Arthur (Big Boy) Crudup, the last self-accompanied blues performer to attain general popularity.

slum

> *Now he throwed me in that dirty old white house, it was so dark I had to*
> *   feel my way*
> *He gave me a slice of bread so doggone thin I could peep through it an' see*
> *   the crack of day.*
> *Now I'd be the one that would get the slum*
> *And the cream would go to those dirty snitchin' rats*
> —Pine Top Smith, "Big Boy, They Can't Do That," 1929

Prison (as well as army) stew; a term derived from *slumgullion* that came into vogue during World War I.

slumgullion

This term occurs in the title of a 1929 Cow Cow Davenport instrumental, "Slum Gullion [*sic*] Stomp," and refers to a watery stew or hash associated with hoboes and the destitute. Originally it connoted a poor-tasting drink, in which sense DAH traces it to 1872; Hotten (1859) defines it as "any cheap, nasty washy beverage." Its transformation into a disparaging term for solid food occurred by 1902, when it was used by Jack London (OED). The word itself derives from *slubberdegullion,* a 17th-century British pejorative meaning "slob" that became obsolete in the 19th century (cf. OED; Partridge).

smack one down

> *If I catch you out with your high brown baby,*
> *I'll smack you down, and I don't mean maybe.*
> —Alberta Hunter, "Aggravatin' Papa," 1923

To thrash one; black slang that may date to the previous century: "... I ... says, 'Nigger, get out of here and don't never come back. If you go back, I'll smack you down'" (Leitman Spinks, as quoted in *Born in Slavery*). This idiom still survives, along with the variant *slapped down,* used figuratively in the following: "Now, I was slapped down to the ground when my son Wade died in 1996 ..." (John Edwards, *ABC World News* interview, 8/8/2008).

smoke one's cigarette

> *Won't you just smoke my cigarette, draw it the whole night long?*
> *Just draw my cigarette baby until you make my good ashes come.*
> —Bo Carter, "Cigarette Blues," 1936

To perform fellatio, an expression perhaps suggested by the catchphrase "She smokes" (or vice versa), applied to women who performed oral sex on males (Partridge).

smoky

> *Say you treated me smoky, but that'll never happen no more*
> *Because if you do not love me woman, it's down the road I'll go.*
> —Walter Roland, "Back Door Blues," 1933

Low, mean; an adaptation from British dialect (cf. EDD).

snake doctor

> *Lord I know many you mens wonderin' what the snake doctor man got in*
>   *his hand*
> *He got roots and herbs, steal a woman at everywhere he lands.*
> —Jelly Jaw Short, "Snake Doctor Blues," 1932

A rustic term for the dragonfly, noted in Southwestern speech by Bartlett in 1877 and in Pennsylvania and Ohio by Clapin (c. 1902). Mississippi blacks of the 1920s believed that the snake doctor had the ability to cure ailing snakes and restore dead ones to life by alighting on them (cf. Puckett, 1925). Presumably, a "snake doctor man" was someone with curative or magical abilities comparable to those of a snake doctor. See *root doctor, root man.*

Snakehips

> *"You know what I like to see you do?"*
> *"What's that, Minnie?"*
> *"That ol' Snakehips; looks like your bones break in two!"*
> —Memphis Minnie and Bumble Bee Slim, "New Orleans Stop Time," 1936

A black dance that became popular before World War I, and later incorporated the passé *Ballin' The Jack* (Bessie Jones). Another dance of that name, an embellishment of the *Shimmy,* was popularized in the early 1930s by Earl (Snakehips) Tucker, a Harlem dancer.

snap

> *An' I feel like snappin' my pistol in your face*
> *Let some brownskin woman be here to take your place.*
> —Blind Boy Fuller, "Pistol Slapper Blues," 1938

To fire or pull the trigger of a pistol; passé standard English (cf. OED, which gives 1857 as its most recent citation). In 18th-century slang, a pistol was termed a *snapper* (Grose, 1796). "I snapped that pistol on him six times before you could bat your eyelid" (Bukka White).

sniggle

> *Everything I do, mama you sniggle an' laugh*
> *An' tell me: "So many suckers daddy, I don't need no cash."*
> —Barefoot Bill, "Snigglin' Blues," 1929

To snigger; snicker; standard English (OED).

so hungry didn't know what to do

> *I got so hungry didn't know what to do*
> *I'm gonna get me a catfish too.*
> —Henry Thomas, "Fishing Blues," 1928

A black catchphrase of antebellum origin; an ex-slave recalled: "We boys in the field used to be so hungry till we didn't know what to do" (Yetman). This expression apparently arose in conjunction with assorted adjectives; in various forms it is still in circulation, as evidenced by a Richmond, Virginia, female's comment: "Just so happy I don't know what to do" (*America's Most Wanted* television program, 10/6/2007).

soak

> *I soaked all my jewelry, you know it was too bad*
> *The dice throwed seven, I lost all the money that I had.*
> —Roosevelt Sykes, "10 And 4 Blues," 1930

To pawn; a slang term of late-19th-century origin (cf. F&H, 1903). See *in so'*.

sociable

> *I met her at a sociable, an' she act just like a crook*
> *She's got this old-fashioned lovin', man it t'ain't in the book.*
> —Blind Lemon Jefferson, "Long Lastin' Lovin'," 1929

A passé American term for an evening party, dating to at least 1826 (cf. OED). Jefferson's protégé Tom Shaw, however, apprehended *sociable* as "a big night-spot."

s.o.l.

> *My woman treat me so mean, till I'm ashamed to tell*
> *If she don't treat me no better, she gonna be s.o.l.*
> —Walter Roland, "S.O.L. Blues," 1935

Shit out of luck, a term dating to World War I, when it was current among Canadian soldiers (STY).

solid (1)

> *Blues jumped a rabbit, run him one solid mile*
> *This rabbit fell down, cryin' like a natural child.*
> —Blind Lemon Jefferson, "Rabbit Foot Blues," 1926

Whole, entire; taken by the OED to modify units of time rather than distance. In the adverbial example below, *solid* (a misnomer for "solidly") appears to connote complete sexual penetration:

> *An' I love you baby, you so nice an' brown*
> *'Cause you, put it up solid, so it won't come down.*
> —Kid Bailey, "Rowdy Blues," 1929

solid (2)

> *Now my name is written on the bosom of my shirt*
> *I'm a solid lover, never had to work.*
> —Julius Daniels, "Richmond Blues," 1927

A still-used black superlative tantamount to *terrific*; misconstrued by the OED as a jazz term of mid-1930s vintage. "He's been a solid, solid individual for us" (Mets' manager Jerry Manual, pregame interview, 8/14/2008).

solid sender

> *Two old maids, sweet an' tender*
> *Two old maids, go on a bender*
> *Two old maids, they're a solid sender*
> *Talkin' about the maids in the bed.*
> —Monette Moore, "Two Old Maids In A Folding Bed," 1936

A swing-era superlative of apparent black origin denoting a particularly exciting female, or enthralling music. As applied to a female it was enshrined in Johnny Mercer's 1944 Tin Pan Alley composition "Conversation While Dancing" ("You're a solid sender") and Little Richard's 1956 rock and roll effort, "Slippin' And Slidin'" ("Oh Melinda, she's a solid sender").

some of these days

> *Some of these days, gonna miss your honey*
> *Some of these days, I am goin' away.*
> —Charlie Patton, "Some Of These Days," 1929

A standard English expression denoting "some day soon, before very long" (OED), that in 20th-century America seems to have been relegated to black or "coon song" use. It served as the title of a 1908 song written by Shelton Brooks, a black songwriter, that became Sophie Tucker's theme song.

somethin'

> *My rider's got somethin', she try to keep it hid*
> *Lord I got somethin', to find that somethin' with.*
> —Charlie Patton, "Down The Dirt Road Blues," 1929

The sex organ, usually put forth in regard to females:

> *I got little bitty legs, me bust isn't oversize*
> *I got somethin' underneath fella, winks like a bo' hog's eye.*
> —Geeshie Wiley, "Skinny Leg Blues," 1930

> *I got nipples on my titties big as the end of my thumb*
> *I got somethin' between my legs make a dead man come.*
> —Lucille Bogan, "Shave 'Em Dry," 1935 (unissued)

sometime woman

> *Now my regular woman stole my pocket change*
> *An' my sometime woman gonna do the same.*
> —*Ishmon Bracey, "Saturday Blues," 1928*

A girlfriend who is seen occasionally, in contrast to one's *regular.* Another performer draws an obtuse contrast between a *sometime* and *always:*

> *Let me be your sometime, till your always come*
> *An' I'll do more for ya than your, always ever done.*
> —*Rube Lacy, "Ham Hound Crave," 1928*

If one always adheres to a particular partner, there is by definition no role for a "sometime" one.

Soo cow!

> *Soo cow!*
> *Don't get slick, or I'll break your leg with a stick.*
> —*Bo Carter, "Sue Cow," 1936*

A shouted farm phrase used to summon cows: "'Soo cow, soo, soo!' That's the way we'd call a cow, and they'd come just a-runnin'. . . . When he say: 'Soo' that means 'Come on'" (Sam Chatmon).

soon

> *I woke up this mornin' mama, blues all 'round my bed*
> *Soon this morning mama, blues all around my bed*
> *Thinkin' about the kind words that my mama had said.*
> —*Bo Weavil Jackson, "You Can' Keep No Brown," 1926*

Early; a once-standard English term used by Chaucer ("I went soon To bedde") that was retained in black speech after becoming obsolete among Southern whites. Its use in Southern speech was noted in an 1869 treatise: "Soon is used adjectively all over the South, as, 'If I get a soon start in the morning, I'll be thar before sunup'" (quoted in Mathews, 1931). Bartlett (1877) records its use among all classes of the South, including (presumably) blacks.

southern can

> *Ain't no need you bringin' no jive here honey*
> *'Cause your southern can is mine, you hear me cryin':*
> *"Your southern can belongs to me."*
> —*Blind Willie McTell, "Southern Can Is Mine," 1931*

Black slang defined by Hurston (1935) as meaning "hips," but quoted in a context in which the meaning "ass" is fairly obvious: ". . . 'Y'all been wearin' Ole Massa's southern can out dis mornin.'"

sow

> Mama mama just look at sis
>
> Standin' on the corner tryin' to do that twist . . .
>
> Come here sis, you ol' stinkin' sow
>
> You tryin' to be a woman an' you don't know how.
>
> —Barbecue Bob, "Easy Rider, Don't You Deny My Name," 1927

A term of abuse for a female dating to the 18th century (F&H, 1903).

spare-made

> She's a spare-made woman an' she's cunnin' as a squirrel
>
> When she starts to lovin', man it's out the world.
>
> —Blind Lemon Jefferson, "Long Lastin' Lovin'," 1928

Thinly built; an embellishment of *spare*, a dated standard English modifier (cf. OED at *spare*, a. and adv., 4.a) retained by blacks of the blues era. David Edwards said of Robert Johnson: "Robert was a tall, skinny, spare-made fella."

special agent

> Now some special agents up the country, they sure is hard on a man
>
> They will put him off when he's hungry, an' won't even let him ride no train.
>
> —Sleepy John Estes, "Special Agent (Railroad Police Blues)," 1938

A railroad detective, empowered to police rail yards and remove hobos from freight trains. The blues singer Bukka White used to impersonate a special agent in order to shake down hobos: "I had me a special agent's [night] stick. . . . I'd walk with it . . . I'd say: 'You got a quarter or fifty cents, you can stay.' If they didn't have that, I'd take a nickel or a dime. I'd search 'em to see if they were lying to me."

spoonful

> "I'm got to go to jail about my spoonful."
>
> . . . Would you kill a man, babe?
>
> "Yes I would!"
>
> Just 'bout a [spoonful]
>
> —Charlie Patton, "A Spoonful Blues," 1929

A dose of cocaine, placed on a spoon to facilitate snorting. A similar idiom, *spoon*, is recounted by Folb to mean a "unit of measure for powdered or crystalline drugs (c. one tablespoon)."

spook

> My doorknob keeps on turnin', it must be spooks all around my bed
>
> I have a warm old feelin', and the hair risin' on my head.
>
> —Robert Johnson, "Malted Milk," 1937

A ghost or *ha'nt*. An ex-slave said of them, in the fashion of the above couplet: "Dey makes de air feel warm and you hair rise up . . ." (Susan Smith, as quoted in *Born in Slavery*). Having one's hair rise was thought to signal the presence of a ghost: "I have been walkin' along and my hair has been standin' up on my head just like somebody take a pair of pliers and pulled my hair up and straightened it up. . . . But I didn't *see* nothin' you know . . ." (Bukka White).

sport (v.)

> *Papa likes his sherry, mama likes her port*
> *Papa likes to shimmy, mama likes to sport.*
> —Ma Rainey, "Barrelhouse Blues," 1923

To have sex; from the noun *sport,* an obsolete term for intercourse that was current in 17th- and 18th-century English and is found in *Othello* ("the Act of Sport") (cf. F&H, 1903).

sport, road

> *My father was a road sport an' a gambler, too*
> *An' he left me here just singin' the blues.*
> —Blind Willie McTell, "Lay Some Flowers On My Grave," 1935

Apparently, an inveterate rambler in pursuit of sexual pleasure. As a term for a male consumed with sexual conquests, *sport* is a black invention.

sportin'

> *One dime was all I had*
> *Tryin' to be a sportin' lad.*
> —Blind Lemon Jefferson, "One Dime Blues," 1927

Devoted to sex and gambling, and, by implication, pimping.

sportin' house

> *My mother an' father both are dead*
> *My sister's in some far an' distant land*
> *My brother's in some (free) sportin' house*
> *And it's what's gonna become of me?*
> —Charley Jordan, "Dollar Bill Blues," 1931

A gambling den or brothel; a term of 19th-century vintage that seems to have gone out of fashion in the early 20th century.

spread (v.)

> *I asked a married woman*
> *To let me be her kid*
> *She said she'd spread*
> *She put that thing on me an' I couldn't keep it hid.*
> —Clifford Gibson, "Don't Put That Thing On Me," 1929

To accommodate a man sexually; said of women. This term first appeared in print in 1692, when Dryden wrote: "What care our drunken dames to whom they spread?" (cf. F&H, 1903).

spread, make a

> She is a little queen of spades, an' the mens will not let her be
>
> Everytime she makes a spread, cold chills just runs all over me.
>
> —Robert Johnson, "Little Queen Of Spades," 1937

A variant of *do a spread*, the latter given by Partridge as a low colloquialism of 1840s origin meaning "to lie down to a man."

spree

> I pawned my watch, pawned my chain
>
> Pawned my gold diamond ring
>
> An' if that don't settle my drunken spree
>
> I'll never get drunk again.
>
> —Skip James, "Drunken Spree," 1931

A period of uncontrollable behavior, usually with adverse consequences; now used primarily with regard to shopping.

squabblin' (a.)

> Got a red-eyed captain, got a squabblin' boss
>
> Got a mad dog sergeant, honey an' he won't knock off.
>
> —Blind Lemon Jefferson, "Prison Cell Blues," 1928

Exceedingly argumentative; given to squabble. The adjectival form is an apparent black innovation; Hayes McMullen described the blues singer Charlie Patton as a "squabblin' scuttlebub" (cf. Calt and Wardlow, 1989).

squall

> I'm not short, I'm long and tall
>
> I've got just what it takes to make you squall.
>
> —Clifford Gibson, "Tired Of Being Mistreated, Part Two," 1929

To emit cries of sexual pleasure; a blues nuance attached to the standard English sense of *squall* (to scream loudly or discordantly; cf. OED) and applied to females.

square

> The first time I seen Mister boll weevil, he's sittin' down on the square
>
> The next time I seen him mama he had his whole family there.
>
> —Sam Butler, "Devil And My Brown Blues," 1926

A planter's term (usually pluralized) for the first green, unripe flower buds appearing on a cotton plant, protected by three triangular leaflets (cf. Brown, 1938). The boll weevil fed on the pollen of the unopened bud, laying its eggs near the base of the bud following the formation of squares.

squatty

> She's low an' squatty, right down on the ground
>
> She's a light-weighted mama, shook her kid man, shook her kid man down.
>
> —Willie Baker, "No No Blues," 1929

A colloquial variant of *squat*, standard English for "[s]hort and thick; dispro-
portionately broad or wide; podgy; thick-set" (OED, which has no post-1826
citations applying to people).

Stack

The Kate's in the bend, the Stack is turnin' round and round
The stern wheel knockin': "Friend I'm Alabama bound."
—*Robert Wilkins, "Alabama Blues," 1928*

The *Stacker Lee*, a Mississippi steamboat operated between 1902 and 1916
as part of the Memphis-based Lee Line, and named for one of the owner's
sons.

Stag O'Lee

Billy Lyons told Stag O'Lee: "Please don't take my life
I got two baby children and a darling, loving wife."
That bad man, cruel Stag O'Lee.
"What'd I care about your two babes, and darling, loving wife?
You done stole my Stetson hat, I'm bound to take your life."
That bad man, cruel Stag O'Lee.
—*Mississippi John Hurt, "Stag O'Lee Blues," 1928*

A misnomer for "Stag" Lee Sheldon, an obscure carriage driver who shot a
friend named William Lyons to death in a St. Louis bar in 1895. After the two
got into a drunken argument about politics, Lyons snatched Sheldon's hat
from his head and refused to hand it back, leading Sheldon to shoot him in
response. The killing became subject of a widespread black ballad that fanci-
fully portrayed "Stag" (variously called *Stack O'Lee, Stacker Lee,* or *Stagger Lee*)
as an outlaw figure who cold-bloodedly killed a man for a trivial theft or (in
some versions) for besting him in a gambling game (cf. Wikipedia, http://
en.wikipedia.org/wiki/Stagger_lee).

stall (n.)

Well if you don't want me, now mama you don't have to run no stall
I can find more good gals than a passenger train can haul.
—*Frank Stokes, "Mistreatin' Blues," 1927*

An act of deception. The term dates to the 19th century (Partridge) and figured
in a contemporary American catchphrase in Swartwood's *Choice Slang* (1915):
"You've got more stalls than a stable."

stavin' Chain' (Chan')

I got a woman, good little woman, she ain't a thing but a stavin' Chain'
She's a married woman and I'm scared to call her name.
—*Ishman Bracey, "Woman Woman Blues," 1930*

A figure in Southern black mythology associated with sexual prowess, eccentrically invoked above in reference to a female, either to suggest like prowess

or to indicate that her only utility is sexual. The same expression is used by a female singer:

> Now you can't ride honey, you can't ride this train
>
> I'm the engineer, I'm gonna run it like a stavin' Chain'.
>
> —Lil Johnson, "Stavin' Chain (That Rockin' Swing)," 1937

The figure generally reported as *Stavin' Chain* was probably surnamed "Chaney" and associated with railroading (cf. *Chaney*). In slightly altered form, the name appears in Zora Neale Hurston's *Cold Keener* (1930): "... we'll do the Parker House and strut like stavin' cheney." In American slang, *staving* stood for very strong or excessive since c. 1850 (OED).

stay

> I was born an' raised in the country, mama but I'm stayin' in town
>
> Hey you don't believe it's pigmeat, mama from my head on down.
>
> —Leadbelly, "Pig Meat Papa," 1936

Reside; a still-used black expression cited in Faulkner's *The Mansion* (1955): "'Hidy, son,' he said, using the old country-Negroid idiom for 'live' too: 'Which a-way from here does Mr Flem Snopes stay?'" This idiom is of 18th-century Scottish origin; cf. OED at *stay*, v.1.b.

steady

> I'm a steady rollin' man, I roll both night and day
>
> But I haven't got no sweet woman, boys to be rollin' this-a-way.
>
> —Robert Johnson, "I'm A Steady Rollin' Man," 1937

A black substitution (or misnomer) for steadily, used in the sense of continuously, or constantly, as in the above and "[y]ou know a cracker is steady looking out for himself all the way" (Gwaltney, 1980).

steady roller

> Went home last night, found a note in my brownskin's door
>
> "Daddy a steady roller has got your room, man you can't live here no
> more."
>
> —Blind Lemon Jefferson, "Deceitful Brownskin Woman," 1927

As in the phrase *steady rollin' man* (see *steady*), a term for one who works regularly. It is less certain that the above also indicates a notable sexual performer. See *roll* (sense 2).

steal

> If you catch me stealin' I don't mean no harm
>
> It's a mark in my family, it must be carried on.
>
> —Trixie Smith, "Sorrowful Blues," 1924

To engage in secret, adulterous assignations; likely suggested by a standard English nuance of the term: "[t]o go or come secretly or stealthily; to walk or creep softly so as to avoid observation" (OED at *steal* v.1 10.a).

stem-winder

Says I'm a good stem-winder

Says I'm a good stem-winder please bring your work to me.

—Blind Boy Fuller, "I'm A Good Stem Winder," 1938

A 19th-century American superlative meaning the best of its kind, or a well-turned piece of equipment (F&H, 1904); literally, a keyless watch (Clapin, c. 1902). This term is still bandied about in reference to political speeches: "She ought to deliver a stem-winder on this kind of issue" (MSNBC commentator, 5/19/2008). The above performer attaches a sexual meaning to it, perhaps on the basis of "winding," which is invoked in the above song as a double entendre referring to sexual intercourse:

My gal say: "You can treat me mean and you can treat me low

But everytime I see you, know I wanna wind some more."

Jelly Roll Morton's "Winding Boy" (1938) was probably rooted in this idiom.

stick candy

He got stick candy that's nine inches long

He sells it fast (as) a hog can chew his corn.

—Mississippi John Hurt, "Candy Man Blues," 1928

Candy in stick form; a once-popular commodity referred to in an interview with an ex-slave: "... she has always liked stick candy" (Aunt Eloie Brown, as quoted in *Born in Slavery*). The above lyric is a double entendre.

'stillery

I hope it keeps rainin', gonna drive my blues away

Goin' to the 'stillery, stay out there all day.

—Robert Johnson, "Preachin' Blues," 1936

Aphetic for distillery. The above couplet apparently refers to a favorite pastime of plantation youths or scroungers, which was to locate a hidden still in the woods and get intoxicated by consuming its mash.

sting

Oh, you done lost your sting

All that wringin' an' twistin', it don't mean a thing.

—Bill Gaither, "You Done Lost Your Swing," 1936

Sexual impact, a sense that underlies the sexual implications of *stingaree* (see *stingaree*).

stingaree

She got somethin' that the mens call a stingaree

Four o'clock every mornin', you turn it loose on me.

—Blind Willie Reynolds, "Third Street Woman Blues," 1930

An unlikely but not uncommon blues or barrelhouse term for *pussy*. Literally, *stingaree* was a synonym of *stinging snake* (Skip James; see *stinging snake*).

The term also stood for liquor, apparently on the similar basis of its ability to stun:

Let me in please Charlie, ain't nobody here but me
I'm speakin' easy, gimme pint of stingaree.
—Barbecue Bob, "Blind Pig Blues," 1928

The above may be a misnomer for *sangaree*. On no discernable grounds, the term was also applied to an insect pest:

Woke up this mornin', heard somebody callin' me
It musta been a weevil, thing they call stingaree.
—Sam Butler, "Devil And My Brown Blues," 1926

stinging snake

I got a stingin' snake, I love sometimes better than I do myself
If the Lord was to take him, I won't be stung by nobody else.
—Memphis Minnie, "Stinging Snake Blues," 1934

A figment of the Southern imagination, supposedly bearing powerful poison in its tail, derived from the appearance of the horn snake, which has a spine-tipped tail (cf. DARE 2). The above application is figurative/poetic.

stirring

That's my gal, stirrin' it now
That's my gal, stirrin' it now.
—Mississippi Bracey, "Stered Gal," 1930

In the above lyric, a literal reference to stirring molasses (see the following quote), given a sexual connotation. "Old Master would call us about 4 o'clock, and everybody had to get up and go 'Stirring.' Old Master had about 30 or 40 sugar trees which were tapped on February" (Dan Bogie, as quoted in *Born in Slavery*).

stomp (a.)

I'm stomp barefooted, can't get no shoes
These Detroit women, leave me with the Detroit blues.
—Bill Pearson, "Detroit Blues," 1929

Elliptical for *stomp-down*, a Southern intensifier meaning downright (WD). The latter appears in black dialogue depicted in Martha Young's *Plantation Bird Legends* of 1902 ("Mister Peacock, he say: 'I'm rale stomp-down hungry …'") and in Ken Kesey's 1962 novel *One Flew over the Cuckoo's Nest* ("'…I figure if I'm bound to be a loony, then I'm bound to be a stompdown dadgum good one'"). For other senses of *stomp-down*, see *stomp-down*.

stomp (n.)

Easy Jones with house rent due
Gave a stomp to help him through
—Virginia Liston, "House Rent Stomp," 1923

A black term for a dance party, so named for the foot-stomping of participants, and short for *stomp down*, a synonymous noun (Hill) now applied to "a
great party with dancing" (Renatha Saunders) that apparently originated as
a variant of similar slave idioms for dance parties: "... I used to go to the drag
downs. Some people say 'hoe down' or 'dig down,' I guess 'cause they'd dig
right into it, and give it all they got" (Charles H. Anderson, as quoted in *Born
in Slavery*). The South Carolina dance parties Gary Davis (b. 1896) attended
in his youth were called *stomp-down frolics*. In various instrumental titles,
stomp is used allusively, apparently to suggest music suitable for consumption at a house party, as in Big Bill and Thomp's "House Rent Stomp" (1927).
See *stomp-down*.

stomp-down (a.)

> Now you'se a stomp-down rider
> You'se a stomp-down rider but you're most too drunk for me.
> —Blind Willie McTell, "Stomp Down Rider," 1931

Dancing or carousing. It appears in Zora Neale Hurston and Dorothy Waring's
Polk County (1944): "She ain't going to like no stomp-down fanfoot round here.
. . ." In blues song it is similarly applied to females:

> I ain't rough, I ain't tough
> I'm just a stomp-down roller an' I like to strut my stuff.
> —Lucille Bogan, "Shave 'Em Dry," 1935

stone-blind

> I beat my baby, man with a rope and a line
> . . . I beat my baby until she went stone-blind.
> —Bo Carter, "Old Devil," 1938

Completely blind; construed as a literary phrase (!) by the OED.

stone pony

> An' I got me a stone pony, don't ride Shetlands no more
> You can find my stone pony, hooked to my rider's door.
> —Charlie Patton, "Stone Pony Blues," 1934

A black superlative applied in pre–World War I Mississippi to "a horse that
can walk through the valley of the shadow of death, and fear no evil" (Sam
Chatmon). He added: "Anything you know that was fine or good, they call
that a stone pony." It may have arisen through the celebrity of Stone Street,
a 1908 Kentucky Derby winner as a 24–1 long shot, which probably produced
the term *stone-blinder*, applied to sure winners on the English turf of c. 1910
(cf. Partridge). Of itself, *stone* was a term for the prize in a horse race (OED).
Another possible derivation rests in the term *stone-horse*, meaning simply
stallion, recorded by Clapin (c. 1902), and apparently derived from *stones* as a
term for a horse's testicles. Apart from the above lyric, where it may refer to a

desirable female, the term occurs once in race recording, connoting a fearless male (the "horse" of Chatmon's allusion):

> *... Take it easy, Lord how can I rest?*
> *If you ain't a stone pony, hard times will bust your vest.*
> —Washboard Sam, "Life Is Just A Book," 1941

A mid-1960s rock group featuring Linda Ronstadt called itself The Stone Poneys, evidently on the basis of "Stone Pony Blues."

stones in my passway

> *I got stones in my passway, an' my road seems dark as night*
> *I got pains in my heart, an' they have taken my appetite.*
> —Robert Johnson, "Stones In My Passway," 1937

A figurative phrase denoting an obstacle or impediment, probably drawn from Lamentations 3: "He hath led me and brought me into darkness.... He hath enclosed my way with hewn stone...." Such interference was proverbially associated with the workings of Satan, as in a slave spiritual that held: "O Satan is a mighty busy ole man, / And roll rocks in my way" (Higginson, 1870). There is no good reason to suppose (as some have maintained) that *stones in my passway* is a reference to being hoodooed; the sense of the phrase is identical with that used by a black speaker with reference to white people: "I could live much better if I didn't have their stumbling stones to worry about" (Gwaltney, 1980). See *stumbling block*.

story

> *Don't tell no story, please don't tell no lie*
> *"Is my gal stopped here?" "No, your little mama kept goin' by."*
> —Blind Lemon Jefferson, "Right Of Way Blues," 1927

A euphemistic term for a lie dating to the 17th century in colloquial speech (Partridge).

straight chair

> *Let me be your rocker, till your straight chair comes*
> *An' I'll rock you easier than your straight chair ever done.*
> —Rube Lacy, "Ham Hound Crave," 1928

Straight-back chair, or any stationary chair designed for upright sitting. The former term was itself colloquial: "She sat upon a straight-back chair. In her 'day' only grandmothers were supposed to sit in rockers ..." (Opie Read's *An Arkansas Planter*, 1896).

strange man

> *Strange man, strange man, let me come close to you*
> *I'm feeling lonely, won't you tell me what to do?*
> —Helen Gross, "Strange Man," 1924

A blues term for a male stranger, derived from the standard English sense of *strange* as meaning unfamiliar (cf. OED).

stray

> *If you see my pigmeat, tell her I said: "Hurry home."*
> *Some low-down bo' hog mama, done strayed my sowbelly from home.*
> —Blind Boy Fuller, "If You See My Pigmeat," 1937

To cause to stray; archaic standard English. The OED offers only a single relevant citation, pertaining to Shakespeare's *Comedy of Errors* (1590): "'Hath not else his eye Stray'd his affection . . .'" (cf. OED at *stray*, v.c., where it is defined as "[t]o cause to err or deviate, to distract").

strut (n.)

> *Up in Harlem every Saturday night*
> *When the high browns get together it's just too tight*
> *They all congregates at an all-night strut*
> *And what they do is tut-tut-tut*
> —Bessie Smith, "Gimme A Pigfoot," 1933

A black term for a dance party.

strut (v.)

> *An' I keep on tellin' my rider: "Keep our shimmies down!"*
> *Lord that jelly you fixin' to strut will make a monkey man leave this town.*
> —Charlie Patton, "Love My Stuff," 1934

To flaunt; an obsolete sense of the word (OED).

strut one's stuff

> *Rooster chew tobacco and the hen dip snuff*
> *Biddy can't do it but he struts his stuff.*
> —Blind Willie McTell, "Kind Mama," 1931

Black slang meaning to show off or exhibit one's best (cf. Fisher [1928], who records it as *do one's stuff*). It apparently arose in connection with dancing, the subject of a Spencer Williams–Ted Koehler composition of 1920, "Struttin' Yo' Stuff." The term now exists almost entirely as a media effusion; runway models are said to be "strutting their stuff" by displaying their wares. In blues songs, to *strut one's stuff* takes on various additional meanings, such as to have a good time or enjoy oneself unreservedly:

> *It takes a little coke to give me ease*
> *Strut my stuff long as you please.*
> —Memphis Jug Band, "Cocaine Habit Blues," 1930
> *Late late last year when the times was tough*
> *I was layin' in a coal yard, struttin' my stuff.*
> —King David's Jug Band, "What's That Taste Like Gravy," 1930

study (n.)

> You is my day study, and you is my midnight dream
>
> I wonder Lord I wonder, what is this woman done to me?
>
> —Arthur "Big Boy" Crudup, "Ethel Mae," 1946

The object of thought; a standard English sense of the word (cf. OED at *study*, n.4.a).

study (v.)

> *I begin to study an' the wind begin to blow*
>
> *I couldn't figure no place for a man like me to go.*
>
> *—Tom Dickson, "Death Bell Blues," 1928*

To think, ponder or reflect on; obsolete English that appears in Shakespeare's *The Tempest* ("'You make me study of that: She was of Carthage, not of Tunis'") and became fastened onto Southern speech (for the latter, cf. ADD). It figures in black dialect depicted by Faulkner: "'I ain't studying no quarter. I got my own business to tend to'" (*The Sound and the Fury*, 1929).

stuff (1)

> *I love my stuff(ie), I want it good an' hot*
>
> *An' my rider's got some way a-shimmyin', swear it just won't stop.*
>
> *—Charlie Patton, "Love My Stuff," 1934*

Sexual activity; copulation. In American slang, this sense of *stuff* dates to the mid-1900s, according to Spears (2001), which would mean it was a newfangled nuance when used in the above lyric.

stuff (2)

> *Stop breakin' down'; please stop breakin' down:*
>
> *"The stuff I got'll bust your brains out baby, it'll make you lose your*
> *   mind."*
>
> *—Robert Johnson, "Stop Breaking Down," 1937*

A still-used black euphemism for *pussy* (Smitherman, 2000). As a less direct term for a female's sexual equipment and sexual attributes, it appears in James T. Farrell's *Father and Son* (1940): "'If she's a mama with the stuff, she must have had a lapse or something, giving you a date,' Heiden said." The above boast ("The stuff I got'll bust your brains out ...") is the recounted saying of females (perhaps prostitutes) who accost the performer on the street.

stuff (3)

> *Look here woman, makin' me mad*
>
> *Come bringin' me somethin', somebody done had ...*
>
> *Let me tell you what these women do*
>
> *Go out an' get stuff, bring it home to you.*
>
> *—Ed Bell, "Carry It Right Back Home," 1930*

Semen; dated by Spears (2001) (on no discernable evidence) to the 1600s.

stuff (4)

She's got good stuff, she got it from a Jew
Lord I'm tellin' you
She got good stuff (2)
Now she got good stuff, I can't get enough.
—*Charlie Spand, "She Got Good Stuff," 1930*

Liquor, in this instance, bootlegged product; a colloquialism found in Opie Read's *Len Gansett* (1888): "I know where we can get some stuff...."

stumbling block

I'm gonna grab me a freight train, ride it till it stops
I ain't gonna be your, low-down stumbling block.
—*Blind Blake, "Stonewall Street Blues," 1926*

Any obstacle one must surmount to succeed; usually applied to things rather than people. It gained its currency in general speech by virtue of an allusion in Romans 14:13: "Let us not therefore judge one another any more: but judge this rather, that no man put a stumbling block or an occasion to fall in his brother's way."

substitute

You have a wife in the morning, Lord a wife at night
And always a substitute to take her place when she's out of sight.
—*Papa Charlie Jackson, "Salt Lake City Blues," 1924*

A female who supplants or "substitutes" for one's regular mistress; used in the title of Jelly Roll Morton's "Sweet Substitute" (1938). The above lyric comments archly on Mormon polygamy.

such as that

"You know I'm a man can't stand such as that."
—*Blind Lemon Jefferson, "Beggin' Back," 1926*

Elliptical for *such a thing as that*, a phrase employed in Twain's *Tom Sawyer* (1876): "I couldn't stand such a thing as that, Tom—nobody could." The shortened form was an evident carryover from slave speech: "I never seed nothing in the way of amusements, except people going to church and going to parties and all such as that" (Ellen Briggs Thompson, as quoted in *Born in Slavery*).

suds, bust

The white folks is done started talkin'...
They talkin' about my no-good man.
They say he is shiftless, they say he is worthless
I know he ain't the worst in the land.
He don't do nothin' but play on his old guitar
While I'm bustin' suds out in a white folk's yard.
—*Irene Scruggs, "Itching Heel," 1930*

To wash clothes; black slang probably coined by domestics. An ex-slave reported: "My daughter's been bustin' the suds for a livin' 'bout thirty-two years now" (Clarice Jackson, as quoted in *Born in Slavery*). A noun form signifying a washerwoman appears in Ellison's *Invisible Man* (1952): "The big woman who looked like a southern 'sudsbuster' was in charge of women's work. . . ."

Sunday clothes

> *When I came to Georgia,*
> *Money an' clothes I had, babe*
> *All my money's done gone, good Lord*
> *An' my Sunday clothes in pawn.*
> —Peg Leg Howell, "Skin Game Blues," 1928

The outfit reserved for church wear; also called *go-to-meetin' clothes*; a standard English but seemingly passé expression, the most recent OED reference (in 1849) involving a farmer's son. A variant, *Sunday pants,* was invoked in the 1978 Lynyrd Skynyrd rock tune, "Down South Jukin'." "There were a lot of women who did nothing but sew, making work clothes for the hands. Their Sunday clothes were bought with the money they made off the little 'patches' the master let them work for themselves" (Shade Richards, as quoted in *Born in Slavery*).

superstitious

> *If you don't think I'm leavin' woman count the days I'm gone*
> *I'm from the South I'm superstitious and I know somethin's goin' on*
> *   wrong.*
> —Luke Jordan, "If I Call You Mama," 1929

Suspicious; a common misnomer among Southern blacks of the blues era.

sure as you born

> *I told that nigger with the black hat on*
> *I'm gonna hit him on the head just as sure as you born . . .*
> —Julius Daniels, "Can't Put The Bridle On That Mule This Morning," 1927

A Southern colloquial catchphrase expressing certainty, found in Opie Read's *Len Gansett* (1888): "'I do, Sarah, sho's you born'd I do.'"

sure God

> *Gonna tell you what a Chinaman told a Jew:*
> *"You don't like-ed me well I sure God don't like you."*
> —William Harris, "Bull Frog Blues," 1928

A black intensifier, apparently invoked as a pious alternative to *sure as hell.*

sure enough

> *"Lord, Lord, I'm gettin' drunk now sure enough!"*
> —Charley Lincoln, "Country Breakdown," 1927

For sure, unquestionably; tacked on a phrase for emphasis. It appears as black dialect in Martha Young's *Plantation Bird Legends* of 1902 ("'Den Br'er Dog, he git mad sho' 'noug'") but originated in white speech. An 1830 specimen of white Virginia dialect records the phrase: "Is it true that Billy's married shoo nuff?" (quoted in Mathews, 1931). As white dialogue it is found in Crane's *Red Badge of Courage* (1895): "'I thought yeh was dead sure enough.'"

sweet

> *Tell all you women, how to make a happy whore*
> *Keep you a workin' man an' leave those sweet boys alone.*
> —Willie Baker, "Crooked Woman Blues," 1929

In the above context, pimping.

sweet back

> *Now I went down Michigan, came up Grand*
> *I saw the sweet backs an' the strutters all raisin' sand.*
> —Frankie "Half Pint" Jaxon, "It's Heated," 1929

A black slang expression for a pimp or a gigolo, perhaps deriving from an obsolete 18th-century meaning of *sweet*, clever, or from *to be sweet on*, a phrase of similar vintage meaning to coax, wheedle, or allure (Grose, 1796). The OED construes the term as "a woman's lover, a ladies' man" in addition to pimp when it at best refers to a gigolo.

sweet man

> *I got the blues for my sweet man in jail*
> *And the judge won't let me go his bail.*
> —Lottie Beaman, "Rollin' Log Blues," 1929

A man who is kept by a woman; noted in connection with Harlem nightspot slang by the *Sunday News* of 11/3/1929.

sweet patootie

> *I'm wild about my 'tootie, only thing I crave*
> *Sweet patootie, gonna carry me to my grave.*
> —Blind Blake, "Tootie Blues," 1928

An approving Jazz Age term for a girlfriend or attractive female dating in print to 1918 (OED). In the above song it has a sexual connotation.

swing (v.)

> *Now down in Georgia they got a dance that swings*
> *There ain't nothin' to it, it's easy to do*
> *They call it Shake That Thing, Lord Shake That Thing*
> *I'm getting' sick an' tired of tellin' you to shake that thing.*
> —Papa Charlie Jackson, "Shake That Thing," 1925

To move in a rhythmically propulsive, supple fashion; a black superlative applied to music or dancing, drawn from ordinary connotations of *swing* as a verb of motion. Upon this seemingly nebulous edifice, a rabid cult of jazz was created in 1935 by white enthusiasts, resulting in the vogue terms *swing/swing music,* and attendant debates as to what "swing" actually meant or entailed. The above represents the earliest documented use of *swing* as a superlative. As applied to music, apart from the 1932 Duke Ellington composition "It Don't Mean A Thing (If It Ain't Got That Swing)," it is first evident in a vocal aside, "Swing now," (Lovin' Sam Theard, "That Rhythm Gal," 1934).

Tack Ann(ie)

(If) you think I'm lyin' just ask Tack Ann
Took many a broad from many a man.
—*George Hannah, "The Boy In The Boat," 1930*

A storied Chicago blues singer notorious for promiscuity; during World War I she was said to have donned a soldier's uniform, infiltrated an army company, and worked as a prostitute (Mayo Williams). She was also said to make a specialty of removing the jeweled tie tacks of unsuspecting males, hence her nickname (Townley, 1976). King Oliver's 1926 jazz instrumental "Tack Annie" was named for this figure.

take

Woman take the blues, she gonna buy her paper an' read
Man take them blues he gonna catch a train an' leave.
—*Willie Baker, "Weak-Minded Blues," 1929*

To be seized by or have an attack of something; a standard English construction that rarely occurs in the active voice (cf. OED). See *taken down.*

take God to tell

Goin' away sweet mama, don't you wanna go?
Take God to tell when I be back here anymore.
—*Charlie Patton, "Screamin' And Hollerin' The Blues," 1929*

A black catchphrase applied to what is unknowable; invoked in Zora Neale Hurston's *Jonah's Gourd Vine* (1934):

"... Wonder whut she thinkin' 'bout?"
"Take uh God tuh tell."

take it as it comes

> *Lord I once was a hobo. . . .*
> *But I decided I'd go down South last night, and take it as it comes.*
> —*King Solomon Hill, "The Gone Dead Train," 1931*

To deal with events as they occur (OED).

take one's time

> *The men don't like me 'cause I speak my mind*
> *But the women crazy about me 'cause I take my time.*
> —*Charley Lincoln, "Jealous Hearted Blues," 1927*

To have unhurried or prolonged sex; generally used to extol males. This idiom is a twist on the standard English meaning of the phrase: "to allow oneself sufficient time (to do something); hence (sarcastically), to be 'quite long enough,' i.e., too long: to loiter" (OED).

take you where you want to go, (it) will

> *I'm crazy about a Packard, but my baby only rates a Ford*
> *A Packard is too expensive, Ford will take you where you wanna go.*
> —*Blind Lemon Jefferson, "D B Blues," 1928*

A saying applied to cars that are serviceable, if nothing else.

taken down

> *"This old soul, you know; the time she left Chicago, you know; old soul*
>   *taken down with the flu, you know."*
> —*Bukka White, "The Panama Limited," 1930*

A Southern colloquial variant of *taken ill*, "to be seized or struck with illness . . ." (OED at *take*, v.6.d), found in an overseer's letter of the 1850s: "The hands is all got Better But anne she was takeing down . . ." (TT). Used with reference to a specific illness (ADD).

talk all out of one's head

> *It was late one night on a milk-white iron bed*
> *I rolled my baby, till she talked all outta her head.*
> —*Otis Harris, "You'll Like My Loving," 1929*

To babble, usually drunkenly, and consequently to say things one later forgets or retracts (Tom Shaw). This expression is an embellishment of a colloquial term for being temporarily irrational, *out of one's head* (used in Erskine Caldwell's *God's Little Acre*, 1935: "'He's out of his head a little,' Ty Ty said. 'He drank too much raw corn.'").

talkin' about

> *If you hear this song, an' don't take my advice*
> *"I'm talkin' about 'an' don't take my advice'; you better take my advice,*
>   *too!"*

It might cause you partner, to lose your life.
—Buddy Boy Hawkins, "Yellow Woman Blues," 1927

A black catchphrase preceding quoted conversation, found in August Wilson's *Fences* (1985): ". . . you ain't done none of your chores . . . and you come in here talking about 'Yeah.' Talking about, 'Baby, you know you'll always be number one with me.'" It was uttered by the presiding judge (a black female) in a court television program, *Judge Hatchett:* "Get out of here! Talkin' about 'I told you!'" (5/25/2007).

tango

I'm goin' to the river, get me a tango rockin' chair
If the blues overtake me, gonna rock 'em 'way from here.
—Barbecue Bob, "Motherless Chile Blues," 1927

Deep orange in color; a shade of apparent decorator origin dating to 1913 (cf. OED).

taste

I know you like my lovin', I can tell from the way you whine
Since you tasted my jelly, you just worries me all the time.
—Otis Harris, "You'll Like My Loving," 1928

To have carnal knowledge of; an archaicism found in Shakespeare's *Cymbelle* (1611): "'If you can mak't apparent That you have tasted her in Bed; my hand, And Ring is yours'" (cf. OED).

tear

When I take the blues, baby, whiskey don't do me no good
Now the best I know baby, tear 'round the neighborhood.
—Charlie Spand, "Dreamin' The Blues," 1930

To rush impetuously or violently; colloquial English (OED).

tear one down

A weak-minded woman will let a rounder tear her down
An' when she get in trouble that rounder can't be found.
—Willie Baker, "Weak Minded Blues," 1929

To devastate; damage emotionally; a still-used colloquialism: "And if it doesn't turn out, don't let it tear you down" (Murder defendant in television documentary *Sin City Law,* 4-7-09). This idiom is an extension of *tear* as meaning "[t]o harrow, wound, 'rend' (the heart, soul, feelings, etc.)" (OED at tear, v.1.d.).

tear one's pants

> *Mean woman, mean woman, you have tore your pants with me*
> *Stayed out all night long, then comin' in 'bout half past three.*
> —*Bill Gaither, "Evil Yalla Woman," 1939*

To get into difficulty by virtue of misconduct; a black expression more often rendered as *tear one's drawers* (Mayo Williams).

tear one's playhouse down

> *The chief of police done tore my playhouse down*
> *No use in grievin', I'm gonna leave this town.*
> —*Maggie Jones, "Good-Time Flat Blues," 1928*

To destroy one's pleasurable or profitable setup, particularly (as in the above) an illicit premises involving alcohol or prostitution.

teasing brown

> *Tell me what time do the trains come through your town?*
> *I wanna laugh an' talk with a long tall teasin' brown.*
> —*Blind Lemon Jefferson, "Black Horse Blues," 1926*

As defined by Gary Davis, "[t]hat's just a woman don't mean nothin' she says and nothin' she do. . . ." It occurs in Zora Neale Hurston's *Meet the Mamma* (1924):

> *When he's out, they're hanging round*
> *All those long tall teasing browns.*

tee-nincey

> *Boats up the river, runnin' side by side*
> *Well you got my lovin' tee-nincey babe, guess you're satisfied.*
> —*Sunny Boy And His Pals, "Don't You Leave Me Here," 1927*

Small, short, tiny; a black colloquial term appearing in Calder Willingham's 1963 novel *Eternal Fire:* "And look at her l'il teeninecy hand, Mr. Handy! My old black paws make two of 'em!" It probably came about by blending *teeny* (i.e., tiny) with *nicety,* a dated standard English term connoting minuteness (OED).

tee-roll (v.)

> *Now there's nothing that I could do, for that old bull has tee-rolled me*
> *When I get myself another heifer, I'm gonna move back to Tennessee.*
> —*Kokomo Arnold, "Milk Cow Blues No. 4," 1935*

To cuckold (Skip James); a black slang term used in Zora Neale Hurston's *Spunk* (1935): "If some other man ain't done tee-rolled you with her." It appeared as dialogue meaning to rob in Iceberg Slim's *Mama Black Widow* (1969): "'We gonna tee roll him,'" which meaning was likely the basis of the foregoing usage.

teddy bear

> *I says fair brown, let me be your teddy bear*
>
> *Tie a string on my neck an' I'll follow everywhere.*
>
> —Blind Lemon Jefferson, "Teddy Bear Blues," 1927

A black slang term for a boyfriend or escort taken for want of a better alternative, contrasted with "big bear" (a preferred suitor) (cf. Puckett, 1925).

tell the world

> *I love my baby an' I*
>
> *"Tell the world I do!"*
>
> *What made me love her, you will come an' love her too.*
>
> —Charlie Patton, "When Your Way Gets Dark," 1929

A variant of the catchphrase *I'll tell the world*, associated with American soldiers during World War I (DC).

terrible

> *"... Shimmy like you talk about it. You know you talk terrible about it.*
>
> *Shimmy like you talk about it."*
>
> —Frank Stokes, "Fillin' In Blues, Part One," 1929

Impressively; a black superlative put to various contexts, as in: "He got a terrible-movin' finger" (Johnnie Temple in regard to the adroit guitar picking of Skip James; cf. Calt). This idiom may have originated in slave speech: "I was a dancin' fool, wanted to dance all the time. I inherited that from my mother. She was a terrible dancer" (Tom Mills, as quoted in *Born in Slavery*).

than the day is long

> *Where it ain't no lovin', sure ain't no gettin' along*
>
> *'Cause you'll have more trouble, honey than the day is long.*
>
> —Bo Weavil Jackson, "You Can't Keep No Brown," 1926

A variant of *as the day is long*, a proverbial 19th-century comparison (DAP). As a figure of speech, it dates at least to Shakespeare, who used the expression *as merry as the day is long* in *Much Ado about Nothing* (1599).

that's your red wagon

> *Now that's your red wagon, you can roll it along*
>
> *Now when you leave me this time, some other woman got your home.*
>
> —Arthur (Big Boy) Crudup, "That's Your Red Wagon," 1945

A black catchphrase indicating that one has a predilection the speaker does not share, or care for; also found in Southern white speech of more recent decades (for the latter, cf. DARE 4 at *red wagon*).

that's what I'm talkin' about

> *"Aw shake it; that's what I'm talkin' about."*
>
> —Memphis Minnie, "Reachin' Pete," 1935

A black catchphrase signifying approval that enjoyed a 2005–6 vogue in television advertising dialogue and has since figured in the rhetoric of Barack Obama: "As he boarded his chartered Amtrak at 30th Street Station in Philadelphia, Mr. Obama pulled on the train's whistle. 'This is what I'm talking about,' he said" (*New York Times*, 4/20/2008). As in the foregoing example, it is used gratuitously, the speaker not having previously referred to what he or she is ostensibly talking about.

they tell me

> Well they tell me that southbound train had a wreck last night
> Sugar the Texas foreman ain't treatin' your railroad right.
> —Blind Lemon Jefferson, "Wartime Blues," 1927

A once-common black colloquialism indicating hearsay, "they" signifying unspecified people, seemingly derived from obsolete white speech: "They tell me 32 houses and the barns belonging to them are burnt . . ." (1675 letter of Massachusetts Bay colonist quoted in Lepore). It occurs in Langston Hughes and Zora Neale Hurston's *The Mule-Bone* (1931): "Dey tell me when dat lady's husband come home Sat'day night, ole Cody jumped out de window."

this black man

> Says I'm on my way back, to that lonesome hill
> 'Cause that's where I can look down, where this black man used to live.
> —Isaiah Nettles, "Mississippi Moan," 1935

The narrator himself. Bartlett (1877) records *this child* as a common Western expression for this person, myself.

this man's town

> My milk cow been ramblin', for miles around
> She been settled for some other bullcow, Lord in this man's town.
> —Robert Johnson, "Milkcow's Calf Blues," 1937

The narrator's town or city of residence; often used to particularize comparisons, as in: "'Divorces are cheap, in this man's town'" (Sinclair Lewis's *Arrowsmith*, 1925). This expression was also declaimed by black females:

> I'm like a red-hot stove, I'm burning down
> And the meanest gal in this man's town.
> —Maggie Jones, "Dangerous Blues," 1925

three six nine

> Ever since you been gone mama, I been 'bout to lose my mind
> But I got another little sweet woman and I don't want your three six and
>   nine.
> —Kokomo Arnold, "I'll Be Up Someday," 1936

Shit; a term fostered by *Aunt Sally's Policy Dream Book*, a popular 1890s publication that assigned policy numbers to various dream subjects. The number three was related to "anything filthy" and "dirrhoea," while both six and nine were related to filth. *Three six nine* still survives in black slang (UD).

three times seven

> *I done told you woman, I been tellin' your partner too*
> *You're three times seven an' you know what you wanna do.*
> —Blind Lemon Jefferson, "See See Rider," 1926

Twenty-one years old and hence, an adult. This expression is apparently of Southern white origin: "'Your po' father uster say that he would quit it jest as soon as he got three times seven, an' he did'" (Opie Read, *Len Gansett*, 1888).

throw a pistol down

> *I gave my baby now, the ninety-nine degree*
> *She jumped up and throwed a pistol down on me.*
> —Robert Johnson, "Stop Breaking Down Blues," 1937

To draw a pistol. This expression occurs in an ex-slave's reminiscence: "... Mr. Littlejohn throw his big old long hoss-pistol down on him ..." (Botkin, 1945). It survives in slang as *throw down*.

throw one away

> *It was early one mornin', just about the break of day*
> *An' my long brownskin come in here and throwed me 'way.*
> —Garfield Akers, "Cottonfield Blues, Part One," 1929

To terminate a relationship, with no possibility of revival; an obsolete Southern colloquialism employed in a 1786 church record: "An accusation brought against Nan belong to Mr. Peter Farror in respect of throwing away her husband and taking another" (TT).

throw one down

> *My baby quit me, man she done threw me down*
> *I wouldn't hate it so bad but that talk is all over town.*
> —Blind Lemon Jefferson, "Booger Rooger Blues," 1926

To discard a romantic or sexual companion; synonymous with *to put one down*. This expression may have entered the blues vocabulary via a pop song of 1907 vintage, "The Girl Who Threw Me Down."

throw oneself away

> *An' I remember one mornin', 'tween midnight an' day*
> *I was way upstairs, throwin' myself away.*
> —Charlie Patton, "Jersey Bull Blues," 1934

? A dated black idiom apparently meaning to lose self-possession or self-control. It was said of Scott Joplin: "... everyone had a lot of respect for Scott because he never threw himself away" (Blesh and Janis).

tight

When a man starts jivin', I'm tighter than a pair of shoes
I'm a mean tight mama, with my mean tight mama blues.
—*Sara Martin, "Mean Tight Mama," 1928*

"Strict, stringent; severe" (OED) standard English of 19th-century vintage that was used by blacks to mean tough, redoubtable, hard (cf. Fisher, 1928).

tight-haired

Here come my tight-haired woman, I can tell by the way she walk
I know she been shakin' that thing, I can tell by the way she talk.
—*Charley Jordan, "Tight Haired Mama Blues," 1931*

Short-haired; a black idiom applied to females. "That gal with that short hair sure could pick a guitar . . . a tight-haired gal, but she sure could pick!" (Sam Chatmon on Memphis Minnie).

tight like that

It's tight like that, beedle um bum
Don't you hear me talkin' to you,
Know it's tight like that.
—*Tampa Red and Georgia Tom, "Tight Like That," 1928*

A Chicago superlative recounted by Tom Dorsey ("Georgia Tom"), who helped parlay it into a best-selling race record: ". . . there used to be a phrase they used around town, you know, folks started saying, 'Ah, it's tight like that! Tight like that!'" (O'Neal and van Singel). Although the term had no express sexual connotations, it would be misconstrued as a reference to "tight pussy" by record consumers such as Henry Hill, probably on the basis of the adjacent phrase *beedle um bum*. This sense is only evident in the following example, remarking on infidelity:

Now Lucy came home, with a big excuse
She left there tight, but she come back loose.
—*Blind Ben Covington, "It's a Fight Like That," 1928*

See *like that, too tight*.

till

I started to kill my woman till she lay down 'cross the bed
An' she looked so ambitious till I took back every word I said.
—*Willie Brown, "M&O Blues," 1930*

That, in black usage; used with *so* (ADD).

till the cows come home

"Rock it till the cows come home."
—*William Moore, "Old Country Rock," 1928*

Forever or practically forever; a hyperbolic saying first recorded as "Kiss till the cows come home" in Beaumont and Fletcher's *The Scornful Lady* (1610). It was based on the false belief that cows never left a pasture of their own accord.

till the sea go dry

> *I love Miss Willie, I 'clare I do*
> *Love her till the sea go dry*
> *An' if I thought she didn't love me*
> *I'd take morphine an' die.*
> —*Skip James, "Drunken Spree," 1931*

Forever; a hackneyed expression dating to Robert Burns's romantic poem "Red, Red Rose" (1794): "And I will luve thee still, my dear, Till a' the seas gang dry."

time, have a

> *If the day was Christmas eve, the morrow Christmas day*
> *"Oh, wouldn't we have a time!"*
> *I wouldn't need my little sweet rider just to pass the time away.*
> —*Robert Johnson, "Hell Hound On My Trail," 1937*

To have an exciting time; a dated catchphrase used in Stephen Crane's *Maggie: A Girl of the Streets* (1893): "'Say,' whispered she, leaning forward, 'Let's go over to Billie's and have a time.'"

tip (v.)

> *She may be your gal but she tips to see me sometimes*
> *She sleeps with you but she got me on her mind.*
> —*Peg Leg Howell, "Fairy Blues," 1928*

Literally, to step lightly or walk on tiptoe (OED). This term is generally invoked in the context of an illicit sexual relationship, making it a virtual synonym of *creep* and *steal*. See below.

tip out

> *I woke up this mornin', 'bout half past three*
> *And to my surprise, my man had tipped out on me.*
> —*Ida Cox, "Mojo Hand Blues," 1927*

African American slang meaning "to have sex with someone other than one's spouse" (Major, 1970).

toby

> *I'm going to New Orleans, to get this toby fixed of mine*
> *I am havin' trouble, trouble, I can't keep from cryin'.*
> —*Hattie Hart, "Spider's Nest Blues," 1930*

A charm, applied in antebellum times to rabbits' feet: "We ate raccoon then and rabbit and keep the rabbit foot or luck, jus' the first joint. The 'Toby' what we call it, and if we didn't have no 'Toby' we couldn't git no rabbit nex' time we goes huntin'" (Andrew Moody, as quoted in *Born in Slavery*). The term is related to the Caribbean term *obeah*, the latter being the prevalent island idiom for conjuring and its accessories (cf. OED, citing *obies* as "amulets, in order to make them [their bearers] invisible"). *Toby* and *obeah* are likely rooted in an unknown African word.

together, to get oneself

> *You can get yourself together,*
> *You can go out with the weather*
> *We don't need no airy man.*
> —*Papa Charlie Jackson, "Airy Man Blues," 1924*

To compose or prepare oneself so as to perform a task; a black expression perhaps dating to slave speech: "... I tryin' to get myself together ..." (Lizzie Davis, as quoted in *Born in Slavery*). It was transformed into 1960s hippy slang, where *to be together* (intact, organized, etc.) was a superlative. The term derives from a 19th-century British colloquialism, *to pull oneself together*, which means "to rouse oneself, to rally" (F&H, 1902).

tommy

> *What make a woman have the blues, she knows a tommy's got her man*
> *Just get you four or good men, woman and do the best you can.*
> —*Lucille Bogan, "Women Don't Need No Men," 1927*

Contemporary slang for a female; from *tomato*.

too bad

> *The walk you got baby, is most too bad*
> *When I see you do it, it nearly makes me mad.*
> —*John Harris, "Glad And Sorry Blues," 1929*

A black superlative (given by Fisher [1928] as meaning "marvelous") indicating that one is favorably impressed; used in the above context to denote a sexually provocative walk.

too bad Jim

> *Tell me pretty mama, why you fool around with him*
> *"I can't tell you papa, it will be too bad Jim."*
> —*Barbecue Bob, "It's Just Too Bad," 1929*

A blues or barrelhouse catchphrase designed to make the negative sense of the conventional expression *too bad* more pointed.

too black bad

> *I wonder why my partner's standin' 'round lookin' sad*
> *"I married a woman an' she quit me, it's gonna be too black bad."*
> —*Blind Lemon Jefferson, "Long Lastin' Lovin'," 1929*

A barrelhouse catchphrase indicating dire consequences, with *black* serving as an intensifier. Tom Shaw, who defined it as meaning "really too bad," related it to an "old saying: 'If you don't do so-and-so, it's gonna be too black bad for you, buddy.'" A rare variant expression, *real black bad*, uses *black bad* as a superlative:

> She's a little ol' gal, 'tween brown and black
> Everytime she love me, it's real black bad.
> —Barbecue Bob, "Doin' The Scraunch," 1930

toodle-oo, toodle-oodle-do

> Every time she blow she blow "Toodlee-oo"
> An' she blow for everybody she meet.
> She could toodle-oo, she could toodle-oo
> That's all the poor girl do.
> —Hambone Willie Newbern, "She Could Toodle-oo," 1929

To fellate; from *'toodle-'loodle*, an obsolete term imitating the sound of a pipe or flute (cf. OED). In the above song it is also used to signify vagina:

> When she went to leave me rat stuck to her shoe
> Fell down an' broke her little toodle-oo-oo.

The related *toodle-oodle-do* likely refers to having sexual intercourse:

> Grandpa came home about half-past two
> Asked grandma to toodle-oodle-do
> —Billie McKenzie and Jesse Crump, "Strewin' Your Mess," 1929

toodlum

> Run here mama an' just look at sis
> She got her hand in her toodlum up to her wrist.
> —Walter Davis, "I Can Tell By The Way You Smell," 1935

Vagina; a variant of *toodle-oo*, perhaps reinforced by *beedle um bum* or *skoodle um skoo*.

too tight

> Too tight, won't behave
> Too tight, make you rave
> Too tight, this rag of mine.
> —Blind Blake, "Too Tight," 1926

A superlative catchphrase based on the outmoded colloquial use of *tight*, which variously connoted anything neat in appearance, trim, tidy, smart, well-made, shapely, or (by the 18th century) skillful, and lively (OED). It occurs in Zora Neale Hurston's *Cold Keener* (1930): ". . . they tells me you got a new mechanic round here that's just too tight." An inverted negative meaning of *too tight* was put forth in some later blues:

> Blind pig, blind pig, sure glad you can't see
> 'Cause if you could it would be too tight for me.
> —Barbecue Bob, "Blind Pig Blues," 1928

too tough

An' everybody say she got a mojo, 'cause she been usin' that stuff
She got a way tremblin' down, an' I mean it's most too tough.
—Robert Johnson, "Little Queen Of Spades," 1937

Too much; a still-used black expression heard in negative formulations, as in:
"Doesn't seem like his punches are affecting him too tough" (Lennox Lewis's
HBO ringside commentary, 5/17/2008).

total ol' shaker

I'm satisfied, satisfied
My total ol' shaker is by my side.
—Memphis Jug Band, "You May Leave But This Will Bring You Back," 1930

A female construed as *pussy*. The term *total ol'* was itself synonymous with
vagina, and was so used in a 1960s Mississippi John Hurt lyric sung from a
feminine point of view:

. . . I pull my dress to my knees
I give my total ol' to who I please.
—"I'm Satisfied"

transom, on the

. . . Some doctor from Tennessee
Has a way of buryin' things on the q.t.
He was buryin' that thing; he was buryin' that thing
Keeps on the transom, he was buryin' that thing.
—James "Stump" Johnson, "Transom Blues," 1929

In private; a black slang expression related to *transom room,* a private room
in barrelhouses set aside for sexual activity. Of the latter, Skip James said:
"They had transom rooms in there [barrelhouses]: you want to take your
gal to a private room, you had the privilege. That'd cost you another dollar"
(cf. Calt).

travelin' man

Travelin' man, I've traveled all around this world
Travelin' man, I've traveled from land to land
—Henry Thomas, "Arkansas," 1927

A euphemism for vagrant, invoked in the following:

Please, help me win my fare
'Cause I'm a travelin' man, boys an' I can't stay here.
—King Solomon Hill, "The Gone Dead Train," 1932

A coarser earlier form, *travelin' nigger,* appeared in an ex-slave's reminiscence:
"I don't know my pappy. Him was what dey calls de travelin' nigger" (Sam
Jones Washington, as quoted in *Born in Slavery*).

traveling shoes (to put on, etc.)

> *You can reach over in the corner mama an' hand me my travelin' shoes*
> *You know by that I've got them Statesboro blues.*
> —*Blind Willie McTell, "Statesboro Blues," 1928*

A figurative black expression denoting departure (cf. Major, 1994). It appears in Roark Bradford's *John Henry* (1931): "... 'git yo' hat, big boy, and lace up yo' travelin' shoes.'"

tremble down

> *An' everybody say she got a mojo, 'cause she been usin' that stuff*
> *She got a way tremblin' down, an' I mean it's most too tough.*
> —*Robert Johnson, "Little Queen Of Spades," 1937*

To dance the *Shimmy* (Moore) or have sex, the latter of which is the most probable connotation of the above couplet. This term appears nonsensically in a spiritual collected by Krehbiel (1914): "Come trembling down ... Safe in the sweet arms of Jesus."

trey

> *Miss Liza was a gambler, she learnt me how to steal*
> *She learnt me how to deal those cards:*
> *"Hold that jack an' trey."*
> —*Henry Thomas, "Run, Mollie, Run," 1927*

A three card. The above apparently refers to cheating at All-Fours, where the jack and low card form half of the lowest trump hand.

trick

> *Tricks ain't walkin', they ain't walkin' no more*
> *And I've got to make my livin', don't care where I go.*
> —*Lucille Bogan, "They Ain't Walking No More," 1930*

A slang term for a prostitute's customer, of likely African American origin (cf. OED). "Tricks ain't walkin'" was likely a streetwalker's catchphrase indicating a dearth of business.

trifle on

> *Caught a train, down to Tennessee*
> *While I was gone, my baby trifled on me.*
> —*Blind Blake, "I Was Afraid Of That," 1929*

To cheat on; black slang derived from the archaic sense of *trifle*, meaning to cheat or befool (OED).

triflin' woman

> *Lord I'm almost dyin', gaspin' for my breath*
> *An' a triflin' woman, waitin' to celebrate my death.*
> —*Blind Lemon Jefferson, "Hangman's Blues," 1928*

A faithless female. Roark Bradford's dialect novel *John Henry* (1931) contains a ministerial denunciation of "... triflin' women.... You bears false witness on yo' friends and unlocks yo' back door to de creepers."

trim (v. 1)

I ain't no lamp, but my wick is burnin' low
Trimmed my wick, 'fore it refused to blow.
—George Carter, "Ghost Woman Blues," 1929

In pre-electricity days, to cleanse or cut level a lamp wick (OED). Southern blacks of the 1920s had almost no access to electricity, except via the electric chair.

trim (v. 2)

I don't need nothin' but my overalls
I done trimmed these womens an' they bound to fall.
—Blind Willie McTell, "Your Time To Worry," 1933

To possess a female carnally; dated slang of 16th-century origin invoked in Shakespeare's *King John* ("a new untrimmed bride") (cf. F&H, 1904).

trim (v. 3)

Now it ain't no use you fooling around, trying to take that other woman's
man
Well now you keep on fooling around, you going to get your head
trimmed down.
—Joe Williams, "Get Your Head Trimmed Down," 1938

To thrash (F&H, 1904).

trouble

Aunt Jane she come a-runnin', tellin' everybody in the neighborhood:
"That man a-mine got the limber trouble, an' his lovin' can't do me any
good."
—Ishman Bracey, "Jake Liquor Blues," 1930

Standard English for "[a] disease, disorder, ailment; a morbid affection" (OED at *trouble*, n.4.a, which contains three citations, from 1726 to 1899). The above couplet refers to impotence, which is put forth as a consequence of drinking *jake*.

trouble, get in

When you get in trouble, it's no use of screamin' an' cryin'
Tom Rushin' will take you, back to the prison-house a-flyin'.
—Charlie Patton, "Tom Rushen Blues," 1929

To get into trouble, *trouble* signifying "unpleasant relations with authorities, esp. such as involve arrest . . ." (OED). As used in the following lyric, it likely refers to prostitutes in need of bail money:

A weak-minded woman will let a rounder tear her down

An' when she get in trouble that rounder can't be found.

—Willie Baker, "Weak-Minded Blues," 1929

See also *weak-minded*.

trouble in mind

Trouble in mind, and I'm blue, but I won't be blue always

The sun's gonna shine, in my back door someday.

—Chippie Hill, "Trouble In Mind," 1926

A misnomer for *troubled in mind*. The original form of this expression (used in what became a famous blues standard) appears in Dickens's *Nicholas Nickleby* (1839): "Meanwhile, Ralph walked to and fro in his little back-office, troubled in mind by what had just occurred."

truck (v.)

Keep on truckin' mama, truckin' my blues away

Keep on truckin' mama, truckin' both night an' day

—Blind Boy Fuller, "Truckin' My Blues Away," 1936

Literally, to dance the Truck, a fashionable swing-era dance originating in Harlem in 1935. In the above song, the intent to convey *fuck* through euphemism is obvious. The phrase *keep on truckin'* entered mainstream English as a result of being featured in Robert Crumb's 1960s artwork and has since taken on the meaning "to persevere; a phrase of encouragement" (OED). (The artist himself derived it from a contemporary recording by Donovan, and was satirizing the dance: "It was a silly dance step or movement. It was, like, stupid to me.")

true

You may go, you may stay

To some far distant place

So be true, be true don't lose your line.

—Henry Sims, "Be True Be True," 1929

To be steadfast or loyal to a mode of conduct, or honest and upright, senses variously regarded as "somewhat archaic" or archaic by the OED. As a term for a rule, *line* is similarly obsolete, and the above admonition itself may have been drawn from pastoral rhetoric.

Turkey Trot

Well men in Kansas City, Lord, doin' the Turkey Trot

The women in Louisiana Lord, doin' the Eagle Rock.

—Leadbelly, "Kansas City Papa," 1935

A black dance of antebellum vintage: "We danced the 'Turkey Trot' and 'Buzzard Lope' and how we did love to dance the 'Mary Jane'" (James Bolton, as quoted in *Born in Slavery*). A like-named white adaptation became a national fad during the 1910–14 vogue for "animal dances" such as the Fox Trot (named for a horse's gait), Grizzly Bear, Bunny Hug, Camel Walk, and Kangaroo Dip.

turn

> *Gonna get up in the mornin', four o'clock*
> *I'm gonna turn that land, turn it*
> *Now hey, hey; I got the cottonfield blues.*
> —Henry Thomas, "Cottonfield Blues," 1927

To plough; standard English (OED).

turn every way but loose

> *Oh you got to stop your forkin' an' raisin' the deuce*
> *Else I'll grab you mama an' turn you every way but loose.*
> —Blind Willie McTell, "Southern Can Is Mine," 1931

To trounce one in a fight (Skip James); a black catchphrase perhaps inspired by the 1896 ragtime song "Mister Johnson, Turn Me Loose." It appears in Ellison's *Invisible Man* (1952): "'. . . if times don't get better soon I'm going to grab that bear and turn him every way but loose!'" A variant occurs in Van Vechten (1926): ". . . making a significant gesture with his middle finger around his throat, he croaked, 'Ah bet you cut him every way but loose.'" *Every Which Way But Loose* became the title of a 1978 Clint Eastwood movie.

turn one's damper down

> *One is a Memphis yellow, the other a Savannah brown*
> *One is a Statesboro darkskin, she'll really turn your damper down.*
> —Blind Willie McTell, "Three Women Blues," 1928

To cool one off (Hill), generally by satisfying one sexually; from a method of regulating heat in fireplaces, by turning the damper (a metal piece within the chimney).

turn one's money green

> *If the jack could win the queen*
> *It would turn your money green*
> *Jack o' diamonds is a hard card to play.*
> —Blind Lemon Jefferson, "Jack O' Diamonds," 1926

To become enriched, if only by replacing one's coins with dollars.

turn up one's toes

> *So dry old bo weevil, turned up his toes an' died*
> *Now there ain't nothin' to do, [but] bootleg moonshine an' rye.*
> —Son House, "Dry Spell Blues, Part One," 1930

To die, a slang expression dating to the mid-19th century (Partridge).

turtle dove

> *Make you weep like a willow, moan like a turtle dove*
> *Life ain't worth livin' if you ain't with the one you love.*
> —*George Carter, "Weeping Willow Blues," 1929*

An erroneous reference to the European dove noted for cooing, the American (ground) dove being the species that was noted for moaning, to the extent of being given the names *moaning* and *mourning dove* (cf. OED; in either event the intent of the first line, promising orgasmic sex, is obvious).

tush hog

> *Mama can't you hear this tush hog, gruntin' all around your door?*
> *But if you give him what you promised him he will soon be gone.*
> —*Bo Carter, "Tush Hog Blues," 1940*

A black term for a quarrelsome, pugnacious person, synonymous with *wampus cat* (Sam Chatmon). In criminal circles, it meant an extortionist (ATS); as an adjective, *tush* remained in post–World War II circulation as black slang meaning belligerent or dangerous (DAS). Literally, a *tush hog* was a wild boar, the term *tush* having been an archaic synonym of tusk (OED).

twelve-pound daddy

> *I got a twelve-pound daddy, eighty-pound one, too*
> *When my twelve-pound one is down, my eighty-pound one will do.*
> —*Pearl Dickson, "Twelve Pound Daddy," 1927*

A man with a large penis (Hill). The comparison is probably to the weight of a hammer.

twist, (that)

> *Mama mama just look at sis*
> *Standin' on the corner tryin' to do that twist . . .*
> *Come here sis, you ol' stinkin' sow*
> *You tryin' to be a woman an' you don't know how.*
> —*Barbecue Bob, "Easy Rider, Don't You Deny My Name," 1927*

? Seemingly, a suggestive hip wriggle associated with beckoning prostitutes. In relation to sexual intercourse, *twist* appears in this lyric:

> *Now I ain't said it man just to be so bold*
> *But I really likes the way she twist her jelly roll*
> *Because she's your cook, she burns my bread sometime.*
> —*Bo Carter, "She's Your Cook But She Burns My Bread Sometimes," 1931*

'twixt

> *Woke up this mornin', 'twixt midnight and day*
> *With my hair on my pillow where my brownie used to lay.*
> —*Barbecue Bob, "Barbecue Blues," 1927*

The aphetic form of *betwixt,* meaning between, a once-common locution appearing frequently in Shakespeare that the OED apprehends as "still in colloquial use in some dialects."

Two Step

> *If I ever catch you down on Hastings Street*
> *I'll do the Two Step on your liver and dare your heart to beat.*
> —*Calvin Frazier, "Lilly Mae," 1938 (LC)*

One of the three bedrock blues dances, along with the *Shimmy* (q.v.) and *Slow Drag* (q.v.), performed to up-tempo songs. It involved two forward steps followed by two backward ones and apparently originated during slavery: "Used to play two steps, one of 'em called 'Devil's Dream' . . ." (Charles H. Anderson, as quoted in *Born in Slavery*).

two to one

> *Says I asked that pawnshop man what the three balls doin' hangin' on*
>   *that wall*
> *Says: "It's two to one buddy you don't get your things back out of here at*
>   *all."*
> —*Blind Boy Fuller, "Three Ball Blues," 1937*

The punch line of the above couplet appears to be based on an old saying; Grose (1796) notes that a pawnshop was known as a *two to one shop,* "perhaps to its being two to one that the goods pledged are never redeemed."

two-way

> *Everybody's talkin' about a two-way woman,*
> *Do you wanna lose your mind?*
> —*Cannon's Jug Stompers, "Walk Right In," 1929*

Dishonest, crooked; ordinarily applied to males (cf. Lighter, 1997, at *one-way*).

typewriter

> *I feel like snappin' my typewriter in your face*
> *Then some shady graveyard baby, be your restin' place.*
> —*Willie "61" Blackwell, "Machine Gun Blues," 1941*

Submachine gun; criminal slang regarded as rare by DAUL.

up (1)

> An' I love you baby, you so nice an' brown
> 'Cause you, put it up solid, so it won't come down.
> —Kid Bailey, "Rowdy Blues," 1929

Up the vagina; a sense probably conveyed in double entendre fashion by the following couplet:

> Now the boat's up the river, an' it won't come down
> I believe to my soul sweet mama it's water bound.
> —Henry Thomas, "Don't Ease Me In," 1928

up (2)

> Sometimes I'm up, sometimes I'm down,
> I can't make my livin', around this town.
> —Lucille Bogan, "They Ain't Walking No More," 1930

"In a state of emotional or nervous stimulation, either naturally or as a result of taking drugs; excited, elated . . ." (OED, which dates this colloquialism to 1942).

up in years

> She may be old, up in years
> She ain't too old for to shift them gears.
> —Tommy McClennan, "Bottle It Up And Go," 1939

Elderly, in Southern black parlance: "We is both way up in years" (Jeff Davis, as quoted in *Born in Slavery*).

upside

> When you catch my jumper, hangin' upside your wall
> Well you know by that baby I need my ashes hauled.
> —Sleepy John Estes, "The Girl I Love, She Got Long Curly Hair," 1929

On; applied by blacks to surfaces but not expressly to their upper half as in the standard English use of the word (cf. OED). This term survived in the black expression *upside the head*, invariably used to indicate a telling head blow, fashionable in the 1960s and 1970s. "They had a bunk up side the wall and a trundle bed" (Felix Street, as quoted in *Born in Slavery*).

up the country

> *Well I'm goin' up the country, won't be very long*
> *Little gal, you can count the days I'm gone.*
> —Bo Weavil Jackson, "You Can't Keep No Brown," 1926

A much-used Southern blues expression that was a corruption of *up-country*, i.e., a part of the country well away from any town (cf. OED, which quotes Kipling [1891]: "I'm going up-country with a column").

used to be

> *I feel a notion, back to my used to be*
> *. . . pretty mama, she don't care for me.*
> —Skip James, "Little Cow And Calf Is Gonna Die Blues," 1931

Former lover; from the adverbial sense of *used to be*, meaning formerly. In white Southern speech, this expression has a pejorative ring and is equivalent to *has-been* (cf. WD). When used adjectivally, it applied to any bygone possession: "'Y'all still talking bout Brazzle's ole uster-be mule?'" (Zora Neale Hurston's *De Turkey and de Law: A Comedy in Three Acts* [1930]).

used to could

> *I used to could get a woman, before I could catch my breath*
> *Now I can't get a break nowhere, an' I talk myself to death.*
> —Bill Gaither, "I Just Keep On Worryin," 1937

Used to be able to; a still-used colloquialism (WD) noted by Bartlett (1877) as "[a] vulgarism used in the Southern States for *could formerly. . . .*"

vag

> *I picked up a newspaper, an' I looked in the ads*
> *An' a policeman came along, and arrested me for vag.*
> —Ramblin' Thomas, "No Job Blues," 1928

Criminal slang for vagrancy (DAUL).

vamp (v.)

> *She don't pay the butcher, one red cent*
> *She vamps the landlord, for the rent.*
> —Laura Smith, "Lucy Long," 1925

To exploit men by using feminine wiles.

vampire

> They call me a vampire, that's why I ain't got no friends
>
> My chief occupation, is takin' money from monkey men.
>
> —Laura Smith, "Two-Faced Woman Blues," 1924

"A person of a malevolent and loathsome character, esp. one who preys ruthlessly upon others" (OED). As used above, the term exemplifies a 1968 definition cited in the OED: "a woman who uses sex to facilitate the acquisition of money...."

viper

> Gonna get me some poison, kill myself
>
> 'Cause the man I love has put me on the shelf
>
> The dirty old viper jumped salty on me.
>
> —Rosetta Howard, "My Man Jumped Salty On Me," 1939

Contemporary black slang for "one who smokes reefer" (Calloway, 1939).

wait, (it) just won't

> Me an' my feets is never late
>
> Me an' my feets just won't wait.
>
> —Blind Lemon Jefferson, "Hot Dogs," 1927

A black or barrelhouse catchphrase applied on blues recording to hurried departure:

> I got to leave Miss'ippi, 'fore it be too late
>
> It may be like '27 highwater, swear it just won't wait.
>
> —Charlie Patton, "Love My Stuff," 1934

It also occurs in the rhythm and blues hit "Rocket 88" (1951).

wait on

> Her head is nappy, an' her feet done got long
>
> Take God Almighty to tell who she been waitin' on.
>
> —Joe Evans, "Down In Black Bottom," 1931

To wait for; a colloquialism dating to the early 19th century (cf. DARE 3 at *on*, 3a).

wake, snake, day's a-breakin'

> *Wake, snake, day's a-breakin'*
> *Peas in the pot and hoe cake's a-bakin'*
> —*Leadbelly, "Green Corn," 1935*

A Southern black catchphrase on the order of "arise and shine."

walking blues, to have the

> *I woke up this mornin' feel around for my shoes*
> *You know by that I had them ol', old walkin' blues*
> —*Robert Johnson, "Walking Blues," 1936*

To be gripped by wanderlust, or a desire to drift. This expression, perhaps originating in blues song, appears in August Wilson's *Fences* (1985): "Ain't you never heard of nobody having the walking blues? Well, that's what you call it when you just take off like that."

walk the floor

> *Blues oh blues, you know you done been here before*
> *The last time you was here you made me cry and walk the floor.*
> —*Ida Cox, "Rambling Blues," 1925*

To pace restlessly by walking back and forth. This colloquial phrase figured in Ernest Tubb's 1941 country and western hit, "Walking The Floor Over You."

walk the streets

> *I love to fuss an' fight (2)*
> *Lord an' get sloppy drunk offa bottle an' bond*
> *And walk the streets all night.*
> —*Charlie Patton, "Elder Greene Blues," 1929*

A variant of *stalk the streets*, 19th-century slang defined by F&H (1903) as meaning "to quest for meat."

wall, to have one's back (turned) to the

> *Now when I was lucky an' on the ground*
> *I had lots of friends to hang around*
> *But when my back was turned to the wall*
> *It didn't seem like I had no friends at all.*
> —*Pine Top Smith, "Nobody Knows You When You're Down And Out," 1929*

To be in dire straits; a clichéd idiom (DC) to which blues singers invariably added "turned," and applied to being imprisoned.

wash job

> *It's comin' a time, these women won't need no men*
> *They'll find a wash job an' money come rollin' in.*
> —*Willie Baker, "Crooked Woman Blues," 1929*

Employment as a washerwoman.

watch my smoke

You don't mean me no good, I can tell by the way you do

"I ain't done nothin' yet, just watch my smoke."

—Bessie Mae Smith, "St. Louis Daddy," 1929; spoken aside by accompanist
  Wesley Wallace

A popular catchphrase indicating that the speaker is about to do something
that will astound or impress others. It appears in Jack London's 1908 novel
Martin Eden ("Wait till I get my stride. Then watch my smoke.") and Sinclair
Lewis's 1920 novel *Main Street* ("Here we go! Watch my smoke—Sam'l, the
ladies' delight and the bridegrooms' terror!").

water-haul

Payday on the Seven, payday on the Yellow Dog

An' I want to meet that payroll and try to make a water-haul.

—Lucille Bogan, "Pay Roll Blues," 1928

A swindle (STY). Conventionally, a *water-haul* stood for a fruitless effort. The
phrase itself originally meant "a haul of a net which catches no fish" (1911
edition of Webster's, quoted in the OED).

water on, to have one's

I'm going to make you wish you had never been born

I just went uptown, got my pistol out of pawn

"Don't start nothin' baby, 'cause your papa's got your bath water on."

—Memphis Jug Band, "Papa's Got Your Bath Water On," 1930

A barrelhouse catchphrase usually rendered as *I got your water on,* meaning
"I'm ready for anything you wanna start, good or bad" (Hill). It is invoked in
the following variant:

When you think I'm gone

I'm standin' right here with your water on.

—Sam Collins, "It Won't Be Long," 1927

weak

Way down South you oughta see the women Shimmy and shake

Got a new way a-wiggle, make a weak man break his neck.

—Blind Lemon Jefferson, "Southern Woman Blues," [1928]

In the blues lexicon, weak for the opposite sex. The blues singer Skip James
referred to the male genitals as "a man's weak spot." See *weak spot.*

weaking down

If I had my right mind, I would write my woman a few lines

I will do most anything, to keep from weakin' down . . .

—Bukka White, "Sleepy Man Blues," 1940

Succumbing to weakness; a corruption of *weakening down* (or vice-versa): ". . .
they commenced to be weakened down from all this mixin' . . ." (Alabama-

born speaker quoted in Gwaltney, 1980). The latter phrase appears in the following:

> When it lightnin' my mind gets frightened, my nerves begin weakenin' down
> And the shack where we was livin', begin movin' 'round.
> —Lonnie Johnson, "Flood Water Blues," 1937

By itself, *weaking* means to grow weaker, and represents archaic English not recorded beyond 1581 (cf. OED).

weak-minded

> A weak-minded woman will let a rounder tear her down
> An' when she get in trouble that rounder can't be found.
> —Willie Baker, "Weak Minded Blues," 1929

Susceptible to the machinations of underhanded sexual consorts; an extension of the standard English sense of the word as meaning lacking in strength of purpose (cf. OED). In the form of *weak mind* this idiom survived in the speech of black youths of the 1960s and 1970s (cf. Folb).

weak spot

> Come on daddy, get down on your knees
> Sock it to my weak spot, if you please.
> —Ora Alexander, "I Crave Your Lovin' Every Day," 1932

Genitals; used with the implication that sex governs one's affections, if not character.

welcome as the flowers in May

> I keep drinkin' malted milk, trying to drive my blues away
> Baby you just as welcome to my lovin', as the flowers is in May.
> —Robert Johnson, "Malted Milk," 1937

A figure of speech apparently drawn from "Just A Little Street Where Old Friends Meet," a 1932 Tin Pan Alley composition by Gus Kahn and Harry Woods:

> Although I'm rich or poor I still feel sure
> I'm as welcome as the flowers in May . . .

what it takes, to have

> So glad I'm a brownskin, chocolate to the bone
> An' I got what it takes to make a monkey man leave his home.
> —Barbecue Bob, "Chocolate to The Bone," 1928

A 1920s catchphrase; as explained in a 1929 issue of *American Speech:* "[t]o avoid using the word *money,* the well-informed user of slang may use . . . *what it takes*" (quoted in OED). In the above instance, *what it takes* more likely refers to sexual prowess.

wheel

I went to the wheel, they wouldn't let me in
I stood on the steps cried out in the wind:
"Mister man, mister man, please open the door
I wanna play four-eleven forty-four."
—*Papa Charlie Jackson, "Four Eleven Forty Four," 1926*

The headquarters of a policy operation, where receipts are banked and betting slips collected; still used. The term probably derives from the turn-of-the-20th-century slang use of *wheel* to mean a business transaction (DAS).

wheeler

"I got a kid, on the wheeler, got a bullcow on the plough
Got a plumb good man bringin' down the job somewhere."
—*Charlie Patton, "Jim Lee Blues, Part Two," 1929*

Side wheeler; riverboat. The above couplet, presented as the boast of a female companion, refers to the occupations of her boyfriends, the *kid* working on a Mississippi riverboat.

where water drinks like wine

And I'm goin' to where Lordie, water drinks like wine
Where I can be drunk-staggerin', staggerin' all the time.
—*Kid Bailey, "Mississippi Bottom Blues," 1929*

A corruption of *where wine flows like water,* a 19th-century figure of speech used in Louisa May Alcott's *Little Women* (1868). In the above and related forms it appears to have been a black catchphrase employed to extol any locality, and is so used in Zora Neale Hurston's *Spunk* (1935): "... Polk County, where the water taste like cherry wine."

whiff

I love my whiskey and I love my gin
But the way I use my coke it's a doggone sin.
Hey hey, honey take a whiff on me.
—*Memphis Jug Band, "Cocaine Habit Blues," 1930*

A snort of cocaine.

whine

A nickel is a nickel, dime is a dime
Don't need no gal if she won't whine.
—*Tommy McClennan, "Bottle It Up And Go," 1939*

To make sounds of sexual transport.

whip (whup)

> *Sometimes I feel like I done been throwed away*
> *"What'ya do?"*
> *Take this old guitar, and whup these blues all day.*
> —*Pink Anderson and Simmie Dooley, "Every Day In The Week Blues," 1928*

To play an instrument vigorously, in such a way as to dominate it. This expression was used as a superlative, indicating proficient musicianship: "He could play a banjo: he could whip a banjo" (Sam Chatmon on Charlie McCoy). In various forms this phrase appears as a vocal aside, particularly during instrumental breaks:

> *"Whup that piano, Mister piano-whupper;*
> *Whup it till it breaks!"*
> —*Blind Lemon Jefferson, "Teddy Bear Blues," 1927*
> *"Whip that box, Bill; whip it."*
> —*William Moore, "Old Country Rock," 1928*

whip it to a cream gravy

> *"Aw whip it; whip it to a cream gravy."*
> —*Blind Blake, "Doggin' Me Mama Blues," 1928*

A stereotyped vocal aside, embellishing the catchphrase *whip it*. A variant appears on Blind Willie McTell's "Atlanta Strut" (1929): "It was a fella up there could whip a mandolin to a slow-down gravy."

whiskey head

> *I drink so much whiskey, it's a wonder that I'm not dead*
> *All around my neighborhood, the people call me a whiskey head.*
> —*"Funny Paper" Smith, "Wiskyhead [sic] Blues," 1931*

Black slang for one who is frequently or generally intoxicated with whiskey. The synonymous *liquor head* occurs in Zora Neale Hurston's *Meet the Mamma* (1924): "I don't give my money to liquor heads." The standard English *pot head* undoubtedly derives from this usage.

whiskey-headed

> *She's a whiskey-headed woman, an' she stays drunk all the time*
> *Baby an' if you don't stop drinkin', I believe you gonna lose your mind.*
> —*Tommy McClennan, "Whiskey Head Blues," 1939*

Alcoholic; drunken.

whistling woman

> *I'm a whistlin' woman, I'm like a crowin' hen*
> *The folks all told me, it come to no good end.*
> —*Bessie Tucker, "Whistling Woman Blues," 1929*

A woman who emulates male conduct in violation of what was perceived as the natural order of things; from the British proverb:

A whistling woman and a crowing hen
Are neither liked by God nor men.

In slave culture, "[a] 'oman that whistled wuz marked to be a bad 'oman" (Amanda Styles, as quoted in *Born in Slavery*).

white folks

White folks, white folks don't work my brown so hard
Solid lover but she did not have a job.
—Julius Daniels, "Richmond Blues," 1927

In the Jim Crow era, a form of address to individual whites: "'Hello, Uncle Nathan,' I called. 'Mornin' white folks,' he answered ...'" (Gertha Couric, interviewer, *Born in Slavery*).

white lightning

Fix my supper an' let me go to bed
This white lightnin' done gone to my head.
—Bukka White, "Shake 'Em On Down," 1937

Corn liquor, the colorless appearance of which prompted the synonym *white whiskey*. Of itself, *lightning* originated as an 18th-century British term for gin (cf. Grose, 1796), and subsequently became attached to American-made corn, presumably on the basis of its stunning or immediate effect.

white mule

Pour me out some white mule, pour me out some sandy rye
I don't want no bug juice, that ol' stuff is too darn high.
—Barbecue Bob, "Blind Pig Blues," 1928

A 1920s term for bootleg whiskey, corn liquor (also called "mule"), or any colorless whiskey (ATS), the comparison to a mule stemming from its kick.

whoop

Well Frankie's mother come runnin', come a-whoopin', screamin', an' cryin'
"Oh Lord, oh Lord, my only son is dyin'."
—Charlie Patton, "Frankie And Albert," 1929

Dated standard English meaning "... to shout, hollo (as in incitement, summons, exultation, defiance, intimidation or mere excitement)" (OED; its most recent citation is 1883).

wild about

I'm wild about my lovin', and I like to have my fun
Wanna be a girl of mine you have to bring it with you when you come.
—Jim Jackson, "I'm Wild About My Lovin'," 1928

"... [V]ery keen on, excited by" (DCS). This expression may have been of black origin; it figured in the title of Sissle and Blake's "I'm Just Wild About Harry" (1922).

wild geese

I lay down last night ... tried to take my rest.

My mind got to ramblin', like a wild geese in the west.

—Skip James, "Devil Got My Woman," 1931

The usual term for Canada geese (goose, in the above instance) when domesticated geese were popular table fare. The association between wild geese and western flight is fanciful; William Byrd's *History of the Dividing Line* (1728) reported: "Now the weather grew cool, the wild geese began to direct their flight this way from Hudson's Bay. . . ."

wise woman

Daddy you done put that thing on me

And I guess you're satisfied.

It took a lot of lovin' and dick honey

To make a wise woman like me smile.

—Sparkplug Smith, "Vampire Woman Blues," 1933

An archaic term for witch or female charm worker (OED); found in Shakespeare's *Merry Wives of Windsor* ("'Was't not the Wise-woman of Brainford?'") and *Twelfth Night* ("'Carry his water to the wise-woman'").

woman rocks the cradle

Woman rocks the cradle, I declare she rules the home

Many a man rocks some other man's baby, and the fool thinks he's rockin'
his own.

—Blind Lemon Jefferson, "That Crawling Baby Blues," 1929

A Victorian-era cliché, popularized by W. R. Wallace's 1865 poem "What Rules the World":

The hand that rocks the cradle

Is the hand that rules the world.

The expression "Many a man rocks some other man's baby" was itself somewhat proverbial among blacks of the blues era (Sam Chatmon).

woogie

"You're cryin' that you been off from Detriot three weeks. . . . Must be have
somethin' in Detroit you're really wild about. You go back there now
you gonna sure get woogie. . . . I believe I feel like gettin' woogie."

—Blind Blake, "Hastings Street," 1929

Pussy, a meaning that may have been understood as the second element of *boogie woogie*. As a term for a female apprehended as *pussy*, it is invoked in the following:

I used to boogie-woogie but I'm sorry to say

My little woogie packed up an' went away

I wonder who's boogyin' my woogie now.

—Oscar's Chicago Swingers, "I Wonder Who's Boogiein' My Woogie Now," 1936

won't don't, just

He'll make you change your mind and don't you think he won't
My man just won't don't.

—Laura Smith, "My Man Just Won't Don't," 1927

A superlative of no appreciable meaning, perhaps suggested by *it just won't quit.*

work, do one's

Now what make mens and womens baby love a rounder so?
'Cause he takes his time, does his work everywhere he goes.

—Frank Stokes, "Memphis Rounders Blues," 1928

In this instance, to engage in sexual activity, *rounders* being otherwise unemployed.

work or leave

I was down in Louisiana, doin' as I please
Now I'm in Texas, an' I got to work or leave.

—Ramblin' Thomas, "Poor Boy Blues," 1928

An ultimatum given to Southern black vagrants during the blues era. Following a 1922 Texas lynching, an anonymous note was left on the door of a local newspaper office at Pilot Point stating: "... Let this be a warning to all nigger loafers. Niggers get a job or leave town" (cf. Ginzburg, 1962).

working (v.)

Says I've got a girl, an' she workin' hard
Say the dress she wear sweet mama says it's pink an' blue.

—Henry Thomas, "Don't Ease Me In," 1928

In this context, working as a prostitute.

working man

There's one thing I can't understand
Why a good-lookin' woman likes a workin' man.

—Ma Rainey, "Shave 'Em Dry," 1924

A man who works for a living at a legitimate occupation.

working woman

I asked the judge, don't hold the trial till two
'Cause I got a workin' woman, let me see what my woman can do.
Here come that woman ... had a hundred in her hand
She had to rock some fatmouth, whose really lookin' for her man.

—Little Hat Jones, "Corpus Blues," 1929

Prostitute; the term *working girl* is still applied to such women by prostitutes, pimps, and police personnel.

world unknown, a

> *I'm goin' away, to a world unknown*
> *I'm worried now, but I won't be worried long.*
> —*Charlie Patton, "Down The Dirt Road Blues," 1929*

Another planet, or extraterrestrial realm; a dated poetic turn of phrase invoked in a slave spiritual, with reference to death: "Am I born to die, to lay this body down, / Must my tremblin' spirit fly into worlds unknown, / The land of deepes shade, / Only pierce' by human thought" (Willie Ann Smith, as quoted in *Born in Slavery*). Another slave spiritual similarly rued: "Mary wept and Martha moaned / Mary's gone to a world unknown" (Sara Pittman, as quoted in *Born in Slavery*). In inverted (and likely original) form, it is found in a 1751 confection, *Dr. Ormond's Recovered Works:* "unknown worlds and heaven's recesses spy."

worry

> *I know you like my lovin', I can tell from the way you whine*
> *Since you tasted my jelly, you just worries me all the time.*
> —*Otis Harris, "You'll Like My Loving," 1928*

"To plague or pester with repeated demands, requests, or the like" (OED); used lightly or hyperbolically. In the following couplet, it is applied to an importuning male sex organ:

> *I said squat low papa, let your mama see*
> *I wanna see that old business, keeps on worryin' me.*
> —*Geeshie Wiley, "Eagles On A Half," 1930*

worry with

> *Baby baby, I ain't gonna worry with you no more*
> *Lord I'm goin' down the country, let you have Mister So and So.*
> —*Walter Davis, "Jacksonville, Part Two," 1936*

To bother with; a black or Southern colloquialism.

wow

> *Too tight, it's a wow*
> *Too tight I'll show you how*
> *Too tight, this rag a-mine.*
> —*Blind Blake, "Too Tight," 1926*

Contemporary slang for a sensational success (OED).

write one's name (on) one's back

> *Put you down under a man they call "Captain Jack"*
> *He'll sure write his name up an' down your back.*
> —*Son House, "Mississippi County Farm," 1942 (LC)*

To flog severely on one's back; a variation of a sporting expression for striking, *write one's name across another's face,* current from the late 19th century until about 1912 (Partridge). Another such idiom appeared in the 1942 film *White Cargo:* "If you show up here again I'll cut my initials across your back."

yard

> *... That must be the bedbug, you know a chinch can't bite that hard*
> *Asked my sugar for fifty cents, she said: "Lemon ain't a dime in the yard."*
> —Blind Lemon Jefferson, "That Black Snake Moan," 1926

House, a sense found in Jamaica: "They seldom speak of going to a friend's home. They say they are going to the yard" (Walter Jekyll, *Jamaican Song and Story* [1907], quoted in OED). See also:

> *My black woman she needs the money, that's why I work so hard*
> *And if I don't keep on rollin', she'll have another black man in my yard.*
> —Buddy Boy Hawkins, "Yellow Woman Blues," 1927
>
> *It must be a black cat bone, jomo can't work that hard*
> *Every time I wake up, Jim Tampa's in my yard.*
> —Lucille Bogan, "Jim Tampa Blues," 1927
>
> *I got a gal in the white folks' yard*
> *She don't drink liquor but she do play cards.*
> —Blind Willie McTell, "Hillbilly Willie's Blues," 1935

The latter is in reference to a domestic.

yas-yas-yas

> *Now the funniest thing I ever seen:*
> *Tomcat jumpin' on a sewing machine*
> *Sewing machine run so fast*
> *Took ninety-nine stitches in his yas-yas-yas*
> —Memphis Minnie, "New Dirty Dozen," 1930

A favorite song euphemism for *ass*, used with humorous intent.

yellow (a.)

> *Black woman's skin stay smooth an' pretty, until the day she's dead*
> *Yellow woman's face get wrinkled, hair drops from her head.*
> —Lee Green, "Sealskin Black Woman," 1937

Along with *black* and *brown,* a standard complexion designation used by African Americans during the blues era, usually applied to females. It was similarly employed in slave speech: "I was a good lookin' yeller gal in dem days and rid free wherever I wanted to go" ("Aunt" Charity Anderson, as quoted in *Born in Slavery*).

yellow (n.)

> *Unlucky with my yellow, unlucky with my brown*
> *The black bitches keep on throwin' me down.*
> —Papa Charlie Jackson with Ma Rainey, "Big Feeling Blues," 1928

A black person of perceptibly mixed ancestry, producing a sallow complexion.

yere

> *Just like a doggone rabbit I ain't got no doggone den*
> *Oh I been in trouble Lord, ever since yere I been.*
> —Charlie Patton, "Joe Kirby," 1930

A dialect pronunciation of *here:* "I wuz baw'n 'yer in Nashville" (Francis Batson, as quoted in *Born in Slavery*). The above lyric transposes "I been here" for the sake of rhyming.

yon, yonder

> *Look over yonder, on the buryin' ground*
> *Yon stands ten thousand, standin' to see them let me down.*
> —Bukka White, "Fixing To Die," 1940

There; over there; regarded as archaic or dialectal English (cf. OED).

you can't tell the difference when the sun goes down

> *I ain't crazy 'bout no yellow, fool 'bout no brown*
> *You can't tell the difference when the sun go down.*
> —Papa Charlie Jackson, "Shave 'Em Dry," 1925

A proverbial sentiment regarding women, expressed by the ancient Greeks as "[w]hen the candle is taken away, every woman is alike"; in *Don Quixote* (1605) as "[a]ll cats are gray in the dark"; and by Francis Bacon ("*Of Unity in Religion,*" 1612) as "[a]ll colours will agree in the dark."

your time now, be mine after while

> *It's your time now, be mine after while*
> *You know that you hurt me, daddy 'cause I seen you smile.*
> —Bessie Tucker, "Bessie's Moan," 1928

A black catchphrase occurring in Zora Neale Hurston and Dorothy Waring's *Polk County* (1944) as: "Your time now, be mine after while." In this instance *time* connotes a period in which one is favored by fortune.

APPENDIX WHAT IS THIS THING CALLED BLUES?

Definitions of blues can only be generalities because the genre had no formal, mandatory compositional features, but rather adhered to stereotyped conventions. When blues were in fashion, black performers were likely to label any material they proffered as being blues in the interests of making it appear more commercially relevant. By the same token, the term blues was employed as a catchall by the music industry, in which light it may be defined thusly:

1. A music industry trade term for any serious-sounding black secular song composed or recorded between 1912 and 1945 that was taken to reflect a racial musical sensibility, distinct from that of whites.
2. A designation for a white-authored song whose lyrics refer to "having the blues."

It was in the latter sense that the first inkling of the term "blues" as a song label occurred around 1906, via a white Louisville performer's composition, "Joy Man Blues," which began: "Tuesday when I awoke I felt so awful blue."

A technical definition of blues, designed to isolate its most typical distinguishing musical features, would run as follows:

1. A name given both individually and collectively to self-accompanied songs of African American street and dance performers of the early 20th century, in which each vocal phrase characteristically ends on the keynote and is followed by a brief instrumental phrase that similarly ends on the tonic, and each vocal phrase forms a grammatically complete statement.
2. Such a song, adapted for stage or ensemble presentation.
3. An instrumental that suggests a blues song.

Even though blues singers concocted thousands of tunes with these characteristics, they did not apprehend blues in actual musical terms. A definition that would attempt to account for the meaning of blues to the bulk of its performers and black listeners alike is as follows: "A term applied to an African American song related in the first person that emphasizes the misfortunes of the singer, depicts an unstable relationship, or expresses strife with others."

It was this understanding of such songs that probably gave rise to the label "blues," which almost certainly came into existence well after the musical characteristics associated with blues were already established. Although blues had no obligatory lyric content, singers who ignored the stereotype of blues as

273

a recitation of unhappy or embittering experiences did so at their own peril. Thus Bo Carter, a purveyor of placid, pleasant blues material, was regarded by his brother Sam Chatmon as something other than a bona fide blues entertainer. "Bo was the best in his field," Chatmon said, "and Ben Mike [another Mississippi singer] was the best in his—that's them pure old country blues, where they could sing *nasty* [employ vituperative lyrics]."

INDEX

Dürer, Albrecht, *Knight, Death, and the Devil*, 121

Durfey, Thomas, *Pills to Purge Melancholy*, 148

Eastwood, Clint, 255
Edwards, Moanin' Bernice, "Hard Hustling Blues," 80
Ellington, Duke, "It Don't Mean A Thing (If It Ain't Got That Swing)," 75, 240
Ellison, Ralph, *Invisible Man*, 6, 8, 94, 107, 238, 255
Estes, Sleepy John: "Diving Duck Blues," 63, 151, 201; "Drop Down Mama," 80; "Everybody Oughta Make A Change," 10, 103; "Floating Bridge," 33, 153; "The Girl I Love, She Got Long Curly Hair," 5, 76, 258; "Mary Come On Home," 113; "Milk Cow Blues," 40, 58; "Someday Baby Blues," 179; "Special Agent (Railroad Police Blues)," 226; "Stack O' Dollars," 171; "You Shouldn't Do That," 82, 127
Evans, Joe: "Down In Black Bottom," 260; "Shook It This Morning Blues," 131
Everetts, Dorothy, "Fatmouth Blues," 89
Every Which Way But Loose, 255
Ezell, Will, "Pitchin' Boogie," 28

Farrell, James T., *Father and Son*, 236
Faulkner, William, *Go Down, Moses*, 103; *The Mansion*, 69, 107, 230; *The Sound and the Fury*, 136, 172, 236; *Sanctuary*, 130, 189
Floyd, Harmonica Frank, xiv
Foster, Rudy, "Black Gal Makes Thunder," 186
Foster and Harris, "Crow Jane Alley," 65
Framer, Eli, "Framer's Blues," 157
Franklin, Benjamin, *Autobiography*, 8, 48
Frazier, Calvin, "Lily Mae," 35, 257
Fuller, Blind Boy: "Black And Tan," 21, 159; "If You See My Pigmeat," 235; "I'm A Good Stem Winder," 70, 231; "Mama Let Me Lay It On You," 146; "Pistol Slapper Blues," 222; "Three Ball Blues," 257; "Truckin' My Blues Away," 254
Fuller, Thomas, *Gnomolgia*, 96

Gaither, Bill: "Evil Yalla Woman," 243; "Georgia Barrel House," 13; "I Just Keep On Worryin'," 259; "Pains In My Heart," 15; "Racket Blues," 147, 181; "That Will Never Do," 41; "You Done Lost Your Swing," 231; "You Done Ranked Yourself With Me," 18, 193
Georgia Tom, 143, 151, 209, 216, 247. *See also* Kansas City Kitty and Georgia Tom; Lucas, Jane, and Georgia Tom; Tampa Red and Georgia Tom; The Hokum Boys and Jane Lucas
Gibson, Clifford: "Don't Put That Thing On Me," 227; "Hard-Headed Blues," 34, 94; "Jive Me Blues," 58; "Levee Camp Moan," 162, 185; "Sunshine Moan," 104; "Tired Of Being Mistreated, Part One," 66; "Tired Of Being Mistreated, Part Two," 67, 228
Gillum, Jazz, "She Keeps On Rickin'," 197
"Girl Who Threw Me Down, The," 246
Glen, Emery: "Back Door Blues," 8, 45; "Blue Blazes Blues," 24
Godrich. *See* Dixon and Godrich
Goodis, David, *Down There*, 129
Graves, Blind Roosevelt, "Bustin' The Jug," 43
Grant, Bobby, "Nappy Head Blues," 168
Grant, Coot, "Get Off With Me," 102
Green, Lee: "Down On The Border," 18; "Maltese Cat Blues," 4; "Pork Chop Stomp," 181; "Sealskin Black Woman," 66, 209, 270; "Wash Day And No Soap," 204
Green, Lil, "Knockin' Myself Out," 99
Grey, Gilday, 215
Gross, Helen, "Strange Man," 234

Handy, W. C., xii, xiv, 66, 161; *Father of the Blues*, 131; "Memphis Blues," 98; "Sundown Blues," 81; "Yellow Dog Blues," 74
"Hangman Johnny," xiv
Hannah, George: "The Boy In The Boat," 34, 240; "Freakish Man Blues," 96
Hardin, Lane: "California Desert Blues," 124, 144; "Hard Times Blues," 118
Harris, Joel Chandler, *Uncle Remus*, 5, 18, 61, 117
Harris, John, "Glad And Sorry Blues," 164, 249
Harris, Otis, "You'll Like My Loving," 241, 242, 269
Harris, William: "Bull Frog Blues," 40, 155,

I Got What You Want," 136; "I'm Alabama Bound," 5, 38; "I'm Looking For A Woman Who Knows How To Treat Me Right," 45; "Jungle Man Blues," 8; "Long Gone Lost John," 24; "Mama Don't Allow It (And She Ain't Gonna Have It Here)," 36, 66; "Mama, Don't You Think I Know?," 52, 88; "Maxwell Street Blues," 156, 184; "Mumsy Mumsy Blues," 167, 211; "Papa Do Do Do Blues," 174; "Salt Lake City Blues," 24, 237; "Salty Dog Blues," 148, 207; "Screaming and Hollering The Blues," 119; "Shake That Thing," 51, 125, 136, 212, 239; "Shave 'Em Dry," 271; "Sheik Of Desplaines Street," 1, 213; "Skoodle Um Skoo," 218. *See also* Jackson, Papa Charlie, with Ma Rainey

Jackson, Papa Charlie, with Ma Rainey, "Big Feeling Blues," 271

Jackson, Sadie, "Original Black Bottom Dance," 22, 69

James, Jesse: "Southern Casey Blues," 165, 176; "Sweet Patuni," 219

James, Skip, 51, 57, 60, 125, 163, 171, 193, 220, 251, 262; "Cherry Ball Blues," 51; "Devil Got My Woman," 103, 196, 267; "Drunken Spree," 228, 248; "Four O'Clock Blues," 201; "Hard Luck Child," 71, 118, 169; "Illinois Blues," 37, 164; "Little Cow And Calf Is Gonna Die Blues," 259; "Yola My Blues Away," 131

Jaxon, Frankie "Half Pint": "It's Heated," 65, 239; "Jive Man Blues," 206

Jed Davenport and His Beale Street Jug Band, "You Oughta Move Out of Town," 174

Jefferson, Blind Lemon, xii; "Bad Luck Blues," 116, 152; "Beggin' Back," 19, 237; "Big Night Blues," 54; "Black Horse Blues," 243; "Black Snake Moan," 52, 270; "Booger Rooger Blues," 42, 135, 150, 157, 206, 214, 246; "Booster Blues," 87, 197; "Broke And Hungry Blues," 22, 47, 141; "Change My Luck Blues," 14, 50, 85; "Chinch Bug Blues," 52; "Chockhouse Blues," 64, 91, 96, 109, 200; "Corrina Blues," 160; "D B Blues," 42, 68, 192, 241; "Deceitful Brownskin Woman," 230; "Dry Southern Blues," 16; "Easy Rider," 83; "Electric Chair Blues," 179; "Fence Breakin' Yellen' Blues," 135; "Gone Dead On You Blues," 105, 139, 181, 194; "Got The Blues," 89, 122, 192; "Hangman's Blues," 252; "Hot Dogs," 22, 28, 260; "Jack O'Diamonds," 255; "Lemon's Cannon Ball Moan," 34, 46, 161; "Lemon's Worried Blues," 12; "Long Lastin' Lovin'," 53, 67, 124, 223, 226, 249; "Low Down Mojo Blues," 162; "Maltese Cat Blues," 99; "Match Box Blues," 92, 156; "Mean Jumper Blues," 25, 137, 157; "Mosquito Moan," 98; "One Dime Blues," 9, 123, 227; "Peach Orchard Mama," 54; "Piney Woods Money Mama," 17, 123, 183; "Pneumonia Blues," 105; "Prison Cell Blues," 153, 195, 228; "Rabbit Foot Blues," 139, 158, 205, 223; "Rambler Blues," 52, 80, 175; "Raising High Water Blues," 119; "Right Of Way Blues," 234; "See See Rider," 74, 197, 246; "See That My Grave Is Kept Clean," 132; "Shuckin' Sugar," 16, 65, 74; "Southern Woman Blues," 36, 214, 262; "Stocking Feet Blues," 83, 178; "Sunshine Special," 99; "That Crawlin' Baby Blues," 68, 267; "Teddy Bear Blues," 185, 244, 265; "Tin Cup Blues," 43; "Wartime Blues," 219, 245; "Yo Yo Blues," xiii

Jenkins, Dorothy, "Sister, It's Too Bad," 85

Jenkins, Hezekiah, "The Panic Is On," 184

Johnson, Alec: "Miss Meal Cramp Blues," 160; "Sundown Blues," 45

Johnson, Blind Willie: "If I Had My Way," 91; "When The War Was On," 195

Johnson, Charles L., "Beedle Um Bo," 16

Johnson, Edith North, "Good Chib Blues," 51

Johnson, James "Stump": "Money Johnson," 37; "Transom Blues," 42, 251

Johnson, Lil: "House Rent Scuffle," 120; "Never Let Your Left Hand Know You're your Right Hand Do," 205, 206; "Stavin' Chain (That Rockin' Swing)," 230; "Take It Easy Greasy No. 2," 57

Johnson, Lonnie: "Don't Drive Me From Your Door," 198; "Flood Water Blues," 263

Johnson, Louise: "All Night Long Blues," 95; "Long Ways From Home," 118; "On The Wall," 55

Johnson, Robert: "Come On In My Kitchen," 169; "Cross Road Blues," 69, 96; "Dead

Shrimp Blues," 107, 166; "Drunken Hearted Man," 151; "From Four Until Late," 5; "Hell Hound On My Trail," 114, 160, 198, 248; "Honeymoon Blues," 120; "I Believe I'll Dust My Broom," 74, 81, 203; "I'm A Steady Rollin' Man," 63, 129, 201, 230; "Kind Hearted Woman Blues," 143; "Last Fair Deal Gone Down," 106; "Little Queen of Spades," 56, 228, 251, 252; "Malted Milk Blues," 154, 226, 263; "Me And The Devil Blues," 70, 86, 105, 123; "Milkcow's Calf Blues," 245; "Phonograph Blues," 86; "Preachin' Blues," 44, 231; "Rambling On My Mind," 71; "Stones In My Passway," 30, 75, 179, 234; "Stop Breaking Down Blues," 36, 55, 58, 172, 208, 236, 246; "They're Red Hot," 35; "Traveling Riverside Blues," 56; "Walking Blues," 261; "When You Got A Good Friend," 90

Johnson, Samuel, 77

Johnson, T. C., "JC Johnson's Blues," 26, 48

Johnson, Tommy: "Alcohol And Jake Blues," 148; "Big Road Blues," 18; "Bye Bye Blues," 44; "Canned Heat Blues," 83; "Lonesome Home Blues," 83; "Maggie Campbell Blues," 7; "Ridin' Horse," 197; untitled Paramount blues, 84

Jones, Bessie, *Ballin' The Jack*, 222

Jones, Jake, "Monkeyin' Around," 163

Jones, Little Hat: "Bye Bye Baby Blues," 194; "Corpus Blues," 31, 181, 200, 268; "Kentucky Blues," 78

Jones, Maggie: "Dangerous Blues," 114, 245; "Good-Time Flat Blues," 243; "Undertaker's Blues," 67; "Western Union Blues," 167; "You Can't Do What My Last Man Did," 79

Joplin, Scott, 246. *See also* Joplin, Scott, and Scott Hayden

Joplin, Scott, and Scott Hayden, *Sunflower Slow Drag*, 220

Jordan, Charley: "Big Four Blues," 95; "Chifferobe," 51; "Dollar Bill Blues," 227; "Hellbound Boy," 118; "Keep It Clean," 9; "Raidin' Squad Blues," 126; "Starvation Blues," 90; "Tight Haired Mama Blues," 109, 247

Jordan, Luke: "Cocaine Blues," 98; "If I Call You Mama," 87, 238; "Pick Poor Robin Clean," 67, 75; "Travelin' Man," 59; "Won't You Be Kind," 68

Judge Hatchett, 242

Judge Judy, 19

Jump Jim Crow, xvii

Kahn, Gus. *See* Kahn, Gus, and Harry Woods; Kahn, Gus, and Walter Donaldson

Kahn, Gus, and Harry Woods, "Just A Little Street Where Old Friends Meet," 263

Kahn, Gus, and Walter Donaldson, "Makin' Whoopee," 154

Kansas City Kitty: "Do It By Myself," 151; "Gym's Too Much For Me," 142; "Killing Floor Blues," 143; "Leave My Man Alone," 142; "Mistreatin' Easy Rider," 83; "Scronchin'," 209, 216. *See also* Kansas City Kitty and Georgia Tom

Kansas City Kitty and Georgia Tom: "Close Made Papa," 26, 54, 102; "Fish House Blues," 92

Kansas Joe: "I'm Wild About My Stuff," 1; "My Babe Blues," 108; "My Babe My Babe," 146; "Pile Drivin' Blues," 115, 182; "Preacher's Blues," 84, 101; "Shake Mattie," 212. *See also* Kansas Joe and Memphis Minnie

Kansas Joe and Memphis Minnie, "Beat It Right" 15

Kelly, Jack: "I Believe I'll Go Back Hime," 94; "Men Fooler Blues," 26; "President Blues," 180; "Red Ripe Tomatoes," 107, 160

Kensey, Ken, *One Flew Over the Cuckoo Nest*, 233

Kid Bailey: "Mississippi Bottom Blues," 13, 36, 128, 264; "Rowdy Blues," 96, 223, 258

Kimbrough, Sylvester, "Bird Liver Blues," 19

King David's Jug Band, "What's That Taste Like Gravy," 235

Kitty Gray and her Wampus Cats, "Doing The Dooga," 76

Lacy, Rube, "Ham Hound Crave," 7, 200, 225, 234

Leadbelly: "Green Corn," 136, 261; "Kansas City Papa," 254; "Pig Meat Papa," 230; "See See Rider," 164

Lee, Bertha, "Mind Reader Blues," 179

To Have My Sweetbread," 34; "Mistreating Blues," 217; "She Got Good Stuff," 237; "Soon This Morning Blues," 13

Sparks, Aaron, "Workhouse Blues," 17

Sparks, Milton, "Grinder Blues," 112

Spaulding, Henry, "Cairo Blues," 26

Springback James, "Poor Coal Passer," 51

Spruell, Freddie, "Tom Cat Blues," 157

Stewart, Priscilla, "Mecca Flat Blues," 158

Stewart, Rex, 33

St. Louis, Jimmy, "Going Down Slow," 106

Stokes, Frank: "Fillin' In Blues, Part One," 244; "Frank Stokes' Dream," 64, 165; "I Got Mine," 112; "Memphis Rounders Blues," 268; "Mister Crump Don't Like It," 66, 125; "Mistreatin' Blues," 229; "Stomp That Thing," 212

Stone, Jesse, "Shake, Rattle and Roll," 212

Stone Poneys, The, 234

Sunny Boy and His Pals: "Don't You Leave Me Here," 243; "France Blues," 59

Swartwood, *Choice Slang*, 229

Sykes, Roosevelt: "All My Money Gone Blues," 217; "Last Go Round Blues," 145; "Papa Sweetback Blues," 104; "Roosevelt's Blues," 144; "10 And 4 Blues," 223

Tampa Joe and Macon Ed, "Wringin' That Thing," 212

Tampa Red: "The Dirty Dozen No. 2," 27; "The Duck Yas Yas Yas," 101; "They Call It Boogie-Woogie," 29. *See also* Tampa Red and Georgia Tom

Tampa Red and Georgia Tom: "But They Got It Fixed Right On," 102, 198; "Tight Like That," 148, 247

Tampa Red's Hokum Jug Band, "Saturday Night Scrontch," 30

Tarter and Gay, "Brownie Blues," 39

Ted Lewis and his Band, "The Monkey Doodle-Doo," 163

Temple, Johnnie, "Lead Pencil Blues," 180

Theard, Lovin' Sam: "Doodle It Back," 75; "Rubbin' On That Old Thing," 29; "She Can Love So Good," 69; "That Rhythm Gal," 2, 240; "Three Sixes," 173; "Ugly Child," 4

Thoma, Hociel, "Fish Tail Dance," 92

Thomas, Elvie, and Geeshie Wiley, "Over To My House," 33. *See also* Wiley, Geeshie, and Thomas Elvie

Thomas, Henry: "Arkansas," 62, 192, 251; "Bob McKinney," 9, 32; "Bull Doze Blues," 40, 126; "Cottonfield Blues," 255; "Don't Ease Me In," 82, 217, 258, 268; "Fishing Blues," 223; "The Fox And Hounds," 131; "Lovin' Babe," 177, 204; "Red River Blues," 186; "Run, Mollie, Run," 110, 162, 202, 252; "Texas Easy Street Blues," 166; "Texas Worried Blues," 33, 78, 110, 211

Thompkins, Jim, "Bedside Blues," 114

Thompson, Edward, "Seven Sisters Blues," 70, 163, 205; "West Virginia Blues," 173, 200

Thoreau, Henry David, 77

Thornton, Margaret, "Jockey Blues," 166

Tin Pan Alley, xi, xii, 10, 16, 49, 74, 154, 212, 224, 263

Torey, George, "Married Woman Blues," 147, 191

Townsend, Henry, "She's Got A Mean Disposition," 147

Tubb, Ernest, "Walking The Floor Over You," 261

Tucker, Bessie: "Bessie's Moan," 271; "Better Boot That Thing," 31; "The Dummy," 80; "Key To The Bushes," 127, 142; "Mean Old Master," 156; "Whisteling Woman Blues," 95, 265

Tucker, Sophie, 2, 224

Tully, Jim, *Beggars of Life*, 177

Tusser, Thomas, *Five Hundred Points of Good Husbandry*, 203

Twain, Mark: *A Connecticut Yankee in King Arthur's Court*, 49; *Tom Sawyer*, 17, 237

Union, 61

Valentino, Rudolph, 213

Vant, Louise, "The Man I Love Is Oh! So Good To Me," 124

Vechten, Van, 32, 39, 57, 73, 84, 116, 128, 209, 255; *Nigger Heaven*, 73

Vinson, Walter, 180, 215; "Every Dog Must Have His Day," 193; "Rosa Lee Blues," 202. *See also* Mississippi Sheiks

STEPHEN CALT is the author of a

biography of Skip James, *I'd Rather Be the Devil,*

and coauthor of *King of the Delta Blues:*

The Life and Music of Charlie Patton.

The University of Illinois Press

is a founding member of the

Association of American University Presses.

———————————————————

Composed in 9.2/13.5 The Serif SemiLight

with Hawksmoor display

by Jim Proefrock

at the University of Illinois Press

Designed by Rich Hendel

Manufactured by Sheridan Books, Inc.

University of Illinois Press

1325 South Oak Street

Champaign, IL 61820-6903

www.press.uillinois.edu